OGALLALA

VOLUME I IN THE SERIES
Our Sustainable Future

Series Editors

Lorna M. Butler
Washington State University

Cornelia Flora
*Virginia Polytechnic Institute and
State University*

Charles A. Francis
University of Nebraska–Lincoln

William Lockeretz
Tufts University

Paul Olson
University of Nebraska–Lincoln

Marty Strange
Center for Rural Affairs

John Opie

Ogallala

Water for a Dry Land

University of Nebraska Press

Lincoln and London

Library of Congress Cataloging-in-Publication Data
Opie, John, 1934-
Ogallala: Water for a dry land / John Opie.
p. cm. – (Our sustainable future ; v. 1)
Includes bibliographical references and index.
ISBN 0-8032-3557-7
1. Irrigation water – High Plains (U.S.) – History.
2. Ogallala Aquifer –
History.   3. Irrigation – High Plains (U.S.) –
History.   4. Agriculture –
High Plains (U.S.) – History.   5. Agricultural
ecology – High Plains (U.S.) – History.
I. Title   II. Series.
S616.U6065 1993 339.9'13'0978 –
dc20   92-26718
CIP

· · ·

To my mother and my father,

two Czechs who loved the land, and

to that useful unit of measure

the acre-foot, or 325,851 gallons

Contents

. . .

Illustrations

．．．

If we lived in a desert and our lives depended on a water supply that came out of a steel tube, we would inevitably watch that tube and talk about it understandingly. No citizen would need to be lectured about his duty toward its care and spurred to help if it were in danger. Teachers of civics in such a community might develop a sense of public responsibility, not only by describing the remote beginnings of the commonwealth, but also how that tube got built, how long it would last, how vital the intake might be if the rainfall on the forested mountains nearby ever changed in seasonal habit or amount. It would be a most unimaginative person, or a stupid one, who could not see the vital relation between the mountains, the forests, that tube and himself.—Isaiah Bowman, "Headwaters Control and Use—Influence of Vegetation on Land-Water Relationships," Proceedings: Upstream Engineering Conference (Washington, D.C., 1937), pp. 76–95.

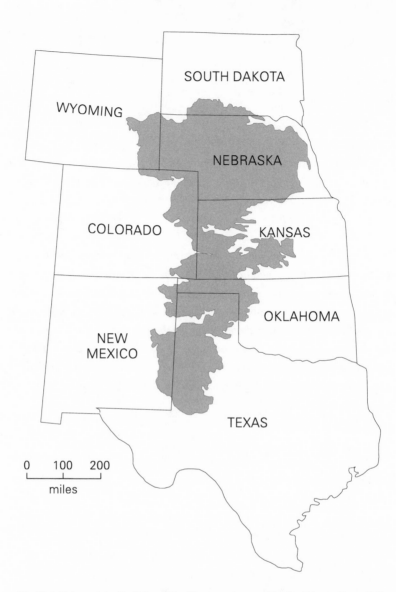

1. The High Plains and the Ogallala aquifer. The groundwater of the Ogallala aquifer underlies 174,000 square miles in eight states, but mostly in Texas, Oklahoma, Kansas, and Nebraska. This book gives special attention to the old Dust Bowl region of southwest Kansas and the Oklahoma-Texas Panhandle because this is the region under highest risk today because of heavy irrigation depletion of the aquifer.

Preface

• • •

This book got its start in the upper atmosphere. My participation in a 1979 workshop[1] on the human consequences of the greenhouse effect drew my attention to the old Dust Bowl region in the south-central High Plains. This troubled farm country would be hurt badly if global warming took hold in the twenty-first century. Always a land of little rain—twelve inches a year instead of thirty in the midwestern Corn Belt—time and again it had succumbed to heavy seasons of extended drought. More recently, however, mechanized irrigation from the underground water of the vast Ogallala aquifer has turned the old Dust Bowl region into the breadbasket of the world. At least for a time.

This book is the story of how access to groundwater, specifically the Ogallala aquifer, revolutionized farming on the south-central plains. Generations of settlers had been tantalized by a rich, deep soil in a flat, treeless region—if only they could find water. When homesteader John S. Gropp arrived in 1887 about twenty miles northwest of Garden City, Kansas, he was willing for two years to roll a large barrel of water three-fourths of a mile from a neighbor's well before he hand-dug his own 220-foot-deep well.[2] Drought broke farmers' backs repeatedly, culminating in the Dust Bowl of the 1930s, but remarkable security rose out of the use of groundwater for irrigation on a vast scale beginning in the 1960s.

This book also seeks to anticipate the effects, by the 1990s and into the twenty-first century, of the rapid consumption and decline of Ogallala groundwater. How well have farmers, water-resource scientists, and government officials understood the Ogallala as a natural resource? What actions were wasteful and downright wrong? What actions can be taken, and are being taken, to sustain productive farming on the plains if the Ogallala is no longer the limitless resource it once appeared to be? The Ogallala problem is not unusual today; it is the kind of problem taken up worldwide in the debates over sustainable development: how to maintain a satisfying standard of living indefinitely into the future. Indeed, the Ogallala problem is one of America's best case studies in revealing how, as a modern technological society, the nation will or will not succeed in sustainable develoment.

Thus far two other books on the subject have been published. Most studies of western water problems focus on the more intense and more glamorous water wars in California and Arizona, while the Ogallala aquifer under the High Plains is relatively neglected. Donald E. Green's pathbreaking 1973 book *Land of the Underground Rain*[3] was devoted to the aquifer under the Texas High Plains. His regional history and technical detail were invaluable, and I am also grateful for his review of my manuscript at its midpoint. Briefer but surprisingly detailed is *You Never Miss the Water Till . . . . (The Ogallala Story)* by Morton W. Bittinger and Elizabeth B. Green, published in 1980.[4] Bittinger and I enjoyed a meeting in Fort Collins early in the project. After more research, extensive travel, many interviews, and several conference papers and articles, this book began to take shape. Its broader scope—in the form of an environmental history, a comprehensive methodology, attention to sustainable development, and coverage of important events during the last several decades—justifies its existence.

I focus on one region because it is at the center of extreme risks and repeated human responses toward water, climate, and farming on the High Plains during the past one hundred years. Southwest Kansas and the Oklahoma-Texas Panhandle, running from the Arkansas River on the north to the Canadian River in the Texas Panhandle, covers roughly 200 miles north-south and 150 miles east-west. This region presents three important phenomena that together offer a particularly meaningful test for American sustainable agriculture: it was the heart of the 1930s Dust Bowl, America's greatest agricultural disaster; it is at the center of intensive drawdown for irrigation of extensive but irreplaceable Ogallala-aquifer groundwater; and it stands at the center of a highly profitable, vertically integrated agricultural industry, including cattle feedlots and beef-processing plants within a 250-mile radius of Garden City, Kansas, that supplies up to 40 percent of the nation's dinner-table beef.

It should also be noted that three hundred miles to the north, Nebraska's lion's share of the Ogallala aquifer now contains 67 percent of its entire groundwater supply.[5] This is the region north of the Platte River underlying the Sandhills cattle-grazing region of western Nebraska. Already Sandhills inhabitants are fighting to prevent their water from being transferred to more parched regions. The more distant future belongs to the Ogallala in Nebraska, but that will require another book; this one is devoted to the old Dust Bowl region as one more often wounded, more often in need, and possibly more of an example of the historic trials of American sustainable development.

Nevertheless, the region has an advantage. Irrigation to save the farmer and maintain production can last longer in the old Dust Bowl than in Colorado, New Mexico, Arizona, or California because there is little competition for groundwater from growing cities or industrial expansion.

The Introduction sketches the problems this book will address, while Chapter 1 describes the central High Plains region as a physical resource, including the geological origins of the Ogallala aquifer as a nonrenewable resource, the surface features and soils, and the natural plants of the shortgrass prairie before settlers arrived. Chapter 2 covers the long, painful, often self-defeating European attempts to settle the plains, America's last frontier, including early quests for water and the short-lived plains version of the national Irrigation Crusade during the early decades of the twentieth century. Chapter 3 is a Dust Bowl history of dryland farming, federal interventions in waterless marginal lands, and the vulnerability of conventional settlement. Chapter 4 depicts the remarkable irrigation revolution, from inadequate windmill technology in the early twentieth century to the deep wells, high-capacity pumps, and center-pivot sprinklers that industrialized the landscape during the 1960s. Chapter 5 compares institutional attempts in Texas, Oklahoma, and Kansas to develop, manage, and conserve Ogallala groundwater on state and local bases. Chapter 6 describes a Kansas farm family, its successful move into irrigation, its fragile future, and the implications for independent family farming on the High Plains. Chapter 7 describes attempts to extend Ogallala groundwater use into a longer future, occasionally moving toward sustainable development. Chapter 8 discusses the effects on water consumption of the most recent severe drought in 1988, together with the possible deeper threat of desertification during a long-term greenhouse-effect climate change. Chapter 9 summarizes the book within the framework of sustainable development, and the Appendix is an essay on environmental historians' views of the High Plains.

A Brief Note on the Advantages of an Environmental Approach

While no book can be all inclusive, this one explores subjects that the traditional history book or policy study would consider irrelevant—economists call them externalities. As an environmental history, it describes the geography, hydrology, soils, and plants of the region, then relates them to human settlement, technology, and civilization. Environmental history reminds us, often in painful ways, that humanity, no matter how technologically sophisticated it is, is still imbedded in nature.[6]

An environmental approach is advantageous. It enlarges our thinking and learning about a subject like the Ogallala aquifer so that we can better understand why it is a troubled resource and why the people who use it are on the edge of failure. Above all, an environmental approach is openly reformist because it is based on the notion that any viewpoint including only the human landscape—its politics, economics, institutions, and culture—is flawed by its skewed focus and limited information. Kenneth Boulding wrote, for example, that "all of nature's systems are closed loops, while economic activities are linear and assume inexhaustible resources."[7] As we explore the history of the Ogallala aquifer and the human actions that depleted it, it is important to recognize that such single-minded, market-driven linear viewpoints have ignored environmental features and thus encouraged runaway water waste, soil erosion, and the exploitation of farmers. The dynamic interactions that hold a historic region together are complex and require comprehensive analysis that can take the complexity into account.

In an environmental approach, human activity cannot be separated from the external three-dimensional physical world, filled not only with rocks and soils, water and air, but also inhabited by living organisms that are born, flourish, and die on their own terms. The human history of the Ogallala aquifer gains new proportions when measured by different time scales of geological epochs, soil building, drought cycles during the farmer's seasons in the field, thirty-year farmland mortgages, quarterly corporate profit-loss reports, and hourly shifts in the commodity markets. By its inclusiveness (everything is connected to everything else), an environmental analysis can account more fully than any single or linear factor alone for the tight bonding between human activities and environmental affairs. Such a holistic approach has an advantage because it examines the glue between humans and nature with equal attention to humans, nature, and the glue. It can recognize that the Ogallala is part of a multipath dynamic system that binds social, biological, and physical forces tightly together.

The transition to this comprehensive viewpoint is not easy, even on the level of what is considered useful information. One person's cluttered noise is another's healthy signal. How to match a theory, or a supposed law, with the raw realities of life? My approach here, discussed at greater length in the Appendix, emphasizes treatment of the Ogallala aquifer as a major element in a larger nonlinear self-organizing system that combines the High Plains region and its human settlers. This throws a conceptual mouthful at the problem but allows us to see the connections among technological, agricultural, environmental, and social forces.[8]

The task is not easy. James Gleick's recent popular study of the new science of chaos describes any ecosystem as "a complicated dynamical system, not with a few points of instability—critical points where a small push could have large consequences—but *instability at every point*."[9] Nothing stays put. Instability at every point is what the Ogallala is, and this is also true of American agriculture. Gleick also notes that "nonlinearity means the act of playing the game has a way of changing the rules."[10] Even while I write about the history of multipath processes of irrigation and food production, including the speed of change, and while the reader works his or her way through this book, the rules are changing. Nevertheless, we can distinguish and hold in mind several continuously variable factors—important ones like local groundwater technology, the family-farm tradition, and farm policy— that can be fixed on, explored as they are running, and integrated into a larger moving whole.

Using the language of self-organizing systems theory, we can better iden- tify small danger points that can become big problems: "fluctuating vari- ables which may be amplified (become critical) leading the system into a qualitatively new state." That is, new goals can emerge from changing con- ditions. Self-organizing systems analysis also allows us to identify more ad- equately each step of the way the "players" and their various interactions (for example, groundwater plus soil moisture plus management skills plus pricing). The objective is also to develop "decision criteria which reflect the prevailing forces, constraints and processes to which management initia- tives must adapt. They will not prescribe a solution, but rather determine the viability of alternative proposals."[11] Policies should not be rigid and ideolog- ical, but flexible and pragmatic.

The issue for the Ogallala region is to what extent human intervention (agriculture is always an intervention) upsets the self-regenerating capacities of the natural ecosystem enough to bring on environmental collapse of a re- gion and subsequently deny human survival there. Or can we identify ways in which human participation in the plains ecology can sustain itself? It is clear that both environments and human agriculture are complex biological and social phenomena not recognized by the marketplace or legislators. Most farmers experience such complexities all too well.

When environmental history is treated as a form of self-organizing sys- tems analysis, it must boldly and continuously shuttle back and forth be- tween the world of human values that characterizes the flow of history on the one hand and the data-laden reasoning of the natural sciences on the other. Here we put a magnifying glass on the historic Dust Bowl region (southwestern Kansas and the Oklahoma-Texas Panhandle) to examine a place "from the bottom up." Here human history is positioned as a piece of a larger natural history, the last few seconds on the face of the geologic clock.

There is hope. When public policy is historically and ecologically informed, it can *optimize* resource use rather than *maximize* it, which inevitably brings extinction and human deprivation. Technologies can be redirected toward sustainable development: resource conserving, pollution preventing, environment restoring, and economically sustainable. Such actions can bring human prosperity at significantly lower environmental costs. The farm bills passed by Congress in 1985 and 1990, despite historic bureaucratic foot dragging, have recognized that low-input sustainable farming has virtues. Claude Levi-Strauss described this redirection as "modesty, decency and discretion in the face of a world that preceded our species and that will survive it."[12]

This study of the Ogallala aquifer is thus both a physical and a human history; it seeks to analyze the biophysical and social processes that shaped the region. By using this approach we can better identify discontinuous (that is, disruptive) change, whether an economic depression or a natural drought, and better comprehend its positive and negative features. We can better identify and track beneficial and harmful impacts of water and land use, soil conditions, appropriate crops, the independent farmer, climate change, and external economic and political forces. Historically, it must be said, these actions have been culturally and economically narrow; more inclusive and responsible policies are possible.

• • •

The list of people who willingly shared their experiences and their information to make this book possible is very long. The following is brief and incomplete. The names of Phil and Linda Tooms, and Roger and Betty Trescott are fictitious, but the people and their places are real. Their need for privacy must be respected. Special appreciation goes to Esther Groves, reporter for the Liberal, Kansas, *Southwest Daily Times,* who wrote many stories about the Ogallala aquifer and put me on track among the people of southwest Kansas and the Oklahoma-Texas Panhandle. Many hours were spent with water-management officials Jeffrey K. Schmidt (and his knowledgeable secretary, Joanne Hall), Gary Baker, Larry J. Kuder, Jerry L. Allen, and Wayne A. Wyatt in Kansas, Oklahoma, and Texas. They generously opened their doors, archives, and copying machines to me. I visited and talked and walked fields and saw the hard-working pumps and sprinklers with B. G. ("Gene") Barby, Gayle Brown, Roland and Bonita Hoeme, Keith and Diane Allen, Paul and Patsy Boles, Ray Clark, and many others. Librarians and volunteers at the Finney County Historical Society and the Finney County Public Library, particularly in the invaluable collections of the latter's Kansas Room, were generous in their assistance. Special thanks go to Edwin D. Gutentag, currently with the U.S. Geological Survey in Denver. Ed was U S G S hydrologist in Garden City for two decades; he opened his personal files to me and located invaluable information and also read relevant parts of the manuscript for accuracy. Wayne Bossert of Kansas District No.4 corrected errors and gave me good advice about the entire manuscript (the errors that remain are my own responsibility). I also thank Michael ("Micky") Glantz of the National Center for Atmospheric Research in Boulder, Colorado, for sharing his insights on the climate-agriculture-water interaction. My apologies to those important folks whose names I have inadvertently omitted. Thanks also to campus colleagues who read the manuscript: Robert Lynch, Michal McMahon, John E. O'Connor, Eric Katz, and particularly Michael Black and Norbert Elliot, who waded through many parts twice and three times. A near-final version was meticulously and thoughtfully analyzed by Patty Limerick of the University of Colorado, I received good advice from a reading by Deborah and Frank Popper of Rutgers University, and Donald Worster lavished generous attention and wise comments. Rose Scarano saved many a deadline with her emergency map pasting, captioning, and photocopying. My wife, Barbara, exercised her prodigious patience, and I tested it.

Earlier versions of parts of this book, but considerably revised since, were published in:

"The Drought of 1988, the Global Warming Experiment, and Its Challenge to Irrigation in the Old Dust Bowl Region," *Agricultural History* 66, no.2 (Spring 1992): 288–314.

"100 Years of Climate Risk Assessment on the High Plains: Which Farm Paradigm Does Irrigation Serve?" *Agricultural History* 63, no.2 (Spring 1989): 243–69.

"Water Runs Uphill to Money. But Will There Be Enough of Both to Keep the Desert Blooming?" *Orion Nature Quarterly* (Winter 1988).

"The Precarious Balance: Matching Market Dollars and Human Values in American Agriculture," *The Environmental Professional* (Spring 1988).

"If John Wesley Powell Were Alive Today . . . The Vagaries of Federal Water Management Policies in the Arid West, 1878 to the Present," *Conference Proceedings: Water for the 21st Century, Will It Be There?* (Dallas: Center for Urban Water Studies, Southern Methodist University, 1985).

"U.S. Water Supplies: Scarcity Amidst Plenty," *Britannica Yearbook of Science and the Future* (Chicago: Encyclopaedia Britannica, 1982).

"What Will We Do When the Water Runs Out?" *The Progressive Magazine* (July 1981).

"For a U.S. Water Policy," *New York Times* Op-Ed Page, December 30, 1980.

"America's Seventy-Year Mistake: Bad Weather in Good Country," *Seminar on Natural Resource Use and Environmental Policy* (Ames: Iowa State University, 1980).

"Research Opportunities in Retrospective Climate Impact Assessment: Case Study in Settlement and Farming on the Arid Great Plains, 1870–1940," *Final Report, Panel on Societal and Institutional Responses, AAAS-DoE Workshop on Environmental and Societal Consequences of a Possible CO_2-Induced Climate Change* (Washington, D.C.: Carbon Dioxide Effects Research and Assessment Program, U.S. Department of Energy, 1980).

· · ·

Introduction

This book aims to inform and persuade as it describes how the Ogallala aquifer came into being. The aquifer did not become a human resource until farmers discovered it and learned to use it, and this book chronicles their repeated failures for more than seventy years to overcome the harsh climate of the High Plains before the aquifer could be used. By 1960 new pumping technologies had created a golden age of irrigation that has continued to the present day; but the irrigation bonanza is now disappearing for wheat, corn, and sorghum farmers on the south-central High Plains because groundwater levels are declining. This book predicts a difficult future that most irrigation farmers have already acknowledged but not necessarily solved and offers some alternate ways of thinking about the connections among groundwater, a difficult farming region, the agriculture it produces, and the types of farming found on the High Plains.

Not many modern workplaces are still directly affected by the weather. Protection from the vagaries of climate has long been one of the major objectives of human tool making and the Industrial Revolution. Jesse H. Ausubel writes: "Humans do not wait guilelessly to receive an [climate] impact, bear the loss, then respond with an adaptation. Rather they attempt to anticipate and forestall problems."[1] Modern technological society has learned to protect itself well against cold and heat, rain and snow; nevertheless, climate still influences construction, transportation, communications, fisheries, forestry, and tourism. Agriculture was, and still is, the human activity most vulnerable to climate: rain, sun, wind, temperature.[2] In the long run, climate, extremely fluid and fickle, is still the part of the environment that humans find most difficult to control or modify.

The history of the south-central High Plains is a series of crisis situations accelerated by repeated drought. As a result, the old Dust Bowl region inadvertently has become an experiment station for crisis management on many levels, from local farming to federal planning. Because of severe environmental limits due largely to insufficient water, when the south-central High Plains was settled as an agricultural region, it also went on permanent alert, experiencing a crisis with no solution and no end. This is particularly true if one sees today's Ogallala irrigation dependency as a mere brief blip in time—1960 to 1990—compared to long-term forces at work. In the context of the new planetary history, environment is the limiter after all.

The Place and its Problem

Each geographical region on the earth was once complete unto itself without humans. When in the 1880s large numbers of energetic and ambitious white European farmers appeared on North America's unplowed High Plains, they accelerated the pace of nature's events and narrowed nature's intentions to suit human needs. One unfortunate result was the Dust Bowl of the 1930s, when fertile soil, no longer protected by native grasses, blew away. Later, through the adept use of technology, farmers learned to mine groundwater to overcome the lack of enough rain. A resource is mined, or developed or exploited, when it is consumed at a pace far beyond any known rate of replacement. A Faustian bargain was struck with the water, and today payment is coming due. This book describes the groundwater, the bargain, and the fleeting opportunity to move beyond a Pyrrhic mastery toward an accommodative sustainable strategy.

The enormous Ogallala aquifer is groundwater trapped below 174,000 square miles of fertile but dry plains farmland. Unlike most of the world's water supplies, Ogallala groundwater is largely nonrenewable because its sources were cut off thousands of years ago. It is essentially fossil water taken ten thousand to twenty-five thousand years ago from the glacier-laden Rocky Mountains before it was geologically cut off by the Pecos River and the Rio Grande.[3] More than 3 billion acre-feet (an acre-foot is a foot of water on one acre, or 325,851 gallons) are stored under the High Plains. One misconception about the Ogallala aquifer (and most groundwater) is that it stands in cavernous lakes or flows in thundering underground rivers. In reality, it trickles slowly southeastward through sandy gravel beds, 500 to 1,000 feet a year, two to three feet a day. These vast water-saturated gravel beds, 50 to 300 feet below the surface, are 150 to 300 feet thick. More than a half-billion acre-feet of Ogallala water was consumed by irrigation farmers between 1960 and 1990, mostly in southwestern Kansas, the Oklahoma panhandle, and West Texas. This is all the more serious because groundwater replacement occurs only from the surface at the rate of less than an inch a year under irrigated ground and 0.15 inches a year under dryland, while pumping is measured in feet per year. It would take a thousand years to refill the aquifer. Nothing can accelerate the flow, and artificial replacement remains impossible. As to alternatives for water-intensive farming in the region, there are no major rivers like the Mississippi or the Missouri, and rainfall is light.

The Ogallala aquifer is still one of the nation's great hidden treasures, containing more than 3.2 billion acre-feet of water to support a region equivalent to three New Yorks, but probably only half that amount is accessible through known pumping technologies and water quality declines as water levels go down. Nonrenewability would not be significant for modern society except that Ogallala groundwater today irrigates almost seven million acres of old Dust Bowl land, turning it into high-production grain fields. New pumping and irrigation technologies have made this part of the High Plains one of the largest and most productive farming regions on the globe. It is rightly called the breadbasket of the world. However, during the next two decades irrigation could fall to two million acres.[4] Even so, with a third of its water consumed and only half of the rest usable, the presence of the Ogallala aquifer below the arid High Plains is still like having the waters of Lake On-

3

tario nearby, ready to be tapped at will to water fields of corn, milo, wheat, and alfalfa.

Today more than 150,000 pumps run day and night during the growing season, feeding water onto crops planted fencerow to fencerow on thousand-acre farms. When they are not shipped overseas according to who can pay on the world market or processed to load grocers' shelves with bread and breakfast cereal, mountains of wheat and corn are added to sorghum and alfalfa and dished out to shoulder-to-shoulder cattle in pens that cover thousands of High Plains acres. Ultimately these animals are slaughtered, cut up, and packaged to fill supermarket meat counters. The world's largest beef-processing plant is just west of Garden City, Kansas, in the heart of the old Dust Bowl.

It was not always so. During the 1930s the loudest noise came not from irrigation-pump motors but from the howling winds of recurring dust storms. The plains farmer, his family laboring at his side, lived as close to the blowing soil as the pioneers. He seemed doomed to lead a substandard way of life. The soil was rich, but it mattered little when spring and summer were rainless and scorching hot, and occasional seasons of rain merely fooled and teased. Mistakes were made, and good people sacrificed their lives. Hence it appeared that Americans were not invincible frontiersmen who inevitably would become prosperous farmers. Wherever the vast grasslands had less than twenty inches of rain a year, farmers did not fare well. Not until pumps and wells, engines and fuels, know-how and cash took over did the situation change.

Today, pumps, wells, engines, and fuels define the High Plains. Local irrigators in the 1980s were successful on a level that the wrung-out Dust Bowl farmers of the 1930s would have found astonishing. Kansans Phil and Linda Tooms, twenty or so crow-flying miles southwest of Sublette, switched from ranching when they learned to irrigate in the early 1960s. Today Phil still irrigates sixteen hundred acres, enjoys his history books in an air-conditioned suburban-style house, and serves on a bank board in Liberal.

A few miles away in the forlorn Kansas Sandhills, where even Dust Bowl farmers never settled, the entrepreneurial Gigot family, father and four sons, irrigates more than fifty thousand acres planted to corn, wheat, and sorghum, using about five hundred circling center-pivot irrigation sprinklers. The operation is nicknamed the Gigot Empire, and the family is worth tens of millions of dollars. The Gigots are not beloved by everyone in the neighborhood.

Sixty or so miles south and slightly west across the border in Oklahoma live Betty and Roger Trescott, both in their seventies. After the pumps appeared in the early 1960s, their ability to flood their wheat fields allowed them to stay when dryland farming would not. Betty in particular is a vocal firebrand who takes on big oil companies and state water boards who want to take Ogallala water from farmers and use it to recover oil from an old field.

Another two hundred miles due south across the narrow Oklahoma Panhandle in Texas at Lubbock is Wayne Wyatt, who in his pre-irrigation youth experienced painful farm losses, who has lived through the entire history of widespread irrigation on the southern High (Staked) Plains, and who now is manager of the path-breaking Texas High Plains Underground Water Conservation District No. 1. The district opened its doors in 1952 to promote "controlled development" of Ogallala water and is gradually being compelled to protect the remaining supply for "beneficial use" only.

Guaranteeing beneficial use has been extraordinarily difficult. Nor has water mining been reduced significantly. Phil Tooms complains that Southwest Kansas Groundwater Management District No. 3 was belatedly organized only after almost half the available water had been consumed, and even the nearby Gigots, despite their deep pockets to buy the newest irrigation technology, admit their future has less groundwater in it. The Trescotts are fighting tooth and nail to keep nonfarm interests from wasting water that morally and legally belongs to growing wheat. Wayne Wyatt clearly understands he is fighting a long battle to keep water available for farmers. He also understands that eventually he will lose.

The dilemma is obvious. Everyone, from the farmer and banker to the state agronomist or federal hydrologist, agrees that intensive and profitable irrigation now faces the serious problem of rapid depletion of Ogallala groundwater. Half the usable water has been spent; the current pace of consumption allows perhaps thirty years, but maybe ten more years or less, if dire greenhouse-effect desertification predictions are borne out. All too soon the remaining water will be reached only by installing prohibitively expensive deep pumps that use costly fuels, a procedure that would require high-priced food (a ten-dollar pound of bread and a sixty-dollar pound of beef in 1990 dollars), an unacceptable forecast in light of America's tradition of cheap food.

This book offers a framework in which to understand the Ogallala aquifer, its implications for humans, and its possible future. Despite decades of trial and error and government intervention, today both groundwater and the farmer continue to exist on the edge of extinction. There is no quick technological fix, and no one in Dust Bowl country would return to the old ways.

Why Is Irrigation So Attractive?

Irrigation on the High Plains is a very comforting technology. At the turn of a valve or the flip of a switch the lucky farmer can flood his fields, sprinkle her crops, or drip water on his vegetables, no matter how dry the weather is. The water is available on demand in defiance of the unpredictable climate of southwest Kansas or the Oklahoma and Texas panhandles. There, a fast-moving thundercloud might unleash a downpour and leave the neighbor's needy field high and dry a mile away. February might not give a farmer the last six inches of snow to guarantee that the field he planted in wheat is saturated with water to a depth of four feet. This was the traditional uncertainty that all farmers faced, not only on the plains but around the world, wherever rain was marginal and rivers ran bone dry in summer.

Today's irrigation farmer, on his 1,280 acres in Dust Bowl country, is now bound to a gushing steel umbilical six to eight inches wide plunging down 250 feet to the once-glacier-fed fresh water of the Ogallala aquifer. At the top end, another finite resource, natural gas, fires up the four cylinders of a new International 605 or Minneapolis-Moline engine or a used and modified Ford or Chevy V-8 engine. The engine's shaft, rotating at twelve hundred revolutions per minute, runs to a reduction gearbox that shifts the torque from horizontal to vertical to power a Johnson or Peerless deep-well vertical turbine impeller pump. The aquifer water rushes up the steel umbilical and into aluminum pipes at 800 to 1,200 gallons per minute, ready to be soaked up by nearby fields overloaded with wheat or corn or sorghum. Corn would take the most water during the season, an astonishing 90 million gallons laid on 130 acres of a 160-acre quarter section, wheat and sorghum half that amount, but alfalfa even more. In 1990, a center-pivot sprinkler system, from drilling the well to watering the milo, cost a farmer fifty to seventy thousand dollars per 160 acres, depending on well depth and field needs. This was twice the 1976 cost, and most irrigators needed six to ten units for efficiencies of size. To pay for it, he needed good wheat or sorghum prices, which in the late 1980s were half of what they were ten years before. His borrowing power, based on land values, fell during the same period by about a quarter.[5]

Most consumers of High Plains groundwater treat it as a "free good," available to the first taker at no cost for the water itself. It takes only fifteen dollars to pump an acre-foot using natural gas and thirty dollars using electricity. Hence this free water has been generously consumed on profligate levels, and there are forces at work that encourage excessive use. Pierre R. Crosson and Norman J. Rosenberg of Resources for the Future, a think tank, write that "markets are not well equipped to protect resources such as water . . . in which it is difficult to establish property rights."[6] Water laws, such as prior appropriation (use it or lose it) counter sustainable development. An imperfect first step is not to try to change the laws but to change economic analysis by including environmental costs. In addition, water is the globe's well-traveled "fugitive resource" and hard to pin down in one place; hence it is contradictorily treated as both private property (whoever owns the land has exclusive rights to the groundwater below) and common property (a free and inexhaustible resource belonging to the public). Since the alternate concept, sustainable development, seeks to combine both environmental and economic factors to devise a more inclusive viewpoint, it may be particularly adept at treating the unique characteristics of water. Clearly, the old distinctions are contradictory and unworkable.

Water waste is multiplied by widespread irrigation of surplus crops, particularly wheat, that is encouraged by government subsidies. Subsidies, intended to keep farmers from collapse, continue to stimulate production even in the absence of demand,[7] and the resultant surplus crops, like obsolete military aircraft, are stockpiled at government expense. When farm subsidies began to cost Western governments, the United States and Europe, more than three hundred billion dollars a year, the 1985 farm bill tried to reduce costs and surpluses by setting aside unplanted farmland as an agricultural reserve. Subsidies also led to transitional unsustainability by inducing farmers to use excessive amounts of pesticides and fertilizers and to waste underground and surface waters in irrigation. It is clear that vast food surpluses are being created at huge hidden economic and human costs. Consumers, grain traders, or foreign buyers may pay less than half of real costs; for their efforts, farmers have less average income than other Americans. Heavy government subsidies ultimately fall on the shoulders of taxpayers but are not seen as food costs. The hidden ecological costs of lost water, soil, and abandoned or exploited farms are not easy to measure in dollars.[8]

Surpluses have in turn promoted an expanding beef industry in which seven pounds of grain produce one pound of beef. It also takes several hundred gallons of water to produce that pound of beef when on the hoof. While Americans today are consuming less beef, over the long sweep of human history, higher meat consumption has been seen as a sign of better living standards; this is true globally. Third World peoples get their protein from beans, rice, and grains, but to them a higher standard of living includes meat in the dinner pot, and beef is still the prime choice. Today the plains are locked into high water consumption to grow the wheat and water the beef.

To this costly equation can be added continued protection of the independent family farm, which some argue should have died out with the horse and buggy. As long as farmers need subsidies and special credits to continue to exist, they will remain the government clients they became in the 1930s. In addition, it is clear that most plains family farmers depend on free water for their survival and would quickly go bankrupt if they had to pay the three hundred to eight hundred dollars an acre-foot that the U.S. Army Corps of Engineers estimates as the cost of "new" water imported from the Mississippi

8

River. Large corporate operations with deep pockets for expensive equipment and costly water may be the only survivors. Not the least, it is also argued that the same independent family farmers who waste High Plains water also receive millions of taxpayer dollars to keep them on the plains.[9] Supporters of the family farm retort that its preservation is a sacred trust and ensures the attractive option of organic low-input farming. Low-input farming is much less capital-intensive but is burdened, perhaps fatally, by heavy labor demands.

Ogallala: Can It Become an American Venture in Sustainable Development?

More and more, today's attempts to lengthen the time farmers can tap the Ogallala are comparable to similar attempts around the world to stretch out the use of limited resources.[10] At worst, if Ogallala water becomes inaccessible over the next ten to thirty years, the region will become unmanageable and revert to a deserted wasteland. At best, rethinking the Ogallala and reworking High Plains agriculture could provide America with a model for sustainable development.

Around the world, the recent record of resource management is not good. The cutting of the last trees for firewood in Africa's Sahel has only made starvation more extreme and ungovernable. Russia's Aral Sea contains only 10 percent of its historic water because of the exaggerated irrigation of a desert, and the reduction of the Amazon rain forest ("the lungs of the world") continues almost unabated. The deepening erosion of America's agricultural soils could be the nation's downfall. Nor is the historic record reassuring: the rugged badlands along the eastern Mediterranean were covered with large forests before civilization took over. The decline of the Roman Empire has been attributed to the erosion of Italy's soils, and Spain's rapid descent from its sixteenth-century greatness occurred in large part because its farmers overgrazed its once-lush central highlands. Wind and water continue to deplete the soil of America's Dust Bowl at a pace faster than that of the 1930s.

The recent concept of sustainable development seeks to balance basic human needs with the protection of scarce resources. It seeks to meet the needs of the present without compromising the ability of future generations to meet their own needs.[11] The debate that swirls around sustainable development is whether the concept is self-contradictory, an oxymoron, because development continues to mean economic growth based on technological innovation that uses up natural resources. Currently, the effort is to make certain that environmental costs and environmental protection are included in any measure of economic growth and that technological innovation is appropriate to human and environmental needs on regional and local bases.

Sustainable agriculture is probably the most challenging aspect of sustainable development in the face of constantly growing world food needs that can be drawn only from shrinking and depleted soils and water supplies. It seeks to balance food production, environmental conservation, and profitability. The American Society of Agronomy says "sustainable agriculture is one that, over the long term, enhances environmental quality and the resources base on which agriculture depends, provides for basic human food and fiber needs, is economically viable, and enhances the quality of life for farmers and society as a whole."[12] This is a tall order. It is also a sharp turn away from industrial farming that measures success by short-term profits. According to a Canadian report, agricultural sustainability is "an economically profitable agri-food system which supplies healthy nutritious food that society needs while preserving and developing natural resources and the quality of the environment for future generations."[13] The same comprehensive language is used in the 1990 farm bill, but its actual impact may be different, as will be discussed later in this book. Sustainable agriculture offers a useful perspective from which to evaluate irrigation's golden age from 1960 to 1990 on the High Plains and the extreme difficulties farmers are having now in their attempts to switch from high consumption.

A farming system that measures success mostly in terms of maximum yields and immediate profits results in too much soil erosion, too much depletion of soil quality, too much groundwater mining, and too much consumption of fossil fuels. Farming is not like any other industry. North Dakota farmer Fred Kirschenmann observed that "a farm is not a factory—it is an organism made up of numerous suborganisms, each alive and interdependent, each affected in numerous, complex ways" by outside forces—

10

money, chemicals, technology, market prices—that are invariably disruptive.[14] "A cow is not a production unit but a biological organism." Kirschenmann worries about the insensitivity of oversimplified analysis (reductionism) to broader and longer-term effects. In their use of insecticides, for example, farmers are urged to measure success by "economic thresholds" that are "based on mathematical calculations that balance the cost of application against the dollar loss caused by the target insect. It causes us to ignore the fact that we may be creating the very problem we are trying to solve by killing off beneficial insects and natural predators and by creating resistant strains of the target pest."[15] Most farmers recognize they are getting less bang for the buck in new technologies. Stephen Schneider writes: "The bigger the technological solution, the greater the chance of extensive, unforeseen side effects and, thus, the greater the number of lives ultimately at risk."[16]

Sustainable agriculture need not be less profitable than conventional agriculture. Field studies by William Lockeretz showed little difference between organic and conventional Corn Belt farms between 1974 and 1978.[17] The farms using alternative-methods had lower yields, but this was offset by lower costs for fertilizer and pesticides; even when increased labor costs were included there was still little difference. In a drier region like the High Plains, organically farmed soils offer the advantage of greater water-holding capacity than conventionally farmed soils. Low-input sustainable agriculture is hampered by federal programs that do not recognize, for example, the rotational system used by alternative-method farmers, who end up sacrificing income support payments available to conventional farmers. For decades conventional farmers have received federal economic incentives that distort their profit picture. What they need instead are economic incentives to change their current unsustainable practices.[18]

Sustainable development rejects boomlike development because it is extremely intensive and short term. Most farmers, but not enough planners and managers of agribusiness, know that farming is a partnership with Nature, but they are constantly urged to exploit their land and water as if there were no tomorrow. Plains farmers were urged, especially in the 1970s, to plant fencerow to fencerow to save the world from impending starvation and, not incidentally, to reduce the balance of payments. It was attractive to be integrated into national and international policies. Boomlike development created vulnerability to a different, unexpected set of risks. The irony of Ogallala irrigation is that it has done so much to conquer perennial disaster from drought, yet at the same time it has created new risks because of its need for heavy equipment investment, new fertilizer and pesticides, integration into outside markets, and dependence on government support, all of which transformed a highly valued farming lifestyle into an industrial operation. Today it is too expensive for a new farmer to start up an entire irrigation operation despite the promised bounty.

Another problem in conventional agriculture is the tendency to treat natural resources as a free commons that has no economic cost. The goal of sustainable agriculture is to identify and track real environmental costs, such as soil erosion and pesticide pollution, as well as aquifer depletion. The plains farmer has for generations received hidden environmental subsidies in free soil and water just as much as the dollar and credit subsidies he receives from the federal government. It can be argued that earlier he was kept on the land by exploiting its fertility, while since the 1960s it was heavy consumption of Ogallala water that allowed him to prosper. Over the long haul, both clearly created a false security.

Sustainable development is not dogmatic; no one desires the total preservation of a frozen asset. Ogallala pumps cannot be suddenly shut down without tearing the social fabric; conversely, better use of Ogallala water would protect the social fabric from environmental collapse. Sustainable development acknowledges that human needs are real and necessary even when they are perceived or imagined needs, socially and culturally determined in ways that are almost impossible to change. Like most environmentally generated viewpoints, sustainable development tends to be cautious and conservative. Indeed, the profit-based development that characterizes conventional farming today is more radical because of its singular loyalty to maximum profits. The satisfaction of social needs and economic growth are not the same. Sustainable development is not pronature and antihumanity. Historically on the

High Plains, consumption of groundwater grew not only with new pumping technologies but also with the perception that the highest levels of food production were worthwhile goals according to profits in the marketplace and a moral duty to feed humanity.

High Plains irrigation farmers already had taken steps toward sustainable development even before the term was used and they learned about it. These steps will be discussed in detail later. But attempts at conservation and efficiency may be only Band-Aid actions until larger conceptual questions about agriculture, environment, and economics are answered. Nevertheless, some of the recent steps are impressive and certainly have slowed consumption. Most important, irrigation farmers organized regional water-management districts in Kansas and Texas or created their own independent associations, as in Oklahoma, to control the number and spacing of wells and pumps, to meter consumption, and to foster conservation and fight waste. Texas High Plains Underground Water Conservation District No. 1 began operations in Lubbock in 1952, with the mission of promoting controlled development of Ogallala water.[19] It has now shifted policies to protect the remaining supply for beneficial use only. This realization that when the aquifer is set aside for farming it serves a fundamental social good that benefits society is also stated in the legislative act that created the Oklahoma Water Resources Board in 1972.[20] But Oklahoma has no local districts, and citizens' groups in the Panhandle often find themselves in conflict with the state board, which they see as dominated by Big Oil. As for Kansas, a local vote in 1976 created the Southwest Kansas Groundwater Management District No. 3, with headquarters in Garden City.[21] Although there is a state groundwater engineer, Ogallala policies and actions in Kansas belong to local boards of irrigators and district officials. Water mining continues, and a physical, technological, and economic limit inevitably will be reached. One radical new development bears watching: In 1990, Northwest Kansas Groundwater Management District Four, established in 1977 and supervising more than thirty-six hundred wells, set a zero-depletion goal to be reached in as little as ten years. To quote a district official, "the declining levels meant zero depletion anyway, so why not opt to reach the same goal earlier while retaining an acceptable quantity of water for future management options."[22] But the district is encountering much difficulty in matching this Draconian goal with the immediate needs of farmers who insist they must irrigate to survive.

Other individual steps are being taken within the framework of conventional agriculture. Ogallala farmers rest their hopes on better management skills. When plains farmers found in 1980 that their groundwater levels were declining two feet a year, they began to practice water scheduling, to serve crops only at critical stages of growth, and water harvesting in tailwater ponds to return runoff to the fields. New and more efficient technologies ranged from center-pivot irrigation in the 1960s to in-ground moisture sensors and drip irrigation in the 1980s and genetically engineered crops that are less water sensitive in the 1990s. There is also interest in new alternative low-irrigation or no-irrigation crops and even the potential return to dryland farming despite its historic limitations. As a result, groundwater decline has averaged one foot instead of two except in times of severe drought.

Low-input sustainable agriculture (LISA) became a small part ($3.9 million) of federal farm policy with the passage of the 1985 farm bill, significantly titled the Food Security Act. LISA was expanded and renamed SARE (Sustainable Agriculture Research and Education Program) and authorized for $40 million in the 1990 farm bill, itself called FACTA (Food, Agriculture, Conservation and Trade Act).[23] It evolved mainly as a reaction to two things: modern industrial agriculture has not protected the environment well, and economic failure continues to bedevil most independent farmers who practice conventional agriculture. Even the staid and generally intransigent United States Department of Agriculture admitted that LISA's appearance is "a criticism of capital-intensive, chemical-intensive monoculture."[24]

LISA sought "to provide an abundance of food and fiber in a way that is harmless to humans and the environment and sustainable for generations to come."[25] Organic-farming advocate Robert Rodale concluded that LISA is the overdue move in agriculture of the historic American conservation tradition that goes back to Gifford Pinchot, Hugh Hammond Bennett, and the Progressive Era and argued for a marriage of conservation and agriculture, since both require wise management methods.[26] Historian Donald Worster concluded that the historic soil-conservation program of New Deal Americans is now coming into its own: "Each generation was to leave the earth in as good shape as it had found it, or in even better shape."[27] Of LISA, USDA official Neill Schaller says "we are talking about an even bolder union—a marriage of agricultural productivity and profitability, resource conservation and environmental protection, and the enhancement of health and safety."[28]

Can traditional soil and water conservation programs be expanded to accommodate broader environmental concerns, or will radically new programs be needed?[29] Environmental constraints will bring changes in conventional farming—now sharply focused on technology, chemicals, and short-term profits—that arose since the New Deal and World War II. At a congressional hearing in 1989 it was said that "no one is more dependent upon a healthy and safe environment than are farmers and ranchers who make their home and their living from the land."[30] Just before his untimely death, Robert Rodale urged Americans to go beyond maintenance and take the next step toward regenerative agriculture.[31] He believed that farming systems have within themselves a large capacity to regenerate, using internal resources. Sustainability should mean forever: "Agricultural environments . . . [can be] designed to promote endless regeneration."[32]

Why Is Agriculture Different and Why Are Farmers Suspicious of Change?

Farming is invariably tied to a piece of land; it is, in current jargon, "site specific." It is also determined by an annual growing season that brings in short-term profits. Ironically, these space and time constraints tend to work against the broad and long-term goals of sustainable agriculture. The rapid exhaustion of Ogallala groundwater results in large part from the farmer's understandable need to think short term. He is caught in a squeeze between weather and markets. High Plains irrigation was truly a great historic victory because it was reliable and because it used free water. The farmer's wheat or corn or sorghum must receive water at critical stages in its short growing season. The ability to irrigate is such a source of security that many plains irrigators flood their fields with massive amounts of water to reassure themselves that each plant is served. The extensive conventional set of institutions and practices, ranging from policies to laws and property rules, will be difficult to overturn.[33]

Recognition that farming is invariably tied to an individual piece of land is not just a view from the High Plains; it is acknowledged globally. A 1987 statement by the influential World Commission on Environment and Development, although it was intended for newly developing nations, can readily be transferred to the American scene in the Ogallala heartland. Just as plains farmers fear being overtaken by Big Agribusiness, the WCED says that "in many developing countries the introduction of large-scale commercial agriculture may produce revenue rapidly, but may also dispossess a large number of small farmers and make income distribution more inequitable." It concludes: "In the long run, such a path may not be sustainable; it impoverishes many people and can increase pressures on the natural resource base through overcommercialized agriculture." Plains farmers say the same thing about falling groundwater levels and soil erosion. Although they are not the small farmers on a few acres in the Third World that the WCED describes, it is still appropriate to agree with the United Nations–sponsored agency that "relying more on small-holder cultivation may be slower at first, but more easily sustained over the long run."[34] Decision making on the local level is an essential tenet of the sustainable-development paradigm. However, local decisions do not guarantee environmental protection, as is shown by the fatal destruction of trees for firewood in the Sahel and Nepal, as well as the human tragedy on the High Plains.

Farmers also worry that sustainable farming will mean a return to hard labor. This is why so many are suspicious about organic farming and appropriate technology, since they see equipment and chemicals as means not only to increase productivity but also to reduce physical labor. Organic farmers who practice sustainability insist that each farm is unique, so that recommended practices and technologies must be uniquely applied to avoid damage to its microenvironment and its microeconomy.[35] Sustainable agriculture needs to be seen more clearly not as a throwback to the less complicated agriculture of fifty to one hundred years ago; instead, it requires of the farmer more knowledge of his farm's ecosystem and its place in his life and society's. In most cases, alternative farming implies diversification rather than specialization. The objective is long-term self-sufficiency to sustain the farm environment and to reduce costs. "Such systems require broad knowledge rather than specialized information or training. They require judgment and flexibility rather than assembly-line repetition. There are no recipes for successful low-input, sustainable agricultural systems."[36]

Whatever the direction, changes in plains farming are inevitable. The zero-depletion plan envisaged by Northwest Kansas Groundwater Management District Four is merely the argument that it is better to control and shape the changes today rather than react to them at the fatal last minute. Many farmers grudgingly acknowledge that access to Ogallala water will gradually become too expensive as water tables decline and pumping costs (equipment and energy) go up. The result is a classic example of the limits set on the use of an environmental resource less by its complete depletion than by rising costs and diminishing returns. For the Ogallala aquifer, the immediate need is physical sustainability. As has been noted, the Ogallala is an unusual water resource where, lacking the usual renewal from rain or river, replacement is measured in inches while consumption is measured in feet. Sustainable development's goal is simple. In the case of the High Plains, more wheat (and alternative crops) can and should be produced using less water, chemicals, soil, fuel, and capital. By necessity, many Ogallala farmers already accept these goals and are moving to achieve them.

The Ogallala aquifer belongs to the world because humankind today is a globally dominant species whose needs cannot be ignored. When food from a radius of thousands of miles enters a single shopping cart or when bags of grain stamped "USAID" avert starvation in Africa's Sahel, the whole world depends on the Ogallala. As a result, the clear fresh waters of the aquifer are being gulped up at ten times their trickling pace of replacement. Over the next fifty years as the world's food needs multiply five or ten times, Ogallala water, fulfilling Adam Smith's eighteenth-century prophecy, will become as precious as diamonds.

The Plains Advantage

Irrigation on the High Plains has definite advantages when compared to irrigation in other regions of the United States and the world. Already the combination of knowledge, prices, and technology has brought expansionary development beyond anything imaginable during the grim Dust Bowl era. Irrigation on the High Plains is positioned well compared with the rest of the world. The cost of new dams, reservoirs, canals, and distribution systems has been rising in Asia, Africa, and Latin America, but High Plains irrigation does not face these large capital costs. It is intensely localized and small in scale, using free-standing in-field pumps and sprinklers owned by individual farmers. In most of the world, including California and Arizona, irrigation involves large publicly owned, debt-ridden systems of dams and diversion projects covering thousands of square miles, with tunnels and aqueducts moving water hundreds of miles from source to farmer and creating much waste through evaporation, besides threatening major environmental degradation. In contrast, the High Plains irrigator is free from distant technological breakdowns, independent of meddlesome collective decision making and complex water regulations. Aside from initial equipment costs and maintenance and energy to fuel the pumps, his water is free, while large-scale projects must attach a price to water and depend on heavy public subsidies to keep costs at a manageable level for intensive-use farming.

In its individualized framework, Ogallala water is translated directly into improved crop yields. On the plains it is the farmer's point of view that prevails, not the bureaucrat's infrastructure.[37] Large systems tend to deliver water on a fixed schedule; the farmer can match water with the needs of crops. Results are far superior on the plains when compared to those in many other irrigation systems elsewhere in the world, notably in India, because independent management decisions can respond to local crop needs. Such freedom is an unexpected benefit from the precarious limitation of the central High Plains: the region has no major rivers or lakes to dam or tap for irrigation. There is no equivalent to the Sacramento, Columbia, or Colorado

18

rivers on the High Plains. The flatness of the land, lacking deep valleys, prevented large-scale dam building by the Reclamation Service.

Another unusual advantage is the absence of major cities on the central and southern plains. Garden City in Kansas, Guymon in Oklahoma, and even Lubbock in Texas will never become a Denver or Los Angeles or Phoenix. Farmers who cannot break even when their water costs reach seventy dollars an acre-foot cannot compete with cities that can afford two thousand to six thousand dollars an acre-foot, as is the case with Arizona. Farming is water intensive. The water a typical plains farmer needs for a year's wheat crop on 1,280 acres could serve twenty-four typical American families annually. The metropolitan pressures that are driving farmers out in California, Arizona, and New Mexico are unlikely to appear on the High Plains. Finally, although industrial use of water is six times more cost efficient than farming, the plains have the advantage of little heavy industry. Except for the threatening increase in the use of Ogallala water for oil recovery, the plains are remarkably free of heavy water pollution.

The central High Plains, for many reasons, are strategically attractive for continued irrigation farming. As cities spread out in the Southwest and consume water once allocated to farmers, the groundwater of the Ogallala aquifer will assume increasing importance in keeping the High Plains a strategic food-producing region. When high prices reflect water scarcity in urban regions throughout the world, the advantages of the nonurban, nonindustrial Ogallala region will make its agricultural sustainability even more attractive. This, in turn, should encourage more intensive water conservation and extend the lifespan of irrigation on the High Plains.

A counterargument involves the parallel realities that the Ogallala region produces grains that are already in heavy surplus, that local farmers have trouble making ends meet on low grain prices, and that the region itself is chronically at risk because of its marginal droughty climate and easily destructible soil and water. Historically, it has been repeatedly abandoned by farmers, and there have been several attempts over time to return it to its original grassland condition, most recently through the federal Conservation Reserve Program of 1985.

Integration into a Worldwide Environmental Economy

Marketplace forces are not likely to be sublimated, subverted, or eliminated in this less-than-perfect world of human frailty and greed.[38] The move toward sustainability cannot escape these forces, nor can the changes be applied everywhere, especially when every farm has a specific geography as its individually unique "living tether." At the moment, world farming is consuming more soil and water and producing fewer human rewards. The Ogallala aquifer's problem is, unfortunately, a common one. Most developing countries and many industrialized nations have discovered that a large part of their wealth comes from the land. American agriculture is history's outstanding example. William C. Clark concludes that "the policy need is to tailor technological innovations to the specific local conditions encountered in various environment-development conflicts around the world."[39] William D. Ruckelshaus's words apply as much to the High Plains as anywhere in the Third World: "A prosperous rural society based on sustainable agriculture must be the prelude to future development in much of the developing world."[40] The Dust Bowl region of southwestern Kansas and the Oklahoma-Texas Panhandle can become a unique model of an environmental turnaround that can teach globally.

The joker in this poker game is global warming. The High Plains region is inescapably threatened by the world's changing chemical climate as ever larger quantities of man-induced carbon dioxide, methane, and other substances are being pumped into the upper atmosphere. According to global climate modeling, the U.S. High Plains is one of several regions around the world that are particularly vulnerable to intensive desertification if the predicted carbon-dioxide–induced greenhouse effect takes place. Global warming would accelerate groundwater consumption at three times the rate of today's conservation efforts and hence would seriously threaten most sustainability strategies. As the greenhouse effect takes hold, warmer weather, bringing more threats of desertification to the plains, will force heavier demands on already-stressed irrigation water. Wrote Jim MacNeill in 1989: "Global warming is a form of feedback from the earth's ecological system to the world's economic system. So are the ozone hole, acid rain in Europe and eastern North America, soil degradation in the prairies, deforestation and species loss in the Amazon, and many other environmental phenomena. A number of communities and regions have already crossed critical thresholds."[41] The greenhouse effect on the plains intensifies the region's well-known primary burden: drought and the constant threat of desertification.

Continuous desertification elsewhere already has made the Ogallala more valuable. The United Nations Environment Program (UNEP) estimates that 60 percent of the world's 8.25 billion acres of arid or semiarid agricultural land is affected by desertification. In 1989 the risk of desertification threated an area larger than the African continent and containing a billion inhabitants. Every year deserts grow by 15 million acres. Simultaneously, water use has doubled worldwide at least twice in the twentieth century and could double again before 2010. Water stress is already the rule in eighty developing nations containing 40 percent of the world's population.[42]

Concluding Note: Searching for the Right Solution

The Ogallala aquifer could have lain forever like a sleeping Behemoth in a bed of gravel and sand under solid rock, but human intervention captured its water to turn a desert into a garden. Although environmental history can be complex, the logic of this book is simple: without irrigation, the region encompassing southwest Kansas and the Oklahoma-Texas Panhandle would have remained a hostile and unproductive frontier environment. It still has hot, windy summers and harsh winters, and wood and water are not easily acquired. Even today dryland farming remains high-risk farming about which the best producers have serious doubts. The Dust Bowl label is appropriate, but the High Plains has become one of the most productive farming regions in the world. The dramatic turnabout from Dust Bowl to breadbasket and feedbag of the world depended on extraordinary technological innovations in irrigation and the industrialization of agriculture. As groundwater levels decline, workable alternatives for sustainable development are being explored; these will have less effect on the natural resource and still serve human needs.

The answer is more political than anything else. William D. Ruckelshaus, reflecting on his experience as director of the United States Environmental Protection Agency and more recently as chief executive officer of an environmental-industry corporation, Browning Ferris Industries, writes: "The central lesson of realistic policy-making is that most individuals and organizations change when it is in their interest to change, either because they derive some benefit from changing or because they incur sanctions when they do not."[43] A self-interested democratic process, whether through a local water board meeting on a Tuesday evening at the Soil Conservation Service office in Liberal, Kansas, or a congressional hearing in a wood-paneled Washington room, can be the means to move toward sustainable agriculture. As long as current consumption is destructive and as long as the marketplace continues to regard environmental and human costs as irrelevant, political intervention is essential.

Ruckelshaus believes that only through political constraints can the market system be bent toward long-term sustainability. The conventional dependence upon technological fixes and normal workings of the market will be severely challenged by environmental barriers. "Business as usual" is pushing against some immovable limits, and alternative crops and markets are becoming more attractive. Ruckelshaus is optimistic about the capacity of American democratic society to accept short-term burdens to meet a long-term goal, citing the historic examples of the high economic risks involved in the mid-nineteenth-century abandonment of slavery, national resolve during World War II, the high-minded postwar Marshall Plan (which consumed 3 percent of the Gross National Product in 1947), and the energy crisis of the 1970s.

Government intervention played an essential role in the recovery of the Dust Bowl region in the 1930s and was instrumental in protecting farmers from the worst effects of droughts in the 1950s and 1970s.[44] Dominant government policy yesterday and today encouraged the overproduction of crops and the overprotection of farmers. The 1985 farm bill finally did include subsidies to encourage, even compel, land retirement. State governments, which claim to own the groundwater on the High Plains, continue to treat water mostly as a plentiful free commodity. Historically, most groundwater agencies have justified their existence by focusing on economic development and the exploitation of resources. It will be no easy task for them to promote sustainable development, which severely restricts farmers. This is the test that Northwest Kansas Groundwater Management District Four has chosen as its model. Responding successfully to a multiple crisis could require a modification of society comparable in scale to the agricultural revolution of the late Neolithic Age and the Industrial Revolution. Past changes were gradual, spontaneous, and largely unconscious; the new changes will be specific and planned. We cannot take nature, or successful agriculture, for granted as past generations have had the luxury of doing. Instead, the future will be what we make of it.

Rewriting the Rule Book: Environment, Economics, and Agriculture

When the best viewpoint or paradigm is sought to understand how a declining groundwater supply is connected with successful High Plains farming, it is not a case of agriculture versus environment. The debate cannot be understood as a simple choice between the survival of farming or preservation of the remaining Ogallala supply. Instead, the picture becomes much clearer when one compares the diverging interests of economics with environmental protection, but even this does not generate a workable model for successful farming above the Ogallala. That must come from somewhere else.

A common confusion today is to reduce agriculture to a subcategory of either environment or economics.[45] Instead, the answer to the problem of irrigation on the plains may be found through neither an environmental approach nor an economic one, but by making both subcategories of a larger agricultural paradigm. Historically, the traditional farm family, reflected in the long-term influence of the farm lobby, is one of the most continuously powerful forces in American history and politics. But new insights concerning the agricultural paradigm also can be gleaned from the concept of sustainable development as a comprehensive model for successful modern agriculture.

The workable model to emulate is a comprehensive agricultural paradigm that is separate, more complex, and inclusive.[46] Agriculture is elusive; it is virtually a floating paradigm with a life of its own. It builds on historic experience but belongs to no historic era. It involves environment and economics but belongs to neither. Sustainable agriculture, in Stephane Castonguay's words, "is dependent upon the autonomy of the agricultural community to practice an agriculture that is environmentally sound."[47] As humanity's oldest intervention in nature, agriculture is not ultimately tied to a specific economic or environmental paradigm or any other ideology because it encompasses a myriad of geographic, technical, economic, social, cultural, and historical factors. One of the most elaborate elements of the agricultural paradigm, the family farm, is discussed in chapter 6. In chapters 7 and 9, connections are made among the family farm, the future of irrigation from Ogallala groundwater, and continuous agriculture on the south-central High Plains.

Irrigation on the plains is still in a self-destruct mode and the Ogallala aquifer is still a nonrenewable resource. As such, the Ogallala today is a representative microcosm of the difficult global search for sustainable agriculture. Ogallala water and irrigation technology are servants to a greater master, but which one?

1

· · ·

The First Half-Billion Years

The soil is the one indestructible, immutable asset that the nation possesses. It is the one resource that cannot be exhausted, that cannot be used up.—position taken by the U.S. Bureau of Soils around 1900

Soil is a temporary interlude for rocks and minerals on their way to solution and to the sea.—soil scientist William A. Albrecht in 1956

Where did the Ogallala aquifer and its valuable landscape come from? All of it migrated from somewhere else, even the plants and people. Hundreds of millions of years of geological restlessness created today's water-saturated underground beds of gravel and sand covered by layers of rock and fertile soil above and undergirded by rolling red rock below. The mighty geological time scale turns human history into an afterthought, for even the Ogallala aquifer lives for only a brief moment as plains soils race from the mountains to the ocean; today's dry landscape is a blink of the Maker's eye. The tall and short grasses of the plains ebb and flow like tides on a beach as they follow fickle shifts in rainfall patterns. Conventional farmers who force corn and alfalfa by draining the underground water supply are a mere interruption, like an itch that is quickly scratched. Other farmers, who see water, soil, and grasses as a collaborating ensemble they must join rather than overcome, will stay a while longer. The successful farmer listens to the nonhuman voices around him; as history has shown, this is not an easily learned skill.

For more than the last two thousand years of the current geological epoch, these forbidding and tiresome grasslands have covered fully one-third of the North American continent, its single most extensive terrain.[1] Some of the same wild grasses—bluestems, switchgrasses, gramas, cordgrasses—range across a thousand miles of middle America, from the southern edge of Lake Michigan to eastern Colorado, from West Texas far north into Canada. They differ in size and lushness, depending on moisture and temperature, and allow us to distinguish between the midwestern tallgrass prairie, the midland mixed-grass country, and the shortgrass High Plains. Since the 1870s, when John Wesley Powell called the High Plains a subhumid region, the description fits an environment where the rainfall is consistently less than that necessary for traditional eastern agriculture. Yearly rainfall is between twelve and twenty inches, compared to thirty to fourty inches east of the Mississippi. Effective rainfall can be much less because of evaporation from the extremes of wind and heat. A favorable factor, repeated by desperate boosters to the point of exaggeration, is that three-quarters of the rain comes during the growing season, April to September.[2]

The Trescotts' Place

Today Roger and Betty Trescott live on a two-thousand-acre Oklahoma Panhandle farm that is compact for a High Plains operation. It is divided into several wheat and alfalfa fields. Their ranch house is white, unpretentious, even small. They have no children and regret it. The yard immediately around the house is sparse and plain. Like most plains farmers, they do not have the familiar steep-roof red-painted barn of the East, but instead several large metal sheds where they keep their equipment and supplies. Inside the house, cleaning is simplified by use of heavy-duty plastic upholstery on some of the furniture. Everything is spotless. When they are out in the wheat fields, the Trescotts are some of the most traditional farmers described in this book because they practice flood irrigation.

The heart of the Trescott home is Roger's and Betty's shared office. He works on farm management while Betty cranks out reports and newsletters to alert fellow farmers and the public about major Ogallala water issues. Despite Roger's recent bout with back trouble, they both devote their attention to these public issues. He is tall, lean, expert, and bemused. Betty is a short ball of fire, blazing with energy, aggressively articulate, and meticulous in her research. Her reputation for presenting hammering testimony at Oklahoma legislative hearings on water abuse now precedes her in the Panhandle and the capital. One event that caught Betty's eye was a landmark December 1984 Oklahoma Supreme Court decision concerning the beneficial use of Panhandle groundwater: was it proper for Mobil Oil Company to draw large amounts of fresh Ogallala water, tens of billions of gallons, to force up the remaining oil in an old field (the process is called secondary recovery), or should Ogallala water, irreplaceable but admittedly existing in large amounts, be saved for the irrigation of crops, as Oklahoma law requires?[3]

Betty represented the Texas County (Oklahoma) Irrigation and Water Resources Association (TCIWRA). With her usual zeal and determination to persuade whoever would listen, she observed that "the late U. S. Senator Robert S. Kerr, Sr., is famous for his often repeated prediction that some day the price of a barrel of water will be higher than the price of a barrel of oil," and commented that "his prophecy is already come true. Right now, at our State Capitol Building and in the very building housing OWRB [Oklahoma Water Resources Board]—the State Department of Health Building—taxpayers are buying bottled water, imported from Arkansas at $33.60 a barrel, while the price of oil on the current (1985) market is $26.53." That would put the price of water at eighty cents a gallon, without doubt an unrealistically expensive example, but Betty Trescott's point was driven home.

Betty noted that Mobil Oil Company was licensed in 1984 by the Oklahoma Water Resources Board to pump fresh groundwater to recover thirty-five million barrels of oil. At a market value of twenty-eight dollars a barrel, $98 million worth of oil would require the use of $19.2 billion worth of water, priced at eighty cents a gallon, a one-to-twenty cost ratio. "In case anyone thinks it is an unfair comparison," said TCIWRA, "to use the cost of imported drinking water at 80 cents a gallon, we would be glad to substitute the value of the destroyed water at the cost of replacement—and then it would become obvious that 80 cents a gallon would be a great bargain."[4] When Ed

Gutentag, for many years the United States Geological Survey hydrologist in Garden City, Kansas, heard of Betty's claims, he first thought she was an environmental kook. He soon concluded, at the OWRB hearing, that "she was one of the few in the meeting room to grasp hydrology. Then I considered her a colleague."[5]

The controversy, of which more will be said in chapter 5, involved the four great geological resources—natural gas, water, oil, and soil—in the Dust Bowl region of the Oklahoma-Texas Panhandle and southwest Kansas. In Oklahoma, fuel from the Hugoton-Guymon field, the largest natural-gas field in the nation (and the second-largest in the world), is used to pump fresh Ogallala water, the largest and most exploited aquifer in the nation, not only for cropland irrigation, but also to recover oil from old fields. The soil of Texas County, rated high-quality Class III by the federal Soil Conservation Service, makes Ogallala water even more desirable to farmers, who in turn find themselves at odds with the oil companies.

The most relaxing spot on Roger's and Betty's land is reached after a brief drive (no one walks in Panhandle country) to their northernmost holding pond, which covers about an acre. The water is refreshing after the hot dusty fields. The pond is ringed by lush green trees, sweetened by the song of birds, and offers an oasis in the middle of the dry, raspy, flat landscape. The steady, noisy pounding of the nearby pump and engine is not an irritant but the symbol of their success as farmers. Roger moved to the Guymon, Oklahoma, vicinity in 1947 after learning to irrigate near Plainview, Texas. He drilled Texas County's fifth well down to the red-rock bottom of the aquifer at 300 feet. It cost him ten thousand dollars, a fortune in the late 1940s, but is now 50 feet deeper than it was when he started. He irrigates 1,720 acres of his 2,000-acre farm from several wells, but now with 30 percent less water than he used in the 1960s. In twenty years, furrow irrigation has lowered his overall pumping level from a depth of 190 feet to 240 feet. Within five years the Trescotts will run out of practical access to water when the pumping level descends 12 more feet; going deeper is too inefficient. They are also facing the crunch between low wheat prices and rising natural-gas costs. The Trescotts' irrigation system, as it floods each field to reach every plant, is also wasteful, losing more than 50 percent of its water to evaporation and runoff. The water is not easy to apply quickly to crops, but a shift to center-pivot irrigation, which has much less evaporation, would cost the Trescotts at least four hundred thousand dollars. If they were younger, perhaps they might have undertaken the transition.

Foundations

Roger's and Betty's farm is eighteen miles north by northwest of Guymon in Texas County, midway on the east-west axis of the Oklahoma panhandle. Their superior-quality soil and the pure groundwater beneath it are geological migrants; it took five thousand years for the Trescotts' soil to build up to its modern fertility before their land was homesteaded in 1911.[6] Underground, the water, now trickling ever so slowly, is ten thousand to twenty-five thousand years old, originally glacier runoff from the Rockies. Everything and everyone is an immigrant. The Trescotts arrived from west-central Texas in the 1940s. Previous farmers brought in dryland wheat, and before that the land supported semiarid grasses, such as buffalo grass. The most recent imports are corn and alfalfa, both demanding so much water that their natural western boundary lies in humid farm country more than three hundred miles to the east. Experts say, and farmers know, that traditional American farming should have halted a hundred miles to the east because there is not enough rain. But the combination of intrusive Europeans, plants and animals, soil and rock, and, above all, someplace else's water, gave rise to the farming that goes on in the Panhandle today. Remove just one of these immigrants and food production ends immediately.

The Trescott place once stood in a vast inland sea. Deep water covered the region for as much as fifty million years at a time. This geologic time span, begun half a billion years ago, is immeasurable on any human scale. The last great flooding took place sixty million years ago when the North American continent looked like a World War II life raft in the ocean, having dry sides but filled with shallow water in the middle and open at the north or south end or both ends. Today's Hudson Bay is the last large shallow remnant of this ancient sea; sixty million years ago it reached as far south as the Dakotas and even earlier as far as the Gulf of Mexico. Called the Rocky Mountain Trough, the inland sea was nearly one thousand miles wide and three thousand miles long. Each time it came, it laid down hundreds or thousands of feet of sediment. Over geologic time, the thick sediments surfaced many times when the seas withdrew, only to be eroded to slivers of nothing, just as the soils of the High Plains today are running to the Mississippi River and into the Gulf of Mexico. Geologic cycling is still in process: for twenty million years or so during the Jurassic Period (two hundred million years ago), the plains may have had a climate similar to that of modern times—dry and brisk—before slipping below the shallow sea again.

The first time Roger's and Betty's farm was under water may have been 580 million years ago (late Cambrian), when thousands of feet of limestone were layered on top of sandstone. After rising above sea level 400 million years ago (Devonian), virtually all of Oklahoma sank again 50 million years later to be rewarded with more thousands of feet of limestone and shale. Then, 275 million years ago (late Pennsylvanian), the land again rose above the waters, but within 25 million years Permian and Triassic seas buried the floor with one or two thousand feet of red sandstones and shales until less than 200 million years ago. The Oklahoma Panhandle and the rest of the region surfaced again before descending under a Jurassic and Cretaceous sea from 150 million to 65 million years ago. These tens of thousands of feet of level "layer-cake geology" marine deposits would have made Oklahoma one of the highest places on Earth were it not for thousands of millennia of erosion by water and dust-storm winds when the land stood above the seas. It is not clear when the region will slip below the waters again, but the record is promising.[7]

The picture changed dramatically about sixty million years ago (early Tertiary times) because of events two hundred miles to the west in the Rocky Mountains. Large amounts of water, active as rain, snow, and ice, have made the surface of Earth far busier than other planets in the solar system. It still is. On a celestial time scale, geologic changes took place at dizzying speed even in the seemingly placid Ogallala country. Activity of uplift and erosion at the Rockies would seem like a speeded-up movie. Rocky Mountain scenery would not be spectacular during the powerful Laramide orogeny (mountain-building period), when the ancestral Rockies first rose and expelled the seas seventy million Cretaceous years ago. The landscape was that of a high rolling country. In a moist and semitropical time, with an abundance of water, it was quickly worn down to a peneplain by the elements as rapidly as it rose. Nevertheless, valley floors still stood thousands of feet above sea level and mountain peaks a thousand feet higher. The continental backbone had appeared. This can still be seen in the upper levels of Rocky Mountain National Park, in the gentle curves that today's Trail Ridge Road (U.S. 36) traverses. The traveler on this highway also sees the sharper and steeper peaks and valleys carved out of the curves by the Pleistocene ice ages between five hundred thousand and ten thousand years ago. Today these mountains stand waist deep in their own tailings, like a candle burned halfway down into its own melting wax. The unthinkable tonnage of rocks and gravel and grit so speedily removed by the glaciers ended up as the surface of the High Plains, carried hundreds of miles by giant braided streams of which the Platte River is a younger and poorer sample.[8] These sediments covered the rolling hills of Roger Trescott's Permian red rock.

The Panhandle country was nudged upward by the same uplift of the Rocky Mountains. It also received a slight tilt of fifteen to twenty feet per mile eastward as the Gulf Coast area began its modern sinking. The Oklahoma Panhandle is midway along the gradual slope of debris running eastward from the Rocky Mountains. Topographic maps of the Trescotts' land show its highest point at 3,239 feet and never less than 3,150 feet. The Trescotts' surface terrain is not ocean-bed material like the red rock and limestone below but came from nonmarine outwash debris. In the last million Quarternary years, the Trescotts' land, from Permian red bedrock to surface soils, began to take on recognizable shape and quality. If Roger Trescott could take a colossal shovel and scrape off the most recent layers from his farm down to three hundred feet or so, he would stand on gently rolling redrock country that had been wearing down for millennia, just as all the other beds of rock, many long gone, had done before it. The oldest rocks under the debris were Permian red bedrock dating back to the watery deposits of broad, shallow, brackish seas 240 million years ago or more. Missing Triassic and Jurassic rocks signal tens of millions of years of rock removal until shallow seas encroached again a hundred million years later and lasted until about 96 million years ago. But the Trescott farm has no sign of the latter shallow seas as does Phil and Linda Tooms's Mesozoic place forty five miles to the north in Kansas. The Trescotts are Permian people.

Today's long-standing geological trend on the High Plains—steady wearing down of steadily rising mountains—became clear about five million years ago near the end of Miocene times. The region's grassland would have been recognizable if we were crossing it today. Between five million and two million years ago, the climate again cycled cooler and drier in a global trend intensified by the rain shadow of the uplifting Rockies.[9]

The rocks, gravels, sands, soils, and water that arrived at Roger and Betty Trescott's future property were a hash of the Earth's entire multibillion-year geologic story. With the Ogallala rock and gravel came the water, or, more accurately, water was a major carrier of debris from the mountains. The flow eastward must have been spectacular in glacial times as it carried away the melting ice and snow with their gravelly burden. Airplane passengers today can still see the miles-wide flow pattern in the vast floodplains of the Platte River system. But the massive flow of water that had already created the Ogallala formation and kept it full was later—thousands of years ago—captured and diverted south by a recent geologic incident: the appearance of two rivers: the southward-flowing Rio Grande and Pecos.[10] What remains in the Ogallala formation is mostly fossil water drawn from the Rockies long ago. There is no massive and perpetual recharge (today it is a paltry inch-a-year trickle down) as was true for most of recent geological history.[11] The High Plains aquifer is like a flat, sandy beach where the tide has recently gone out; no new water comes in at the upper (western) end, yet it is naturally draining out the lower (eastern) end directly into streams and springs. Nevertheless, the scale of water held the Ogallala formation is almost beyond reckoning: over three billion acre-feet (9.78 trillion gallons) under 174,000 square miles in gravel beds up to three hundred feet thick, moving east on an average of a foot a day.

All this geologic history tells us that the Panhandle country is a very changeable place. The top hundred feet or so of Roger and Betty Trescott's land also came from somewhere else. Some was rock and gravel from glacial times, but chewed up several times over by rivers as they moved it from place to place. Other parts came with the wind, either in vast moving dunes or simply blown there during several centuries of recurring dust bowls.

The Tooms Land

Forty-five miles north by northeast from the Trescott farm in Kansas is the three thousand-acre farm of Phil and Linda Tooms. They live in the northwest corner of Seward County on the western bank of the now-intermittent Cimarron River. When he drilled his first well in 1965, Phil Tooms reached his red bed at 465 feet. His share of the Ogallala wet gravels, as they filled in and leveled off the ancient hills and valleys, is about 250 feet thick. This is topped by about 215 feet of young mountain debris imported by water or wind during the Quaternary or Pleistocene ice age. Hence Tooms's farmstead stands at 2,750 feet above sea level, while his solid-rock red bed is at 2,285 feet.

The story of the Tooms's land is mostly similar to the Trescott account. It is made up of the scant remains of discontinuous seabed layers and leftover scraps of the Rocky Mountains, the rest still dribbling east toward the Mississippi and the Gulf of Mexico.[12] But about a mile south of Phil Tooms's house and farm and 2,400 feet underground, the Trescotts' 230-million-year-old Permian red seabed slips down northward at the rate of 15.4 feet per mile unconformably (layers of rock are missing) underneath an upper Jurassic–lower Cretaceous red bed that is a mere 135 million years old. Ninety-five million years of Triassic and Jurassic seabed has disappeared downhill and east into Oklahoma, Missouri, Louisiana, and underwater.

Phil Tooms is lucky when it comes to water in the Ogallala.[13] His land is smack-dab in the middle of a U–shaped rock structure thirty-seven miles southeast of the Bear Creek Fault and thirty-four miles west of the Crooked Creek–Fowler Fault. Over tens of thousands of years, a seventy-mile-wide stretch of rock running northeast to southwest was undermined by salt dissolution and collapsed into itself. Today the groundwater sits in a large seventy-mile-wide covered bathtub with the cover tilted southeast about 12.5 feet per mile. But the tub is not simply full of water; its bottom and lower sides are the red bedrock lying 465 feet deep on the Tooms farm, and it has been filled with 250 feet of unconsolidated silt, clay, sand, gravel, and caliche aquifer set down by Pliocene, Pleistocene, and Quarternary braided streams across an ancient floodplain before being covered by a lid of wind-blown modern soil.

Climate

When the emerging High Plains began their most recent rise above the inland sea, no great mountain barriers to the west shut off the flow of moisture-laden winds from the nearby intruding Pacific Ocean. The most fleeting migrant moving west to east across the plains was another fluid, in this case damp air. The water was picked up from the prehistoric Pacific shore only halfway as far west then as it is today: about where today's Colorado-Utah border is. Ten to five million years ago, when it was not under water, the vast American center from South Dakota to Texas was a moist, low-lying semi-tropical region with heavy vegetation, perhaps with valley forests and hilltop shrubs similar to today's neighborhoods around San Antonio, Texas, and Monterrey, Mexico.[14] The region is likely to become fecund again in the geologic future. In due time, the ancestral Rocky Mountains intervened to cut off rainfall to make the region as dry or drier than it is today. Today the High Plains stand under this rain shadow that forces clouds to give up their burden two hundred miles farther west than in earlier geologic time. The decade of rains in the 1880s that fooled so many aspiring settlers was not a promise of immediate change.

A worldwide cooling, begun a little more than a million years ago and still in process until a century ago, brought more arid and more contrasting climates than those of today. Dust storms raged across the plains as they had in every dry phase, becoming the major movers of today's rich loess soil. The landscape may have been as harsh as the modern drifting dunelands of Africa and Asia. The droughts and dust bowls that cycled in the recorded history of white explorers and settlers in the nineteenth and twentieth centuries are but phases in a longer history. Scientists who contribute their days and nights to poring over prehistoric and historic tree rings, wide for wet times, narrow for dry, tell us that twenty-two-year cycles of dry and wet times can be discerned, seemingly associated with fairly regular sunspot incidents. Short term or long, the High Plains have not been a good place for man or animal for tens of thousands of years if the prehistoric records of animal depopulation and the historic human depopulations are any indication. There were no permanent American Indian settlements in the Dust Bowl region. No doubt the immediate human future will see more droughts and blowing soils. The greenhouse effect, the human-induced warming caused by carbon dioxide released into the atmosphere from two hundred years of industrial coal burning, may quickly skew the data (see chapter 8). No doubt, on a geological time scale, the wet climate will return, together with the rising inland seas, but today's thousand-year pattern points toward continued and increasing dryness.

Through all this the vast waters of the Ogallala aquifer waited underground, unknown and untapped, inexorably trickling eastward, surfacing occasionally in eastward-dipping riverbeds, then disappearing again, unreplenished and hardly consumed.

Soil: Ecological Capital and Albrecht's Dilemma

The great modern naturalist Loren C. Eiseley said the greatest magic on this planet is the wonder of water. Together with Earth's other magnificent fluid, the atmosphere, water is valued because it is extremely interactive. It makes living things happen. On the High Plains, water's work is to make the good soil spring to life. In turn, soil is complex and dynamic, and, fortunately for us humans, it is extremely interactive with the plants that must feed upon it. Soil is potent, always in motion, as soil scientist William A. Albrecht stated so eloquently in the epigram at the beginning of this chapter, a vigorous and flowing medium ready to be used by wild grasses or set to the plow for wheat or sorghum. The irony of soil is its fluidity.[15] It is predestined to flow eventually to rivers and the sea just as much as the rocks inevitably broke from mountains to become soil.

35

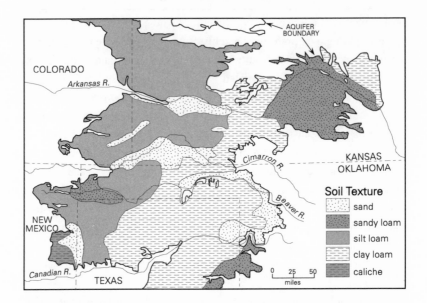

2. The soil types overlying the Ogallala aquifer of the central High Plains range mostly from sand to clay in southwest Kansas and the Oklahoma-Texas Panhandle. With irrigation, they proved to be some of the most productive in the nation. Redrawn from Richard R. Luckey, Edwin D. Gutentag, Frederick J. Deimes, and John B. Weeks, *Digital Simulation of Ground-Water Flow in the High Plains Aquifer in Parts of Colorado, Nebraska, New Mexico, Oklahoma, South Dakota, Texas, and Wyoming: Regional Aquifer-System Analysis,* USGS Professional Paper 1400-D (Washington, D.C.: Government Printing Office, 1986), 28.

What turns High Plains soil into good farmer's soil is a miraculous ecological balance between the right chemical salts and the presence of the right amount of water. Calcium, magnesium, potassium, sodium, and hydrogen, as well as nitrate and phosphate, in the top six to eighteen inches of the ground, mixed with the right amount of moisture, are necessary for the electrochemical exchanges between the roots of plants and ingredients in the soil. All the grains, every seed, and every morsel of the fruits and vegetables we consume depend on these exchanges. As a secondary result, we also can have meat to eat—beef, lamb, pork, chicken—because animals consume the plants, many inedible for humans. Animal and human survival depends on the ionization that makes the plants grow.

36

Root hairs, like the ones the weekend gardener sees in transplanting his tomatoes or her azalea, are enveloped in hydrogen carbonate. Hydrogen is a hyperactive element, and the solid nutrients, in the form of salts, are acquired by the plant in the hydrogen exchange between soil and root. The higher the concentration of chemical dynamics in the soil, the larger and better the crops. This is what makes Roger and Betty Trescott's soil into a world-class dirt—Richfield sandy loam—so prized that it commands the highest prices in Oklahoma's Texas County. The balance is delicate; if the soil lacks the nutrients or has too many salts or if moisture is too high or too low, plant growth is limited, as in the worn-out lands of Appalachia, or virtually nonexistent, as in Nevada's Great Basin.

An enduring soil has consistently offered each human civilization its long-term security, its ecological capital, which deserves to be reinvested rather than squandered. Good life-giving soil maintains a proper physiochemical-electrical balance. The old phrase "salt of the earth" turns out to be remarkably appropriate.

In the broad sweep of human history, the closest approximation to an enduring artificial farm soil created by agricultural tillage is that now covering the great plain of western and northern Europe. Pioneering soil historian Edward Hyams called it "the perfect artificial soil."[16] It models the desirable combination of fertility and stability. In contrast to the insane devouring of North American soils over the last fifty years, European agricultural land advantageously emerged slowly from forest to farm over seven or eight thousand years. European society was largely an agrarian culture for most of its history and did not change until the last two hundred years. The heavy demands of rapid population growth, industrialization, and urbanization are recent happenings when measured by the millennia of a soil-making time scale. Elsewhere on the globe, the long-term results of grassland farming have not been good if the debilitation of China's wind-blown loess, the soil mining in India's history, and the shift from fertility to badlands across the Near East are representative. The quest for new virgin soils under the tropical forests of Brazil is a failure. Speaking of white European settlement on Oklahoma's soils, Hyams argued that in the United States fertility and stability in the land were sacrificed to the American commitment to individual freedom (for example, private property) at all costs.[17] In Europe, by contrast, local geology, climate, technology, and social systems merged to create an ideal cultural balance which coddled the soil instead of the individual.

Unlike hydrogen, nitrogen is underactive. It does not easily combine with other elements for plants to absorb through their roots. Yet nitrogen is essential to every family of living things on earth. How is this riddle solved? How is nitrogen, which exists in the atmosphere, acquired by plants? The process is called nitrogen fixing.

Nitrogen fixing became even more mystifying when in 1837 a French chemist named Boussingault discovered that the soil of a field planted in clover, a legume, actually gained in nitrogen while a nearby wheat field showed no such gain. Somehow, it seemed, clover and other legumes took nitrogen from the air. Later in the century, in 1889, a Dutch scientist discovered that the strange nodules, called warts or galls, on the roots of legumes, such as beans, peas, and clover, were filled with millions of bacteria. The plants gave bacteria their energy through carbohydrates; the bacteria in turn captured nitrogen from the air and made it available to the plant. Once captured by the bacteria, the nitrogen took the form of nitrates, which plants captured chemically and converted into proteins. These proteins in turn were consumed by animals and humans. Usually one strain of bacteria to one plant did the job. It was a symbiotic relationship, since neither plant nor bacteria alone could achieve nitrogen fixation. Of the importance of nitrogen fixing, Peter Farb wrote in 1959: "Should some calamity overtake these bacteria, or a sudden change occur in the environment of the planet, that their numbers might be so seriously reduced . . . [the event would] collapse our superstructure of life, which is hinged to the nitrogen fixed by these microbes."[18]

Humanity's utter dependence upon the thin layer of rocky debris called soil is summed up in Albrecht's dilemma, so called after pioneering Missouri soil scientist William A. Albrecht. In order to feed himself, man intervenes in nature by plowing up virgin soil, planting crops which produce more useful food than would naturally grow on the land, but in the process he speeds up the depletion of nutrients from the soil with high levels of mineral solutions to feed his plants. The brief geologic moment of productive soil, "a temporary interlude for rocks and minerals on their way to solution and to the sea," is dangerously hastened by necessary human interference. On the High Plains, today's soil and wind erosion matches or surpasses the horrific Dust Bowl years.

A significant part of the soil above the Ogallala aquifer is windblown dust, or loess mantle, blown to the High Plains for the past million years from the crumbling rock of the Rocky Mountains by incessant strong winds. Dust storms are hardly a new phenomenon, nor are they entirely man made by poor land management. Over several thousand years, countless dust bowls of transitory loess deposited the incredibly rich clay soil so prized by nineteenth- and twentieth-century pioneers and immigrants. Today it commands premium farmland prices. Such soil has been named chernozem, a Russian word for black or dark brown earth (*chernyi* means a dark brown or black color), and by implication a rich and fertile substance. In contrast, forest soils, with their underlayer of gray, are called podzols, from the Russian *pod zola,* for ashes. Soil science got its start among observant peasants in Ukraine.

The American chernozem is the best in the world: early plains settlers who abandoned worn-out eastern forest farmland marveled that such soil still existed and that there was so much of it. Tradition told settlers that only forest soils were worthwhile. Hence tales of a new cornucopia of abundance captured from the plains soils reached incredulous ears; the notion that plains soil was unbeatable cannot be overestimated for its impact on American and world history. Even as early as 1673 explorer and missionary Louis Joliet exclaimed, "At first, when we were told of these treeless lands, I imagined that it was a country ravaged by fire, where the soil was so poor that it could produce nothing. But we have certainly observed the contrary; and no better soil can be found, either for corn, or for vines, or for any other fruit whatever. . . . Sometimes we saw grass . . . five or six feet high; hemp, which grows naturally here, reaches a height of eight feet. A settler would not there spend ten years in cutting down and burning the trees; on the very day of his arrival, he could put his plough into the ground."

Man cannot live by pulverized rocks alone. The soil that produces our food is more than an inanimate matrix of rocks and minerals; it is an organic living entity: bacteria, fungi, and microbes on one scale, insects, roots, the all-important earthworm, and such animals as the mole on a larger scale. A good little-bluestem acre on the arid Great Plains includes two and one-half tons of plant material in the first six inches of soil. The roots absorb the nitrates and other mineral compounds, absorb soil matter, and hold the plant in place. Farmers quickly learned not to cut their bluestem less than four inches above the surface, nor to allow their animals to graze it down excessively, or the underground sod would suffer, since the above-ground growth produced the sugars and starches the roots needed. The dense roots of quality bluestem withstand drought and can carry cattle through dry spells and winter. Prairie sod is a final synthesis of the entire plantscape; it is the great compromise between parent material, slope, climate, and previous plant life.

While many soils are created over a long time by the forces of climate and vegetation, in Texas County, Oklahoma, Roger and Betty Trescott's soil came during the Pleistocene as a thin mantle that combined silt and fine-textured sand (loess) brought by wind. It built up very gradually into virgin sod under native shortgrasses, taking much more time than in a moist climate. This mature soil is named Richfield sandy loam after its type area near Richfield in Morton County, Kansas.[19] It covers about 10 percent of Texas County, is listed among the most productive soils in the county, and commands premium prices on the local land market. A deep, dark, clayey soil, it is now about six inches thick and was less affected by Dust Bowl windstorms because of its medium texture. Sandier soils blew away faster and to greater depths. But almost eighty years of off-and-on cultivation has burned up a good deal of the fertility of the virgin sod.

It was easy to lose the advantage of virgin soil. When first plowed in the second decade of the twentieth century, virgin soil in Texas County sometimes yielded seventy-five bushels of wheat per acre, but by 1933, only twenty years later, 95 percent of the county's wheat land was abandoned under the pressures of soil depletion, drought, and depression. In 1961 it would average only eight bushels under typical dryland farming, but irrigation would revitalize production. When many of today's old-time irrigators began watering in 1961, wheat yields rose to 45 bushels per acre and grain sorghum yielded from 3,300 to 6,000 pounds per acre, depending on "common management" or "improved management."[20] Irrigation today also allows between 3.5 and 6 tons of alfalfa, which cannot be grown dryland.

Richfield sandy loam is Soil Conservation Service (scs) Class III soil, superior for a region with little rain and significant wind erosion. (Classes I and II are more productive, but because of climate conditions they do not exist in Texas County.) According to national scs standards, Class IIIs are "soils that have severe limitations that reduce the choice of plants, or that require special conservation practices, or both." Without irrigation, Richfield sandy loam can grow dryland wheat and, when the rains are good, sorghum. Central plains farmers, when they can pause to look and read, are told in their soil-survey manuals that

> these soils need to be protected by a growing crop or a heavy stubble to help control wind erosion. . . . Use a cropping system that fits the moisture conditions. Fallow 1/4 to 1/3 of the field. . . . Wheat is likely to fail if it is sown in soil that is moist to a depth of less than 24 inches. Delay tilling fields that have been left fallow, until the danger of soil blowing has passed in spring. . . . Strip-cropping will help to reduce wind erosion, and the stubble will help conserve moisture by catching snow. Avoid excessive tillage and tillage that will leave the surface soil loose and powdery.[21]

Farmers are reminded that their use and management of the soil hinges on the realities of High Plains climate: low rainfall, strong winds, high temperatures in the summer, and low humidity. If the rains come late in spring, they are right for planting sorghum but too late to help wheat mature. Rains late in summer are good for planting wheat but too late to save a sorghum crop. In late winter and early spring, strong winds rip and tear at the soil and it must be protected. In summer, hot winds and low humidity bring high rates of evaporation.

Farmers also know that water is the key to successful farming. Immediately underneath the Panhandle topsoil is a dark grayish-brown compacted clay that is six to twenty inches thick. It advantageously stores large quantities of water. The 1961 edition of *Soil Survey of Texas County, Oklahoma* said few farmers "have access to an ample supply of [irrigation] water and have enough time and money to irrigate all of their land."[22] It added: "Farmers cannot control the weather, but they can adjust their farming methods to protect the soil from extremes of climate, to keep moisture in the soil" to depths at planting time between two and four feet. The 1961 techniques included crop residue (leaving crop debris on fields), stubble mulching, delayed fallow, strip-cropping, terracing, and contour farming. Farmers were warned that if there was not enough cover to protect the soil from wind and water erosion, emergency tilling, or roughening the surface with chisels, shovels, or listers, could provide quick protection, "but it does not provide long-term benefits. It dries the soil and breaks down its structure." Nothing was, or is, easy or clear cut on the plains.

There is the story of the plains farmer who, on being congratulated for a banner crop, grumbled, "Yes, but look what it did to the soil." He was all too aware that his equipment, interest on his outstanding loans, his house, barn, and outbuildings, his own living costs, and any crop profit for the year were paid out of his soil fertility and that it had limited capital. The fertile loess soil of the arid grassland, he knew, was originally so healthy as to continue almost indefinitely, but any farmer working the land every season spends a little more of this capital that is locked up in the thousands-year-old soil.

Albrecht's dilemma is at bottom an ethical paradox in both human and environmental terms. It is the conflict between the inevitability of soil destruction by farming and the imperative of soil construction to ensure continued food for a hungry world. At risk is the well-being of future generations.

When the newly arrived plains farmer hitched his newfangled lightweight John Deere polished-metal shear plow to his horses or oxen and sliced into the virgin sod to plant, cultivate, and harvest his corn or wheat, the soil took on a particularly granular body. If he was on quality land, the farmer judged its potential productivity when, in Albrecht's words, "he took a handful of soil, allowed it to run between his fingers, and said, 'This will be a good place to farm.'" The granular soil does not pack down but allows air and water to percolate through it; the microbes, bacteria, nitrogen, and carbon dioxide work more freely. Rainwater (and later irrigation water) does not run off immediately but filters into the soil, which in turn holds the all-important moisture. Even moderate drought can be endured by crops if water is stowed in porous soil.

Paradoxically, this mechanical shaping of granular soil, with all its physical and chemical benefits, also means that soil is vulnerable. Heavy rainfall pounds it into a gummy slush that quickly closes off further penetration of water. Additional water runs off, erodes the fertile surface soil, and carries it away. Both water and soil are lost in the breakdown of soil body. The effect includes chemical changes as well, since some salts—calcium and magnesium—encourage granulation, while hydrogen, sodium, potassium, and other salts encourage the goo. Farming the land, which increases the carbon dioxide and acidity levels, also encourages the making of goo rather than granules. The soil shifts from being physically stable to being unstable. Water does not seep in and stay; instead, it quickly erodes the soil. When soil loses its fine physique, it also loses the physical environment that allows the all-important chemical and mineral feeding of the plants that are grown in it.

Grasses

Little is left today of the lonely immensity that unnerved the first Europeans. High Plains space is still vast, but now it includes eye-catching markers: farm buildings and geometric fields; roads that run to a vanishing point in infinity; and the ubiquitous grain elevator in towns fourteen miles apart, because that was the round trip a farmer could make to town with a loaded wagon. The monotony that travelers see on the plains is in fact dispelled by the variety, colors, sizes, and shapes of the original tallgrass, midgrass, and shortgrass prairie.[23] The best time is early morning, although boots and jeans get soaked wading through the wet dew of the hip-high plants. Even the multiplicity of names, often for the same plant, provide a surprisingly diverse and pleasantly Middle American lexicography: ripgut grass, scarlet globe mallow, rubber rabbitbrush, blazing star, ironweed, puccoon, beardtongue, chickweed, blue grama, fescue, gumweed, red three-awn, spiderwort, phlox, prairie shoestring, big-leaf pussytoes, threadleaf sedge, silky sophora, fringed sagebrush, broom snakeweed, butterweed, coneflowers, buffalo grass, poverty catgrass, witchgrass, sand dropseed, Johnny-jump-ups, skeleton plant, muhly, switchgrass, lovegrass, pinweed, poppy mallow, sloughgrass, tumblegrass, violet wood sorrel, yellow tansy mustard, greenthread, big and little bluestem, porcupine grass, sideoats grama, purple lovegrass, false boneset, curlycup, gumweed, needle and thread, skullcap, and woolly loco.

The best time of year to enjoy the prairie is late July and early August, not the spring flowering. The weather is hot and dry and the stems and leaves of the grasses such as big bluestem, have lengthened and outgrown early flowering forbs or nongrass prairie plants (broad-leaved herbs, such as prairie cat's foot and wildflowers). Where it has not been farmed, the land is like an organic kaleidoscope, a veritable flower garden, as the wind blows and the weeks pass. There are multiple layers competing for space and sun, soil and water. Against a luxurious silver-green background, the summer-blooming plants—larkspur, roses, coneflowers—are met in midsummer by the first yellow and golds of the autumn-blooming forbs: ironweed, gentian, asters, sunflowers, goldenrod. The midcontinent grasslands are so vast that one could follow this process for a thousand miles from south to north, east to west, depending on altitude, geography, and season.

Geography and altitude, together with rainfall, also bring a progressive change between grasses in the humid eastern prairie and the dry Great Plains. Where rainfall is thirty-five inches a year or more, tall grasses, such as big bluestem and the hardy sloughgrass, dominate, while very arid plains are covered by blue grama and buffalo grass. The tallgrass prairie extends to a roughly north-south line a hundred miles beyond the western borders of Minnesota, Iowa, and Missouri, with a westward finger going across two-thirds of Nebraska. There is a mixed-prairie zone of both tall and short grasses until one hits the line of twenty inches of rain or less and an altitude of fifteen hundred feet or higher, roughly along the ninety-seventh meridian, cutting the Dakotas and Kansas into east-west halves and marking the Texas-Oklahoma Panhandle as dry country. It is convenient to keep in mind these three zones: eastern tallgrass prairie, a broadly transitional midgrass zone, and the western shortgrass plains.[24] It is not entirely rainfall that controls these differences today; it may be overgrazing in the west, first by buffalo and later cattle. The zones shift over the years as well, the tall grasses working west during heavy rains, as in the 1880s, or retreating during the big and little dust bowls of the 1930s and 1950s. Presumably, the drought of the summer of 1988 began to force the tallgrasses to retreat before the advance of the western shortgrass.

Learning to Read the Prairie-Plains Landscape

Often the first response of a pioneer farmer to open prairie country was to look for something better because he firmly believed that only forest soil was fertile enough to farm and that open country was a desert. Whoever left the protective forest shelter and crossed the eastern side of the American prairie rarely troubled himself to mention the ocean of tall grasses, despite the fact that the big bluestem, prairie sloughgrass, switchgrass, and wild rye of the eastern prairie stood taller than a man and reached unremittingly to the horizon. Foreign accounts like that of German explorer F. A. Wislizenus in 1839 or the official American report of John C. Frémont in 1842 were instead preoccupied with sightings of occasional trees and shrubs—oak, elm, cottonwood, hickory—strung along streams as if they were markers or reminders of a more familiar and benevolent world.[25] The all-important grasses, which signaled good and bad land, went unseen at first.

The pioneer's highest priorities were to find water, get away from the interminable wind, and get out of the hot sun. He looked over and beyond the grasses for a cluster of trees in the distance, indicating water. Settlers who found themselves on the exposed open land would find many emergency uses for thick, tall clumps of sloughgrass.[26] Tall enough to hide a horse, cow, or buffalo, it dominated the wetter bottomlands along river courses and in swampy areas of the gently rolling midwestern tallgrass prairie. Also called prairie cordgrass, it quickly acquired the name ripgut grass because its four-foot-long coarse leaves had razor-sharp sawtooth edges that lacerated bare arms and hands. The Indians were using the tangled sloughgrass as thatching that could be covered with earth; white pioneers used it to cover haystacks and corncribs. As winter came, these immigrants in this treeless country burned sloughgrass as a barely adequate fuel. According to an 1884 account,

> large wisps of this are twisted, doubled, and tied by hand, being thus brought into compact and convenient form for putting into the stove. One or two of these twisted bunches are supplied every five or ten minutes, and they maintain a hot fire and serviceable as that of wood or coal. The amount of hay thus used in a year for heating in an ordinary room is from eight to twelve tons. An hour's time is sufficient for twisting up a winter day's supply of this fuel.[27]

Sloughgrass also made good hay. Farmers could mow it two or three times a year, which encouraged rapid new growth and protected soil from erosion. However, the stems and leaves usually tangled so much that only a strong man could pitchfork a load, and it had to be cut from the stack with a hay saw. This prairie cordgrass also bunched into a classic prairie sod and spread by seed and by rhizomes (underground outward-creeping roots impervious to fire and cold).

Even more important to the first white settlers who struggled to settle the land were the big-bluestem communities that blanketed the eastern prairie for thousands of square miles. Bluestem grew in large soddy clumps, taking over the top two feet of soil with roots reaching down a dozen feet. It was also called turkeyfoot because its stalks, up to eight feet tall, usually branched into three parts. Farmers learned to "read" big bluestem as a sign of prime well-drained prairie bottomland soil, particularly in the Flint Hills of Kansas and the eastern half of Oklahoma. For forage, pioneer livestock preferred big bluestem to other grasses; fortunately, it is unequaled for both quality and quantity. But this grass was killed out over most of its original vast prairie range until farmers learned to save the lower six or eight inches during cutting to allow fast regrowth and guarantee good ground cover.

Between the massive stands of sloughgrass in the wetlands and the big bluestem in the drylands stood sod-making switchgrass, with broad branching stalks three to six feet high. Switchgrass tolerates the severe winters and hot summer droughts well, persisting as a nutritious food for livestock in the form of green forage or prairie hay. Switchgrass is joined by Canada wild rye, also known as nodding wild rye because its seed heads curve downward from upward-pointing stems. It is also valuable for livestock as long as it is harvested early to avoid ergot infestation.

Moving onto the upland mixed-grass prairies of western Oklahoma, Kansas, Nebraska, and South Dakota, one enters the region of the great cattle drives of the 1870s and 1880s from southern Texas to the Kansas railheads of Abilene, Fort Dodge, and Atkinson. This semiarid rangeland was little-bluestem country, equal in nutrition, abundance, and staying power to the larger midwestern big bluestem. Little bluestem's bunches have dense root systems, and the seed stalks, waving like peacock feathers in the wind, grow two to five feet high. It grows well on sandy, shallow, rocky soil as well as deep sod. The cattle trails, therefore, were used to fatten up the herds on rich middle-prairie grasses not available in the southern rangeland. Before European intrusion, little bluestem may have been the most abundant grass in the American heartland, and it is still the most useful in the Flint Hills and Oklahoma. Today cattle are still shipped from the South and Southwest for this superior little-bluestem forage. Successful grazing requires stubble four to six inches high or little bluestem is wiped out, and less-productive plants take over. It can also be harvested by combines, yielding three-quarters of a ton to two tons of hay per acre, and has been successfully seeded on large areas of once-farmed but abandoned plains land.

Little bluestem is joined by sideoats grama, the name taken from the attractive rows of oatlike seeds hanging on one side only of the long stem. Eighteen to thirty-six inches high, with short roots, it provides high-quality animal nutrition, even on uplands, ridges, and rocky fields. When a range is abused, sideoats grama replaces taller grasses unless it is grazed closer than two to three inches. Sideoats grama is so easily seeded by man as to be almost fail-safe, good for the conservation of eroded land, and it can be nitrogen-fertilized for better production. It is in turn joined by prairie (puffsheath) dropseed, with its seeds recessed into the stems. This dropseed is only three to twelve inches high, with shallow roots, and prospers in dry, sandy soil un-

47

less forced out by taller, denser grasses. More nutritious and grown in small bunches is porcupine grass, or needlegrass. Two to four feet tall, it is good eating but sometimes a bother for cattle during seeding season because the sharp, pointed seeds stick in the animals' mouths.

At that invisible line, the ninety-seventh meridian in arid western Oklahoma, Kansas, and Texas, as the altitude rises westward from fifteen hundred feet to more than three thousand feet at the Colorado border, the annual rainfall declines from a less-than-acceptable twenty inches down to a downright desertlike twelve inches a year.[28] Even under drought pressures, when mixed grasses were driven eastward, buffalo grass and blue grama remained to feed millions of buffalo and later the beef cattle that still symbolize American food abundance. The erect bunches of blue grama, ten to twenty inches high, although reproducing only by seed, will withstand extreme drought and alkaline soils and will grow rapidly under favorable conditions. As the seed heads mature, they usually bend into a curve resembling a human eyebrow. Buffalo grass is found with blue grama, spreading through seeds and strong surface runners. The plants are usually less than five inches tall, which protects both buffalo grass and blue grama from overgrazing. Because of its excellent ground-cover quality, aggressive spread under use, wide climate adaptation, and relative ease to establish and spread, buffalo grass is ideally suited for erosion control on ranges and pasturelands where the soil does not contain too much sand.

Two secrets of why the vast midcontinent grasses persisted under harsh natural conditions are now clear: many plants were perennials, unlike farm crops, and many plants grew from the base rather than the tip, allowing them to withstand grazing by buffalo and cattle.

Prospective settlers on the open tallgrass prairie quickly learned to read the grasses for the type and quality of land that would be good for agriculture. Large stretches of big bluestem meant well-watered superior soil, while nodding or Canada wild rye succeeded best on medium-texture soils. The wild rye was called a decreaser, signaling the rise of less-valuable plants and a possible decline in land and range quality. Among the middle grasses, little bluestem was too widespread to provide information about what lay under it, but sideoats grama was an increaser, indicating that the land had good potential. Perhaps the new settler could buy land cheaply and build it up through proper management. Prairie drop grass told of dry, sandy soil that was of little use to the farmer unless irrigated and fertilized at high cost. Weedy June grass (Japanese brome, a foreigner) signaled land so badly abused as to be in very poor condition. "Don't buy it even if the price seems right!" Buffalo grass sends out different signals, depending on the environment. When found on middle or mixed-grass prairie land, it points out overgrazed but good land that still has potential for farming. Dominant on the arid Great Plains, it indicates good pasturelands that are not too sandy. Blue grama, the companion to buffalo grass, is often deceptive. It is an important increaser that can build up abused or overgrazed land, but it can successfully mask high-drought regions or alkaline soil because it can survive both.

The new settler who could read the landscape was rewarded well. Domesticated food grains had the same forms, soil needs, and climate demands as the native grasses, if one learned which matched which.[29] Only the species changed, although the difference between native grasses as perennials and domesticated grains as annuals is still more often misunderstood when it comes to plains sustainability. Tallgrass prairie of sloughgrass and big bluestem went readily to their tall counterparts: corn and soft winter wheat. Mixed prairie of little bluestem and sideoats grama was transformed into fields of hard winter wheat and dryland grain sorghums. Amid shortgrass plains went also the hard winter wheat and some sorghums, and where the buffalo once roamed, cattle soon grazed on the same blue grama and buffalo grass.

The absolute importance of wheat, corn, and grain sorghums to human survival—starches, oils, proteins—was in itself enough to justify the settlement of the difficult plains by skilled farmers and it still justifies the extraordinary effort to keep it in production. Of more than two hundred thousand known flowering plants throughout the world, including the grasses called grains, only three thousand have been used to any extent for human food. Only about two hundred of these could be called domesticated, and only a dozen or so stand between us and starvation, with wheat, corn, and sor-

49

ghums high on the list.[30] They are concentrated foods, give high yields, are relatively easy to collect, travel well, and may be stored for long periods of time. Today more than 70 percent of the world's farmland is planted in cereals to provide more than 50 percent of humanity's calories. Water-hungry and cold-vulnerable corn is the least adapted to the plains climate, while the best-adapted crop is either wheat or the sorghums. Soft wheat failed on the plains, but the specialized import, Ukranian winter wheat, prospered with limited water. On the other hand, grain sorghums grow in severe climates worldwide but demand more water than the plains naturally provides. Wheat, corn, and sorghums are even more attractive today because of hybrids and highly successful mechanization; each has a major role in today's capacity of each American farmer to feed six dozen others, and for the nation to prosper despite the fact that less than 2 percent of Americans work on farms, and half of those are on the plains.

Most often the frontier settler quickly discovered a simple and unique test to measure good land. Could it yield a large crop of corn? The problem was that corn, needing water, would not grow west of the tallgrass prairie, yet settlers moving west persisted in trying to raise it. Nor could they grow the soft wheats to which they had been accustomed. This stubbornness and inability to grow corn and their accustomed crops did much to guarantee that settlers avoided the plains and later encouraged human failure there. Ironically, corn would be the crop of choice for the irrigators of the 1960s. James C. Malin, historian, naturalist, and plains veteran, concluded that the excessive hardships repeatedly encountered between settlement in the 1880s and the Dust Bowl were partly the settlers' own doing because they could not adjust to an agricultural system without corn or soft wheat. Only belatedly and reluctantly did the plains farmer turn to hard or durum wheats.[31]

But the exchange was not quite equal. The original grasses, in all their variety, lived in a symbiotic balance with one another, even as plant domination ebbed and flowed. Even with fire, climate fluctuations, animal grazing, and low-level American Indian interference, the grasslands would have continued indefinitely for millennia.

Sustaining High Plains Farming

Today the Land Institute at Salina, Kansas, led by the indomitable Wes Jackson, is working to return parts of the High Plains to the original prairie landscape and also create a sustainable, natural, food-producing agriculture with perennial plants. An institute researcher writes:

> The prairie ecosystem existed as a complex web of interdependent relationships among plant, animal, and microbial species. Critical nutrients were garnered, retained, and recycled efficiently by the prairie's biota. Generations of prairie grasses, thriving during the moist springs and hot summers, then drying in autumn and winter, accumulated thick mulches of leaves and stems that gave rise to deep dark soils. These rich prairie soils have made the highly-productive Great Plains granary possible.[32]

Agricultural plantings of corn, wheat, rye, and sorghum last only a season. If the land is abandoned, within months the prairie soil, weakened by the exchange, is open to drift and erosion. Weedy native plants take over, as was true in Dust Bowl years. The intervention of modern agriculture on the High Plains is not a balanced or durable intervention that would continue another season without direct participation of the human hand. Hence, the Land Institute says,

> the agriculture we envision, modelled on the prairie, would be composed of herbaceous perennial seed crops grown in mixtures. These mixtures will take advantage of differences among species in growth period, nutrient use, and water requirements. We will incorporate into the design of perennial polycultures various principles of ecosystem function discovered in studies of the prairie ecosystem. Thus we will address nutrient cycling, ecological succession, long-term stability of yield, and biological management of insects, diseases, and weed within agroecosystems. The herbaceous perennials we are developing for polyculture, eastern grama grass, wild rye, and Illinois bundleflower, have either been derived from native prairie or are analogous to species occurring in native prairie.[33]

Concluding Note: The Paradox of Farming

The move from prairie diversity to today's monoculture fields stocked with wheat, milo, or corn (and narrowly specialized versions of each) breaks the first rule of ecology: diversity brings health while simplicity results in death. Soil, plants, climate, and other natural forces, alone and together, generate the complexity of ecological creativity. In Wes Jackson's words, "to maintain the 'ever-normal' granary, the agricultural human's pull historically has been toward the monoculture of annuals. Nature's pull is toward a polyculture of perennials."[34] The struggle for human health on the plains requires a greater loyalty to diversity than human history has usually shown. The distinction between what is food and what is weeds goes back, of course, to the original Agricultural Revolution, but it is refined to the highest degree in modern plains farming. Today's monoculture inevitably means ecological destabilization. The plains grassland had its own rational stability. The objective of the Land Institute, for example, is to build a diverse agriculture that can prosper on the plains, as once the wild grassland did, and serve human food needs as well. Wes Jackson argued in 1980 that plains farming, like farming everywhere since the beginning of the Agricultural Revolution twelve thousand years ago, destroys more than it builds and that nowhere is this more vivid than on the difficult plains.[35]

In the 1980s and early 1990s, appropriate and sustainable agriculture on the High Plains has new momentum. The trend, described in more detail later in this book, is signaled not only by the Land Institute but also by water- and soil-conservation legislation in Congress, the environmentally protective Conservation Reserve Program of the 1985 farm bill, and the well-received support for low-input sustainable agriculture (LISA). These have been enhanced in the 1990 farm bill. Not the least, in September 1989 the National Academy of Sciences reported that farmers who apply few or no chemicals to crops can be as productive as those who use pesticides and synthetic fertilizers. The academy recommended changing federal subsidy programs encouraging overuse of agricultural chemicals and advocated natural farming practices. Historically, farm policies of Congress and the United States Department of Agriculture have discouraged farmers from trying natural techniques. Federal subsidies stressed high-yield production that required heavy chemical applications of costly and toxic herbicides, pesticides, and artificial fertilizers. Current policies, costing almost fourteen billion dollars in 1989, actually encouraged practices that were destructive to the environment. The academy urged priority for so-called organic or alternative farming, which had been seen by farmers and government policy-makers as unorthodox and incapable of generating harvests that match those produced with chemicals. "Well-managed alternative farms use less synthetic chemical fertilizers, pesticides and antibiotics without necessarily decreasing, and, in some cases, increasing per-acre crop yields. . . . Wider adoption of proven alternative systems would result in ever greater economic benefits to farmers and environmental gains for the nation."[36] At least 5 percent of the nation's 2.1 million farmers, said the National Academy of Sciences, have adopted such techniques. But for a century after the earliest white settlement in the 1870s, farmers on the plains worked their fields in traditional ways, failed, learned to irrigate, and were persuaded to load their declining fields with chemicals.

2

. . .

Finding the Water: Boom and Bust, 1870–1940

From the 98th meridian west to the Rocky Mountains there is a stretch
of country whose history is filled with more tragedy and whose future is pregnant
with greater promise than perhaps any other equal expanse of territory
within the confines of the Western Hemisphere.—
Farm historian A. M. Simons in 1906

Extensive areas of the Great Plains . . . must be classed as unsuited
to sustained cultivated crops, and should therefore never have been plowed.—
National Resources Planning Board, Public Works Administration,
United States Department of the Interior, 1936

If the Atlantic coastline of North America had been dry prairie instead of an extended forest, settlement might never have taken place. Europeans might have contented themselves with fishing its shores. Ingrained Old World opinion told them that treeless open land could not be turned into fertile farmland. The best poor man's country was hewed from forest: no trees, no crop. After the eastern forest land had been cleared and settled and Americans again looked westward, they were not happy with what they saw. The midcontinent grasslands seemed no more than a worthless rangeland in the distant western backcountry.[1] The plains stood primarily as the obstacle— America's empty quarter—for migrants headed for garden spots in Oregon and California.

54

"A Forever Dangerous and Useless Place, Deserving Only to be Passed By"

The plains were bad news from the first. When Coronado began his surprisingly deep venture below the Rio Grande and tramped as far north and east as the wild Kansas country in 1540, he reported that the ocean of grass had "no more landmarks than as if we had been swallowed up in the sea . . . because there was not a stone, nor a bit of rising ground, nor a tree, nor a shrub, nor anything to go by."[2] The expedition had to navigate by sun and stars as if it were on the open ocean. Coronado had difficulty finding water, and he found neither gold nor clues to a passage to Cathay; instead he was forced to halt for roaming herds of massive buffalo as awesome as the land itself. Five soldiers on Zaldivar's 1598 expedition deserted in panic when they entered the endless plains; they were more willing to risk capture by Indians than penetrate the lonely land.

Historic doubts continued. About 1787, James Monroe set the stage when he flatly told Thomas Jefferson that the entire United States west of the Appalachians was no bargain: "A great part of the territory is miserably poor [and] consists of extensive plains which have not had from appearances, and will not have, a single bush upon them for ages. . . . The districts therefore within which these fall will perhaps never contain a sufficient number of inhabitants to entitle them to membership in the Confederacy."[3] Based on experience in Europe, the British Isles, and east of the Appalachians, the only land worth farming was that hewn from forests. No wonder Jefferson concluded that it would take a hundred generations before Americans would settle the continent to the western sea. (The actual total would be fewer than five generations.) The plains were too remote and inaccessible, devoid of the major rivers that had opened up so many other American regions. One early advantage of this geography was that no attacking army could sustain itself to invade the weak United States at its vulnerable backside. Even with major logistical support, a large-scale military force would disappear into the vastness. However, Jefferson, always the optimist, rushed in 1803 to accept Napoleon's offer to sell the 830,000-square-mile Louisiana Purchase wasteland at fifteen million dollars—three cents an acre.

The problem was that the American grassland could not be compared with any part of western Europe, while the Atlantic coast was forested like Europe. Like the distant steppes of central Asia, the American grassland might as well have been a moonscape to the first European visitors. The visible scene was a minimalist landscape of unbounded grasses, the flat surrounding horizon, and the infinite sky; any human presence shrank into nothingness. In 1810, Lt. Zebulon M. Pike shaped American opinion about the nation's new western territory when he reported that "a barren soil, parched and dried up for eight months in the year, presents neither moisture nor nutrition sufficient to nourish the timber. These vast plains of the western hemisphere, may become in time equally celebrated as the sandy deserts of Africa."[4] In 1821, Major Stephen H. Long reported his unhappy passage through the same Great American Desert; the land was unfit for cultivation and hence uninhabitable by pioneer farmers. Edwin James, a botanist with Long, spoke of a landscape of "of hopeless and irreclaimable sterility."[5] He wondered how animals survived. Unrequited forest man Washington Irving wrote in horror when he crossed the prairie in the 1830s that "there is something inexpressibly lonely in the solitude of the prairie . . . an immense extent of landscape without a sign of human existence . . . the consciousness of being far, far beyond the bonds of human habitation; we feel as if moving in the midst of a desert world."[6] The experience of marching for days, never emerging from formlessness and void, never seeing an end to emptiness, depressed other early travelers, such as Francis Parkman, and filled them with foreboding. Charles Dickens, already displeased with his American travels in 1840, took an instant dislike to the open country. "Looking toward the setting sun, there lay stretched before my view a vast expanse of what scarcely amounted to a scratch upon the great plank . . . a few birds wheeling here and there, with solitudes and silence reigning paramount around . . . oppressive in its barren monotony."[7] As late as 1856, Joseph Henry, the influential secretary of the new Smithsonian Institution, concluded that "the whole space to the west, between the 98th meridian and the Rocky Mountains, denominated the Great American Plains, is a barren waste . . . a country of comparatively little value to the agriculturalist."[8] After the Civil War the military commander of the plains region, Gen. William Tecumseh Sherman, reported that western settlement reached its workable limits at the ninety-ninth meridian. "There began the Great Plains 600 [*sic*] miles wide, fit only for nomadic tribes of Indians, Tartars, or buffaloes."[9] Today, for the 98 percent of Americans who do not live and work on a farm, the great grassy flatness covering the thousand miles between Chicago and Denver on Interstate 80 seems interminable, with few scenic or picturesque stops. Today's travelers still conclude that it is a mediocre and commonplace zone between the cosmopolitan East and the spectacular Rocky Mountains.

So much for the High Plains grasslands, a land of uninhabitable extremes. Pioneers understandably shrank from the sun-baked, waterless flatlands. The incessant wind too often fanned raging prairie fires, and the same wind brought nerve-wracking summers and fierce winters. Nor was there wood for fuel, buildings, or fences. Even on the midwestern tallgrass prairie it would take decades to dispel doubts before settlers edged nervously onto the benign Illinois and Iowa prairies. There they would discover the world's best, deepest, and easiest-to-work chernozem soils. But the waterless High Plains region was not the well-watered midwestern prairie. Far-reaching pioneers who dared to think of settling on the plains did find good soil under the blanket of grass, but only with water could it be put to work. Water became the plains obsession, and still is today.

As American expansion pressed across the Mississippi, adventurers, explorers, and settlers soon peered into that ominous landscape which was an affront to Manifest Destiny. Nevertheless, a few observant settlers soon deduced that the soil was unusually fertile, had no trees or rocks to clear before plowing, and was "nowhere too steep for the wagon or the plow." As early as 1811 the English botanist John Bradbury, deep in the Dakota plains, concluded: "It can be cultivated. . . . It will be one of the most beautiful countries in the world."[10] In a complete turnaround from Coronado, Pike, Long, Henry, and Sherman, a newly arrived plains wife could write: "We must pronounce this the most charming country our eyes have ever beheld. Beautiful rolling prairie, undulating like the waves of the sea, high limestone cliffs with immense bottom-lands, stretching into thousands of acres as rich as it is possible for it to be, high tablelands, with a soil a number of feet in depth."[11] In 1831, Joshua Pilcher told Congress that anyone who saw the open grasslands as an impossible obstacle "must know little of the American people, who supposes they can be stopped by anything in the shape of . . . deserts."[12] A western booster agreed: "The skill and enterprise of American farmers will find the means of obtaining comfort and wealth in those regions, both of Kansas and Nebraska, which many are disposed to condemn as worthless."[13] Indiana senator G. S. Orth, member of an 1867 Republican junket onto the plains, announced that "our good 'Uncle Sam' has come here, and he brings with him science and civilization. He intends to plant permanently a part of his great family; for he is now founding empires."[14] A journalist asserted that the Great Plains offered "a garden three times the area of France."[15]

The midcontinent grassland was a novelty. To the aspiring young husband and wife of a farm family, rumors of a vast grassland, but under rainless skies, were not encouraging despite the national passion that Everyman deserved his God-given share of the virtually free land carved out of the public domain. The trick was to make a small amount of water go a long way, but wheat or corn for cash and survival needed more than a trickle. Irrigation was known to succeed in California, but where was the water in western Kansas? Year-round streams were rare and their banks were quickly captured by the first round of settlers, who claimed exclusive riparian rights.

The open country also required technological innovation and new farming practices. Back East, 20 or 40 or even 80 acres could be worked with hand tools, a plow, and horses, but not 320 acres in a half-section or 640 acres in the full section required to prosper on the plains. The new dryland farming required far bigger farms to field a decent crop, plus machinery to cultivate the bigger farm. A new farmer saw a treeless, arid, and desolate landscape. What features in the land would allow him to apply new skills and tools to guarantee his survival? He knew that he could plow the land and that it was extremely fertile. The potential for success seemed better with the appearance of John Deere's steel moldboard plow. Word spread that it "cut through the sod like a hot knife through butter." The new farmer could figure out how to get along without trees; the invention of ready-made wood-frame houses and barbed wire for fencing gave him a boost, and railroads would soon connect him with the East. The Indians had been subdued and pushed westward, and the 1862 Homestead Act offered (but often failed to deliver) free prime farmland to a settler committed to five years of toil and survival to prove up his property. A rush of new inventions offered him hope and may have made him overconfident by including windmills with the steel plow and barbed wire. Cyrus McCormick began selling a workmanlike mechanical reaper. It alone multiplied eightfold the land a farmer could harvest and seemed destined to guarantee success for dryland farming. Back East, the new roller process for milling wheat for bread encouraged larger plantings on more land, so the farmer's natural hesitancy was overcome by these technological advances. He had in his mind a successful picture to repeat: the bonanza farming of the Red River of the North bordering the Dakotas and Minnesota. Wheat, if not always water-hungry corn, could be grown profitably. In time, large-scale farming covered hundreds of acres instead of tens of acres. The new mechanized equipment seemed designed for flat, open country.

When Did the Frontier End and Successful Farming Begin?

One of America's premier geographers, Carl Ortwin Sauer, argued that the midcontinent grasslands were where the nation's frontier history really began.[16] In the eastern forests the first waves of white settlers deadened trees, cleared openings, and planted fields in ways little different from generations of European forebears. If frontier means an encounter with strange conditions requiring new responses, then the American frontier began not at the Atlantic coastline or the Appalachian Mountains, but at the prairie peninsula that edged onto today's Indiana-Illinois state line. The midland grasslands marked the starting point for a distinctively American history and American space.

High Plains historian Robert G. Athearn called the post–Civil War rush to the plains "the initiation of the final assault upon the American frontier. When the movement ended, a new nation stepped forth into the family of the world."[17] When does a frontier end? Not until 1912 did the Santa Fe Railroad

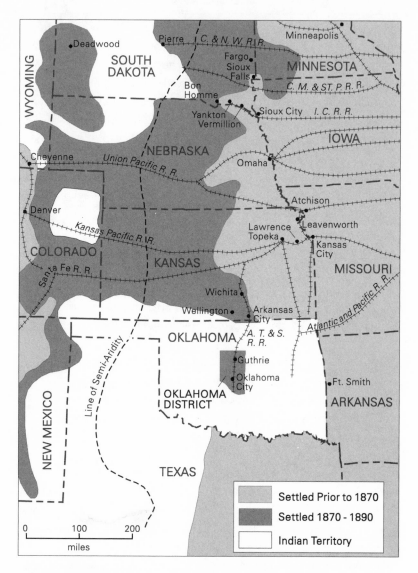

Settled Prior to 1870

Settled 1870 - 1890

Indian Territory

3. The farmer's frontier, 1870–90. Note the vertical twenty-inch rainfall "Line of Semi-Aridity" and early railroad expansion. Redrawn from Ray Allen Billington, *Westward Expansion: A History of the American Frontier*, 4th ed. (New York: Macmillan, 1974), 655, with permission of Macmillan.

intrude on the grasslands of southwest Kansas by building a branch line from Dodge City to Satanta along the old Dry Fork of the Santa Fe Trail. Before then, settlers bounced their wagons along the ruts of the centuries-old trail. There were no broad, smooth-flowing rivers like the Ohio or Mississippi to raft a farm family and its household goods, animals, and tools into the central High Plains. Roads and bridges (across dry washes) did not exist before 1912 in the sandy country on the north bank of the Cimarron River; wandering families simply rattled on cross-country. During the 1870s the Santa Fe had built its Pacific line along the Arkansas River thirty-five miles to the north, but that was a two-day roadless wagon ride away from farmsteads along the Cimarron. The Santa Fe was more intent on getting across the plains than on serving its cash-poor population and sparse resources. In 1888 the Rock Island reached the spot just north of the Oklahoma-Kansas border that would become Liberal, Kansas.

As for the Oklahoma Panhandle, in 1890 there was nothing in that no-man's-land except huge undeveloped ranches where buffalo and Indians recently roamed. The Denver and Fort Worth Railroad speculated by running tracks across northeast New Mexico into the Texas Panhandle. It found a limited seasonal business with the spread-out cattle ranchers, such as the Bates and Beals L-X cowboys, who set up temporary shop in the far southwest corner of Kansas (present-day Morton County) in 1877.[18] Not for fifty more years, in 1927, did the Santa Fe complete its line from Satanta across Grant and Stanton counties into adjoining Baca County in Colorado. Settlers then rushed in to capture still-cheap but now-accessible land; a railroad line meant they could get their wheat, corn, and alfalfa to market. Haskell County, the eastern terminus of the Santa Fe branch-line-off-the-branch-line, grew 93 percent in the 1920s. Next door to the west, Grant County boomed to nearly twice its 1920 population, and Stanton County on the Kansas-Colorado line in the late 1920s had fourteen people for every ten people earlier. Gradually the small towns north and south across Panhandle country were linked by a network of tracks. In 1930 the Rock Island connected Liberal with Amarillo, Texas. Not until the late 1920s and early 1930s

would southwest Kansas and the Texas-Oklahoma Panhandle region overcome its frontierlike isolation.

If the frontier ended when railroads crisscrossed a region, then the
Ogallala heartland had barely graduated from frontier status before the Depression and Dust Bowl devastated its towns and farms. If the frontier ended
when the traces of civilization appeared—schools, churches, stores, law
and order—then the region had moved from frontier to rural status decades
earlier. If the frontier ended only when the geography had been domesticated, then the Ogallala heartland was still an untamed frontier region in the
1940s. If the frontier ended when local people could abandon a subsistence
standard of living, then the central Great Plains had its first taste of prosperity in the 1950s, not so much from wheat or corn or alfalfa as from natural gas
from the nation's greatest underground pool. Such industrial prosperity,
however, also included the extreme swings of a boomtown economy. The
frontier may have ended only when the farmer's tools matched his needs.
Not until new irrigation technologies took hold in the 1960s would the previously undertooled local farmer substitute groundwater for rain to bypass environmental constraints. How temporary an environmental conquest this
would be is still to be seen.

Regional historian James C. Malin offered an environmental test in the
1940s when he was one of the first to argue that the plains frontier ended only
as settlers moved from primitive short-term exploitation to long-term conservation.[19] "The worst manifestations of soil blowing as related to agricultural operations occurred during the pioneering process," Malin wrote.
"The country was new, the population was not settled-in on a firm and sta-
bilized foundation in harmony with the new environment."[20] On these
grounds the frontier has not yet ended in the region; in the long run, geography may never be conquered. Neither the tractors and mechanized harvesters of the 1920s nor the machinery for deep wells and full-field irrigation
of the 1960s nor entrepreneurial motives behind both eras reflects a mature
commitment to the conservation Malin sought. They are forms of continuous frontierlike exploitation. Whether the land-saving policies initiated by
the 1985 Farm Security Act can bring major changes is still to be seen. On

environmental grounds, the Ogallala heartland is still in the thrall of frontier conditions.

America's Seventy-Year Mistake: The Beginning

Waves of farm families filled with Jeffersonian idealism and Manifest Destiny moved onto the plains through the second half of the nineteenth century. To their surprise, they were often forced back by the lack of rain or groundwater, so they tried again. They learned that the myth of the desert was not entirely a myth. Like troops sacrificing themselves on the battlefield, fresh waves seemed always ready to step forward. New settlers learned painfully that less corn or wheat would grow on 160 acres in western Kansas than sprang forth on 40 acres in Illinois or Iowa, despite more hard labor and personal risk. The combination of drought and heat that struck in two succeeding summers, 1859 and 1860, forced hundreds to flee the territory. No soaking rain fell. Winter snows and their life-giving moisture were so light that for the first time in memory they did not hide the ground from view. A crop of less than five hundred bushels was harvested from 4,000 acres in Shawnee County as both winter and spring wheat failed. The settlers who remained survived only on charity coming from such distant points as Wisconsin and New York.[21]

The settlers who endured the grasshoppers in the summer of 1874 and the desperate winter of 1874–75 conceded the harsh limits of the plains. They reluctantly shifted from corn, the symbol of American prosperity, to wheat, strange new winter wheat instead of spring wheat. The hard red winter wheat, Turkey red, of new German-Russian Mennonite communities spread widely to become the new staff of life. American settlers also learned dryland farming techniques from the immigrant communities. Russian tillage methods, not those of the humid eastern United States, worked in the unfamiliar plains soil and climate, and Americans learned to let their fields lie fallow in alternate years to build up subsoil moisture from two years' rain, which in turn offered enough wetness to grow a single crop.

Congress tried to legislate an environmental fix to re-create a more familiar landscape: cover one-quarter of the region with forest to duplicate eastern farmland. The Timber Culture Act of 1873 promised to change the climate.

Whoever planted trees on 40 acres of his 160-acre quarter section and kept them growing for ten years received title to the entire 160 acres. This was so unlikely that the requirement was reduced to 27,000 trees on 10 acres with a 25 percent survival rate. Trees and climate change failed. In 1877, Congress tried again with the aptly named Desert Land Act, which discounted a full section of 640 acres to settlers who would water their land. Irrigation ditches were often no more than plowed furrows that ran uphill and downhill. Both acts produced more fraud and speculation than honest results. It also became abundantly clear that by restricting settlers to an inadequate 160 acres, the celebrated Homestead Act of 1862 failed to suit conditions beyond the ninety-seventh meridian. In early 1881 the Kansas legislature took an unusual step by assigning twenty-five thousand dollars, barely adequate even for that day, for immediate relief of farmers.

Despite these warnings, plains boosters reviled the renowned scientist and explorer John Wesley Powell as a doomsayer when he prefaced an 1878 government report with his view that realistically in the American West, including the High Plains, "the climate is so arid that agriculture is not successful."[22] Since "practically all values inhere in the water," the only land which the government ought responsibly to offer settlers was parcels where "the water could be distributed over them."[23] Using Utah as a dubious average, Powell concluded pessimistically that only 3 percent of the West could be so farmed. His argument was clear, direct, and precisely what potential settlers did not want to hear. It was possible to begin farming but impossible to succeed. Within five years everything would be lost. With dryland farming as a risky alternative, Powell urged a sixteenfold expansion of the homesteading quarter section to a minimum of two to four sections (1,280 to 2,560 acres, two to four square miles) to offer the best chance for success.[24] At the very least, he concluded, the day of the independent farm family that prospered on the famous quarter section was long gone and would never successfully settle the High Plains. Enemies drove Powell from his government post in the U.S. Geological Survey; he would receive more attention in the 1980s than in the 1880s.

Climate Anomaly: 1878–87

Then a miracle happened. In 1844, Josiah Gregg wrote that "the extreme cultivation of the earth might contribute to the multiplication of showers."[25] Now for a decade—approximately 1878–87—extraordinarily heavy rains fell on the High Plains country west of the ninety-seventh meridian from Texas to Canada. The rains encouraged frontier farmers to move into the region because they believed they could perpetuate the change from dry to moist weather. They could alter the forces of nature by the ordinary field practice of plowing the sod. "Rain follows the plow" became the popular slogan. These farmers, together with government agents, private boosters, and the American public at large, concluded that the weather had permanently changed and farming could begin in unlikely western places. The power of ordinary but Bunyanesque Americans to dictate favorable geographical change was not a strange claim in the age of Manifest Destiny. Mormon settlers happily reported that the level of the Great Salt Lake rose when they began irrigating and cultivating nearby land.[26]

The theory of increasing rainfall by plowing the land gained credence as a widespread scientific fact when it was endorsed by Joseph Henry of the Smithsonian Institution, the new American Association for the Advancement of Science (A A A S), and the most famous explorer-scientist of the day, F. V. Hayden, director of the U.S. Geological Surveys of the Territories. In 1880 Nebraska scientist Samuel Aughey concluded that, "after the soil is broken, a rain as it falls is absorbed by the soil like a huge sponge."[27] Then the soil evaporates a little moisture into the atmosphere each day, receiving it back at night as a heavy dew. Ironically, Washington's Government Printing Office was at the same time turning out hundreds of copies of John Wesley Powell's much-abused warning about the arid lands of the West. Powell's pessimism was countered by Aughey and real-estate promoter turned pseudo-scientist C. D. Wilber. They said that west of the 100th meridian the soil was fertile and rainfall was gradually increasing.[28]

Farmers and boosters in the western parts of Kansas and Nebraska were delighted with the new science. This was not intentionally bad science. In fact, it was not bad science for its day, but it was inadequate science to explain climate modification. In addition, it was widely believed that the spread of the railroads and telegraph lines also brought rains because the iron and steel rails and electric wires modified natural electrical cycles in an arid zone to induce the fall of moisture. Civil War veterans remembered that artillery fire, such as that at the Battle of Gettysburg, seemingly contributed to the deluge that followed. If Sherman would use more cannon to clear the plains of Indians, it might have the added benefit of bringing rain.

Boom and Bust: The Plains Experiment

The wonderful combination of more rainfall, better crops, cheap fertile land, and the beginning of an interlaced network of railroads was too good to resist. In 1878–79 the land office at Bloomington, which had jurisdiction in southwest Kansas, entered homesteads totaling more than 307,000 acres.[29] The spell of good rain encouraged a Chicago newsman to say in 1884 that "Kansas was considered a droughty state, but that day is past, and her reputation for sure crops is becoming widely known. . . . Land is cheap and a good home can be made to pay for itself in a few years."[30] Congregational minister Jeremiah Platt, visiting in the mid-1880s, concluded that "I am more and more convinced that there is a Great Western Kansas which, in fifteen or twenty years from now will be as rich and productive and valuable as is the eastern part of the state, making Kansas the greatest and grandest agricultural state in the union."[31] Modern agricultural historian Gilbert C. Fite wrote that new arrivals in western Kansas were undeterred when they rode past deserted claim shanties abandoned during the drought that occurred three or four years earlier. He quotes the *Larned* (Kansas) *Optic* claim that "the largest immigration ever known in the history of the state is now steadily flowing into southwestern Kansas" and the *Kinsley Graphic*, "Come on! There is still plenty of room, land is cheap here yet, and thousands of acres for sale." Edwards County was "literally spotted with new frame and board houses with here and there a sod house."[32] Unexpectedly fast settlement in western Kansas led to county-seat wars, including fatal gunplay over whether Hugoton or Woodsdale would be the Stevens County seat. Between 1885 and 1887, the population of the western third of Kansas rose 370 percent, from 38,000 to 139,000 people, just as the rains halted.

66

The boom ended more suddenly than it began, its collapse accelerated by disastrous blizzards in early 1886 in which 80 percent of all range cattle died. The decade of heavy rains ended unexpectedly, and drought returned in the late summer of 1887. In the successive summers of 1889 and 1890, farmers got only two and one half bushels of wheat an acre in the western counties and an even less-productive eight bushels of corn. Farmers in Grant County could not survive, much less prevail, when a dry summer gave them four bushels of corn or wheat per acre. One farmer reported that he had no wheat or rye at all from twenty-two acres, and his corn crop totaled less than a bushel.[33] Widespread crop failure was made worse because the previous boom times had encouraged many settlers into overexpansion and heavy debt. With disastrous overconfidence, settlers in western Kansas had put their first crops into feed corn instead of the seed corn that would have avoided outright starvation. Crops, boomtowns, and optimism withered, replaced by "the blues badly" and return to "relatives east, poorer, sadder, and much wiser." Western counties, such as Pawnee, began losing people who had come only two or three years before.

"Most all the people here that could leave have done so and what is here are too poor they cannot get away," said a Grant County inhabitant in late 1889.[34] Farm families holding some of the world's most fertile land were living, they said, on "Andersonville fare," remembering the notorious Civil War prison in the South. In early 1890, despite a mild winter, word went out that the state would have to supply seed corn (which a farm family ate only out of desperation) or see western Kansas abandoned. Most settlers were still too proud to accept direct relief, but Kansas farmers could accept seed corn. Drought took hold more severely in the summer of 1890 than it had in earlier years and spread from the Texas Panhandle to the Canadian border. Few people were ready to acknowledge that dry times were the norm rather than the exception, and most settlers (and bankers and businessmen) waited expectantly for the next rainy season and a return to "normal" weather. The rains returned in 1891 and 1892, but a combination of more drought and the Panic of 1893 once more created desperate conditions in western Kansas. This was followed in 1894 by one of the driest years on record (only eight to nine inches of rain) and a particularly heavy plague of grasshoppers.

Between 1890 and 1900, the number of farms in the twenty-four counties of western Kansas declined from 14,300 to 8,900. The entire decade of the 1890s brought only two years of good crops and five consecutive years of failure. By the mid-1890s, Hugoton's dozens of new houses emptied and its population stood at a mere 308 in 1915. Throughout the western counties people left behind only shuttered or windowless homes. Grass grew in front of rows of brick business districts as monuments to a fantasy that had no link with reality. In a colorful phrase, one observer complained about population claims of boomtowns in western Kansas: "Census returns prick the bladder of this inflation."[35]

The five years of homestead residency were soon called "the period of starvation." Plains historian Walter Prescott Webb wrote that "the government is willing to bet the homesteader one hundred and sixty acres of land that he'll starve to death on it in less than five years." A popular song told of "starvin' to death on my government claim." Passage of the Three-Year Homestead Act in 1912 admitted that the point of starvation was far short of five years: "Consequently it would be humane to shorten the required time of residence to three years."[36] By 1895, more than 184,000 people abandoned their farms and left Kansas.

The shadow of drought constantly hung over people of the plains as they entered the new century. Hence, Webb concluded, their existence focused on one element: "this primitive and elemental desire for rain."[37] The heavy rains had not persisted and would not return, but the myth of climate change did. For over seventy years, until the hammer blows of the 1930s, settlers were lured to the plains by the dream of more rain on the rich soil. First corn crops went dry, then sorghums and wheat, and finally the farmyard gardens so tenderly nourished by well water.

The fabled American homesteading dream broke down on the devil's anvil of the plains. By losing their capacity to be self-sustaining, starving farmers felt betrayed and, paradoxically, believed they had betrayed the American dream in their failure. Government agents had encouraged

68

farmers to stay on the land despite the return of drought and economic pressures to abandon the land. Farmers themselves believed it was unpatriotic (and possibly even sinful) to desert their homesteads.

The unexpectedly harsh environment forced Americans to rethink their vaunted frontier settlement. First, it became clear that the plains were a permanent frontier because no one could bring more moisture to the land. Reclamation leader Frederick H. Newell of the USGS announced in the 1896 agriculture yearbook that the High Plains region was fated to succumb to periodic drought and periodic famine.[38] Second, hardships that farmers accepted because they were temporary and therefore conquerable were deep seated; permanent problems were inherent in dryland agriculture. In 1901, USGS official Willard D. Johnson called the rush to plains settlement an "experiment in agriculture on a vast scale . . . it nevertheless ended in total failure . . . [resulting in] a class of people broken in spirit as well as in fortune."[39] Third, the plains farmer was undercapitalized, undertooled, and underinformed to cope with the challenges he faced. Only a new type of credit economy and government cash, not to arrive until the New Deal, would bring a share of national prosperity to the plains. It also turned plains farmers forever into government clients.

Two failed frontiers marked the plains as a hard place. Webb writes of the short-lived but high-romance cattle kingdom of dryland ranchers before the farmers came.[40] Despite its well-financed British and German backing, it did not survive the winter of 1885–86. Nor could the cash-poor sodhouse farmers who followed—"nine children and eleven cents"—cope with the 1889–95 drought. Since large parts of the grassland remained in native sod, dust storms did not blow, but without rain the settlers concluded that "there is no god west of Salina."[41] The Great Plains, at first reviled as the Great American Desert, then celebrated as the Great American Garden, became a three-hundred-mile-wide, near-empty swath ranging from Canada to Texas. By the mid-1890s, the central plains had reverted to its virtually uninhabited prefrontier state. Even the Indians had never lived there except as hunters and nomads.

The First Struggle to Find Groundwater: Well Diggers

The first farmer to turn sod and look hopefully heavenward for rain in Finney County did so in 1878. Before the farmers arrived, there were ranchers, often Civil War veterans who parlayed the Homestead Act into significant spreads. But even hardy range cattle needed water, and the old Z6 or OX or XY Ranch staked itself out along the Arkansas River.[42] It took no genius to see that southwestern Kansas lacked enough rain. Springs and ponds and pothole-like playa lakes were rare. Despite this fatal flaw, adventuresome or desperate farmers were drawn to the treeless, fertile, and flat land so ready for the steel-tipped John Deere shear plow. Within a year, Finney County had 2,905 acres planted to crops. In an era when a farmer was mighty pleased to turn sod on four acres a day and plant seed on eight, this was energetic progress.[43] Getting to a reliable source of water quickly became a dire necessity.

In the early wet 1880s, new settlers in southwestern Kansas assured themselves they could farm successfully by drawing water from shallow wells, wet-weather draws, buffalo wallows, the rare spring, and, if they were lucky in choice of farm site, the Arkansas or Cimarron rivers. By the mid-1880s, the best access to water was already taken by earlier homesteaders and hopeful late arrivals were virtually doomed to failure, not by lack of skill, but by unlucky timing. Where there was a town well, a common sight on the open prairie was a horse-drawn wagon or even a box on skids bumping along loaded with water barrels covered with burlap. When homesteader John S. Gropp arrived in 1887, he had to settle on waterless land about twenty miles northwest of Garden City. For two years he rolled a large barrel of water three-fourths of a mile from a neighbor's well before he hand-dug his own well and had the hard luck not to find water for 220 feet.[44]

Nineteenth-century farmers knew that well digging was a nasty chore, but they did not anticipate the months-long hard labor to get one's own water on the plains. Back in the tallgrass prairie of Missouri, where many had come from, a family chore given to children was carrying buckets of water from the nearby stream or shallow well. A more convenient family well might occasionally descend twenty or thirty feet, lined with stone or brick or not finished at all. Water was brought up hand over hand in the two-bucket system using the familiar crossbeam and pulley. On the High Plains, not only was the water fifty or one hundred or more feet down, but settlers were dismayed by the layers of dense soil, sandy clay, and rocky conglomerate they had to dig through. Soon the part-time well driller appeared, often a neighboring farmer or town mechanic or an itinerant. He alone possessed the equipment to drill a six-inch hole which, if the homesteader was unlucky, went down more than two hundred feet. The six-inch hole would be sheathed in an iron casing, not only to prevent the collapse of the well, but also to offer a smoother journey for the unusual bucket, about four feet long but only three inches in diameter.[45]

Many farmers lucky enough to hit water under fifty feet might take on the major construction and engineering job of a well three or four feet wide. Water for a family and small garden patch meant a long spell of sweaty well digging on an open, sun-burnt and windy site. Hand-dug wells often went through a ten- or fifteen-foot stretch of sand that had to be laboriously curbed out with four-foot pieces of wood sawed and nailed into place. Hundreds of wells were dug by the homesteaders themselves, work that led to crippling accidents and deaths. As a local historian put it, "picture a digger down a hundred or two hundred feet watching an 80 or 100 pound bucket of dirt ascending to the top. . . . If the rope broke and dropped the load, he flattened himself against the wall as close as he could."[46] A falling hammer or shovel or piece of curbing, not to mention the collapse of a well wall, made him fearful of the slightest sound or movement. A dry well was not unusual, forcing the hard-pressed farmer to start all over again.

In a few rare cases, a good deep well lucky enough to tap the aquifer supported two hundred head of cattle, while typical wells barely furnished water for the sod house and a few barnyard animals. Very rarely, to the envy of all his fellows, a farmer might enjoy an artesian well, but most artesian wells were in the Dakotas. In hand-dug wells the water was lifted laboriously in the old-fashioned two-bucket system: one in the water when the full bucket was on top. It was an arduous and time-consuming task to lift the heavy bucketful of water by hand. At first, few farmers could afford the newfangled windmill, tower, and pump and were reluctant to throw hard-earned cash at an untested device. To keep up with the needs of ten or twenty cattle was probably impossible; watering an uneconomical twenty acres of wheat, much less water-needy corn, was unthinkable. No tinkerer, much less a manufacturer, had come up with a pump for the plains. In the first two decades of the twentieth century, however, the self-regulating factory-built windmill (see chapter 4) would water enough land, five to ten acres, to enable the homesteader to hold on when all others had to leave. But windmills did not feed the thirsty crops on a farmer's quarter section, much less a spread covering an entire square mile.

"Big Ditches" from the Arkansas River: The Garden City Experiment

Today, USGS survey maps show many intermittent streams in southwest Kansas. Local people call them wet-weather streams or dry draws. They can still be traced for twenty or fifty or even one hundred miles, sometimes with still-visible depressions where buffalo once pawed and wallowed to make a damp place deeper and wetter. Today the Arkansas River, once a full-flowing river from Colorado into Kansas, barely trickles when dust does not blow through its channels. One reason for today's barrenness is the declining water table as Ogallala water is drawn down. Another is that for decades upstream irrigators around Lamar, Colorado, have captured the river's water long before it reaches the state line. But at the turn of the century, the river flowed well through Garden City, Kansas; it got national attention, and the town's name seemed appropriate.[47]

For water to supply a growing population of irrigators, the Arkansas River got most early attention.[48] In the 1870s the river ran wide and deep; even in severe drought it flowed at least one to three feet deep and one hundred feet wide. After an upstream storm, it would rage through a channel four hundred feet wide. The biggest early problem was throwing a bridge that could span the channel. The river flow, fed from the Rocky Mountains, usually did not vary more than five feet between high and low water, although it did once go completely dry in the spring of 1883. Two Garden City farmers with irrigation-ditch experience, one from Colorado and the other from California, told stories of the wonders of irrigation projects that spread for miles along rivers in those states. They got more attention when drought hit again in 1879, the second year of settlement in Finney County. Farmers had barely turned the new sod before they looked around for water. Fear of no crops brought fresh interest in irrigation. The farmer with Colorado irrigation-ditch experience was apparently W. H. Armentrout; the California irrigator may have been George Finnup. They were joined by banker A. G. Landis from nearby Sterling. The three walked the banks of the Arkansas River and found, three miles west of Garden City, a place where an inexpensive earthen dam between an island in the river and the north shore would force water into an east-flowing ditch. In 1880, with money lent by Landis, Garden City's first irrigation canal was laboriously dug by local farmers; it was four miles long, eight feet wide, and two feet deep. Finnup reminisced in 1922: "We figured the expense to make the dam, cut the ditch to Garden City, and a few laterals would cost about seven or eight hundred dollars."[49] It eventually cost Armentrout two thousand dollars to divert water for one hundred acres. His ditch also served Squire Worrell, whose irrigated farm produced five crops of alfalfa in 1881 alone, a sharp contrast to his drought losses on the same land in 1879.[50] Successfully completed, the project worked so well that it was extended twice to run twenty miles northeast, well beyond Garden City.

The Garden City experiment received nationwide attention as part of the popular Irrigation Crusade that linked western prosperity to intensive irrigation.[51] In 1893, national irrigation spokesman William Smythe, applying his usual booster hyperbole, hailed Garden City as "the center and inspiration of irrigation development." Another ditch was dug between June 1880 and July 1881 by a group that called itself the Kansas Ditch Company. It was improved in 1882 to run more than thirty miles and extended again in 1901–1902 and renamed the Farmers Ditch by its new owners. As Garden City's fame spread, investors from as far away as Ohio financed the successful Southside Ditch on the south bank of the Arkansas River.

Garden City became an irrigation boomtown. Investors from Lawrence, Kansas, joined local speculator C. J. ("Buffalo") Jones to support the Great

73

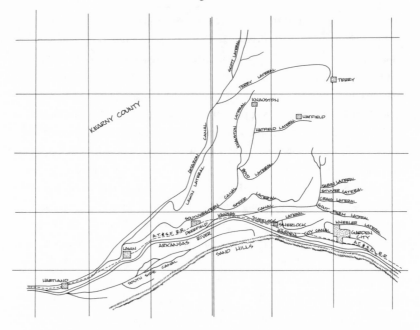

4. Garden City canals, ditches, and laterals tapping upstream Arkansas River water in 1892. These were the only large-scale community irrigation projects on the High Plains. But the Arkansas too often went dry early in the twentieth century, so the use of surface water alone proved inadequate for farming in the region. Twentieth-century groundwater irrigation would be on individual farms only. From the *Garden City Imprint*, May 7, 1892.

Eastern Canal, which spread a network of ditches and laterals 30 miles north of the Kansas Ditch. The Santa Fe Railroad promised funds, using income from its sale of railroad sections, but then it backed out and the canal was turned over to participating farmers in 1883.[52] By 1889 the Great Eastern, including its main laterals, extended 96 miles across the previously unsettled dry uplands north of Garden City at a cost exceeding one hundred thousand dollars; a year later the Great Eastern badly needed repair and served few farms.[53] Buffalo Jones also guided construction of the long-lived Amazon Ditch, which supplied farmers in Finney, Scott, and Kearny counties from 1890 into the 1960s. To build the Amazon Ditch forty-five-feet wide and nine feet deep, records show that the experienced construction team used a crew

74

of fifteen men, thirty horses, two excavating graders, and several two-horse slips. They built the ditch and its farmstead laterals in less than two years for about one hundred thousand dollars. It eventually ran for 102 miles.[54]

This era of big ditches, totaling 336 miles of main canals to irrigate about 70,000 acres (far below Buffalo Jones's estimated 600,000 acres), encouraged a population explosion along the Arkansas River valley: from 10,000 residents in 1884 to 70,000 by 1888.[55] By 1882 a journalist could boast that the hardy farmers of Garden City had created

> a great newly-made garden [that] was laid out in beds of large size, each with a foot-high ridge around it, like the bottom crust of a pie. These are the dykes through which the water is let on the beds. Running the length of the fields parallel with the river was a ditch with swift-running water one or two feet deep; the water ran like a mill-race, and did not creep as in a canal, then there were lateral ditches crossing the fields, a ridge on each side preventing overflow. . . . I walked about over the little fields. The earth was soft like ashes. There is not a stone as big as a baby's foot for miles and miles. All sorts of vegetables had been planted; some grain was growing, and there was a field of the curious dark-green alfalfa, which sends its roots to water, six, eight, or ten feet, and can be cut four or five times a season.[56]

Fields were flooded two or three times a season. Field leveling involved horse-drawn scrapers made of wood and a length of railroad iron. Crop yields doubled and tripled with irrigation: up to seventy-five bushels of oats per acre, twenty-five bushels of wheat, and forty bushels of corn, as well as ten tons of alfalfa a year. Prosperity in southwest Kansas was linked entirely to water from the laterals and ditches off the river. In 1899, virtually all irrigation in southwest Kansas—95 percent of 200,000 acres—used Arkansas and Cimarron water. Irrigated farmland offered stability and hope for the future as nothing else ever did in the dry region. For a time, the population in and around Garden City took on boomtown proportions, growing from 1,315 in 1880 to 26,260 in 1890.

Despite old optimism about the return of heavier rainfall and new optimism about the success of water-conserving dryland farming, by 1889 most settlers in southwest Kansas admitted that irrigation was a necessity, not an optional improvement, for successful farming. Farmers who had settled the arid low hills north of Garden City, where the ditches could not run, were without a regular water supply. Beyond the irrigation ditches, only twelve families held out on the arid northern stretches of Finney County and only thirty families were spread out over the vast "north flats" of Kearny County. Foster Eskelund recorded that they supplemented their skimpy farm income by hiring out to work on ditches and by leasing their land to irrigation farmers who generally also invested in sizable herds of cattle.[57] The profitability of irrigation was clear. A newspaper correspondent wrote in September 1887: "There will be no more building canals and then waiting for the people to be converted. They are already converted by the strongest argument in the world—hot winds, protracted drought, and consequently almost total failure of crops."[58] But even the irrigators repeatedly compounded their own problems by having no interest in irrigation during a season of rains.

With the large Amazon Ditch, a new problem arose: there was not enough water in the Arkansas River to fill its main canal and laterals. Upstream Colorado irrigators were on the verge of diverting the entire flow of the Arkansas. As early as July 1888, the Garden City Ditch Company tried to protect irrigation by damming all but twelve feet of the river's remaining flow. In July 1890 the river went dry, and in 1893 rainfall declined to less than twelve inches for western Kansas; no water entered irrigation ditches until the last week in June, too late to save the burned-up crops.[59] The upstream irrigators in Colorado delivered the coup de grace in 1905 when about one hundred ditch systems serving over seven thousand farmers irrigated nearly half a million acres using Arkansas River water. USGS maps began to show the river as an intermittent stream when it entered Kansas. In 1907 a landmark U.S. Supreme Court decision, *Kansas* v. *Colorado,* established a concept of equity in economic terms but failed to deal with environmental and economic realities. Much later, in 1949, the Arkansas River Compact treated water solely as a commodity, but, despite local optimism, it had little effect on the future of irrigation in southwest Kansas.[60]

Farmers began to resist water contracts costing $500 over ten years and guaranteed by a first mortgage on the farmer's land.[61] New speculation in canal development was attracted by the promise that an irrigation system could be constructed for about fifty cents an acre, while the standard charge for existing irrigation stood at a dollar an acre a year. Irrigators complained that much of the new irrigable land lay "year after year in a state of nature producing nothing more valuable than weeds or buffalo grass" because it stood in the alternate sections of the Santa Fe land grant, too costly at $2.50 to $10.00 an acre.

Drought in Finney County, combined with a dry riverbed, meant that wheat production collapsed from an average high of twenty-five bushels per acre in 1889 to three bushels in 1895 and 1896. Corn fell from thirty bushels in 1889 to five bushels in 1893 and 1894. The 1890s brought investment from England, cooperative irrigation companies, and large landowners involved in sharecropping, "but even English capital could not raise crops in western Kansas in the 1890s."[62] Farmer irrigation associations acquired the bankrupt Kansas Ditch, the Garden City Ditch, and even the vaunted Amazon. When some rain reappeared in the mid-1890s, farmers aggressively planted wheat on 26,600 acres, compared to predrought planting of less than 1,000 acres. But profitable production on an intensive scale now depended on irrigation more than rainfall. Between 1895 and 1899, 10 percent of the remaining farmers hung on by reluctantly becoming dryland ranchers, shifting from grain crops to cattle. By the time another drought struck in 1900, planting collapsed to a low of 409 acres. No alternative dryland crops were known and the land was simply abandoned. As a result the population west of the 100th meridian in Kansas fell from 81,000 in 1889 to less than 50,000 in 1895, not to rebuild until the next century.[63] Wheat acreage would not rise above 26,000 acres again until 1908 during the so-called Agricultural Golden Age of high productivity and high prices. Homesteaders would not again risk their fortunes in the region until the palmier days of 1906–1907. It appeared that farming on the Kansas High Plains, despite the best new technologies and hardier wheat, would always remain a risky enterprise with low

Cost of Irrigation

Cost of irrigation under ditch, from 50 cents to $1.00 per acre per year.
Cost of irrigation from pump, as follows, according to lift:
RULE–"Eight cents per acre foot for every foot of lift."
Per acre foot we mean, sufficient water to cover an acre of ground to the depth of one foot, and you will not use to exceed, if your land is properly prepared, over from 3 to 5 inches per irrigation.

Table of Cost as Follows:

20 foot Lift	$1.60 per acre, foot	Per irrigation about	55 cents per acre
25 foot Lift	2.00 " " "	Per " "	66 " " "
30 foot Lift	2.40 " " "	Per " "	80 " " "
40 foot Lift	3.20 " " "	Per " "	$1.05 " " "
50 foot Lift	4.00 " " "	Per " "	1.35 " " "

Per acre foots we Cost of irrigation under ditch, from 50 cents to $1.00 per acre per year per acre foots.Cost of irrigation under ditch, from 50 cents to $1.00 per acre per year.

Crop Yields Under Irrigation Last Year

Wheat	30 to 63 bushels per acre	Corn	30 to 65 bushels per acre
Barley	35 to 65 " " "	Oats	40 to 90 " " "
Maize	40 to 60 " " "	Alfalfa	5 to 7 " " "
Irish Potatoes	200 to 300 " " "	Sweet Potatoes	200 to 400 " " "

These results will depend on the kind of farming and the amount of water used, yields varying as in all localities, the better the farming the more production.

Crop Yields Under Dry Farming Last Year

Wheat	15 to 35 bushels per acre	Corn	20 to 40 bushels per acre
Oats	20 to 35 " " "	Barley	15 to 35 " " "
Rye	15 to 30 " " "	Maize and Kaffir	15 to 35 " " "

These crops vary, as to the kind of farming and the amount of rainfall, and we are offering a large acreage of fine wheat lands, from which a single crop has more than paid for the land on which it grew.

ANNUAL RAINFALL AT GARDEN CITY, KANSAS, FOR THE PAST TEN YEARS.

Month	1920	1919	1918	1917	1916	1915	1914	1913	1912	1911
January	.20	.10	.70	.30	1.09	.45	.27	.15	.28	.00
February	.23	1.73	.75	.00	.00	2.54	.20	1.15	3.04	3.53
March	.21	1.45	2.48	.60	.60	.95	.13	.50	.98	.86
April	1.52	4.42	.92	3.52	2.50	2.98	1.73	1.05	2.36	.40
May	2.22	.98	2.67	3.60	.33	4.36	4.34	1.42	.67	2.91
June	3.79	1.14	1.88	2.48	3.56	2.28	2.54	3.28	4.16	1.46
July	3.45	3.19	4.01	2.23	.55	2.29	1.93	1.14	1.57	3.50
August	3.78	.54	.66	3.26	3.83	7.68	1.01	2.00	3.91	1.81
September	2.00	4.23	2.14	1.58	.87	2.61	.10	5.21	1.04	.22
October	2.10	1.23	4.44	.13	1.05	1.75	1.45	.23	.15	1.54
November	.69	1.28	.10	.30	.00	.12	.00	1.19	.29	.95
December	.33	.27	4.80	.16	.50	.13	.41	2.92	.05	1.66
Total	20.52	20.56	25.55	18.16	14.88	28.14	14.01	19.74	18.50	18.84

Average Rainfall 19.89 inches. For Past Ten Years.

The above table shows we have sufficient rainfall to supplement irrigation, which is a great advantage over the wholly arid irrigated sections, and yet we do not have enough rain to hinder farm operations and damage crops.

expectations. By 1949 less than 40 percent of southwest Kansas irrigation came from stream water; by 1966 it was less than 10 percent.

Discovery of the "Underflow" and Federal Reclamation

The canal companies tried to save themselves from the vagaries of river water by tapping into the "underflow." New settlers and old-timers alike took comfort in their belief in a vast underground body of "sheet water" that was constantly replenished, either from the Rocky Mountains or even the remote Arctic. Garden City residents, including a newspaper editor, went further by insisting that a cavernous underground river thundered along with more water than the Arkansas River had ever contained. It had the advantage that it was inexhaustible and would not go dry. The editor of a Texas Panhandle monthly, *The Earth*, wrote of "a water sheet . . . that is inexhaustible" and that could be "counted upon in all cases."[64] Did not artesian wells in the Dakotas already easily tap a strong underground flow? Yet there were no artesian wells in southwest Kansas and the Texas-Oklahoma Panhandle.

An unidentifiable Captain Livermore, with even more flimflam than most promoters, claimed that underflow water was glacier water from the Arctic, although how it traveled thousands of miles and then fanned out widely "is a matter to be worked out." But the water was so reliable that "the only power that could ever exhaust the Plains water supply would be an earthquake that would crack the flint bottom and give the water another channel."[65] The myth of a gigantic underground river underlying the Great Plains would not be abandoned easily. The Arctic theory remained a popular notion into the 1950s, the Ogallala's inexhaustibility into the 1960s—until irrigation-well levels began to decline noticeably. A historian of the Ogallala in Texas, Donald E. Green, observed that "the very massiveness of the

OPPOSITE: 5. The contents of the back page from a 1921 irrigation-land promotional brochure of the Garden City real-estate firm Charles I. Zirkle and Company vividly illustrates the contemporary boomer mentality. Zirkle made the best of marginal rainfall by claiming, "We have sufficient rainfall to supplement irrigation, which is a great advantage over the wholly arid irrigated sections, and yet we do not have enough rain to hinder farm operations and damage crops." From the Kansas Room files, courtesy of the Finney County Public Library, Garden City, Kansas.

Ogallala formation was partly to blame for the misconception. Early irrigators could pump a thousand gallons per minute from the extensive subsurface lake [*sic*] day after day without exhausting the supply."[66]

An 1891 United States Geological Survey investigation gave scientific credibility to popular belief in the underflow: it originated as runoff from the Rockies that flowed eastward, refreshed along the way by percolation from surface rain and snow.[67] In 1895 an official of the Kansas Geological Survey, Erasmus Haworth, reported: "The citizens throughout the tertiary areas of Kansas almost as one man have an unshaken faith that the waters precipitated along the eastern slope of the great Rocky Mountains very largely pass eastward and constitute at least an important proportion of the great body of water."[68] The idea was to tap the underflow by digging an irrigation ditch upstream to intersect the underflow and gravity-feed it into canals, laterals, and fields.[69] In 1889 the visiting U.S. Senate Committee on Irrigation and Reclamation of Arid Lands was urged to provide survey and experiment funds, which, if successful, would be augmented by an "abundance of private capital."

The search to identify the size of the underflow led the Kansas legislature in 1905 to order a Board of Irrigation technical survey in which twenty irrigation wells were to be drilled in several counties, using unoccupied school lands. Eastern Kansas interests ridiculed the attempt to find large groundwater supplies, but it was worth wasting thirty thousand dollars on a final, unsuccessful search, one said, to put the western "bow-wows" in their place.[70] Federal geologist W. D. Johnson visited Garden City in 1897 and encouraged capture of the underflow, although in his 1901 United States Geological Survey report he would conclude, as Powell had twenty-three years earlier, that "the absolute verdict must be that they [the High Plains in general] are non-irrigable . . . the only possible agricultural land of the High Plains belt lies within the valleys, where small patches here and there are irrigable." More confident was federal geologist Charles M. Slichter, who in 1904 took the trouble to drill several wells in a line across the river valley just west of Garden City. He concluded wrongly that the underflow moved eight feet every twenty-four hours, but he was on target when he claimed the flow was constant and that large amounts of water could be pumped if a cheap source of power could be found.[71]

In 1890 work began on an underflow channel at the head of the Great Eastern Canal. Costs were estimated at six thousand dollars but immediate benefits were set at twelve thousand dollars because the new water would enter the canal at more than nine hundred cubic feet a minute. However, the river flooded in the spring of 1891, destroyed the channel, and the experiment was not repeated. As late as 1902, newspaper editorials still urged construction of steam- or gasoline-powered pumping stations: "Cut the ditches loose from the river and install pumping plants."[72]

By the early twentieth century, only a trickle of Arkansas River water occasionally reached Garden City. Residents clamored for an experimental government-financed underflow-capture project, and as a result, one of the first projects of the new federal Reclamation Service was a series of pumps to capture thirty thousand acre-feet of water, half the estimated underflow of the Arkansas River. The Newlands Reclamation Act of 1902 released funds from the sale of public land to be applied to irrigation projects. The farmers who consumed the water were to repay construction costs to the federal government in a minimum of ten annual installments. Imitating the successful irrigation colonies of Utah's Mormons, California communities, and the well-known success at Greeley, Colorado, citizens organized the Water Users Association and enthusiastically oversubscribed the project, pledging more than twelve thousand acres in December 1905. Despite his belief in the reality of the underflow, Charles Slichter, now with the Reclamation Service, was convinced initially that no more than eighty-six hundred acres could be irrigated, although he later raised his estimate to twenty thousand. Slichter was soon to argue that the project would raise land values so much that it would be paid for easily by "those under the ditch."

Garden City's steam-powered electric station began transmitting power on April 1, 1908, to twenty-three pumps at one-thousand-foot intervals along a four-mile concrete conduit. Each pump, a No. 10 vertical double upper-suction centrifugal device, was connected to nine or twelve wells fifteen inches in diameter and thirty to sixty feet deep in clay.[73] The year was the severest drought year in a decade and provided a good test of the project's effectiveness under dire conditions. In 1908, water drawn directly from the river irrigated 2,900 acres, while the new pumping plant covered 5,100 more. How much water actually reached the fields is not known, but engineers, farmers, and businessmen were disappointed in the coverage and stared in disbelief at the 75 percent that was lost to evaporation and seepage.

In August 1908, Secretary of the Interior James A. Garfield arrived to assess the results. He told the Water Users Association that "it is not right to charge the patrons for something they did not receive. . . . The patrons did not receive the water at the time when it was needed the worst."[74] On his return to Washington, however, he insisted on full payment of $3.50 per acre plus a building charge of $2.75 per acre for maintenance. Few farmers, with or without water, could afford $1,000 a year for ten years to service a 160-acre quarter section, and the association refused to pay. The next year, 1909, was a better one, with river water irrigating 9,400 acres and pumped water going to 6,500. This fell far short of the most conservative estimates; per acre costs shot up from $25 to $37.50 and finally exceeded $100. The government quit pumping in 1910 and sold out after World War I to the Garden City Company, which operated the system indifferently into the 1930s.

Arkansas River underflow had been misinterpreted; it would later be identified as part of the Ogallala aquifer, but it was not the answer to dry times and a dried-up surface river until new technology and new fuels became available. Charles Slichter repeated the common complaint about Kansas farmers, even those who became irrigators: they stubbornly stuck to large-scale wheat farming in the face of certain defeat while in the rest of the West small-scale irrigators were prospering. In 1908 he argued:

General agricultural crops grown in large tracts and farmed after customary methods for such crops will not pay a large return on the cost of pumping irrigation water. It is necessary to divide land into small holdings and to cultivate special crops such as melons, sweet potatoes, fruit or sugar beets in order to realize profitable results. In communities that have been accustomed to the cultivation of forage crops . . . it is probable that a complete revision of agricultural methods may be

82

necessary. . . . It will be advantageous for the [Garden City] farmers to reduce the size of their farms.[75]

Slichter concluded in 1911 that "the plant itself is not a failure, but the people will not try to make it a success." In 1912 the new secretary of the interior, Walter L. Fisher, refused to intervene and blamed local intransigence: "The project at Garden City was taken up on the urgent request of the citizens of Kansas. . . . The works were built, were partly used, and any lack of success is due mainly to causes within the control of the persons who are now seeking relief."[76] Reclamation projects were booming in California and private entrepreneurs established irrigation communities, such as Greeley, Colorado, but the people of southwest Kansas rejected centralized and cooperative irrigation. The Garden City Water Users Association felt unjustly abused. It would gladly pay the $3.50 per acre per year if it got the promised two acre-feet of water per year. "But when the experiment showed conclusively that the plant was unable to deliver the promised water, what else could we do?" A state irrigation official wrote in 1913: "The big plant with its wasted $400,000 stands there idle, today, a monument to a theoretical dream."[77]

Industrial Crop Irrigation and Local Processing

Even before the rise and fall of Garden City's troubled federal reclamation colony, private industry saw an opportunity.[78] By 1900, sugar-beet companies in Colorado were operating successful irrigation-based processing plants and were looking to expand into western Kansas. Garden City businessmen organized the Cooperative Sugar Beet Growers' Association to join the American Sugar Beet Company of Rocky Ford, Colorado, in a five-hundred-acre experiment. Climate and soil conditions were excellent, but sugar beets required almost thirty-seven inches of rain a year compared to Garden City's nineteen-inch average rainfall. Similar conditions had been mastered by the irrigation colonies in Colorado and estimates suggested costs of eight dollars an acre to raise beets, with a practical minimum of five acres; the Kansas legislature chipped in a dollar a ton for "beets grown in Kansas and actually used for sugar manufacturing."[79] In 1901 almost three hundred acres planted in sugar beets produced 295,000 tons of beets. A processing plant in Holly, Colorado, bought more than 8,000 tons of Kansas sugar beets grown on almost seven hundred acres, and the state paid farmers a ten-thousand-dollar bounty. Business interests quickly moved into Garden City and quietly bought sixteen thousand acres, together with ownership of the Great Eastern, South Side, and Garden City ditches; thirty thousand dollars from businessmen soon sweetened the deal.

The $250,000 factory was large: a brick refinery 273 feet long, several office buildings, and 700 feet of beet sheds.[80] When in full operation in 1909, it could process eight hundred tons of sugar beets daily, consuming up to six million gallons of water in the process. The United States Sugar and Land Company established the United States Irrigating Company to clean, maintain, improve, and expand the irrigation canals it now owned. This included a 30,000-acre-foot reservoir named Lake McKinney, five miles by two and a half miles, created by an earthen dam several miles long. Fed by pumps and the intermittent Arkansas River, Lake McKinney kept sugar processing going during the severe drought of 1908. In addition, the company took full advantage of improved pumping technologies to establish a pumping plant of seventeen stations, nine wells, and a central gas-fired power plant. The entire operation was valued at $5.5 million, far beyond the $500,000 of the federal reclamation project. With $500,000 poured annually into the local economy, Finney County's population doubled between 1905 and 1907.

The sugar-beet operation, an early version of vertically integrated agribusiness, seemed to be the wave of the future on the High Plains wherever large quantities of groundwater could be found. By 1919 the company owned fifty-two thousand acres of sugar beets, ran its own Garden City Western Railway, processed waste beet pulp into cattle feed, operated an alfalfa mill, and supplied its own electric power to the sugar factory, irrigation pumps, and the public. But sugar beets require about the same heavy irrigation as corn, cultivation is labor intensive on small acreages, international markets are extremely competitive, and new processing technologies are costly. After struggling for many years, the beet factory closed in December 1955; the operation never expanded beyond its level in 1919, when it created almost four hundred seasonal jobs. By the 1960s the company operated primarily as a land-management business, leasing out almost twenty-three thousand acres, and was the largest absentee owner in Finney County. On its land, mostly north of the Arkansas River, groundwater depletion at 50 percent is the most serious in the county.[81]

Against the Kansas Grain: Frederick H. Newell's
Intensive Irrigation Farming

As early as 1894, C. H. Longstreth, director of the state horticultural society in eastern Kansas, stated the prejudice against farmers in southwest Kansas: "The irrigation question is simple. It means intense culture." Large-scale dryland farming, to which the western farmers were so unreasonably committed, would invariably fail in the face of extended drought. The task was to turn farmers into small-plot irrigators. The new nationwide Irrigation Crusade, strongest in California, announced that ten acres to a maximum of forty acres, well irrigated, was sufficient to support a family. Intensive farming meant raising onions, cabbage, sweet potatoes, tomatoes, grapes, cherries, and apples, with which a farmer had his hands full on twenty acres. Although there was not enough water to cover quarter sections, irrigation could serve small tracts. According to B. P. Walker, president of the Kansas Board of Irrigation in 1913, many farmers "have lived in western Kansas too long to be able to confine their labors to a small irrigated farm, since they have been accustomed all their lives to farming a [640-acre] section or more of land by dry-farming methods." In 1907, western Kansas farms averaged 800 acres, with 120 acres under regular cultivation. In the Arkansas River valley near Garden City, irrigators worked farms that averaged 160 acres, but even this was excessive to Irrigation Crusaders. They irrigated fields of alfalfa, sugar beets, and small grain crops like wheat, oats, and barley. They found that irrigation increased production by a third to a half, but they strongly opposed intensive farming.[82] Walker went so far as to urge that stubborn plains settlers be replaced with dedicated irrigators.[83]

Longstreth and Walker were the Kansas agents of the national Irrigation Crusade led by William E. Smythe, Frederick H. Newell, and Richard J. Hinton. Smythe was introduced to the virtues of irrigation at Kearney, Nebraska, in 1888. He took the lead at a statewide irrigation congress in Lincoln in 1891 and built the National Irrigation Movement, which later received the public blessing of President Theodore Roosevelt. When Smythe organized the Los Angeles Irrigation Congress of 1893, he was joined in the proceedings by Judge J. W. Gregory of Garden City, James S. Emery of Lawrence, and Joseph L. Bristow, the new editor of the *Irrigation Farmer* at Salina.

In 1894, Smythe returned to the plains to address an irrigation congress in Hutchinson, Kansas.[84] With his usual florid rhetoric, he called the new Garden City irrigation project the "beacon light for Kansas" and warned his audience, "You cannot afford to blunder. This is one of the times when blunder is worse than crime. You must not raise another crop of false hopes, a plant that has already been too prolific in Western Kansas." He repeated the new irrigation credo: "Wherever water can be had to irrigate forty acres of Western Kansas soil, every industrious family can win both a living and a competence." He told his audience that during the last forty years each Utah Mormon family on twenty irrigated acres had averaged $1,357.25 a year, or $482.25 over its cost of living. In Kansas a family of five that owned forty acres could support itself on twenty acres and net $500 a year from the other 20 acres. "Wherever a quarter section is now occupied by one family there ought next year to be at least four families, provided there is water for irrigation." Owners of quarter sections would profitably subdivide into twenty- to forty-acre parcels and use the proceeds to pay for a water supply.

> Remember that this is an entirely different sort of development from the old boom in town lots and wheat fields. All of that rested on a speculative basis. We are not planning a development that rests on self-sustenance first and then a wise surplus, which in ordinary years will bring us a reasonable profit. . . . It hurts me to ride through Western Kansas and see the desolate houses that serve as homes. We will change all this with irrigation. We will have little homes of pleasing architecture. We will surround them with pretty lawns, we will fringe them with trees and hedges, we will drape them with vines and deck them with roses, in a new Kansas dedicated to industrial independence.[85]

Smythe's overwrought prose gained credibility after Frederick H. Newell published his sober report, "Irrigation on the Great Plains," in the 1896 yearbook of the Department of Agriculture.[86] While Smythe was a journalist and promoter, Newell had credentials as chief hydrographer of the United States Geological Survey. But the message was the same: large dryland farmers foolishly waste the land and are doomed to failure; industrious smallholders on irrigated land are virtuous and will prosper.

Newell anticipated the debates of the 1930s and 1980s when he condemned the way the plains had been settled. Admittedly, during a rare good year a plains farm will bring "wonderful crops," but it will also encourage the useless plowing of thousands of acres. The "irregular and scanty rainfall" of the plains means that "total loss of crops and bitter disappointment inevitably follow, and the unfortunate settlers, if not driven from the country, alternate between short periods of prosperity and long intervals of depression."[87] These misled, inept, and intractable farmers have already damaged one-sixth of the nation's land when, properly irrigated and professionally tended, it could provide farmsteads "for millions more." Newell argued that the plains offer "boundless tracts of fertile soil" where, tragically, "the temptation to the settler is [still] to make his farm as wide reaching as the horizon, and to spread his efforts over hundreds of acres. The ever-recurring droughts stimulate him to try and till more land, in the hopes that he may recoup his losses in a fortunate year. He is in a certain sense a gambler, staking everything upon luck, and with the chances against him . . . it is almost impossible for him to see that his own hope of permanent success lies in limiting his operations to a comparatively few acres."[88] Newell acknowledged that plains farmers were stubborn and would rather emigrate than practice "un-American intensive farming."

Newell proposed that farmers abandon western Kansas and that, barring intensive irrigated farming, migration be cut off in order to return the region to pastureland. "Has the world not heard enough of droughts and crop losses, of famines and suffering, of abandoned farms and worthless Kansas mortgages? Why interpose to prevent the country from going back to its former conditions? It was, and can be, a magnificent grazing land."[89] He recommended government intervention, since the federal government was still the plains' largest landowner. Any attempt to irrigate a field on the scale of a quarter section is costly, unnecessary, wasteful, and deceptive. "The idea that any man on the boundless plains would concentrate his energies on 10 acres has seemed ridiculous. Yet this is what stern necessity is compelling the farmer to do, and is making him unlearn his old habits and methods, turning them over perhaps to grazing, and giving his main attention to the few acres almost within a stone's throw of his door."[90] This included abandonment of wheat or corn, which are too low in value for irrigated land and should be left to farmers in Illinois and Iowa.

Newell argued that intensive farming is high grade, diversified, and risk free. In a prophetic statement anticipating the technologies and practices of the 1960s, he concluded that plains farming depends upon individually controlled wells to tap groundwater supplies, since surface streams are uncommon and often intermittent. "It is often possible for the farmer to dig or drill the well himself, and he can purchase, sometimes on credit if necessary, the machinery, windmill, or pump for bringing the water to the surface."[91] In an open appeal to the crusty independent plains farmer, Newell argued that intensive farming thus preserved democratic freedom for the individual farmer, which he might have lost under a large irrigating colony. Newell then described state-of-the-art pumping and windmill technologies, believing that steam and gasoline power offered great promise in the future. He also emphasized skilled management techniques for the application of water and the cultivation of crops. Following these recommendations, any industrious farmer could begin to prosper on three to five acres. The Jeffersonian dream of the citizen farmer thus could still prevail in the arid West.

Newell's small-farms plan for the plains was resurrected during the Dust Bowl era. Agricultural extension agents in Meade, Grant, and Ford counties in western Kansas promoted live-at-home programs to encourage self-sufficiency when cash crops failed. Farmers were piously told to work harder toward diversification involving a combination of row crops for feed and grain; a mix of cattle, pigs, chickens, and turkeys; and gardening.[92] The Ford County agent preached that wheat had destroyed the region, that federal aid had failed, and that farmers loafed away three-quarters of their time because eight hundred acres of wheat needed only 411 hours a year. Farmers wryly observed that animals and gardens did not do well under Dust Bowl conditions.

Newell's Kansas reclamation crusade was reinforced by a colleague, Richard J. Hinton. Originally a newspaperman like Smythe, Hinton came to know the West as a government agent and writer for private industry, including the Southern Pacific Railroad. In 1886 he was commissioned by Congress to write *Irrigation in the United States,* perhaps the most important federal land study after Powell.[93] As Powell had done with Utah, Hinton gave special attention to California's ever-increasing water needs and the High Plains received secondary attention. But as Powell's influence declined, Hinton's rose. In 1889 he turned his attention to central plains farmers, in such destitute condition, he announced, that they would in the future be "the largest part of the population to be benefitted by irrigation."[94] Hinton followed Newell's lead and warned that existing large-scale dryland farming guaranteed an "element of [permanent] insecurity" as well as certain collapse in the face of endemic drought. The moral solution to plains poverty was still intensive low-acreage farming—"small detailed works" built through "neighborhood and individual exertion."

Despite his errors concerning the potential for artesian wells in southwest Kansas,[95] Hinton was right on target about plains groundwater. He concluded that the Arkansas River underflow did not exist but a very large, slow-moving, and "mysterious" aquifer did.[96] He supported USGS scientists in their conclusion that the aquifer was composed of slowly moving water that seeped eastward with little local recharge because of soil conditions and high evaporation rates.[97] Despite the conservation implications of this new information, Hinton proposed leaving groundwater to private development. A Walter Rusinek article on Hinton argues that "he appeared to advocate private control and pricing of water, a popular trend today dubbed 'privatization.'"[98] Rusinek concludes that in the long run Hinton did not advance plains irrigation with his privatization argument. "Inefficient pumps, low crop prices, expensive energy, and a government policy that fa-

vored surface works kept groundwater development too costly for wide use
on the Great Plains until the 1950s. This . . . resulted in too little use during
the severe drought of the 1930s and overuse in the post-war years."[99]

The High Plains Way: Decentralized Irrigation

With the ephemeral promise of California-style irrigation from the Arkansas
River, wheat farmers around Garden City mortgaged themselves to buy hundreds and even thousands of acres in the dry open country, to dig costly irrigation ditches and peripheral canals, and to dream of abundant crops. Then,
with the return of drought, coupled with upstream use in Colorado, the river
ran empty on the "dazzling plain without timber and with little water." With
communal failures like this, it is not difficult to explain why commitment to
decentralized irrigation would become the High Plains way. The answer also
may be the persistence of independent farmer values, each family living and
working autonomously and determined to make or break in privacy. Neither
the Garden City Sugar Company irrigation plan nor a major Reclamation
Bureau project nor the cooperative or communitarian styles that succeeded
elsewhere would become the irrigator's style in southwest Kansas. Farmers
there also rejected Newell's criticism of large-scale irrigation; it insulted
their plains know-how. The plains farm family was individualistic, settled
on its own independent tract of land, and disinclined to share and divide responsibilities with a larger group, even a cooperative among neighbors. Personal success was measured by no machinery debts; all the land paid for; a
ready supply of food and fuel, clothing, and a few conveniences; and deep
loyalty to the perceived fundamental virtues of rural American thrift, hard
work, and self-discipline. Cooperative ventures and centralized irrigation
may have been extremely successful in California, but the plains farmer remained committed to ownership of his own total irrigation system, including
wells, pumps, engines, ditches or piping, and all the costs and personal labor
they involved.

In still another try, as crop prices rose, southwest Kansas farmers by 1909
had put down 684 pumps irrigating almost two thousand acres. In 1921 a Garden City farmland sales agent wrote this pitch: "Irrigation: Dollars for you

where Water Means Wealth, in the Garden City district, America's Land of Promise, combined with Good Land, Rich Soil, Low Prices, and Reasonable Terms."[100] By 1924 the area had some twenty thousand acres "under pump" and eighty thousand "under ditch." Kansas Irrigation Commissioner George S. Knapp concluded after a 1,300-mile tour of the state that irrigation had reached its limits because since it was too costly outside the few river valleys in the west. Although Riverside, California, irrigators could pay for pumping from one hundred feet or more below ground because they could afford twenty dollars per acre on a two-thousand-dollar-orange grove yield, Knapp asked, "What crop could they raise in western Kansas which will make such a return as that?"[101] Irrigation, he said, was limited to pumping when the cost did not exceed 10 percent of the value of the crop and where the water table was not more than twenty feet below the surface so that it could be reached by windmill power. But Knapp also observed: "How do you suppose the farmers back there would like to throw a switch and save their corn crops this year at the cost of $1 an acre?"

The local farmer fought tenaciously to preserve his way of life. Sometimes he would plow up more ground for a bigger crop as prices fell; other times he would sell off cattle at a loss. The farm family had a stubborn pride that made it imperative to stay on the dried-out plains rather than face the gritty factories and boss-ruled politics of a distant industrial America. Dust Bowl historian Donald Worster noted that "the people of the [Arkansas] country were land- and machinery-rich . . . but in other respects they were closer to the sod-house era than to our own."[102] The frontier still held sway on the High Plains.

3

· · ·

From Dryland to Dust Bowl:
Not a Good Place to Farm

On a small corner of the leeward side of a field, a particle of soil, broken loose by the wind, struck a cluster of soil particles like a cue ball striking the racked balls. The avalanching effect of soil erosion gathered force as it moved across the field. By the time the effects of one tiny wind-driven soil particle reached the opposite side of the field, a mighty force was assembled to assault the neighboring abandoned field. Soon a dirt storm was burning any living plant, while the soil around the plant's roots was joining the race across the stricken land.—Dust Bowl historian Paul Bonnifield

It is useless to single out any one set . . . the farmers, the bankers, the land speculators, the agricultural teacher or scientist—and blame one group or all of them for what has happened. We have all had a hand in it. . . . We wound our country and threaten its future by thoughtless actions which are . . . an inherited way of thinking—not thinking—about the land.—Secretary of Agriculture Henry A. Wallace in the 1930s

In his magisterial 1931 history of the Great Plains, Walter Prescott Webb concluded that the future of the region did not belong to irrigation. Neither Webb nor John Wesley Powell fifty years earlier anticipated the remarkable technological breakthroughs that gave plains farmers access to large amounts of Ogallala groundwater by the 1960s. Nor did they foresee the enormous capacity of the aquifer. Webb recognized that large-scale irrigation projects were under way in California and in irrigation communities like Greeley,

Colorado, but he correctly concluded that these did not suit the widely spaced independent farms of the plains. Individual plains farmers fended for themselves (and they often insisted on their independence at almost any price) in an environment rigidly limited by less than twenty inches of rain. More than half of the precious rain was evaporated by hot winds and bright sunshine. Fortunately, most rains came in the spring.

Under these conditions, despite the rash of failures, Webb urged dryland farming: "The conservation of soil moisture during dry weather by special methods of tillage."[1] It was not no-rain farming but low-rain farming in which certain soils, such as the common Dalhart sandy loam of the Texas-Oklahoma Panhandle, held some of the rainfall ready to be tapped. When a midwestern corn farmer showed up to try his luck on the plains, he turned the sod deep with a moldboard plow and tilled the fields smooth, but neighboring dryland farmers warned him that this hard work would only lead to soil blowing. The new settler learned to prepare the land by listing—"cutting the stubble with a double plow that split the slice"—and to leave untilled ridges as barriers against the wind. Always keeping the wind and moisture holding in mind, the farmer learned to plant his corn or wheat or sorghum in the shelter of the furrow. The rough fields offended the traditional sense of good farming and "critics regarded the trashy seedbed as careless farming," but it worked in the windy and droughty region.[2] Frequent harrowing and disking turned the soil and kept it moist. Besides drought-resistant crops, deep plowing, and frequent cultivation, farmers learned the critical importance of timing. A field had to be cultivated within a few hours after a rain to limit rapid evaporation in the low-humidity atmosphere. Using dry farming's careful management of resources, early twentieth-century farmers in southwest Kansas turned the corner toward prosperity without tapping the hidden and unknown waters of the Ogallala aquifer. Like so many solutions to the severe problems of the plains, it was a temporary victory.

"Successful dry farming also depended upon plant adaptation," Webb wrote. The first settlers experimented with Turkey red hard winter wheat, the sorghums, and kafir, the fodder crop "that never failed—that is, almost never."[3] The U.S. Department of Agriculture, although it cautiously played

93

down dryland farming as the salvation of the plains, identified drought-resistant grains, particularly durum wheats for use in macaroni and spaghetti. The agency also encouraged mixed farming in wheat, sorghums, and millets so that farmers might not go down if one crop failed. Corn and alfalfa also were mentioned, but both were water-intensive crops and clearly needed irrigation; corn would return as a major crop only with the spread of modern irrigation. Alfalfa was new to plains farmers and they tried it only occasionally in a leftover field. Reminiscent of Irrigation Crusaders, bright-eyed dry-farming advocates also insisted that if the farmer found the right combination of trees, shrubs, grains, fruits, and vegetables, he could succeed on less than a quarter section. Pioneering agricultural scientist John D. Widtsoe claimed in 1911, one of American agriculture's most triumphant years, that the independent family farmer with four horses and basic equipment could live on 160 acres, even if he kept 80 acres in alternating summer fallow.[4]

For a time early in the century, dry farming would make the plains into "the last and best grain garden of the world." Wrote Webb: "[S]ettlers swung their plows into the [apparently] hopeless sagebrush lands, planted their wheat, waited, watched and prayed. To their amazement the seed sprouted and the young plants stood up bravely in the scorching sun and yielded a bountiful crop."[5] In 1910, in the middle of the pre–World War I boom time called the Golden Age of Agriculture, the central and southern plains had 11,422 farms averaging 520 acres each. Farm prosperity was so good and living standards so nearly matched the new urban wealth that 1909 to 1914 have been called the parity years ever since. In early 1918 a manager for the Texas Land and Development Company optimistically wrote that although Plainview, Texas, had only ten inches of rain, "a good wheat crop was produced and considerable feed was grown without irrigation."[6] During 1917 the company had easily sold seventy-five thousand dollars worth of unimproved land at twenty-five dollars an acre for dryland farming.

With the appearance in the decade before World War I of integrated mechanization—gasoline tractor, combine, and gasoline truck—dryland farming, never workable on a few acres, turned into farming on thousands of acres because the machines allowed rapid plowing and intensive cultivation. When machines and mechanical power became commonplace, they offered seemingly unlimited access to the flat, open grassland. Between 1910 and 1930, the man-hours needed to produce wheat fell by a third while land in wheat rose a third. A hundred years earlier it took fifty-eight hours to harvest an acre of wheat; by 1930, an efficient mechanized wheat operation on the plains could do the same in three hours.[7] When farmers believed they could get $2.50 for a bushel for wheat, they invested in high-priced land and expensive equipment.

In 1915 there were approximately 3,000 tractors in all of Kansas. Wartime demand and the appearance of the mass-produced and low-cost Fordson populated Kansas with more than 17,000 tractors by war's end. By 1930 there were more than 66,000 tractors, and despite the Great Depression the numbers exceeded 95,000 in 1940. According to a writer for *Harper's* in 1938, tractors like the International Harvester Farmall, the Fordson, the Case, and John Deere's two-cycle "poppin' johnny" changed the farmer from "a clod into an operator; from a dumb brute into a mechanic."[8] In 1926, farmers overcame the problem of tillage with Charlie Angell's one-way disk plow. Although it doubled or tripled the sod a farmer could break compared to the venerable moldboard plow, the one-way plow left behind a pulverized granular soil that would easily blow away.[9] Yet the organic material in a smooth, pulverized soil produced tremendous wheat crops. Forty-seven hundred combines in 1925 grew to more than 24,000 in 1930 and 42,800 in 1940. Harvesting, from on-field header to in-town market, declined from sixteen men to two, and the grain was handled only once or twice instead of five times. Efficiency in one area created bottlenecks elsewhere: the problem of hauling grain to market disappeared when the gasoline-engine truck replaced the team of horses. In 1920, Kansas farmers owned 3,900 trucks, which accelerated to 33,700 by 1930 and 42,600 by 1940.[10]

This triumph through mechanization put an entirely new cash pressure on the farmer. In earlier decades, equipment came from the local blacksmith when tools were not homemade. The majority of southern and central plains farmers in the 1920s still lived on their small quarter-section tracts of 160 acres; raised milk cows, pigs, and chickens; and generated a small cash crop from wheat, sorghum, or broomcorn. Donald Worster writes that during the 1920s, when more and more farmers wanted to buy a tractor, truck, and combine, they found they had to generate $4.00 an acre in new money to cover mechanization costs alone, equal to ten bushels of wheat at forty cents each. During the 1920s, when wheat averaged $1.03 a bushel and yields ranged from eight to eighteen bushels an acre, a farmer's mechanization costs were about 40 percent of his gross income, not to mention seed cost, hired labor, and land mortgage debt.[11] Few plains farmers would have their debts and loans paid off when wheat collapsed to twenty-five cents a bushel in the 1930s.

European famine after World War I encouraged vast new plantings that expanded plains plow-ups on more millions of acres. In Finney County, Kansas, 76,000 plowed acres in 1914 had grown to 122,000 by 1919.[12] In a 1986 essay, Donald Worster lays blame for plains failure upon "the Great Plow-up," which between 1914 and 1919 expanded plains wheatlands by 13.5 million acres, including 11 million acres of native grass; this allowed American farmers to enter world markets during World War I by shipping 330 million bushels overseas, a third of the nation's entire production and equivalent to the total annual wheat harvest during the Golden Age. Wrote Worster: "The war integrated the plains farmer more thoroughly than ever before into the national economy . . . [and] into an international market system. When the war was over, none of that integration loosened; on the contrary plains farmers in the 1920s found themselves more enmeshed than ever, as they competed fiercely with each other to pay off their loans and keep intact what they had achieved."[13] These bonds have never since loosened and mostly have become tighter. The promise of mechanized dry farming encouraged new settlement on the central and southern High Plains immediately after World War I. In southwest Kansas, 2 million wheat acres in 1925 became 3 million in 1930. Worster writes of a Texas wheat farmer, H. B. Urban, who in 1929, with one hired man, used his two International tractors to break 20 more acres each day.[14] In the last five years of the decade,

5.25 million acres were plowed up and wheat production rose 300 percent, bringing a severe glut by 1931.

The combination of mechanization debt, widespread plow-ups, and historically depressed wheat prices was terrible for plains wheat farmers; they collapsed under the fourfold hammer blows of wheat glut, prices that fell through the floor, and the arrival of both drought and depression. In his 1979 book *Dust Bowl: The Southern Plains in the 1930s,* Donald Worster argues that when the dryland plains farmers entered the world of modern industrial capitalism, it was not the salvation they expected. Instead, mechanization costs would accelerate the collapse of their independence and force them into bondage to market forces they could not control. Worster concludes that a widespread disregard of economic realities, plus public indifference to farmers, "was the work of a generation of aggressive entrepreneurs, imbued with the values and world view of American agricultural capitalism. They smelled an opportunity to create a profit on the Plains and . . . they started out to create that profit—to derive from the land both personal wealth and status. . . . they made the region say money instead of grass."[15] Worster says this is still the dominant policy toward plains farming today.

The tragedy of the plains lay in its contradictions. It had fertile land "in which a furrow can be plowed a hundred miles long." New plows, harvesters, and combines were designed specifically with the plains in mind. The region was inhabited by skilled, energetic, and eager people, but there was still not enough water to exploit the new technologies and bring lasting prosperity to hard-working farmers. Wrote Walter Prescott Webb: "This search for water has been the continuous and persistent movement that has gone on in the Great Plains country."[16] He wrote prophetically when he doubted that groundwater, whether from artesian wells or pumped by windmills or any other advanced technology, would turn the plains into a perpetual garden, since they "are paying out a store of water which has been long in accumulating."[17] He had no idea of the scale of Ogallala water storage, but he worried about rapid overconsumption: "Such utilization over a broad area would call for a re-supply 'beyond the possibilities of even the most humid climate.' . . . the ground water is an accumulation which has been made over long periods. It is a bank account of great size maintained at a given level by a balance of small deposits and small withdrawals annually."[18] But he thought the discussion was academic: "Throughout the region water lies below economical pumping depth for irrigation on any considerable scale."

Worster also concluded that mechanization and the speculative capitalist economy behind it pushed the plains ecology far beyond its limits and thus transformed an ordinary drought into the extraordinary Dust Bowl. These conditions further enfeebled the Jeffersonian farmer lifestyle that had been the American model since the earliest plains frontier settlement.[19] The answer, industrial capitalism, was worse, claimed Worster, than a harsh frontierlike life. Americans dedicated to farm life on the open plains began in the 1920s to abandon their frontier-outpost lives to become small businessmen. They went to the bank and borrowed money; crossed the street to use the money for a tractor, truck, and combine; rented another quarter section or two; and went into business to make money to pay back the bank.

Submarginal Land: A Bad Place to Farm

Considering past experience, some government officials concluded that farmers, even good farmers, had no reasonable justification to stay on the plains. Despite all other improvements, only access to water would bring survival, and there was not enough water. Local dryland farmers disagreed; they argued they could grow crops and prosper if prices were right. The 1930s would test both viewpoints and bring a confrontation.

In July 1931 dryland farmers in southwest Kansas harvested the biggest crop they had ever seen. Extensive fall rains and winter storms offered water-laden fields that farmers rushed to plant, cultivate, and harvest, but wheat had fallen to only twenty-five cents a bushel, one-tenth of its price at the end of World War I. In the middle of abundance, farmers were going broke. Then plains farmers experienced the second blow: a rainless August and September so severe they burned next season's feed crop. The dry spell continued into the winter. Reeling from this double stroke of misfortune, many farmers had abandoned their bare fields by the spring of 1932. March's strong winds built up into more than twenty dust storms that drifted blowing topsoil as high as fencerows. The farmers who planted a spring crop averaged only five bushels per acre, although fortunate farmers near Hooker, Oklahoma, and Liberal, Kansas, surprised themselves with nearly thirty bushels.[20] There was no national grain surplus, yet prices hovered between thirty and thirty-six cents a bushel. More fields were left abandoned and more bare soil lay exposed.

In 1933, scientists at the Panhandle A & M Experiment Station at Goodwell, Oklahoma, recorded 70 days of severe dust storms in 1933. A neighbor ten miles away in Texhoma recorded 139 dusty days and 195 clear days from January through November 1933. With wry humor, farmers said they now "dusted" their seed into the soil. The wheat harvest would be the poorest of the entire Dirty Thirties. Whatever remained of alfalfa and wheat and milo went down to plagues of grasshoppers and rabbits. Farmers were soon stacking Russian thistle (young tumbleweed), bitter and laxative, to feed their cattle in the winter. Many were forced to sell their milk cows, losing the household's supplementary cream check. Farm families with nothing left in the fields or bank book ate rabbits; a rabbit drive in Kansas or Oklahoma might round up two thousand animals on a section or two of land. As a final blow, many farmers in the southern plains lost their gas leases when the oil and gas industry collapsed in the mounting Great Depression. Government relief programs would not start until 1934; that same year recorded the lowest level of rainfall during the entire 1930s drought. But hope for an end to bad times revived briefly when Goodwell, Oklahoma, recorded only 22 days of severe dirt blowing. This was smashed in 1935 with 53 days of dirt blowing at Goodwell, followed by 73 days in 1936 and 134 days in 1937, more than a third of the entire year.[21] Popular folk singer Woody Guthrie visited the area and reported that people were flocking to churches because it was the end of the world.[22]

The land drifted into desertlike dunes, the topsoil gone and hardpan exposed like a flayed skin laid open. The 1934 crop was good in Morton County, Kansas, but a total failure in neighboring Beaver County, Oklahoma. Wheat prices offered a morsel of hope when they finally crept up to seventy-five cents in July and ninety-four cents in August. But New Year's

Day 1935 opened with a severe dust storm, followed by repeated blowings in February and damaging winds of hurricane force in March. On the night of March 15 in Boise City in the western panhandle of Oklahoma, moviegoers could not manage the few blocks to their homes; a businessman returning home abandoned his car in town and spent the night in a hotel. Respiratory diseases, including "dust pneumonia," received attention in newspapers throughout the nation. The emotional strain of months and years of wind and blowing dirt led to suicides, beatings, and murders.[23] Few people who experienced it will forget the blackness and confusion of the apocalyptic dust storm of April 14, 1935, which darkened skies from Colorado to the East Coast and layered dirt on ships three hundred miles out in the Atlantic Ocean. It was fixed in American popular culture by Woody Guthrie's new song from Pampa, Texas: "So Long, It's Been Good to Know Ya."[24]

By the spring of 1932 vast acreages were abandoned to bare dirt. The swing was dramatic: in southwest Kansas's Hamilton County, 16,000 acres under wheat in 1929 rose to more than 103,000 in 1931 and then collapsed to 48,000 in 1932. In Morton County, it rose from 33,000 acres in 1929 to 113,000 in 1931 and fell to 59,000 in 1932. Seward County saw 139,000 acres in 1929, 170,000 acres in 1931, and 86,000 acres in 1932. Grant County went from 114,000 acres in 1929 to 196,000 in 1931 and down to 27,000 in 1932.[25]

If Dust Bowl farmers could not raise wheat, they believed they could temporarily return to cattle raising, since their land had once been ranchland. Unbeknownst to them, the detested "socialist" bureaucrats in Washington had plans to move now-hapless dryland farmers off submarginal land in Kansas and Oklahoma and replace them with cattle-grazing ranches spread widely across the plains. Ironically, fifty years later, in the 1970s and 1980s, both farmers and ranchers would be served by prosperous feedlots supplied by irrigated green fields of alfalfa and milo covering hundreds of acres in southwest Kansas and the Oklahoma-Texas Panhandle. Increased cattle grazing did help sustain Dust Bowl farmers until the beef market fell through the floor in 1933; lack of rain threatened the herds in 1934.[26] Any extended revival of ranching succumbed to drought: cattle could not wait for another year of bureaucratic delays before getting emergency feed. Ranchers had not helped themselves by habitually overstocking and overgrazing their over-burdened land. Several million acres of pastureland in the Dust Bowl region produced only 30 percent of the normal crop of grasses.

More water was the answer, but until the right technology could reach the deep-seated Ogallala groundwater, this need could be met only by more rain. Instead, federal relief came in the spring and summer of 1934. The New Deal would spend more than two billion dollars to keep the independent plains farmers on the land. Ranchers who took personal pride in their self-sufficiency now accepted federal loans to import cottonseed cake and al-falfa. Despite their fierce independence, stockmen in 1934 and 1935 gladly sold their cattle at rock-bottom prices as low as four dollars a head to an emergency government program, which then destroyed diseased or useless animals and distributed the remaining tough meat free to unemployed Amer-icans.[27] Drought also brought the invasion of federal "locusts," who wanted to tell already-resentful ranchers how to improve pastureland, manage their scarce water better, and improve their herds.

The New Deal: Getting Good Farmers Off Waterless Submarginal Land

The question was raised in the 1890s, put to the test in the 1930s, and raised again in the 1950s. Could farming succeed on the central High Plains? De-cent, hardworking farmers appeared to be sacrificing themselves repeatedly on land that lacked enough rain.

In a controversial 1979 book, Paul Bonnifield, trained historian and plains farmer, argued that in the 1930s the Roosevelt administration con-cluded that the settlement of the Dust Bowl had always been on submarginal land, that the region ought to be depopulated, farmers resettled elsewhere, and the land turned back to native grass.[28] Without extensive irrigation or some other significant improvement, the region did not offer practical habi-tation. Farmers damned the idea as "communist" intervention. A 1936 fed-eral statement would hardly reassure them:

> Although crop failure, speculative expansion, absentee ownership,
> and depressed price levels were among the factors that precipitated the

relief situation . . . the frontier philosophy which assumed that the individual, if given complete freedom, will pursue an economic course that was to the best interests of society, led to the present dilemma of stranded communities, bankrupt farmers, and widespread unemployment.[29]

Nor was the problem of private ownership resolved. An enforced federal buyout from unwilling landowners was widely perceived as a direct attack on the inviolable constitutional right of private property. Any landowner, whether farmer or speculator, had no restrictions on what he did with his land; he could with impunity plow it to dust or let it wash down into the Gulf of Mexico. The new thrust toward conservation and land management heralded a revolutionary shift from this unfettered and historic laissez-faire philosophy.[30]

Decades earlier, Irrigation Crusaders Smythe, Newell, and Hinton had castigated plains farmers for foolish and inappropriate practices. In its 1936 report the new federal Great Plains Drought Area Committee blamed the extremes of the Dust Bowl on historic federal land policies that had encouraged settlement on submarginal land between 1880 and 1910. Dust Bowl hardships were made worse by misguided agricultural policy that had urged widespread and environmentally harmful plow-ups between 1910 and 1930. Plains farmers had been mistakenly lured onto the land and then wrongly urged to hang on. Echoing the sentiments of John Wesley Powell almost sixty years earlier, the 1936 report said: "The basic cause of the present Great Plains situation is our attempt to impose upon the region a system of agriculture to which the Plains are not adapted or to bring into a semi-arid region methods which are suitable, on the whole, only for a humid region."[31] In compensation "the federal government must do its full share in remedying the damage caused by [1] a mistaken homesteading policy [and 2] by the stimulation of war-time demands which led to over-cropping and overgrazing." These provoked "a system of agriculture which could not be both permanent and prosperous."[32]

As a result, the committee concluded that the Dust Bowl region had collapsed into seriously degraded environmental conditions far below its original frontier conditions; it was government's duty at the very least to return it to frontier status. Despite repeated attempts at settlement, the plains could never thrive as an agricultural heartland; instead, famine stalked settlers under the implacable dryness. At best the central Great Plains could serve as a grazing land to support a small number of hardy ranchers. The Great Plains Committee also admitted that the inhabitants, despite the double hammer blows of depression and Dust Bowl, "were in no mood to abandon their land. . . . They were willing to do all that was humanly possible to save it."[33]

As the committee saw it, the central plains were not terribly important to guarantee the nation's food base because the nation had a surplus of good farmland. The agricultural boom of the 1910s and 1920s involved a combination of expanded acreage and revolutionary advances in plant genetics, soil science, and mechanization. This technological revolution brought on a farmland glut. As early as 1923 a federal land-use management proposal, "The Utilization of Our Lands for Crops, Pasture, and Forest," had been developed by Lewis C. Gray in the USDA yearbook. With aggressive USDA backing, Gray urged the creation of clearly defined and specifically graded agricultural districts based on soil, climate, agricultural science, farm technologies, location near population centers, and even historical and cultural factors. Since the central Great Plains region lacked essential water and was beset by uncontrollable climate extremes, it failed to measure up to Gray's standards for good agriculture; hence the plains should cease to exist as a farming region. His plan would restrict new settlement, pull back from low-production hardship farming, and discourage further costly improvement of plains farmland. Instead the nation should put its resources into more improvement of the prosperous farming in the humid midwestern and eastern agricultural belts. In 1924 the Bureau of Agricultural Economics argued that there were "pathological farming areas" on the plains. This unfortunate label identified "diseased" areas that had been created by a combination of natural and human conditions.[34] At a 1931 conference on farmland use in Chicago, the keynote speaker reported that "the boomer days are over."[35]

Gray urged that submarginal lands be closed down entirely and allowed

103

to revert to their natural state for future recreation, wildlife, or pasture. The people who mistakenly had been allowed to stake out submarginal land would be resettled on subsistence homesteads elsewhere. In many circles this USDA plan was considered progressive and humanitarian, based on the latest scientific land-use planning.[36] (This was also the era of Soviet collectivization, which was being watched with much interest throughout the world). Gray's plan failed to gain support in Congress, but the USDA continued to promote agricultural districting and resettlement as the Draconian answer to falling farm prices and failing farms. In its 1930 yearbook the agency argued that "much of the economic hardship suffered by farmers has been caused by too rapid expansion. . . . The eagerness of land-owning interests and selling agencies to induce farmers to occupy undeveloped areas, public encouragement to land settlement, and other influences have contributed to overrapid agricultural expansion."[37] Plains farmers had been devastated not only by the forces of nature, but also by private economic interests and political policies that were, it seemed, socially destructive and inappropriate for the plains. This statement stood in sharp contrast with aggressive land-sale promotion of the previous 150 years. With passage of the Taylor Grazing Act in 1934, a century and a half of selling off the public domain to promote on-site family farming came to an end. The act itself restricted most of the remaining public domain to grassland—80 million acres—and took it off the market. The government reversed the historic public sales by buying up devastated farmland to return it to grass.

In 1933 the incoming president, Franklin D. Roosevelt, strongly advocated agricultural districting and resettlement from submarginal lands. He followed up his controversial 1933 Agricultural Adjustment Act with appointment of a National Planning Board in the Public Works Administration of the Interior Department. The National Planning Board was packed with advocates for redistricting and resettlement. In 1934 it reported that "extensive areas of the Great Plains . . . must be classed as unsuited to sustained cultivated crops, and should therefore never have been plowed, but retained in grass for stock raising." Both the National Planning Board and the powerful Great Plains Committee damned the Homestead Act of 1862 for encouraging settlement on too-small 160-acre farms on submarginal land. The ghost of John Wesley Powell and his 1878 arid-lands report must have been hovering nearby.

The New Deal treated plains agriculture as a matured economy in decline,[38] yet there was regret over the apparent abandonment of the family farmer as a national symbol. Historian Donald Worster notes that federal officials, such as Rexford Tugwell and Lewis Gray, admitted that farming was an important cultural phenomenon, a major feature of the American Dream and Manifest Destiny, as well as an economic problem and that it deserved attention for its central role in the preservation of a national identity in troubled times. In a statement that would shape and color farm policy well into the 1980s, they said plains farming was "a valued way of life, not merely another 'industry.'"[39] Hence farmland policy was duty bound to seek to insulate the lifestyle of the independent farmer from the negative pressures of overproduction, commercialization, land destruction, and family poverty. Farm policy in the 1930s supported regional self-sufficiency and encouraged the remaining dryland farmers to graze cattle on locally grown sorghum silage. Fifty years later, in the 1970s and 1980s, the same region would be sustained in large part by large feedlots using locally grown silage. The difference was that the large amounts of silage would be grown under irrigation.

Lewis Gray's views were confirmed by an influential 1936 report, *The Future of the Great Plains*. The National Resources Board sought to eliminate "the numerous farm families now engaged in crude, self-sufficing systems of farming" unlikely to experience mechanization, afford costly irrigation, or accept other improvements. In angry reaction, Oklahoma soil scientist H. H. Finnell complained in a Boise City newspaper article in 1934 that "recent agitation for the abandonment of the plains on the grounds the land is submarginal or even marginal are [*sic*] not founded on any knowledge of the actual potentialities of our resources nor of the technic [*sic*] of utilization."[40] Finnell's answer was not abandonment, but appropriate dryland-farming techniques for a semiarid region. The USDA's 1935 yearbook complained that farm use was uncoordinated and that "wrong land uses" were still not put in check: "New uses had to be discovered for land withdrawn from production for export, submarginal farming had to be discouraged, and crop adjustment had to be coordinated with land utilization in general."[41] At first, desperate local farmers asked the federal government to declare an emergency, put the Dust Bowl under martial law, and create a "Dust Bowl Authority."[42] A local "Farm Practice Committee" naïvely fell into a federal trap when it argued for federal purchase of submarginal land and its return to grass. As land-retirement plans became reality, farmers soon balked at their loss of independence and property rights.

How was submarginal land to be identified before it could be bought, taken out of production, and restored? The problem of definition was not resolved. The word "submarginal" remained poorly understood by government agencies, the public, and the affected farmers: it was not measured by soil quality or water quantity, but by the more complex capacity of the farmer to sustain himself on his land. The federal answer was the intensive industrialization of agriculture, which left out the low-scale original settler, who did not have the cash, machinery, or know-how to industrialize. Submarginal came to mean the incapacity of historic farm practices to support large-scale mechanization, including irrigation technologies. If farmers had blindly rejected Smythe's and Newell's small-plot irrigated farming, they were not likely to support large-scale mechanized irrigation, but in the 1930s no one could agree whether technology was the cause of the Dust Bowl or its salvation or both.

A submarginal designation was very often arbitrarily determined by farm size. Sometimes the farm was too large: a 1937 on-site federal wind erosion survey concluded that most Kansas wheat and sorghum farms that ranged from 320 acres to over 640 acres could not be worked by financially strapped and undertooled farmers. Sometimes the farm was too small: 160 acres did not produce enough of a cash crop for a farmer to survive under conditions of drought and low prices. The National Resources Board offered opinions on social conditions and moral duty that angered plains farmers:

> The poor land areas are replete with social and economic maladjustments . . . they are literally the slums of the country. Incomes are low . . . credit is expensive, the people are often poorly housed and ill fed;

educational and cultural opportunities are meagre, while governmental services are either at a minimum or are provided at high expenses to both the community and the larger public. . . . [The government has the duty toward] the rehabilitation of the present occupants of the purchase areas now living a socially degraded existence as a result of their inadequate income, poor schools, and roads, and infrequent contacts with an outside civilization.[43]

Even farmer psychology came under scrutiny. Called colonists by the Great Plains Committee, Dust Bowl farmers were criticized for their lack of understanding of Great Plains land and climate and for their habitual application of unsuitable farming practices brought from the humid East. Their "rehabilitation" required revision of "deep-seated attitudes of mind."[44] The Great Plains Committee wrote that "erosion is . . . closely related to farm management and land-use practices. . . . The legislative program should encourage . . . modification of those land-use and cropping practices which are undesirable."[45]

Historian Paul Bonnifield concluded that the federal government had revived its old Indian-removal policies and now applied them to drought-stricken farmers.[46] Dust Bowl areas set aside for "permanent retirement" included parts of Meade County and the land south of the Cimarron River in Morton, Stevens, and Seward counties in Kansas, including the towns of Liberal, Hugoton, and Elkhart. In adjoining eastern Colorado, most of Baca, Prowers, and Bent counties joined the list. In May 1935, farmers were being offered a fire-sale price of $2.75 an acre to retire fifty thousand acres in Stevens County, but a timely rain, dramatic news of a natural-gas strike, a $10 million natural-gas pipeline construction project, and opportunities for on-farm gas leases left the Resettlement Administration empty handed. A 1935 census report noted that the average value per acre of land in Stevens County was $22.50 instead of the offered $2.75. In Morton County, where gas development was slower and farm conditions more desperate, land prices averaged $13.66 per acre, but a few farmers had already sold out to the administration for $3.00 to $5.00.[47] In late 1934 the National Resources Board received funds for the retirement of seventy-five million acres of unprofitable or waste land, and in April 1935 the Resettlement Administration was authorized to proceed (in 1937 the Farm Security Administration took over, and in 1938 the Soil Conservation Service). Seventy-five million acres of submarginal land on the plains, as well as in Appalachia and around the Great Lakes, was almost 8 percent of the nation's total agricultural land. Federal planners argued for government purchase of several million acres of privately owned farmland in the Dust Bowl region.

As for the farmers who insisted on remaining, they would be regulated on farm size, denied credit, and excluded from federal relief programs. They were to be left—abandoned—more on their own than the original settlers. Whether an advanced groundwater pumping technology that independent farmers could use, as described in the next chapter, would arrive soon enough was doubtful. It did the Dust Bowl–stricken small farmer no good when the Great Plains Committee urged "the enlargement of undersized operating units . . . through extension of credit under suitable restrictions." Only larger, wealthier operators with bank credit could expand their holdings. These "suitable restrictions" had been written into the Taylor Grazing Act.

By 1938 the new federal Kiowa Grasslands covered 91,173 acres. The project was made up of 4,133 abandoned acres, the rest purchased at four to eight dollars an acre of land under "serious misuse."[48] Cimarron National Grassland was created from 53,590 acres in Morton County, Kansas. In its attempt to restore the land, the federal government did not do much more than imitate the land-stabilization procedures used on private farms: listing and planting with forage sorghum and broomcorn and using winter rye instead of winter wheat.[49] When the program died in 1947, a national total of 11.3 million acres had been purchased, mostly on the plains, but far less than originally scheduled.

The first step toward federal reorganization of the nation's superior farmland was the creation of local soil conservation districts along geographical rather than political lines. There were precedents. As early as 1894 a Weather Bureau unit in the USDA had been assigned the mission of studying agricultural soils; it was to integrate "the relation of soils to climate and organic life."[50] In 1895 it became the Division of Soils in the Department of Agriculture and in 1901 gained the elevated name Bureau of Soils. With the Dust Bowl debates on soil erosion, marginal lands, and appropriate crops and land use for the plains, the Soil Erosion Service joined the Department of the Interior in 1933 and was shifted to the Department of Agriculture in 1935, where it became the Soil Conservation Service.[51] The SCS had the incredible luck to have for its first chief Hugh H. Bennett, "one of the few immortals of agricultural history." In a set opening talk as he preached the SCS gospel, Bennett said:

[W]e tried to imitate nature as much as we could. We abided by the following basic physical facts, (1) land varies greatly from place to place, due to differences in soil, slope, climate and vegetative adaptability; (2) land must be treated according to its natural capability and its condition as the result of the way man has used it; (3) slope, soil, and climate largely determine what is suitable protection in all situations. . . . Above all . . . we tried to imitate nature.[52]

Bennett brought to the SCS a broad vision of public service, a deep allegiance to comprehensive soil conservation, and a dedication to the American farmer.

Nevertheless, farmers feared that the new SCS would spew forth restrictive regulations, for federal relief assistance often was available only to Dust Bowl counties that organized soil conservation districts. A 1937 editorial in the *Spearman* (Texas) *Reporter* dreaded government interference in the farmer's daily life. The Resettlement Administration, it said, would "plan gardens . . . determine what quantity and kinds of foods . . . supply the family's dietary needs; determine . . . foods . . . during the growing season and what foods . . . during the winter months; plan the family's clothing budget," and divide labor among household, kitchen, garden, and field work.[53] In 1937 the Resettlement Administration intensified these fears when it urged significant changes in Dust Bowl farming practices away from wheat to a combination of livestock and alternative crops. Farmers responded by voting down soil conservation districts. Eventually, new emphasis on local rule within the SCS made the districts palatable[54] and brought soil and water conservation districts to the High Plains. Few farmers could agree on a common course of action. Existing practices of overtillage pulverized the soil into more dust, and stubble burning reduced organic materials and soil building. Abandoned farms belonged to no one, yet an unattended farm blew severely.[55] Leaving the land alone was no solution.

Despite the move toward government-planned agriculture, federal help was not immediately forthcoming. The new and inexperienced Soil Conservation Service tried eastern water conservation practices, such as contour plowing. In its article on soil erosion, the 1934 USDA yearbook said nothing about wind erosion, although hundreds of dust storms had ravaged the plains, but when contour rows were in line with the wind, they often accelerated soil blowing.[56] Commonsense practices of listing, terracing, strip cropping, check dams, soil pitting, deep tilling, soil mulching, and summer fallow were intended to prevent water erosion and conserve moisture and had some effect on breaking the force of the wind. One of the first specific attempts to control wind erosion was made in Texas County, Oklahoma, by farmer Fred Hoeme, who invented the Hoeme Chisel, a cultivator that went as much as twelve inches into hard, dry soil below the dust, and it brought up large clods that broke the power of the wind and simultaneously created a listerlike trench to hold whatever rain might fall.[57] To use new conservation equipment often cost farmers much money and drove them deeper into debt to buy bigger and more powerful tractors with rubber-tired wheels. Even so, all attempts at water conservation and wind erosion control were bandaids without access to more water. Only sufficient water would shift Dust Bowl land from its submarginal status.

High Plains Boom and Survival During Repeated Dust Bowls

Nature and the market teased farmers at harvest time in 1935. Wheat prices went from seventy-nine cents in July to more than a dollar in August and to $1.21 in September, the best since 1929. But farmers who got 30 bushels in 1934 faced bare fields in 1935. There was the rare oasis of harvest: Beaver County's crop, which had failed in 1934, produced more than 148,000 bushels in 1935. In eighteen Dust Bowl counties, the 1936 harvest was about the same as 1935: less than a subsistence crop, but enough to allow the remaining farmers to hold on another year. Revived gas and oil leases helped. In 1937, harvests doubled in Texas County, Oklahoma, and the weather generally was less severe in the region. Prices dropped from $1.09 to eighty-eight cents per bushel between July and August, but it was enough to sustain farmers for another year. A grasshopper invasion in 1937 and 1938 seemed a final blow, to be followed by army worms; stretches of the Oklahoma Panhandle and eastern Colorado roads were slick with dead insects. Prices again collapsed in 1938 to less than sixty cents a bushel, but the worst was over in 1939.

Rain and war, a strange mixture of good and evil, revived plains life for the second time in the early 1940s. In 1942, even in places where five or six inches of topsoil had been lost, the central plains produced a record wheat harvest that surpassed the bumper crop of 1931. As a portent of the future, the record was set on a smaller acreage with more machines, better moisture management, and superior agricultural science. The 1942 crop record was topped in 1943 and again in 1944 as farmers patriotically set themselves to offer more food for a war-ravaged globe. The war ended in 1945, but postwar famine threatened hundreds of millions of victims and victors alike. Farmers doubled the 1939 yield, using only 2.5 million more acres on the central and southern plains.[58] Farm income rose 165 percent in the war years, 1939–45, while farm mortgage debt declined almost 20 percent. But, as Donald Worster noted, while production in the Texas Panhandle country rose $37,737,000 in value between 1935 and 1942, it cost taxpayers $43,327,000 in federal aid.[59]

The rules for survival on the plains, despite lessons taught by the great plow-ups from 1914 to 1929, were still being ignored. Between the mid-1930s and 1946, as much as 4,000,000 acres were replowed on the central and southern High Plains, 3,000,000 of which had previously been labeled unfit for cultivation, creating worse results than in the Dust Bowl era. Cheyenne County in eastern Colorado abutting the Kansas border, for example, had 512,000 farmed acres in 1935 and over 931,000 acres in 1945. Once again postwar bumper crops, high wheat prices, and soaring land prices encouraged farmers to capitalize on good times by reworking abandoned land.

By 1950, land that cost three or four dollars an acre in the 1930s sold for up to sixty dollars an acre, a sizable increase, even accounting for inflation. A new breed, the so-called suitcase farmers, who did not live on the land but directed hired laborers from a comfortable distance, were buying land in 5,000-acre parcels.[60] Corporations were formed specifically to plant profitable crops on parcels of 10,000 acres or more. It was not difficult in 1946 to make a million dollars, as one new corporation did on 28,000 acres in southeastern Colorado. Success was guaranteed by more and better machines, superior plant science, and field techniques that grew more on less water, aided by government money and advisers. For a while, industrial farming could be as profitable a money machine on the plains as anywhere else.

In Haskell County in 1947 it was difficult to argue with five million bushels of wheat that generated $3,333 per county inhabitant. After visiting the plains in 1947 a national magazine staffer wrote that "the voice of two-dollar wheat is far more persuasive than scientific facts on wind, rain, sun and soil."[61] Although he was impressed with the dramatic changes since the 1930s, he wondered about overconfidence in the newly industrialized farmers: they were "belligerently positive about their ability to take care of their land, no matter what happens." The new hope for the plains farmer in the postwar era was no longer self-preservation on a bone-dry landscape, but how to have a full share of the postwar boom.

The shift from simple land stewardship by the family farmer early in the century to exploitation for profit seemed irrepressible. Instead of conservation of the unique and limited resources of the plains, the answer seemed to be more cash for better equipment as farmers finally joined the rest of the United States in rushing toward a high-tech future. This was aided by agricultural exports. The Department of Agriculture repeatedly urged fencerow-to-fencerow plowing, and for the next forty years it would continue to press for high production. Postwar big-scale farming began to pull free from the constraints of government conservation so elaborately constructed in the 1930s—terraces, shelterbelts, soil-conservation-district rules—while hanging onto the safeguards of federal subsidies.[62] The conditions were right for the next step in heavy industrialization: pump large amounts of underground water for high-production irrigation. However, writing in a national magazine in 1947, Agriculture Secretary Clinton Anderson, who had experience on his own New Mexico farm, warned that "what we are doing in the western Great Plains today is nothing short of soil murder and financial suicide."[63] Better rains had also returned, averaging fourteen to seventeen inches in the 1940s, but when the hot dry winds came to eastern Colorado again in late 1948, not enough grass remained to anchor the soil.

Oklahoma soil scientist Howard Finnell had warned in 1947 that "we are heading into the same conditions that gave us the old Dust Bowl. The next Dust Bowl will be bigger and better. . . . We have been overrun by the plow-up. Soil conservation districts, organized by farmers to promote good land use, haven't had the backbone to stand up to the money pressure behind the plow-up." Kansas State College agronomist R. I. Throckmorton advised that ten million acres on the central and southern plains, including replowed marginal land, were again in harm's way.[64] Twenty years after the Great Dust Bowl, the rains once again failed in southwest Kansas and the Texas-Oklahoma Panhandle. A hot sun seared the landscape. Winds blew the topsoil away. As early as December 1948, the wheat land of southwestern Kansas received eastern Colorado soil blown its way and sent it flying eastward with its own load. Not since the 1930s did railroad crews have to halt their trains and shovel tracks clear. In mid-January in 1950 the topsoil was powder dry and as easily blown away as in the worst 1930s dust storms. At the end of March 1950 the lack of rain set all-time records. By mid-April, daytime darkness and zero visibility were again commonplace. As much as $275 million worth of wheat was lost.[65]

By early 1950 the wheat crop, devastated by lack of rain, could not hold the soil it was planted in. Land lay bare everywhere: new plowed land lost its grass cover, wheat fields failed, and intensive cattle raising meant overgrazed ranchlands. During the summer of 1950 the drought spread from Kansas and Colorado into the Oklahoma-Texas Panhandle, and farther south. In February 1952, winds that reached eighty miles an hour created a dust front to an altitude of twelve thousand feet; the soil drifted in dunes. By 1952 large tracts of land had lain open for three or four years. Colorado's

Baca County lost more than 70 percent of its 500,000 acres of wheat to the wind; 95 percent of the 250,000 wheat acres in Prowers County blew out or silted over. Hamilton County, Kansas, lost 95 percent of its wheat, worth $1.5 million. In early 1954, several inches of topsoil had been removed from the entire old Dust Bowl region, damaging about 11,700,000 acres.

In the first five months of 1954, only one inch of rain reached the ground. Garden City, Kansas, after the heaviest dust storm of the decade struck on February 19, 1954, next received a heavy load of snow, and townspeople waded through quagmires of mud on the streets and sidewalks. March 1954 was the worst month in several years of dust storms, with familiar results: wheat fields blown out, choking cattle, streetlights on at noon, stranded travelers. The agricultural experiment station at Garden City had recorded thirty more dust storms by June 30. Soil was blown off twice the acreage between 1954 to 1957 than had been lost from 1934 to 1937.

By the spring of 1955, dunes thirty feet high were not unusual. In one storm the dust cut a swath from Denver to El Paso and ran as far east as Wichita. The following spring of 1956 saw dust cover forty thousand square miles, resulting in closed roads and damaged hospital equipment. High abrasive winds scoured paint off license plates and smashed plate-glass windows. Normal rainfall, as farmers still hopefully called it, did not return until the spring of 1957, ten years after the first signs of drought in 1948.[66] Whether Dust Bowl conditions coincided with heavy sunspot activity or not, it became painfully evident that dry times and black blizzards would reappear in a predictable two-decade cycle.

There was less helpless inertia than in the 1930s. Unlike federal shakiness during the Depression, the postwar government was the richest in the nation's history and could generously aid farmers. It also helped that farmers still lived in boom times and were not already weakened by another long-term farmer depression, which in the 1920s had already broken agriculture's back by the time the Dirty Thirties rolled in. The Korean War of 1950–53 would hold farm prices at good levels. Without waiting for government aid, farmers in Morton County, Kansas, set their one-way disks for fourteen to twenty-four inches to conserve about five thousand acres. In 1955 a new technique called pitting offered better endangered-field conservation: disks on one-way plows were set off center. The rotating disks dug pits three or four feet long and several inches deep. These would catch and hold any rainwater and give native grasses—crested wheatgrass, bluestem, grama, and buffalo grass—a good start.

After delays the United States Department of Agriculture allocated $25 million in 1954 and 1955 for emergency tillage. Each farmer was now offered seventy-five cents an acre for listing, fifty cents for chiseling, and $1.25 for contour strip cropping to total no more than $1,500. In addition, farmers were paid for feed and hay. Federal aid programs, many set up in the 1930s, again came into play. The Dust Bowl–era Great Plains Drought Area Committee, for example, had identified policies to carry farmers through disaster, including foreclosure moratoriums, relief, and feed loans. The 1950s provided crop insurance, government supports (forward pricing), long-term loans with variable payments, grain and feed storage, short-crop alternatives, and sophisticated livestock marketing.[67] By August 1954 the Farmers Home Administration (FmHA) provided emergency loans for designated disaster areas covering thirty Kansas counties, thirty-seven Oklahoma counties, twenty-four Colorado counties, seventy-five Texas counties, and twenty-four in New Mexico.[68] To stave off bankruptcy, 3-percent loans could be used to purchase feed, seed, fertilizer, replacement stock and equipment, maintenance of buildings, and fence repair. These efforts kept the farmers solvent and on the land. Their creditors were told to stand by while they recovered.

The drought of the Filthy Fifties was frequently as severe as the one in the 1930s. Almost twenty-one million acres had been seriously damaged and remained vulnerable to more harm. Resettlement and reversion to grassland became unthinkable alternatives, leaving the search for more water as the only acceptable answer. Even after it rained in May 1955 and farmers could expect a good crop, sixteen million acres were still ready to blow.

The 1970s would see another severe drought, and a repeated cycle can be anticipated in the 1990s. In the drought year 1974, with rain seven inches below average, irrigators ran their pumps nearly twice as long as in the normal year 1973 and energy consumption rose 64 percent. Farmers recorded that their groundwater levels declined as much as three feet a year. These high figures continued until the return of normal rainfall in 1978.[69] An orbiting satellite scanning Earth in the late winter of 1977 clearly showed newly seeded West Texas farms blowing dust into Oklahoma as neighboring New Mexico grassland held steady.[70] But now geographer John Borchert could write, there is "a widespread belief that, though there will be future droughts, there need be no future dust bowl."[71]

Plains farming had transformed itself. Beginning in the 1950s, the historic family farm in many cases became a private, heavily capitalized and mechanized industrial operation. Today plains farmers resemble the nation's small businessmen more than their pioneer forebears.[72] Well-managed dryland farming could still offer the power to endure and prosper on the High Plains, it was believed. When fallowed ground was returned to production, it yielded twice as much wheat as unfallowed. Terracing improved wheat and sorghum yields. Worster wryly wrote: "Agronomists promised [the plains farmer] anew the tomorrow world of infinite abundance, when all the land would be contoured to the horizon, every drop of water captured and used, straight even rows of trees planted wherever they would grow—a landscape of engineering and efficiency."[73] Years earlier, SCS conservationist Hugh Hammond Bennett had concluded that "farming will become an expert profession; the inexpert and inept will be forced off the land."[74]

The gospel of efficiency took over on the High Plains. By the late 1970s more than half the market value of Kansas's farm production came from those counties with more than twenty thousand irrigated acres.[75] Ogallala water was pumped onto the fields in a use-it-or-lose-it (prior appropriation) policy. By planting fencerow to fencerow at the highest efficiency, farmers could participate in the nation's ebullient postwar expansion. It was get big or get out. Farm size in Kansas doubled, irrigation acreage tripled, and the number of farms decreased more than half between 1940 and 1983, from 159,000 to 76,000. But whenever drought reappeared, it accelerated groundwater consumption to keep production up.

Disadvantages and Advantages of the Plains

The debate over marginal farming and resettlement is not over. Dust Bowl conditions marked the High Plains as an unusually harsh land where settlers and farmers would remain perpetually disadvantaged. It was the last major region frontiersmen settled. The history of repeated plains depopulation, including today's gradual outmigration, reveals inherent weaknesses in the land's capacity to support farmers and towns. Nor does this old Dust Bowl region appear to be essential to the survival of the United States as a prosperous and powerful society. Many irrigated crops, such as wheat, corn, sorghum, alfalfa, and the lesser grains, are surplus. Taxpayers are beginning to protest all-important federal subsidies. Why should American agriculture, no longer shaped by the family farm and now turned into big business, receive special privileges? The farmer is now the government's client, if not its ward. Most successful on the plains are large-scale, vertically integrated corporate operations; their commitment is less to the plains than the mining of its land and water for profit.

The question of removing grain farmers from submarginal plains land and returning the land to light grazing or empty grassland reappeared in a 1983 report compiled by the influential Office of Technology Assessment, an arm of Congress. In seeking to balance out the pros and cons of High Plains farming, the OTA is pessimistic about the future. The combination of food surpluses, low prices, depletion of groundwater, and reduced federal supports demonstrates inability to sustain current levels of agriculture and promises the possibility of another Dust Bowl.[76] The OTA recommends that Congress's limited agricultural appropriations be focused on "protecting and maintaining the long-term productivity of rain-fed agricultural resources" elsewhere at the price of limited commitment to irrigation or dryland farming on the plains:

> The problem of cultivating marginal or unsuited lands ("plow-out") has become particularly critical in the semiarid lands of the Great Plains . . . where the land is especially vulnerable to erosion. Some Federal agricultural programs encourage cultivation of fragile lands and thus contribute to resource degradation.[77]

One option OTA recommended to Congress was that it "withdraw those Federal programs that induce conversion of rangeland to uses not suited to that land and thus cause resource degradation that ultimately limits long-term productivity."[78] Unsuitable laws have already encouraged the conversion of rangeland, plow-ups, and extensive resource degradation, so, "Congress could withdraw Federal incentives that induce conversion of rangeland to cropland use where that use is not suitable for the resource . . . e.g., price supports, commodity loans, and disaster payments."[79]

The 1983 OTA report reviewed irrigation growth on the High Plains from 2,000,000 acres in 1944 to 13,000,000 acres in 1974. It noted that when the Ogallala aquifer is depleted under a farmer's land, he reverts to dryland farming (over 500,000 acres, mostly in Texas, between 1974 and 1979) and compensates by plowing up more rangeland (1,400,000 acres in Colorado and South Dakota between 1974 and 1983). OTA concluded that

> this trend has alarmed Federal and State Officials who fear that this land is too fragile for intensive cultivation and that the "Dust Bowl" days of the 1930s will return if irrigation water is in short supply or if a lengthy period of dry weather occurs.[80]

Limited ground cover, rainstorm runoff, and soil loss keep the land vulnerable for a repeat of the Dust Bowl. "If these areas are converted [to dryland farming] but later abandoned, how can they be rehabilitated and made productive again, and who should bear the costs of reclamation?"[81] The massive rescue provided by the New Deal in the 1930s (and recycled during the droughts of the 1950s and 1970s) should not be repeated. Irrigation transformed the High Plains, but as the aquifer runs dry, the landscape will shift to larger farm size, more nonsite ownership, changing land-use patterns, and more intensive integration of land values into global investment patterns. Food, land, and water on the plains will be transformed into costly commodities and on-site operations will be drastically unlike current plains farming. The OTA suggests that the changes will bring more, not less, degradation of land and water. According to this view, in the long run plains farming will be unsustainable, which, after all, is the definition of submarginal.

The most radical proposal was offered by land use planners Frank and Deborah Popper in late 1987.[82] Let us finally admit, they argued, that more than a century of repeated farm abandonments, dust bowls, costly government interventions, and environmental destruction has resulted in repeated failures. America's rural past, and technological civilization, has surrendered to environmental adversity in a wide swath of the Great Plains counties running from Texas to North Dakota. "Over the next generation, the Plains will, as a result of the largest, longest-running agricultural and environmental miscalculation in American history, become almost totally depopulated."[83] Federal resettlement programs in the 1930s were right on target. Depopulation should be aggressively encouraged to allow the plains to revert to their preagricultural condition. Frank Popper said this must include deprivatization to create an open and publicly owned Buffalo Commons, not only in the old Dust Bowl region, but selectively throughout the entire High Plains from Canada through Texas, almost one-sixth of the land area of the lower forty-eight states.

Despite stormy criticism from High Plains inhabitants, the Poppers seek to "recreate the 19th century. It will be the world's largest historic-preservation project, the ultimate national park," since Americans have failed to make much of the High Plains an economic or human success. "The brute fact is that in any plausible use, the bulk of Plains land is insufficiently competitive with land elsewhere. The only people who want it are already on it, and most are increasingly unable to make a living from it." Could a compromise be reached through partial nationalization if irrigation would be accepted as a land-conservation strategy for the rest? It requires only two irrigated acres to produce three acres' worth of dryland corn, sorghum, wheat, and cotton.[84] The answer, however, depends on today's heavy groundwater consumption and thus offers no long-term solution. The Poppers' critics, and they are many, might instead ask: Why not create federal relief zones like the proposed business enterprise zones?[85]

Frank Popper's proposal is too politically explosive to succeed. At the same time, it once again raises the question of Ogallala groundwater. If the surface land were set aside as a national preserve, would the stored water under marginal land be available for transfer elsewhere? If water under protected land was valued at five dollars an acre-foot and prime land next door could be irrigated at forty to fifty dollars an acre-foot, would a transfer benefit the region and the nation?[86] The debate about mining for minerals or drilling for oil under national parks might have ramifications that could be applied to Ogallala water. Reserved water rights, as they are protected in wilderness areas, could also apply.

But even the OTA admits that the High Plains, including the Dust Bowl region, has certain advantages that deserve attention.[87] Pioneering farmers spoke with pleasure of the wonderfully fertile soil and noted that the land was flat, rockless, and treeless. Any Missouri or Pennsylvania farmer who had struggled uphill and down behind his plow and horses, only to encounter innumerable tree stumps, found real satisfaction in plowing the plains. In addition, compared to the humid East, the plains environment was dry and therefore relatively disease-free for his crops. Low humidity meant many more cloud-free days. In more recent years, the High Plains have the advantage that they do not suffer from competition for water from booming cities as is the case in California and Arizona and Colorado. Industrial development is not the major problem (aside from water flooding for secondary oil recovery described in chapter 5) for the plains as elsewhere in the West. Thus the privatization and free-market debate does not currently include water ownership, rights, and pricing. As long as pumping is economically feasible, Ogallala water belongs to agriculture on the High Plains as nowhere else. Farmers can continue to produce crops in otherwise impossible areas, such as the Kansas Sandhills. They can experience higher yields than with dryland farming. Some other western water problems, including the long controversy over federal water subsidies and farmer paybacks, are not problems for the High Plains.

Concluding Note

Have the plains ever moved beyond their frontier exploitive status? Regional ecologist and historian James C. Malin argued that in the 1930s southwest Kansas and the Texas-Oklahoma Panhandle, much of it the last frontier not homesteaded until the early 1900s, were still in their pioneering or early exploitive stage, which had only been intensified by the tractor and mechanized harvester. True postfrontier mature settlement, he believed, should include conservation of land and water for long-term support of a successful rural agricultural society. The 1930s drought was a national tragedy because it overwhelmed the High Plains before maturity took hold, but in the future a well-conceived government assistance program and proper land management could, Malin believed, carry the region into its delayed agricultural prosperity. Plains historian Walter Prescott Webb, who wrote before Ogallala irrigation took hold and who advocated dryland farming, would cautiously agree. But geographer Carl Sauer believed that an ecological balance between successful farming and resource conservation would be possible only through the less mechanized and less capitalized world of small family farmers. Environmental historian Donald Worster concluded that the plains were rapidly becoming a helpless victim of capitalist exploitation.[88]

The plains during the 1930s were, as they always have been, a complicated and dynamic environment-human system. This chapter suggests many critical points of instability—dryness, soil blowing, low prices, low yields, farm-family weakness, poor or wrong information—where a small push anywhere had large consequences everywhere. The question today is not whether plains farming is in harm's way, but whether a small push—greenhouse-level drought or a fresh influx of federal credit to buy equipment and pesticides—will consume Ogallala water at an accelerating pace and bring the entire delicate agricultural house of cards crashing down.

4

. . .

From Windmills to Gigot,
Center Pivots, and IBP

Successful irrigation means high-grade farming. It means the employment of intelligence and persistent labor. Unlike wheat farming, for instance, the work of the year is not concentrated into a few weeks or months, but for good results must be continued in one form or another almost every day.—Frederick H. Newell, writing in 1896 on the new industrialized work habits required for irrigation farming.

WE SELL RAIN!—1969 irrigation equipment advertisement.

The windmill is the familiar symbol of the independent plains farmer. It appears in political cartoons, Dust Bowl photographs, and a recent run of romantic farm films. It failed in its promise because windmill technology could not water large fields.[1] A farmer's windmill could usually draw water from a maximum of thirty feet below, so he was frustrated when he learned that good water lay directly underground a tantalizing fifty feet close and yet too deep. Windmill technology deserves credit because it was a good substitute for water raised laboriously bucket by bucket from the hand-dug well, but this could supply only the home and barnyard, or at most five acres of wheat or thirty head of cattle. The windmill would not become another major force in the remarkable technological revolution that Walter Prescott Webb said transformed the plains and raised farmers above survival levels, including Glidden's barbed wire, John Deere's shear plow, McCormick's reaper and Colt's revolver.[2] While the irrigation ditches of the federal Reclamation

122

Service would transform California in the first half of the twentieth century, the plains by contrast stood on the verge of abandonment.

It appeared that Zebulon Pike and Joseph Henry were right when they saw only the Great American Desert in the midcontinent. Since four 12-foot windmills were needed to water 40 acres, a quarter of a quarter section, southwest Kansas could not turn the corner to prosperity. Scrambling pioneer farmers would have been incredulous at today's irrigated abundance. The notion that corn, which needs more than ninety million gallons laid by center pivot on 130 acres of a 160-acre quarter section, could ever be a major crop on the High Plains seemed laughable when it was not a dangerously self-deluding fantasy.

The need was obvious. Webb said plains farmers sought "a mechanical device that would raise water to the surface, one that would be economical in construction, inexpensive to operate, and capable of making slow but constant delivery."[3] In 1894, Joseph L. Bristow and his *Irrigation Farmer* championed a Kansas irrigation revolution, but not by using the dams, reservoirs, and centralized irrigation canals and ditches of the Reclamation Service. Instead, Bristow spoke for individual on-farm pumps, each powered by its own windmill. He became private secretary to the governor of Kansas, and in 1895 the state established the Board of Irrigation Survey and Experiments to test irrigation pumps. Not the least, a farmer who could pump his own water would be independent of the uncertainties of the irrigation ditch and the costs of the irrigation company. He would fit the Jeffersonian mold better than California farmers. He could regulate the flow of water to his crops without dependence or intervention from the outside. He could stop worrying about river, ditch, and peripheral levels, no longer keep an eye out for the ditch rider to turn the water off, and bring an end to annual water rents. He need not keep another eye cocked skyward for a promising thunderhead. But enthusiasm was dampened by cost: up in South Dakota, farmers had painfully learned that their artesian wells, requiring no windmill or pump, still cost three to five thousand dollars per well for drilling and casing.

As early as 1872 the newfangled windmills situated strategically along the Santa Fe and Union Pacific railroad tracks did not escape farmers' attention.[4] These were not the large, creaky windmills, with their massive wooden sails and revolving millhouses, that characterized the landscape of Holland or Spain, but leaner wood and metal devices spinning twenty- or thirty-foot blades set on top of a simple platform. An old western Kansas saying had it that the trains ran only on days the wind blew. This was not because the engines needed the push. When the wind did blow, which was most of the time, windmills pumped water into strategically located water tanks to replenish Santa Fe steam locomotives, for the Santa Fe had spanned southwest Kansas by the end of 1872. Each tank was on a ten-foot-high platform, the train crew jerked down a metal spout to pour water into the locomotive's water jacket. Occasionally, "jerkwater towns" grew up around the windmill, tank, and maintenance crew. Nor did it go unnoticed that smaller homemade windmills allowed cattlemen to fence their land into separate fields, each herd supplied by windmill and tank. But by comparison, crop farming demanded much larger quantities of water than cattle or locomotives.

Legend has it that as early as 1854 an old midwestern pump doctor, John Burnham, weary of constant repairs, suggested to a young Connecticut mechanic, Daniel Halladay, that if a windmill could be made self-governing, it might well transform western farming. Halladay devised a windmill that turned itself into the wind and controlled its speed, all by the centrifugal force of a weight. The response was astonishing. Halladay moved to Chicago to be closer to potential dryland markets and large-quantity orders from railroads allowed the United States Wind Engine and Pump Company to dominate the new industry by 1862. By 1879, as the railroads spread across the plains and independent plains farmers became a significant market, sixty-nine manufacturers sold more than a million dollars' worth of windmills. Competitive shakeouts reduced the number of manufacturers to thirty-one by 1919, while sales reached nearly ten million dollars.[5] Important refinements in that period included reduction in size from thirty-foot diameters to a range of four to sixteen feet, with eight- or ten-foot windmills becoming standard. The introduction of curved steel blades led to more efficiency, reductions in size, and lower cost. And the wonder of the self-oiling mechanism delighted the farmer, who otherwise climbed up in the middle of a blizzard or dust storm to lubricate the linkages. Manufacturing guidelines established by Fairbanks, Morse and Company summarized the features that successfully sold windmills to farmers, townspeople, and railroads on the windy, waterless plains:

1. Ability to be shipped knocked down and yet readily erected with simple tools by ordinary mechanics;

2. Interchangeability of parts;

3. Durability;

4. Minimum amount of material used, keeping down cost of material and transportation as well as erection;

5. Simple lubrication;

6. Self-governing, both as to staying in the wind and as to maintaining a uniform speed regardless of velocity of wind.[6]

The pumps under the spinning vanes ranged from five- to twelve-inch-bore cylinders with a stroke of six to twelve inches. Farmers were told to use a pump cylinder smaller in inches than the windmill diameter in feet: a twelve-foot windmill to serve a ten-inch pump. The well underneath the windmill and pump was usually a four- or five-foot square pit excavated down to the water table and had to be relatively shallow.[7]

By 1895, farms around Garden City sported about 150 "wind-reservoir irrigation" operations. They typically included one or two windmills, a reservoir, and up to five acres under irrigation, planted in vegetables and fruits for human consumption or alfalfa for animals. A Kansas official revived the Irrigation Crusade claim that a farm family could live well on five irrigated acres and become rich on twenty. Journalists visited Garden City; articles in *Review of Reviews* and *Scientific American* gave the community a national reputation as America's center of windmill irrigation.[8] But one Kansas farmer complained that the windmills were overrated. The wind, apparently so constant, was in fact so irregular that the windmill ran only a third of the time. To make matters worse, he lost half his reservoir water through evaporation.[9]

Most farmers found windmills and pumps too costly and constructed their own. Even local shop-made windmills were beyond the means of cashless farmers; homemade mills took their place for a decade or more. A common home-built version was called the Jumbo:

> It is a simple home-made contrivance. Four posts are planted in the ground, then covered or boxed with boards. An axle with from four to eight spokes fastened to it, with paddles generally made of wood nailed on the end of the spokes like a steamboat's paddle wheel, is set on the box east and west to catch the prevailing south and north winds. A crank on one or both ends works the pump or pumps. The box shields the lower part of the wheel, while the top is fully exposed to the wind, and from its spinning round with a kind of comical merriment in a good south "prairie zephyr" it has probably [also] earned the name of "Go-Devil."[10]

The largest practical Jumbo, twenty-one feet in diameter, could in theory pump 700 gallons a minute with a fourteen-foot lift and cost $20 in scrap wood. In contrast, the average windmill kit a farmer could buy from a local manufacturer cost $75 for an eight-foot mill, $100 for a ten-foot mill, and $135 for a twelve-foot mill. As costs declined, in 1909 a farmer could build his own reservoir and install two twelve-foot windmills with ten-inch pumps for $330. Theoretically, one twelve-foot windmill could irrigate ten acres.

Casting theory aside, farmers learned regretfully that their costly $330 investment might at best water a total of eight acres.[11] Contemporary observer Erwin H. Barbour wrote of the delicate balance between failure and survival: "The mill may not net its owner over $100, but if the rest of the crop is a total failure, this is worth more than one hundred cents per dollar. [But] the mill may easily exceed the profits of the rest of the farm during exceptionally poor seasons."[12] The inherent pumping limits of windmill technology were reached quickly and did little to help the wheat farmer on his one-square-mile section. An 1895 report by the Kansas Board of Irrigation Survey and Experiments was uncharacteristically pessimistic: the minimum survey tract of forty acres (quarter of a quarter section) required twenty-four windmills mills for an average of less than two acres per 8-foot windmill.[13] In 1911,

6. A homemade jumbo windmill, ca. 1890s. Many farmers could not afford three hundred dollars for a factory-made windmill, so they often worked from rough sketches they made after looking at a neighbor's jumbo. Frequently a windmill was made from scrap wood lying around in the farmyard. Courtesy of the Nebraska Historical Society.

Scott County farmer Fred Mahler constructed a "windmill irrigation plant" made up of a circular 200-foot-wide, 4-foot-deep reservoir supplied by ten 10-foot windmills to irrigate fifty acres of alfalfa. In 1912 a neighboring farmer, E. E. Coffin, put together a 210-foot-square reservoir 5 feet deep with water from six 12-foot windmills, also for fifty acres of alfalfa.[14] Neither farmer found it economical to expand his windmill irrigation operation.

Clearly, windmills could not provide the resources for successful farming on the High Plains, yet Walter Prescott Webb wrote in 1931, at the end of the windmill era, that "these primitive windmills, crudely made of broken machinery, scrap iron, and bits of wood, were to the drought-stricken people like floating spars to the survivors of a wrecked ship . . . transforming the so-called Great American Desert into a land of homes."[15] But windmills did not offer a new ship to continue the journey. Webb exaggerated the windmill's conquest of the plains when he concluded, "Without it large areas would long have remained without habitation." He did admit in his monumental history of the Great Plains that "the windmill mitigated the thirst of the Great Plains but did not assuage it. The search for water had to go on."[16] The answer to human permanence on the plains lay elsewhere. Early windmill technology did not create a new rush of settlement as did the rainy early 1880s. Curiously, Webb ignored technological developments that had existed since the opening of the twentieth century: (1) a pump capable of drawing a steady and large volume of water from a deep well, (2) powered by a low-cost and suitable power plant, (3) fueled by a low-cost energy source, (4) supported by known well-drilling technologies.

Back in 1901, federal scientist Willard D. Johnson described plains farming since the 1880s as "the agricultural experiment . . . in ignorance or disregard of the fairly abundant data, indicating desert conditions. . . . Though persisted in for several years with great determination, it nevertheless ended in total failure. Directly and indirectly the money loss involved was many millions of dollars . . . [and resulted in] a class of people broken in spirit as well as in fortune."[17] Webb quotes farm historian A. M. Simons, who wrote in 1906 that the region had a future "pregnant with greater promise than perhaps any other equal expanse of territory" in the Western Hemisphere but "whose history is filled with more tragedy" that left "a mass of human wreckage in the shape of broken fortunes, deserted farms, and ruined homes."[18] Irrigation advocate Frederick H. Newell wrote off the Great Plains in 1896: it was "a region of periodical famine."[19] Desperate farmers' rush to use windmills was the reaction of desperate men to an inadequate technology. As the 1880s boom fell apart, those who could do so abandoned their farms and headed back East or went West, and those who were condemned to stay turned to any device that might make water available. There is no more vivid example of an undertooled high-risk situation in American history.

Garden City farmer C. J. Longstreth set up a fourteen-foot Halladay windmill that powered a quality eight-inch Gause pump producing forty-four hundred barrels of water a day, enough to irrigate fifteen acres. His venture pushed windmill pumping to its limits. Probably no more than a thousand acres were ever irrigated by windmills around Garden City, compared to more than forty-two thousand acres irrigated from the old ditches and peripherals in 1905.[20] The ebullient irrigation promoter William E. Smythe was unconvincing when he wrote in his 1905 classic, *The Conquest of Arid America,* that Garden City windmills have "saved an enormous district from lapsing into a condition of semi-barbarism."[21] Smythe's Jeffersonian image of the happy and prosperous farm family on its ten or twenty irrigated acres would not take hold on the plains. By World War I, windmills were being phased out in favor of electric or gasoline-powered pumps.

A brief spell of rain in the mid-1890s again revived hope and eroded interest in the costly Irrigation Crusade. The Kansas Board of Irrigation Survey and Experiments lost most of its influence, and Bristow's *Irrigation Farmer* shut down. A plains newspaper hoped: "We have passed from the drought period and have entered an era of old time moisture supply. We will now stop talking about irrigation."[22] But by 1900, when drought returned, farmers again talked of the underflow and the mysterious aquifer. Deep groundwater would be the next solution and turn the plains into the "land of the underground rain." To raise large amounts of the groundwater to the parched fields successfully was another matter.

The First New Ingredient: The Centrifugal Pump

In the 1890s a major step forward in mechanical pumping technology began to appear on the plains. A new version of the century-old English centrifugal pump was made far more efficient by means of a revolving metal impeller with diffusion vanes housed inside a cast-iron circular chamber with far closer tolerances. Water was pulled into the center of the chamber and the impeller forced the water against the outside walls (hence centrifugal pump), where it exited outward and upward through a discharge pipe. The pump could deliver the several hundred gallons per minute needed for crop irrigation. Without valves that could clog easily, it was far easier to maintain. Its primary drawback ultimately meant its failure: it had to be located no more than twenty feet above water level. Thus a wide pit had to be dug down close to water level, so the pump was practicable only where groundwater levels were still relatively shallow. The depths of the Ogallala, fifty to three hundred feet below the surface, remained mostly inaccessible.

In addition, the limits of existing power transfer technologies, no matter whether steam, internal combustion, or electric, created serious difficulties. Engines had to be on the surface for running and daily maintenance and connected to the pump by a long belt and pulley, which required constant adjustment, or, less successfully, by a long, carefully aligned vertical shaft that wore out its bearings with alarming regularity.[23] In addition, farmers and mechanics complained that the leather belt broke or slipped as it tightened in winter and stretched in summer and had to be restitched repeatedly. Replacing, lubricating, or adjusting belt or shaft bearings was a dangerous job: the farmer descended into the well pit alongside a wildly spinning belt or shaft and, once down to the pump, might have heavy overhead equipment come crashing down on him. An East Texas farmer wrote: "Imagine getting down into the pit to oil the pump with the mess of rope running at the velocity of the outside diameter of the 54″ fly wheel with 6 or 8 fifty pound weights dancing on the tightener above your head. BAD DREAMS."[24]

By 1896, irrigators around Garden City, Kansas, were using the new pumps and power sources to tap shallow water levels, less than ten feet from the Arkansas River water table; they could avoid the difficult and dangerous pits. Using steam power, a No.2 pump with a six-inch pipe delivered 245 gallons per minute, a larger No.3 pumped 625 gallons, and at Hutchinson, Kansas, several No.6 pumps at a meat-processing plant delivered 1,300 gallons per minute, equaling today's pumping levels. Such pumps were already raising irrigation water in eastern Colorado, western Arizona, and the Sacramento Valley in California.[25] But at a time when a prosperous plains farmer

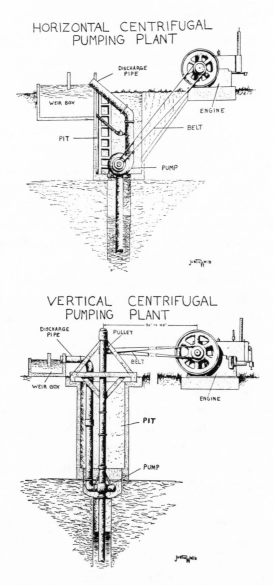

7. Late-nineteenth-century setups for a centrifugal pump. More efficient and reliable impeller pumps, together with the internal combustion engine, helped bring the first irrigation revolution to the plains. Reprinted by permission from Donald E. Green, *Land of the Underground Rain: Irrigation on the Texas High Plains, 1910–1970* (Austin: University of Texas Press, 1972), 44.

generated only a few hundred dollars a year, and long before easy credit and federal subsidies, the centrifugal pumps were generally too expensive. The smaller No.2 pump, with its delivery of 150 to 250 gallons per minute, cost $230 to $390, excluding power plant and well-digging costs. Irrigation engineer Frederick H. Newell, who generally sought to put forward the best opinion, admitted in 1902 that centrifugal-pump irrigation costs were "considerably higher than the amount yearly paid for the maintenance of canals and ditches in the arid region, or the amount paid annually to a canal company for delivering water. It is rarely below $2 per acre irrigated, and from this as a minimum, may rise to $5 or even $10 an acre."[26] Crops had to be far more profitable than the contemporary prices paid for wheat, sorghums, or corn. The demand remained for a mechanically simple, inexpensive, easily powered pitless pump.[27]

Aside from cost, few farmers (despite their jack-of-all-trades reputation) had enough mechanical know-how to take on the industrial technology of pumping systems. It was one thing to straighten a bent bar on a mechanical reaper, but it meant entering another world to fiddle with a motor, belts or shafts, and a pump. Donald Green quotes Hereford, Texas, farmer Roland Loyd in 1914: "Worked about half of afternoon trying to start pumping outfit gave it up as bad job and cut weeds rest of afternoon. . . . Worked 'til 3:30 P.M. trying to start big engine. Then gave it up and went to town."[28] Before gearing became workable and inexpensive, the long leather belt that connected engine and pump demanded constant adjustment as it expanded or contracted with the weather. If it was too loose, it was inefficient; if too tight, it wore down pump shaft bearings. Roland Loyd wrote in the summer of 1914 that he cut the belt down on June 29 when the temperature reached 103 degrees, resewed a piece in on July 21, cut it again on July 30 and again on August 1. These constant maintenance problems also kept farmers from irrigating at night. As a result, peak irrigation from a well averaged only about seventy-two acres in 1919. This was remarkable in comparison with windmills but not enough to save wheat farming.

The still-rare steam-powered tractor of the 1890s was a behemoth the size of a small railroad locomotive. The eighty-horsepower steam engine that worked irrigation pumps for a prosperous farm near Mesa, Arizona, in 1900 demanded two trained engineers to service the engine and two firemen, who also cut wood for fuel. The running cost was $9.25 a day. Irrigation engineer and advocate Elwood Mead estimated the cost, with all expenses, at $2.27 per acre-foot: "The expense of raising water by steam power is very great indeed . . . such water is too costly for constant use in ordinary farming operations."[29]

Electric irrigation pumps existed, but power lines from distant stations did not. Only large enterprises, such as the United States Sugar and Land Company at Garden City, could generate their own electricity. In 1909 its plant used an oil-fired 400-horsepower engine to run a 350-kilowatt steam generator for electricity which in turn went out over fifteen miles of power line to fourteen pumps. Each pump could deliver 1,800 to 2,000 gallons per minute to irrigate thirty-five hundred acres.[30] If a central plains farmer in 1908 wanted to use electricity to run a five-inch centrifugal pump to raise 450 gallons per minute from a depth of seventy-five feet, he would have to pay almost four dollars per acre-foot. This was unacceptable. Costs included the power line to his pump, high kilowatt-hour rates, and usually a surcharge based on the horsepower of the electric motor.[31] Even with a four-man crew steam power was significantly cheaper but still uneconomical.

The Second New Ingredient: The Gasoline Engine

Steam engines to run large pumps remained expensive for low-income farmers; one used near Holcomb in 1904 could pump up to twenty-five hundred gallons per minute but it cost twelve thousand dollars, the equivalent of three years' gross income for a prosperous farmer. Gasoline or oil engines were new, unreliable, and not generally available until after 1900. As gasoline pumps became commonly available, the picture would change. By 1912 more than fifty gasoline pumps irrigated sixty-five hundred acres. Internal-combustion engines burning cheap fuels would become the power source of choice, but they were yet without a clear-cut technological direction. In the late 1890s, low-compression oil-burning Hornsby-Ackroyd type English-design engines were sold to early pump irrigators in the Gulf Coast

133

rice belt, in California and Arizona, and occasionally on the Great Plains. These were simple one- or two-cylinder "hot bulb" spark-plugless engines with large and heavy (up to four feet in diameter) cast-iron flywheels generating up to seventy horsepower. The hot bulb protruded from the engine head, where it was heated with a torch. The heat was conducted into the cylinder head by a "spoon" or "lip," where it ignited the oil while the flywheel was rotated by hand in small engines or by compressed air into the cylinder head on larger engines. Then the engine ran itself by reheating the hot bulb with each ignition. However, the engine did not start easily in cold weather, it was inefficient, and it was costly, usually nineteen hundred dollars delivered and connected. Advantageously, the heavy crude oil it used cost three to seven cents a gallon, less than a third the cost of gasoline in 1916.[32] Anticipating the future, a Kansas farmer jacked up the rear of his car and ran a small centrifugal pump through a belt from his rear axle. In 1907 the cost of a 12-horsepower gasoline engine, a No.6 centrifugal pump, and a well ran twelve hundred dollars, but its promise was its ability to irrigate one hundred acres. The difference was dramatic. Conversion from a twelve-foot windmill to a gasoline engine and centrifugal pump increased irrigation capacity from five to fifty acres.[33] Larger ranchers and farmers quickly took advantage of the new technology but small settlers still could not. The King brothers north of Garden City operated five wells going down as much as 150 feet to irrigate four hundred acres at a total cost exceeding three thousand dollars.[34]

The combination of the pitless pump, the rotary drilling rig, and the internal-combustion engine would become the wave of the future, once efficiency and reliability went up and costs and servicing went down. In 1912 a Kansas State Board of Agriculture official wrote optimistically that "these large, deep wells, with the centrifugal [pitless] pumps and powerful cheap oil-engines, are the means by which the underground waters will be utilized to irrigate the lands of this great territory." Irrigation historian Donald E. Green described the changed High Plains scene and found it as revolutionized as England's Midlands or New England's river valleys during the

Industrial Revolution. Quiet rural countryside became an industrial landscape:

Not only could one locate such a well easily by sight [a squat thirty-foot wooden tower], but the distinctive sound of the huge oil engine—some models weighed several tons—also identified it. Both four-cycle and two-cycle engines were used. . . . Both could be audibly identified by a slow, pulsating, unrhythmic pop-pop-pop. Some models were capable of blowing extraordinary blue smoke rings out their exhausts and high into the atmosphere. . . . A house was usually built over the pump, belt, and engine to protect the machinery from the weather, and the derrick jutted into the sky above one end of the house.[35]

World War I gave the plains new life with global demands for wheat, and put cash into the farmer's palm, but it delayed the spread of the irrigation revolution. It seemed unpatriotic to turn potential cannons into irrigation pipe to flood the fields when dryland farming would do just as well. Lack of experience and poor information about water use did not help neophyte irrigators. Most farmers turned on their pumps only as a last resort, when plants were already withering, nor were they certain how much water would flood the fields. Know-how on land leveling for flood irrigation also was limited. Ditches were badly dug and choked with weeds or Johnsongrass. Nor were farmers, still in the age of the horse-drawn cultivator and the wagon, particularly adept at operating or repairing the new internal-combustion engines. Pump maintenance was still a Zen-like mystery to most farmers.

Many new irrigators became disenchanted with the complexities of the newfangled method. Four out of five buyers of irrigated farms from the Texas Land and Development Company could not continue their payments and lost their farms in less than a decade.[36] The irrigated wheat fields of the plains did not offer the rewards of the irrigated vegetable fields or fruit orchards of California, and California's vegetable fields and fruit orchards could not be established on the High Plains. The collective effects of high winds, temperature extremes and threat of hail, and distance from markets limited farmers, it was believed, to wheat or alfalfa. Besides, "it may rain."

Irrigation equipment was by far the most sophisticated and costly farming item the plains farmer might consider. Green reports that in 1912, John H. Slaton paid $2,350 for digging a well and installing a pitless pump and a thirty-two-horsepower engine,[37] this in a day when a good farmer was tickled pink if he had $500 ready cash for a year's worth of "improvements." Cheaper pit-type pumps caused too much trouble and were useless for water more than 30 feet deep. Drilling and casing a twenty-six-inch well ranged from $4.00 to $5.25 per foot, which meant $500 to $600 for a 100- to 120-foot well. The Layne and Bowler pitless pump ran another $500, and another $1,000 might quickly go for lumber and construction of the derrick and pump and engine shed, a fuel tank, air compressor and tanks. The new gasoline engines were still costly, particularly since used ones out of Fords, Dodges, and Chevrolets, so commonplace later, were neither available nor reliable. Twenty-five- to sixty-horsepower stationary oil-burning engines— the less costly ($1,000 to $1,600) made by Charter, Van Sevrein, or Herr and the more expensive ($1,800 to $2,500) made by Primm and Bessemer—often put irrigation out of farmers' reach. The cost of a turnkey well, ready to start, could easily exceed $6,000.

Using another measure, state agricultural economists of the day concluded that the cost per acre-foot of water ranged from $5.00 to $6.25, including depreciation, credit costs, fuel, and maintenance. Many farmers who saw their future in irrigated alfalfa fields were told to expect to pay $12.50 to $15.60 for two and a half acre-feet of water per acre, or more than $1,000 for an eighty-acre tract. If the farmer harvested three tons an acre at $15 a ton, he would gross $3,600 and then would deduct $1,000 for irrigation and $600 for harvesting, plus taxes and interest, depreciation on equipment, and the cost of seed and labor. These optimistic figures did not factor in the vagaries of weather or fluctuating market prices. Most farmers on the plains in the 1910s and 1920s concluded they had their hands full without risking their farms and future on irrigation.[38] Between June 1920 and December 1920 the price of wheat dropped from $2.58 a bushel to $1.43, effectively ending any remaining interest in costly irrigation. Plains farmers stayed with land-extensive dryland farming rather than try complex capital-intensive, technology-intensive, and irrigation-intensive means of production.[39]

Compared to the halcyon days before the war, a plains farmer in 1920 unknowingly stood on the verge of a twenty-year depression. Farmland prices were 57 percent of prewar value in 1921 and would collapse to 17 percent by 1928. By the spring of 1921, farmers' purchasing power declined to 63 percent of their prewar purchasing power with the same crop production. The agricultural conundrum of the 1920s was not only low prices for farm products and land but also overproduction. The national Irrigation Crusade ground to a halt. One remaining irrigator on the Texas High Plains reported that his seventy-four-acre tract with one well provided a net profit in 1924 of $196.53 after taxes and expenses, a figure that did not encourage the effort and cost of irrigation.[40] Not until money arrived from an entirely new source—New Deal Agricultural Adjustment Administration government-subsidy checks in 1934 and 1935—did interest revive in farm mechanization, but mostly in trucks and tractors rather than wells, pumps, motors, and pipes.

The Revolution Takes Hold

After World War II, irrigation spread across the plains to help insulate farming against a repeat of the Dust Bowl. In the late 1930s, new technologies, lower-cost equipment, and trouble-free pumps had trickled onto the plains. The individual elements of a high-capacity pumping system had been available in the 1920s but the entire system did not come together until the 1940s. In the 1920s the size of the well needed for pitless bowl centrifugal pumps, which could bring water from three hundred feet, decreased to twelve inches or smaller. This improvement depended on a huge increase in revolutions of the pump from 850 to 1,200 revolutions per minute to 3,600, based on advances in lubrication and bearings. The pump was in production by 1930 and was used by municipal water systems, for irrigation in the Far West, and in Gulf Coast rice fields. The deep-well turbine pump, in turn, depended on new engines that could exceed the 250-rpm pre–World War I oil-burning internal-combustion engines. By 1935 in the burgeoning irrigation country

137

IRRIGATION LEGEND

NAME	Location	Date Drilled	G.P.M. APPROX.	Depth	Size Pump	TYPE ENGINE	Static Draw Down	Fuel Used	Gravity Spin
Lee Larrabee	NW 16-32-33	1947-1948	1200		8"	LeRoi		Nat. Gas	288
R.A. Boles	SE 4-35-34	1950	1100	290	8"	MM605	88'-90'	Nat. Gas	509
Jack Massoni	NE 12-33-33	1953	1000	140	8"	MM605	8'	Nat. Gas	spr. 250
Harold Lower	NE 18-31-32	1947	1800	382	10"	Cat	184'-10'	Nat. Gas	240
Harold Lower	SW 9-31-32	1954	1800	385	10"	Cat	184'	Diesel & Nat Gas	316
R. Fields	SE 4-31-32	1948	1300	368	8"	LeRoi	170'-24'	Nat. Gas	480
Harold Stapleton	SE 6-31-32	1947	1300	387	8"	Cat.	177'-7'	Diesel	1127
Harold Stapleton	NW 6-31-32	1949	1300	387	8"	Cat	177'7'	Nat. Gas	400
Loyd Marteney	NE 19-32-34	1949	750	308	6"	Waukesha	200'-7"	Nat Gas	600
Loyd Marteney	NE 20-32-34								390
Dale Beard	NW 18-31-34	1951	900	375	8"	MM605	180'-40'	Nat. Gas	211
Don Priefert	NE 10-34-31	1952	700	297'	3"	Ford P-N	90'	Nat. Gas	20
C.C. Snyder	SE 17-32-34	1950	1200	336	8"	MM	205-10'	Nat. Gas	450
Kenneth Metcalf	SW 7-34-33	1953	400	345	8"	Chrysler		Nat. Gas	130
C.J. Conover	SW 6-31-33	1947	700	348	8"	MM605	210' 50'	Nat. Gas	189
E.H. Good	SE 21-31-33	1950			18"	MM1210		Nat. Gas	471
Hitchland Cattle Co.	SW 29-32-34	1950	1526	350	10"	LeRoi	180'-12'	H+2	1142
Hitch Land & Co.	SE 22-32-34	1950	1500	300	10"	LeRoi	190'-15'	Nat. Gas	255
G.R. Downing	NW 19-32-34	1953			10"	Buda		Nat. Gas	294
Forrest Simpson	SE 4-31-33	1950	1500	400	8"	MM1210	185'-12'	Nat. Gas	388
E. Boles	SE 10-32-34	1950	700	300	6"	IHC450	205'-20'	Nat. Gas	202
Henry & Hitch	SW 14-32-34	1953			6"	Chrysler		Nat. Gas	
J.N. Hatcher	NE 18-32-32	1953	1800	400	10"	MM1210	160'	Nat. Gas	320
Lombard Cattle Co.	SW 16-32-33	1953	1800	397	10"	MM1210	186'-20'	Nat. Gas	266
Edna Guthrie	NE 22-32-33	1953	1800	430	10"	MM1210	185'-20'	Butane	318
Emery Ball	NE 16-34-32	1953	1000	370	8"	MM605	190'-35'	Nat. Gas	160
Richard etc. Cobb	NW 24-32-34	1954	1800	410	10"	Waukesha	160'-50'	Nat. Gas	550
Ted Lofland	NW 18-35-32	1953	250	393	6"	220P Elec	170'	Elec.	140
Fred Schmidt	SW 5-31-32	1955	1800-2000	389	10"	Waukesha	150'-19'	Nat. Gas	150
David Schmidt	SW 11-31-31	1954	1900	360	10"	Buda 1290	166'-34'	Nat. Gas	586
A.E. Cotton	W 10-43-33	1954	1800	352	10"	MM1600		Nat. Gas	712
Fran Dufield	NW 14-32-33	1955	1300		8"	GMcV12		Nat. Gas	291
Keith Rosson	SW 29-32-31	1955	1950	418	10"	Buda	158'-48'	Nat. Gas	611
Dean Printz	NW 12-32-32	1955	2100	410	10"	Waukesha	185'-24	Nat. Gas	480
M. Parter (J. Davis)	NE 23-31-32	1955			10"	Hudson		Nat. Gas	459
Jessie Thomas	NW 21-31-32	1955	1600	403	10"	LeRoi	170	Nat. Gas	319
O.S. Wilkins	NW 1-34-31	1955	2000		10"	Cat		Diesel Nat Gas	580
Hitchland Cattle Co	NW 17-32-34	1954	1396		8"	MM800		Nat. Gas	609
Hitch Land & Co.	SW 12-32-34	1954	1000		8"	MM800		Nat. Gas	800
Henry Hitch	NE 21-32-34	1955			10"	2 Chrysler		Nat. Gas	253
F.H. Wallenberg	SE 20-31-32	1955		400	10"	Budda		Nat. Gas	158
Raymond Halt	SE 18-32-34	1955	1400	406	8"		225'-11'	Nat. Gas	153
John Grover	NW 10-35-31	1955	1000	353	8"	605MM	90-190	Nat. Gas	285
Lombard Cattle Co.	N. 20-32-33	1955	1800	400	10"	Waukesha	185-20	Nat. Gas	374
Joe Pittman	SW 17-31-33	1955	1800	300	10"	Buda	160-40	Nat. Gas	593
Don Priefert	NW 10-34-31	1955	800-900	505	8"	MM800	110-200	Nat. Gas	193
Randall Bird	NW 2-31-32	1955	1500	360	10"	GMc V12	180-260	Nat. Gas	300
R. Pittman	SE 17-31-33	1955	2000	455	10"	Waukesha	179-17	Nat. Gas	320
R.L. Dunlap	SE 16-34-32	1956	1300	230	8"		100-100	Nat. Gas	177
Ted Lofland	NW 15-35-31	1956	1300	321	8"	Waukesha	173-12	Nat. Gas	310
C.C. Snyder	SW 34-32-34	1956	2000	435	10"	970 Buda	100-40	Nat. Gas	320
Waldo Wills	SW 26-32-34	1956	1800	390	10"	2 Chrysler	179' 30'	Nat. Gas	497

8. Original tally sheet of the first modern irrigation wells in southwestern Kansas as recorded in the offices of the USDA Soil Conservation Service in Liberal, Kansas. Important historical data include the name of the pioneering irrigator, location of the pump, date drilled, flow in gallons per minute, depth to water, size of pipe, type of engine, and fuel type. Some of these wells are still in use, usually with deeper drilling and new pumps and well casings. Original file, USDA Soil Conservation Service Office, Liberal, Kansas.

around Plainview, Texas, used and cheap automobile engines provided the necessary speed. In Hale County, Texas, a farmer in 1938 could acquire a fancy Ford V-8 engine for $310 and a lesser but equally workable Chevrolet engine for $235. Even then the investment was not trivial. The dangerous and inefficient belt that drove the pump from the engine was also replaced by the right-angle geared pump head. It had been available since the teens but would not have worked with the slower engine. By making the gear on the engine shaft larger in diameter than the gear with which it meshed on the pump shaft, the pump could be made to rotate faster at lower and more efficient gasoline-engine speeds. An 800-rpm engine could provide 1,200- to 1,600-rpm pump speed.[41] Even better would have been electric motors, because of their flexibility, but they were costly, as was electricity; poles and power lines to the pumps were still beyond farmers' means, although the Rural Electrification Administration would inch toward plains farmers in the next two decades.

"Rain when you want it" became the slogan for irrigation advocates. When rain failed to appear in the 1930s, interest in irrigation predictably revived. In 1937 the first deep well outside Liberal, Kansas, brought a public celebration, including a parade sponsored by merchants. "The parade then wound its way to the well, where hundreds of people and cars gathered to watch the spudding ceremony."[42] By the late 1930s, the cost of drilling and casing a well, for pump, gear head, motor, and housing, was a third of what it had been in the 1910s and 1920s, down from $6,000 to $2,000. A well 250 feet deep cost $650 for drilling and $3.25 a foot for casing; a pump was the most costly item at $850. The gear head, which raised efficiency dramatically and delighted farmers who hated the old belt, cost $270, but the handy farmer was likely to recycle an engine from his junked auto. The shed for the entire unit would come to about $50 if not handmade from farmyard scrap. In sum, a determined farmer could get into irrigation for less than $2,000.[43] Compared to earlier operating expenses at about $6.00 per acre-foot, the 1938 irrigator could flood his field for $3.20 to $4.50, including installed well and equipment, interest and depreciation, and fuel and maintenance. He still planted alfalfa, grain sorghums and wheat, but a hundred acres in

139

wheat might now net $1,200. Around Plainview, Texas, from 1930 to 1936 the number of wells doubled from 170 after declining since the 1920 high of 250. At the beginning of 1935 there were 35,000 irrigated acres, which grew to 80,000 at the end of 1936 and then doubled again in 1937 with 1,150 wells.

Advances in technology soon gave the ordinary farmer access to irrigation, but two more decades would pass before it was commonplace.[44] Two thousand dollars was usually beyond the reach of plains farmers. Even a small farmer often worked an entire 640-acre section and would need four units, since one well and pump served only a quarter section of 160 acres at the most. Large operators had no trouble arranging credit based on farm value and production, but small farmers seeking to shift from dryland farming to irrigation to move into high production needed loans based on future production. Their existing equity was often too small, a Catch-22 situation.[45] On the High Plains, if irrigation technology was too costly for the independent farmer, it might as well not exist.

In the late 1930s, federal policies first concentrated on better dryland farming through soil conservation rather than industrialization through irrigation. Despite the availability of efficient irrigation technology at reasonable cost, the Great Plains Drought Area Committee concluded in 1936 that "irrigation at best can cause only minor changes in the economic life of the Great Plains."[46] It identified only a few favorable areas with access to shallow underground water, and it generally discouraged federal financing. Additionally, irrigation would only mean more overproduction of wheat, alfalfa, and grain sorghums. Unlike the extensive support given dryland farming by the new Soil Conservation Service, no public agency, including the Reclamation Service, took an interest in plains irrigation. Irrigation historian Donald E. Green concluded that only independent local entrepreneurs, such as banker Artemus ("Artie") Baker of Lockney, Texas, in Floyd County, offered the credit that small farmers found unavailable elsewhere. Baker even arranged for shipment of steel well casings, Ford V-8 engines (a boxcar lot of fifty at $125 each), gear heads, pumps, and even professional well-drilling rigs and personnel.[47] Baker required no down payment, although when the Peerless Pump Company set up its equipment office in

9. Typical modern pumping systems in southwest Kansas. *Top:* centrifugal pump using a rebuilt V-8 automobile engine fueled by natural gas, serving water to an open ditch for flood irrigation. *Bottom:* One of Keith Allen's commercial large-scale pumps and natural-gas engines used to flood his alternative-crop fields. Photos taken in 1988 by the author.

Plainview in 1935 it required a $500 down payment for a $2,000 turnkey irrigation system.

Despite the moves by federal agencies toward dryland farming or resettlement, a number of farmers began to believe that irrigation was a real alternative. The combined effects of depression and Dust Bowl convinced farmers in the Texas counties of Floyd and Swisher that "when drouth and the depression had swept everything from us, we decided to give up dry farming and irrigate." "I was 'flat broke' and ready to move when I installed a well on my place in May 1936." With a well, "you were sure of a crop; without a well you were sure of a failure."[48] Some farmers were beginning to conclude that dryland farming was unprofitable over the long run—it would not pay debts or meet annual expenses. Green suggests that a turning point was reached when "farmers began to think of irrigation as more than simply 'crop insurance' to be used during abnormally dry years." A Floyd County farmer said he finally realized that if he turned to irrigation only as a last resort, he misused it: "The average irrigation farmer watered with an eye on the sky for possible rainfall and usually waited until the last possible moment before he used his well. Consequently, his crops did not show sufficient margin of profit over that of the dry farmer." Instead, irrigation should be used "with an eye to producing capacity crops."[49] This view became the norm for irrigation throughout the High Plains. It would also encourage overproduction and the heavy drawdown of Ogallala water.

Equally revolutionary, irrigation farmers broke with long-standing tradition by watering night and day and also on Sunday, which in farm communities had been zealously guarded as a day of rest. Fabled American rural virtues, so enthusiastically protected even during the Dust Bowl, would be abandoned only reluctantly. As their neighbors trooped to see stands of irrigated wheat, the new irrigators were called "modern rainmakers" who could "place moisture where and when needed," guaranteeing "abundant crops in spite of cloudless skies and torturing suns."

Gigot and Center Pivot

Despite its cost since the 1930s, government credit was a Band-Aid to struggling plains farmers as long as most of them were still without water. Very gradually a sprinkling of irrigation units appeared in southwest Kansas, mostly in Finney County.[50] Momentum grew during the Filthy Fifties, and in the 1960s a man-made deluge of "walking water" began to be pumped from underground. For example, in the heart of the old Dust Bowl country of southwest Kansas today, Garden City farmer Clarence J. Gigot (starts like *jig* and rhymes with *spigot*) does not worry about drought as he did when he was a young man in the 1930s.[51] He now operates hundreds of circles of center-pivot irrigation sprinklers spread across submarginal land. Each covers a 160-acre quarter section. No matter how dry and dusty it is, he can water surprisingly lush green fields of wheat, alfalfa, grain sorghums, and even corn. Others have followed Gigot's lead, but he continues to dominate Kansas Sandhills irrigation. In 1965, eleven center pivots watered 1,760 acres of Finney County's 150,000 acres of Sandsage Prairie. Nine years later, in 1974, there were 590 pivots, and in the early 1980s, Gigot's center-pivot circles peaked at more than 700.[52]

In the 1960s, Clarence Gigot and his four sons turned the desert into a garden when they introduced center-pivot irrigation in the long-abandoned Sandhills. The family owned 2,800 lightly grazed Sandhills acres that troubled it as underused. Hearing of a new irrigation device, Clarence and sons Dean and Terry traveled over three hundred miles into Nebraska to see a center pivot in action, they bought one directly from the factory, and set it up twelve miles southeast of Garden City. In its first year the quarter section yielded a remarkable 120 bushels of corn per acre.[53] Today Gigot fields consistently yield two to three times more grain than those of his dryland-farming neighbors. With their accustomed venturesomeness, the Gigots planted their growing number of circles mostly in water-consuming corn, with some alfalfa and only a little barley and wheat. Now they work more than 50,000 irrigated acres, using laser-beam technologies to ensure proper land levels and even water flow. They depend on computerized management of the fertilizers and pesticides used on their fields, as well as the nutritional feed mix for the cattle in their feedlots. A Gigot manager observed that every effort is made to reduce labor, energy, and water costs, that each field is measured for the best balance between gallons of water per minute and bushels of corn or wheat per acre. The Gigots are reputed, by both friends and critics, to control "the most finely tuned irrigation management in western Kansas."

As for the future, the Gigots expect to continue advanced-technology water-conserving irrigation for a long time, yet a Gigot Feeders manager thinks the lowering of the Ogallala water level eventually will shut everything down and return the region to submarginal scrubland. Dean Gigot told a Wichita newsman who came out to report on their achievement, "It's not raping [the land] to pump water. Water is something put there to use and I hope that I'm using it to the best of my ability."[54] He told another interviewer, "Should we be using [the groundwater]? Damn right we should! The same doom sayers are claiming that the buffalo and the Indians should still be here. . . . The water is there for man to use, same as the soil, the trees and the oil. Use it with all the abilities that you have." He also acknowledged high consumption: "We are overpopulated out here. My family's contention is stop the drilling, put in a five-year moratorium on new wells, and get a real good monitoring situation in place."[55]

But Gigot did not say that his family drilled its wells before state regulations went into effect and can continue to take as much water as it chooses. Kansas groundwater official Gary Baker observed to a reporter that "the time will come when we'll be real sorry that the Sandsage Prairie [Sandhills] was ever developed. There's a tremendous amount of wind erosion already, especially on the irrigated prairie that you wouldn't otherwise be farming. Once you take away the natural vegetation cover on this land, there's no way to restore it. I sure don't want to live here when the aquifer goes dry, because this place is never gonna stop blowing. It's gonna be a new desert."[56]

In the meantime, Gigot family assets no doubt far exceed the thirteen million dollars reported in 1980. Despite some retrenchment, they still include more than five hundred circles, mostly under Circle Land and Cattle Company. The family's operations also include the equipment dealership (Gigot Irrigation), and the two massive feedlots (Gigot Feeders and Circle Feeders), together with Southwest Corn (the Gigot grain elevator company), Maxima Corporation (the Gigot fertilizer company), and Circle Research Corporation (the Gigot gasohol operation).

Down in Texas County, Oklahoma, Roger and Betty Trescott have not invested in center-pivot units; instead, their four pumps provide water for flood or furrow irrigation on their exceedingly flat Oklahoma Panhandle land. Modern flood irrigation does not use expensive center-pivot equipment and can offer the same crop yields, but it demands more labor and consumes much more water for the same results. Simple flood irrigation once required the farmer to spade out part of a ditch wall to channel water into each field row, then close the gap when each row was saturated. Then he could channel his water farther down the field into the next set of rows. The rush of water in such sets eroded ditches and rows and required repetitious, muddy, and back-breaking shoveling to repair breaks and overflows. New World War II materials brought postwar civilian plastic, rubber, concrete, and aluminum piping and siphon tubes to carry and measure water from ditches down field rows. More than 50 percent of flood-irrigation water is still lost to seepage and evaporation in open ditches between pump and field rows; enclosed (closed-conduit) pipes help to conserve water for direct application to crops.

The commonly used flood system began with a ten- or twelve- or fifteen-inch concrete pipe laid three or four feet underground to carry water from the pump to the field, where it was connected to aluminum pipe at two hundred-foot intervals. Installed concrete and aluminum pipe in 1949 cost $0.95 to $1.40 per foot, depending on diameter.[57] An important benefit of the closed-conduit system was that water under pressure could be delivered to a field higher than the pump level and on mildly rolling terrain. Mechanical land leveling remained important but was less critical for successful irrigation of large tracts. To encourage mechanization and conservation, the USDA paid approximately one-third of the cost of installing such a system. By 1958, 50 percent of the irrigated farms on the Texas High Plains had installed a closed-conduit system, mostly between 1954 and 1958. Even when water is apparently abundant, most farmers are averse to waste.

Farmers on the High Plains became familiar with terms like "make a set," "check the water," "change the water," "prewater," and "tailwater."[58] The soils are deep, hold moisture well, and are nearly level in much of southwest Kansas and the Texas-Oklahoma Panhandle. When many farmers began flood or furrow irrigation in the late 1950s, they could figure on a reasonable five- to ten-dollar cost to get the 326,000 gallons in an acre-foot of water on a field.[59] But even modern flood irrigation requires the daily routine of channeling water to the fields, shoveling rows open, closing off wet rows, and continual maintenance against erosion and rodents. More convenient gated pipe, with outlets along its length, still needs individual management and adjustment of each plant row. Flood irrigation can require two weeks to cover 150 acres, compared with three to five days under center-pivot irrigation.

Invented about 1950 by Colorado farmer Frank Zybach, the center-pivot irrigator was called in a *Scientific American* article "the most significant mechanical innovation [worldwide] in agriculture since the replacement of draft animals by the tractor."[60] This "novel rotating machine . . . enables the farmer to irrigate large tracts of land automatically." It caused a revolution because, although irrigation has existed since the early human experiences with agriculture ten thousand years ago, irrigation was always synonymous with hard work for long hours.

The center pivot is a thirteen-hundred-foot-long six-inch pipe (itself eight feet off the ground) supported by a row of seven or more towers on large wheels. Sprinklers are attached at regular intervals, pointing up or down. One end of the pipe is set in the middle of a 160-acre quarter section around which the pipe and wheeled towers circle. Water from the center flows through the pipe; its pressure at the end of the pipe actuates a mechanism, the Trojan bar, that moves the outermost tower on a broad circular route, and the rest of the towers follow, led by an alignment device to keep them in line. As this center-pivot irrigation mechanism circles over a crop, a farmer can selectively apply small amounts of water as needed. His circular pattern leaves out the corners of the typical 160-acre quarter section; between 120 and 132 acres are actually irrigated, although various types of corner arms can be attached to cover an extra 19 to 45 acres, up to 96 percent of the field, or even an irregular field. A center-pivot device can track a complete circle in twelve hours, applying about three-eighths of an inch of water in the traverse, although the farmer can slow the pace by adjusting the outermost tower. Typical irrigation scheduling calls for one traverse every three to five days.

10. Two examples of center-pivot irrigation in the 1980s, the top photo illustrating the original and less efficient high-level sprinklers that wasted water through wind and evaporation and the bottom photo showing a more efficient (up to 80 percent) drop sprinkler. Center-pivot irrigation also has the ability to water gently rolling country, as in the Kansas Sandhills, whereas flood irrigation required flat farmland that in some cases was laser-leveled by the SCS. Photos supplied by Valmont Industries, Valley, Nebraska, and reprinted with permission.

Clarence Gigot took advantage of another opportunity allowed by the new technology. Gigot, now in his late eighties, experienced the Dust Bowl firsthand. The land he owned in the sunburned Sandhills had been designated submarginal by the USDA to prevent attempts to do anything more than graze cattle on it: one steer to 160 acres. At the point where Kansas, Oklahoma, and Colorado meet, much of this scrubland, mixed with blowing dunes, was turned into federally owned grassland reserve during the Dust Bowl troubles, with the government offering to resettle drought-broken farmers elsewhere.

While virtually everyone else abandoned their Sandhills property, Clarence Gigot bought up more of Finney County's scrubland. At that time it must have appeared foolhardy, even at a bargain-basement five dollars an acre, but since the 1960s Clarence appears to have been incredibly shrewd. Center-pivot systems can apply water lightly and frequently, perfectly suited to submarginal Sandhills land, which was notorious for its inability to hold water. Good loamy soil can hold two or more inches of water per foot of soil, while sandy soil soaks up water quickly but holds less than an inch per foot.[61] Center-pivot irrigation offered several lighter sprinklings instead of a single heavy flood application. Crops otherwise entirely unsuited for the Sandhills could prosper: corn, alfalfa, sorghum, and wheat, even sugar beets and potatoes.

Gigot also benefited because the center-pivot system could carry liquid fertilizer in its water and overcome the inability of sandy soils to hold nutrients usually suspended in water. When high-capital, low-labor center-pivot irrigation brought a field to maximum production, it also required the use of commercial fertilizers to replenish soils that now became rapidly depleted. Sophisticated irrigation thus encouraged technological soil mining. Traditionally, the farmer protected his soil by using the ancient methods of crop rotation and animal manure, but the new maximum-yield industrial farming does not easily allow for crop rotation into fallow fields or low-cash-value soil-building crops. As a result, beginning in the early 1950s, the ubiquitous high-pressure stationary or wheeled steel tanks containing anhydrous ammonia (the business in which the notorious Billy Sol Estes made his fortune) dotted the landscape. This chemical fertilizer in convenient gas form, more than 80 percent nitrogen, filled the need of irrigation farmers to replenish nitrogen in the soil rapidly after each harvest of grain sorghum or wheat. It seemed most efficient at first to put the liquid into the irrigation water between the pump and the field, but soon it was applied directly to the soil during plowing through nozzles attached behind the plow points of chisel plows.

In addition, center-pivot irrigation seemed predestined to make Gigot prosper because it could adjust to slightly hilly terrain. Most of the Sandhills is gently rolling terrain where ordinary flood irrigation would always be impossible. Besides, soil quality was so bad—classified by the USDA as unfit for cultivation—that the effort seemed wasted.[62] Most of Gigot's neighbors abandoned their attempts at dryland farming because sandy soil soaks up massive amounts of water, making it virtually impossible to run water down rows as on tighter soils. Answers to problems created more new problems in the Sandhills. Deep-break plowing techniques tightened sandy soil by bringing underlying clay to the surface. Contrarily, where the landscape was rolling, water ran downhill too rapidly to soak into the soil.[63] Gigot's move to controllable sprinkler systems produced little runoff. Center-pivot irrigation offered scheduled man-made rains on demand, not man-made rivers of canals and ditches. Grades to 30 percent can be covered, although usually the center pivots stay with 10 percent or less because of the threat of erosion and gullying.

Each time they set up a center-pivot system on 160 acres, the Gigots turned the Sandhills desert into a garden. In the 1960s they acquired an additional 22,000 acres that no one else wanted, and between 1972 and 1974 alone they applied for and drilled more than one hundred wells, mostly in the Sandsage Prairie of the Sandhills. Their timing was remarkable. The Gigots were already well established as center-pivot pioneers when the first irrigation boom arrived in the late 1960s and early 1970s. Sandhills land prices in the 1970s soared from a low of $25 an acre to $250 an acre, and irrigated center-pivot land hit $1,200 to $1,500.

High Technology Irrigation on the Prosperous Plains

With their new prosperity, irrigators could afford fully automatic sprinkler systems with all the latest bells and whistles in technological innovation. They enjoyed buried water-supply lines, electrically operated and even computerized valves, low-pressure spray nozzles, and moisture sensors imbedded in the soil, all devices that improved crop watering versatility and conservation efficiency. Nebraska plant and water scientist William E. Splinter writes that "for the normally dry climate of the Great Plains the microclimate of a field being irrigated by a center-pivot system is quite similar to that of an oasis in a desert."[64]

Computer modeling of the interaction between plant-growth patterns and water application led to better irrigation scheduling that conserved Ogallala water. Scheduling involves strategic or critical-stage irrigation during tasseling and silking, head emergence, or pod and bean development. Data on light intensity, air temperature, and length of day, combined with soil-moisture levels, allowed precise information on corn, for example, that covered leaf area, carbohydrate production, dry-matter weight, and grain yield.[65] It was discovered that since corn grows about 20 percent per day in its early stages, lack of water at specific times creates stresses that can cause irreversible damage to the future of the crop. With a device called a contact auxanometer, which measures the diameter of a plant's stem, a change in growth rate can be detected within five minutes. Plants have biological clocks and they have stress days: it takes a total of one thousand degrees Fahrenheit over a number of days for a corn plant to shift from germination to forming a tassel.[66] Tasseling is the most vulnerable time for corn, and irrigation is critical at that time, but a crop like sorghum is not as easily stressed. Another device called a lysimeter measures the water being evaporated from the soil or transpired through the plant leaves from sun and wind.

Irrigators who invested in the new systems went deeply into debt. In the late 1970s a bushel of corn peaked at $3.00 a bushel before collapsing down to $1.25. As a result, land prices also fell almost half from $920 an acre to $500. Many Sandhills irrigators suddenly lost two-thirds of their borrowing power. At the high point of new installations between 1971 and 1976, a complete sprinkler-and-well system ran $25,000. By the mid-1980s, a minimum-cost turnkey irrigation system on a quarter section cost $70,000. This was $437.50 an acre, about the cost of owning the same acre of land. Two hundred thousand dollars for a state-of-the-art system is not unusual, nor is $1,250 an acre. This does not include other production costs: seed, equipment, fertilizer, insecticide, labor, and amortization. If 140 bushels per acre of $3.00 corn is produced on 133 acres, the farmer grosses $420 an acre. Simultaneously, energy costs had soared. A typical center-pivot unit consumes about fifty gallons of diesel fuel per acre per year to apply twenty-two inches of water, or ten times the fuel needed to raise and harvest a nonirrigated corn crop.

Cattle Kingdom Redux

Even in hard times the Gigots discovered that their irrigation costs could be covered if they turned their operation into a vertically integrated cattle business. They had no middleman between the soil, water, and sun at the start of the process and the beef markets at its end. They even sold and serviced the center-pivot irrigation systems. They continued to profit because they could make adjustments to buffer themselves when high costs invaded one or another of their operations. In the mid-1980s, Gigot and his four sons were the biggest corn producers in the entire nation. When corn was cheap, they fed it to cattle in their feedlots and benefited when cattle prices rose from twenty-nine dollars per hundredweight in mid-1973 to fifty dollars in July 1985 to seventy-eight dollars in May 1988.[67] But because corn prices had fallen in the short term (and water levels declined for the long run), the Gigots protected themselves in 1984 by switching a significant part of their production from risky water-intensive corn to more reliable wheat, which could even be dry-farmed. When a wheat glut brought federal restrictions, they could follow the lead of Texas irrigators by planting grain sorghum, partly for feeder livestock and partly to bypass the restrictions on wheat production.[68] They also switched cultivation to a moisture-preserving no-till operation. On center-pivot land where a grain crop was no longer profitable, they could successfully graze cattle on irrigated grasses. Dryland open-range beef production stood at twenty-seven pounds per acre, while cattle that consumed cool-season grasses under a center-pivot unit virtually guaranteed between seven hundred and nine hundred pounds of beef per acre.[69]

Gigot venturesomeness has paid off handsomely, but it is a conservative gamble: the Gigots work hard to make certain the dice will roll their way before they place their high-stakes bets. One of their most controversial gambles, and most profitable, was a water depletion-allowance case. When the Gigots purchased most of their irrigation land in the 1960s and 1970s, the price of land overlying the aquifer had already risen substantially, while groundwater supplies began to decline significantly. In a 1963 court case, *U.S.* v. *Shurbet,* a Texas farmer established his right to a cost-depletion income-tax allowance for the decline in the aquifer level underlying his land, since it also reduced the cash value of his land.[70] The Gigots went to court and in 1980 got a Justice Department ruling that they were entitled to the deduction. They had asked for more than $30,000 in income-tax refunds. As a result of the ruling, farmers in the Midwest and High Plains could save more than a billion dollars, and Kansas irrigators alone could enjoy tax relief totaling fifty million dollars a year. For a single quarter section of irrigated land, the annual depletion deduction would be $2,400.[71] But farmers who were too farsighted and acquired their land in the 1940s and 1950s, before prices went up, would receive no benefits.[72]

Kenny Ochs, sales manager for Gigot Irrigation Company, summed up the current blueprint for future survival on the old Dust Bowl High Plains: "As long as cattle make a profit, everyone profits." Comparative 1988 supermarket shopping figures support Ochs's argument.[73] A farmer's share of a five-pound bag of all-purpose wheat flour retailing at $1.02 is $0.27, or 26 percent. A pound of choice beef costs the shopper $2.42, of which the producer earns $1.38, or 57 percent. He gets 12 percent of the cost of potatoes and 7 percent of the cost of a loaf of white bread. A farmer might do better with a combination of eggs, (62 percent) and chicken (50 percent). Alternative-crop advocate Keith Allen near Sublette, Kansas, is looking into poultry for the High Plains, but beef usually has accounted for the lion's share of the consumer's cost.

Beef production no longer means the traditional steers of "home on the range." Instead, they are crowded onto grassless feedlots and fattened at high speed on concentrated feed and nutrients set at scientifically designed mixes by computer. Ron Crocker, manager of Gigot Feeders (the highway sign says "Custom Cattle Feeders. Open to the Public"), proudly shows visitors the vast open bins of thousands of tons of grain piled up like coal at a power plant and the computerized feed mixes dumped into trucks from overhead hoppers. Much of the grain comes from the fifty thousand acres of Gigot irrigated fields. Large supplies of corn, milo, wheat, and alfalfa became possible only as irrigation turned the traditional extensive farming on the High Plains into intensive farming as well. But Ron Crocker openly agrees that when the Ogallala water is gone, the feed grains will be gone and everything will shut down, including the feedlots.

Gigot Feeders services as many as twenty-five thousand cattle each week. Ten percent are Gigot owned, the rest on contract from ranches as far away as Missouri and Texas. The slaughterhouses and beef packers in the region consume ninety thousand head a week. Four of every ten cattle in the United States are slaughtered within 250 miles of Garden City (ranging from Pueblo, Colorado to Wichita, Kansas). Neither Chicago nor Cincinnati nor Kansas City is any longer the nation's meatpacker, nor have they been for three decades. The meat-processing business moved itself to where the beef or pork was rather than spend money shipping animals to central locations. In the Garden City area, where the corn, milo, wheat, and alfalfa grew, the first meat processors appeared in 1950 and the steers got fat in the first feedlots in the early 1950s.

According to a shiny full-color brochure handed out to visitors at Gigot Feeders, within a ninety-mile mile radius of the Gigot feedlots, packinghouses have been established by Val Agra, Excel, Hyplains Beef, National Beef, Swift, and IBP. Thirty percent of America's livestock passes through packinghouses in Dodge City and, especially, Holcomb, Kansas. The IBP plant in Holcomb, built in 1981 eight miles west of Garden City, is called the largest and most efficient beef-processing operation in the world under one roof. Visitors and reporters receive IBP's own brochure, "The Cutting Edge." Production consumes four hundred gallons of water to process one head of beef. The plant slaughters up to 5,000 head per day, or as many as 1,000,000 head a year, requiring six hundred million gallons of water pumped from the Ogallala. If, as Ogallala supplies diminish, the rights to use water are sold at market prices (both conservatives and conservationists now recommend this), it is unlikely that irrigators or feedlot owners could compete with IBP for the water. Finney County's irrigators, who started Kansas's irrigation industry, would go high and dry because they cannot afford costly water.[74] The right to Ogallala water is inescapably and forevermore the key to success on the Kansas High Plains.

At the plant, streams of cattle are crowded up a long ramp. A reporter, officially unwelcome but posing as a tourist, made the rounds in the plant:

I enjoy eating meat, and I know that the cows must be killed. . . . A laborer clamps a chain around the hind leg of each steer and heifer. Another places a foot-long cylinder against each of their heads, and fires a steel rod into the skull. A huge chain sweeps down from an overhead trolley line. It swings the cattle upside down, and sends them clanging a couple of feet apart down a long chute. . . . And the disassembly process begins. Man and machine merge to separate the various parts in stages. The workers use electric knives. . . . No chaps or spurs necessary, just ear plugs, rubber boots, belly guards, and chain-mesh gloves. . . . Within fifteen minutes, 1,200 pounds of corn-fed steer have been reduced to tenderloins and rib eyes.[75]

Iowa Beef Processors (the name was changed to IBP in 1987), which became part of the Occidental Petroleum conglomerate in 1981, deserves a book to itself.[76] In the 1970s, when 35 percent of the nation's beef-packing plants were going under, A. D. ("Andy") Anderson of IBP created boxed beef and captured a quarter of the nation's beef business. Old-line meatpackers—Swift, Wilson, Armour, Hormel, and Oscar Mayer—quickly lost their lead to boxed-beef newcomers IBP, Excel, and ConAgra. IBP's Holcomb plant never delivers the carcass to the supermarket butcher's door, as had always been done when Swift and Armour were big. Instead it arrives, mostly bone out, in manageable boxes. Not the least, when beef carcasses were hung up to cure before delivery to retailers, a considerable amount of water-weight was lost. With boxed beef, the water stays and each cut of meat weighs more. The Holcomb disassembly line does the heavy and difficult work before the boxes go out the door. The new plant itself immediately doubled the largest earlier capacity, claiming an annual kill capacity exceeding one million head.

Economy of scale thus dominates all levels of High Plains agriculture, from the spectacular amount of water in the Ogallala aquifer through the heavy pumping of water onto fencerow-to-fencerow high-yield crops of thousand-acre farms and the feeding of those crops to cattle in crowded pens covering hundreds of acres to the serving up of carcasses to rows of bone-sawing and meat-cutting disassembly lines.

People in and around Garden City expected to have the lion's share of the thirty-three hundred new jobs, but when IBP opened Holcomb's doors, it admitted that "six out of seven workers who would leave jobs in the community to work at the plant would find the work too hard and distasteful and would quit."[77] In several of its plants, IBP has been cited by the federal Occupational Safety and Health Administration (OSHA) for "shocking and dismaying working conditions." A study by the Kansas Rural Center concluded that

> meat packing is the second most dangerous industry after underground mining. Most workers stand on a production line and cut the same piece of meat with a knife all day long. . . . The most common physical complaint among workers is sore and cramped hands, due to gripping a knife all day in a 30–50 degree Fahrenheit environment. Workers often develop [sic] tendonitus, bursitus, arthritus, muscle strain, or back strain, besides constant fatigue.[78]

Hence IBP, known for its tough labor policies, brought in its own immigrants: Cubans, Laotians, Vietnamese, and Mexicans, workers resented by local citizens. In 1982 the company paid a base wage of $6.00 an hour compared to $10.50 at an old-line packer like Wilson.[79] But no one disagreed that the IBP plant would keep irrigation pumps running on the surrounding farms and that many people would receive their share of the profits in the chain that ran from the water to the steaks. Whoever controlled the chain could control southwest Kansas. However, local big fish could be swallowed by larger fish from the outside, so feedlot owners wondered what had happened to their hard-earned influence when it hit them that they would receive lower prices for their cattle, not higher, after IBP arrived.

Summary: Irrigation Brings the Central Plains into the American Consumer Mainstream

Bolstered by the reliability of Ogallala irrigation and the combination of fields of wheat, sorghum, and alfalfa serving cattle feedlots, farmers after the 1950s believed they had finally left the frugal days behind. They were no longer frozen in time on a sodhouse frontier. They enthusiastically entered America's postwar consumer binge: new kitchens and new cars, vacations to Florida or California, the latest farm equipment, and teenagers playing organized high school sports instead of toiling in the fields. A successful Haskell County farmer took pride that he and his family, and their kitchen appliances and living-room television set, looked no different from the families and homes pictured in advertisements in *Life* or *Look* or *Collier's*.

In 1957, Haskell County made twice as many bushels for four times the money from half the wheatland of 1936.[80] The wartime exodus from the hard life on the farm to high-paying urban factories was slowed by the new agricultural prosperity. Young men returned from the war to the farm and felt encouraged to stay. Farming became mechanized, irrigation guaranteed that fields were safe from drought, and government payments meant the nation recognized farmers' importance. Historian Donald E. Green provides a representative example:

In Lamb County [Texas] a disabled World War II veteran owned 8 acres and rented 100 acres in 1945. By 1946 he had made a down payment on an 80-acre farm and borrowed money from a local bank to install an irrigation plant. With 70 acres in cotton in 1947 he produced 102 bales, enough to pay for the irrigation unit and the land. The veteran then made a down payment on another 115 acres, bought some new farm equipment, and drilled a well on his newly purchased land. By the end of 1948 he had 195 irrigated acres clear of debt.[81]

With new resources thrown onto the battlefield for plains survival, it seemed that all-out crop production and the farmer's newfound prosperity were the ordained wave of the future. After decades of bitter and disappointing delays, America's Manifest Destiny had finally reached the plains.

This belated boomer psychology, not seen since early in the century, depended on widespread access to Ogallala water. In the early 1900s farmer enthusiasm had been tied to the sweep of flat, fertile land, good rain, and new machines designed for the plains. The new boom turned on pumping and irrigation technologies that, together with the security of government programs, gave the plains its second life. The 1950s Little Dust Bowl pushed farmers further toward heavy irrigation. There are usually three reasons a new agricultural technology is adopted: a crisis, for better production, to reduce risks.[82] Farmers slowly made the important switch from treating irrigation as a last resort and temporary safeguard against crop failure to a major installation to guarantee increased production. A 1948 Texas experiment-station study reported that irrigators did not use their potential: they "seldom strive for maximum per-acre yields. They choose instead to spread water over the greatest possible acreage with the accent on increased total production rather than on the highest per-acre yield."[83] Soon, however, irrigation from the Ogallala aquifer would no longer be an emergency measure when all else failed.

Farmers turned their increased wartime and postwar profits not only to consumer goods, accelerated mortgage payments, and more land purchases, but also to pumping plants and complex irrigation systems. Commitment to irrigation came earliest on the Texas High Plains, where the number of irrigation wells rose from more than 2,500 in 1941 to 4,300 in 1945. The Little Dust Bowl on the Texas Plains lasted from 1947 through 1956, a longer drought than that of the 1930s. In response, Texas farmers drilled more than 5,000 wells each year in 1953, 1955, and 1957. Compared to 8,400 wells in 1948, there were more than 42,200 wells by 1957 that irrigated 3.5 million acres on the Texas High Plains alone. After three decades of prosperity, by

1977 farmers on the Texas High Plains could afford over 71,000 wells, each pumping furiously. The least-expensive well and pumping system doubled its 1938 price to about $4,000. Drilling and casing a basic well ran approximately $1,300, the pump and gear head about $2,200, and a small automobile engine five hundred dollars.[84] The machinery fulfilled its promise by making farming much more efficient and reliable. Farmers pridefully believed, as they watched the throbbing engines and pumps, shiny pipes, and gushing water, that they had at long last entered the modern machine age.

The extended postwar era of extraordinarily cheap fuels lasted until the energy crisis of 1973. Gasoline sold for 11.5 cents a gallon in 1947 and would not top 35 cents until the early 1970s. It assured the widespread use of internal-combustion automobile or specialized industrial engines. There seemed to be little interest in shifting to more flexible electric motors when the federal Rural Electrification Administration brought electricity to remote farmsteads in the southwest Kansas and the Oklahoma-Texas Panhandle after World War II. Typical cost for the occasional electric pumping motor was 49 cents an hour in 1947, compared with 26 to 37 cents' worth of fuel an hour for a butane-powered engine and 40 to 52 cents an hour for a gasoline engine.

Often irrigators could depend on free natural gas tapped from gas and oil wells on their own land. The world's second-largest field of natural gas, the Hugoton-Guymon field, had been known since 1904 to exist under the Dust Bowl country, but its promise for irrigation energy was first promoted in 1927. A Plainview, Texas, dealer reported in 1949 that he sold liquefied petroleum gas (LPG) for more than 5,000 irrigation and tractor engines; by 1952, almost two-thirds of the 16,500 irrigation units on the Texas High Plains were powered by newly commercial LP, butane, or propane gas.[85] It is relatively easy to convert gasoline engines to propane. In 1947, fuel from a farmer's own storage tank cost about eight cents a gallon. Widespread access to natural gas meant that by 1958 more than two-thirds of Texas High Plains farmers had shifted to it, compared with only 3 percent before 1952. The cost of natural gas per acre-foot (including depreciation, interest, taxes, repairs, and other costs) of irrigation was $5.15, compared with electricity's $6.58 per acre foot, $7.53 for LP gas, and $8.70 for gasoline. Nevertheless, many

158

farmers were most comfortable with their long experience with gasoline engines.

Once committed to irrigation, the plains farmer found that his work habits changed. His physical labor was different, but not eased. He had less direct contact with his soil and water and more with the mechanisms—pumps, gearboxes, motors, valves, and piping—of his watering systems. Sometimes he worked like an unskilled factory laborer in the daily maintenance of his leaky, grinding, noisy machinery. Frederick H. Newell had predicted as early as 1896 that the irrigation farmer would no longer work like the traditional seasonal farmer.[86] His work became both intensive (tied to the seasons) and extensive (year-round activity). Donald E. Green writes:

> Labor began with preparing the soil in the winter. . . . Preparation included discing, chiseling, and applying fertilizer. Preplanting irrigation was required in the early spring if little moisture had accumulated during the winter. In the spring farmers also watered wheat. . . . Irrigators . . . harvested wheat, and planted grain sorghum in June. During July and August . . . grain sorghum required cultivation and irrigation. And through the summer, farmers "side-dressed" their crops with fertilizer and periodically sprayed insecticides on growing plants. Then in the fall winter wheat had to be planted . . . and combines gathered the grain sorghum crop.[87]

Green also describes the intensive labor of long daily and even nightly hours:

> Farmers often had to "make a set" during the late night or early morning. The spectacle of pickup trucks driving down country roads at 2:00 A.M., the bobbing of flashlights across distant fields, and the incessant distant roar of hundreds of irrigation engines became commonplace during what had once been the still of a plains summer night. As one reporter described the scene, ". . . big business is going on, and big engines are pumping a drink for the crops from several feet under the ground." A spade and a pair of rubber boots in the back of a mud-splattered pickup truck marked the High Plains irrigator.[88]

The mechanization of irrigation promoted intensive farming on the High Plains instead of traditional extensive dryland farming. Mechanization and new technologies reduced the heavy labor needs and farmhand costs required to manage the old mud ditches. Equipment investment for irrigated land was two to three times more than that for dryland farming. In the late 1950s a 320-acre dryland farm typically had about $6,600 worth of equipment, while a 320-acre irrigated farm invested in $18,000 worth of equipment.[89] Irrigated farms averaged 250 acres and used water from as many as five wells. Land values rose rapidly for productive irrigated land: Dust Bowl land in 1935 cost no more than $20 or $30 an acre; by 1948, dryland farms ranged from $50 per acre to as high as $125, while irrigated land sold for as much as $300 an acre and no less than $150 an acre. To the south, in Lubbock, Texas, where irrigation long had prospered, farmland was valued at more than $400 an acre.[90]

By the late 1950s, the machinery for widespread irrigation was in place to exploit the vast soaked beds of gravel and sand of the Ogallala aquifer. To the plains farmer, the prize was worth the effort. How long he would enjoy the prize, two billion gallons of usable Ogallala water, is another story.

5

. . .

A Tale of Three
Water-Conservation Districts

Farmers typically refuse to treat water as a regular economic good, like fertilizer, for example. It is, they say, a special product and should be removed from ordinary market transactions so that farmers can control conflict, maintain popular influence and control, and realize equity and social justice.—Arthur Maass and Raymond L. Anderson in a 1980 study

The current paradox of High Plains irrigation is how to have one's cake while also gulping it down. Plains farmers are as dependent on irrigation as cigarette smokers are on nicotine: they cannot break the habit without paying a heavy price. Nor can corn and alfalfa survive without their seasonal fix of thirty inches of water. Cattle in feedlots demand a bare minimum eight gallons a day per animal, often soaring to fifteen gallons a day. As water levels decline, there will be a ripple effect on what had once been called "externalities."[1] Suppliers of irrigation equipment will shut down, bankers will be forced to foreclose on worthless land, scarce grains will inflate consumer prices of bread and beef, and American foreign policy might have no grain surpluses to influence needy nations. Almost thirty years of water on demand since the late 1950s has created a lulling security that has masked the tremendous struggle to grow abundant crops under Dust Bowl conditions.

The transition from exploitation to conservation of Ogallala groundwater is not going smoothly. The idea of conservation goes against the conventional stream of American progress, and plains irrigators during the 1960s,

1970s, and 1980s were still celebrating their victory. For generations Americans saw limitless resources on an unpeopled continent, and European visitors were amazed at American wastefulness compared to their own stewardship in crowded countries. Environmental historians Joe Petulla and Roderick Nash have chronicled the difficult break from wastefulness.[2] Postwar industrialization soaked up resources faster than ever, and until recently few plains irrigators paid any attention to the reality that Ogallala water levels were beginning to drop one or two or three feet each year. Those state agencies specifically appointed to manage the water joined the irrigation boom.

Whatever their claims in favor of conservation, the first objective of the three agencies described in this chapter is the profitable consumption of groundwater. The oldest, dating from 1951, is the regional Texas High Plains Underground Water Conservation District No. 1, followed by the statewide Oklahoma Water Resources Board in 1972 and the regional Southwest Kansas Groundwater Management District No. 3 in 1976. On the High Plains, "groundwater management" is still a surrogate phrase for "economic development." Today, even with well-meaning local control, groundwater mining is still five to ten times bigger than any recharge.

As a result, modern Cassandras still speak ill of plains prospects. In 1984, California law professor Frank J. Trelease wrote: "Only two states [New Mexico and Colorado] on the fringes of the [Ogallala] aquifer have recognized that irrigation use of this water is a mining process, and that when the water is exhausted (or fallen too deeply) the overlying farmland must revert from irrigated crops back to dryland wheat or cattle grazing."[3] Earlier, in 1977, a federal General Accounting Office report described dangerously high "ground water overdrafting" levels on the Texas High Plains that would predictably make irrigation fall from almost 8 million acres in 1975 to 2.2 million in 2020, leading to "significant social and economic dislocations. . . . A return to dryland farming could substantially reduce the income of the farmers in the area [whose] per capita income was less than the national average and was projected to decline over time."[4] Despite their common hostility toward the radical plans of Frank and Deborah Popper, all the farmers interviewed for this book acknowledged that the end of widespread irrigation is inevitable.

Still, the High Plains have a distinct advantage over other water-needy parts of the country. Agriculture is by far the highest consumer, taking 90 percent of plains water. The old Dust Bowl region of the High Plains—southwest Kansas and the Texas-Oklahoma Panhandle—has no major metropolitan cities to compete for water. Lubbock and Amarillo in Texas, Guymon in Oklahoma, Liberal and Garden City in Kansas are unlikely to become new Denvers, Phoenixes, or Tucsons. Elsewhere in the West, the uncontrolled growth of cities brought on water wars (depicted in the movie *Chinatown*) in California, Arizona, New Mexico, and Colorado. Outside the plains, western water, historically applied to farm fields, is being shifted more and more to crowded populations that can pay a thousandfold more for it than farmers. Sixty-two miles north of Denver, for example, water supplied by the Big Thompson project is being transferred from "underutilized" farm use at forty dollars an acre-foot to urban use at more than twelve hundred dollars an acre-foot.[5]

For a long time irrigators were tranquilized by the size of the resource. The three billion acre-feet of water in the gravel beds of the Ogallala, which allowed hundreds of thousands of gallons to be pumped daily from individual wells, made Ogallala water seem inexhaustible. Or irrigators, like early settlers of the Texas High Plains, continued to believe that it was an inexhaustible resource, a massive fast-flowing subterranean river instead of irreplaceable water trickling slowly through gravel beds.[6] The original myth told of a grand underground river that swept down from the snowfields of the Rocky Mountains as far away as Canada. An outlandish Captain Livermore, who told stories of subterranean rivers from the Arctic, found his way into reminiscences of old-timers in the Texas Panhandle. Don H. Biggers, who began irrigating land in Lubbock County in 1911, remembered that the water moved across the bottom of his pit well at a mile an hour. "Livermore was right. It was not melted snow from distant mountains, but glacier water from the Arctic, thousands of miles away. How it gets to the Plains and then spreads out is a matter to be worked out."[7] Ironically, the most ambitious construction project proposed in the 1970s was the multibillion-dollar North American Water and Power Alliance, which was to bring water from northwest Canada to the plains through vast sluices shaped from the valleys of the Rockies.

Popular belief in the inexhaustible resource lasted into the 1950s; geologists and hydrologists, however, had been drawing less-sanguine conclusions since the 1910s. Contrary to that state's usual optimism, the first accurate analyses came from Texas. In 1938 the senior hydrologist of the U.S. Geological Survey, Walter N. White, warned at a Texas groundwater conservation meeting that "practically everywhere that large supplies of water can be obtained from wells the popular belief has developed that the water is inexhaustible. This belief in many parts of the United States has led to disastrous over-development."[8] At the time White gave his warning, early versions of efficient and powerful pumps already had begun to lower water levels on the Texas High Plains. In 1939 the Texas Board of Water Engineers reported that "there has been a general decline in the water table in the principal pumping districts of the High Plains during the last few years." In Deaf Smith County, water levels began to drop more than a foot a year, and in 1949 the board warned of exhaustion "within 5 to 10 years."[9] Accelerated by the stresses of the Little Dust Bowl of the 1950s, groundwater levels in the irrigated Texas High Plains averaged a decline of forty-three feet (and as much as one hundred feet in parts of Hale, Lubbock, and Floyd counties) in the twenty-two years between 1937 and 1959, well before the heavier demands of center-pivot irrigation systems were felt. The measure of water inexhaustibility depended not on the water itself, but on the speed and scale of the technology that could consume it.

High consumption was also encouraged by conflict over property rights and freedom of action. The problem of prior appropriation is not nearly as intense on the High Plains as in California or Arizona. The earliest irrigators, who got the best rights to use water, tended to overappropriate and overuse,[10] but the same general philosophy, use it or lose it, pervaded western irrigation everywhere. Overlapping drawdown cones between wells too close to each other made aggressive irrigators rush to flood their fields with groundwater before falling levels gave them dry wells. More cautious irrigators complained that aquifer levels were declining far too rapidly because of unnecessary consumption of too much water by others, sometimes for unneeded crops. A good supply of groundwater under a farmer's land not only assured him of on-demand water for crops, but doubled and tripled his property value and thus his borrowing power.

Usually the first legal step to regulate Ogallala groundwater was to restrict it to agriculture. Groundwater has been a public resource owned by each state since the federal government separated water from land in the Desert Land Act of 1877 and turned water over to the western states. All three states in this study adopted the guideline "reasonable beneficial use" and by it meant agricultural use. This was not only for economic survival, but because water dedicated to farming was regarded as an essential social good.[11] That is, its free use kept the independent farmer on the land, the productivity of irrigation guaranteed food surpluses, and thus it kept the nation strong and independent. Private use of this public resource was conditional; the irrigator could not waste the water he could rightfully take under his land by either nonagricultural or excessive use. Furthermore, the preambles of all the High Plains water agencies state that groundwater must be dedicated to farmland production. This is an unquestioned moral good. According to a 1936–37 Oklahoma Supreme Court decision, water use in the state must be controlled by "beneficial use" and "greatest need" for "agricultural stability."[12]

The second step is more efficient management of agricultural watering. Reasonable beneficial use is difficult to establish. Wasteful practices, declining water levels, questions of ownership, preservation of the farm economy, and, not least, fear of heavy-handed government intervention encouraged the creation of self-governing groundwater conservation districts on the High Plains.[13]

From the beginning, the High Plains water management agencies combined economic development and democratic participation. However, as Ogallala depletion becomes more extensive, these same interests are provid-

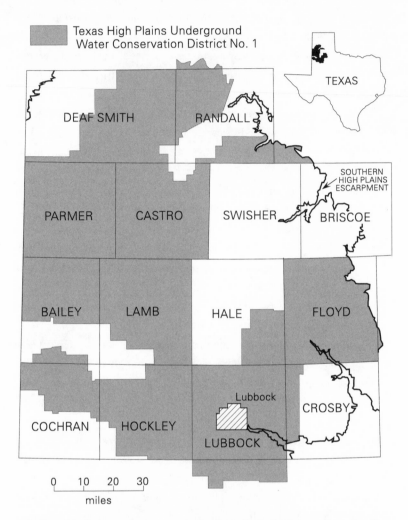

Texas High Plains Underground
Water Conservation District No. 1

TEXAS

DEAF SMITH   RANDALL

SOUTHERN
HIGH PLAINS
ESCARPMENT

PARMER   CASTRO   SWISHER   BRISCOE

BAILEY   LAMB   HALE   FLOYD

Lubbock

CROSBY

COCHRAN   HOCKLEY

LUBBOCK

0   10   20   30
miles

11. Outline of the first groundwater management district in the Ogallala aquifer region, Texas
High Plains Underground Water Conservation District No. 1, with headquarters in Lubbock.
Original boundaries were established by local vote in September 1952 and expanded to their current version in May 1967 and April 1969. Farmers in Swisher, Briscoe, and most of Hale counties refused to join. Redrawn from cover map, "Estimating Soil Moisture by Feel and Appearance," *Water Management Notice,* Texas High Plains Underground Water Conservation
District No. 1, Lubbock, Texas, September 1985.

ing the means to create long-term water conservation programs. Further, to a remarkable degree, the combination of development, conservation, and localism are consistent with recent global philosophies of sustainable development.[14] Conservation policymakers can keep long-term economic needs in mind even as they bring a shift away from raw economic exploitation for higher profits. The transition is helped by the fact that most High Plains farmers agree that their golden age of intensive irrigation, approximately between 1960 and 1990, is closing. The water economy of the High Plains (except for the water-rich Sandhills of western Nebraska) is moving from its exploratory-expansionist phase to its mature conservation phase.[15] Peak heavy use may have been recorded between 1978 and 1983 when irrigated land reached a high point of seventeen million acres, then declined to sixteen million acres in 1990.[16] During the past few decades, the very success of heavy irrigation from the Ogallala aquifer forced decisions to protect the flow from accelerated decline and the unacceptable phasing out of irrigation. Local populist management may be the way to shift from today's destructive development to a transitional conservation management toward sustainable development.

Texas High Plains Underground Water Conservation District No. 1
Unlike their Kansas counterparts two decades later, Texas High Plains irrigators in the 1940s lobbied vigorously against state legislation to regulate groundwater. If the Ogallala failed, farmers were convinced that there were stronger and deeper aquifers to make up deficits, and that new technologies, yet to come, would guarantee high recharge levels.[17] Plains farmers are determinedly independent, and Texas irrigators were unsurpassed in their prideful self-assurance.

The issue headed over the rights of private property. In 1947 the *Southwestern Crop and Stock* journal editorialized: "It is unsound to advocate to a farmer that he curtail pumping when with top market prices he can pay for his irrigation installation in the first year of its operation."[18] A November 1948 editorial pronounced that "West Texans can consider the water their own—to use or waste as they please."[19] But in 1949, Texas set a precedent by legislating the first underground water-conservation districts on the High

Plains. Its bedrock goal was to ensure the continued profitable industrialization of a depressed region. District No. 1 would be headquartered at Lubbock, where depletion was the worst. It would issue drilling permits, control well spacing, regulate water consumption, develop workable recharge (to refill the aquifer), and prevent water waste. Most important to the success of these measures, which appeared so radical, the groundwater district itself would be governed by a board of local irrigators. Individual landowners would continue to have exclusive rights to their water, but it would be managed water.

Virtually no one accepted the notion that the irrigator should give up his personal right to underground water. One Hockley County irrigator represented public opinion when he told the local newspaper, "I favor no control, but if we must have it, let it be local." Management by a state board was out of the question; federal control was unthinkable. Yet virtually everyone agreed with a 1950 editorial of the *Tulia Herald* of Swisher County: "If there is not some regulation of water pumpage there is a real danger—note the fall of the water table this year—of this country having to exist on dry farming and range economy." As the debate heated up, the *Amarillo Sunday News-Globe*, in a special report on May 28, 1950, quoted a farmer as saying, "What's caused this underground water crisis . . . Abuse of our natural resources, that's what caused it. . . . It's those who want to squeeze every last drop of wealth from the land every year." But another said he was "somewhat puzzled about all this excitement over the wells going dry. . . . My well has been going good since 1936, and it's still going strong." Another reflected the dominant mood: "All the water under my land belongs to me. No government, no association, nobody can tell me how to use it. I've never wasted any water in my life. I couldn't afford it. . . . I don't intend to live in a country full of Hitlerism laws."

In a regional vote on September 29, 1951, two entire counties—Lubbock and Parmer—and parts of eleven other counties—Lynn, Lamb, Hockley, Deaf Smith, Floyd, Castro, Bailey, Armstrong, Randall, Potter, and Cochran—voted to form Texas's first groundwater management district. Significantly, three of the most intensively irrigated counties, Hale, Swisher, and

Crosby, refused to join. (In May 1967 parts of Hale County did join, followed in April 1969 by parts of Crosby County.) Ultimately, an area of 8,149 square miles, or 5,215,600 acres, would be served by the new district. Texas High Plains Underground Water Conservation District No. 1 opened for business in April 1952 and on February 1, 1953, set forth its first regulations covering all full-scale irrigation wells (pumping 100,000 gallons per day or more). Compliance was voluntary. In the meantime, land under pump expanded from 650,000 irrigated acres in 1946 to 2,700,000 irrigated acres in 1954.[20]

The district regulations did not provide immediate relief. Between 1951 and 1958, the average water level fell twenty-eight more feet. In 1954, at least six farmers who started irrigating in 1953 were back into dryland farming. The general manager of the district concluded that "our conservation program is about twenty-five years or more too late." In June 1950 the *Tulia Herald* had asked, "Which is better, a super abundance for a few years and then nothing or reasonable abundance for many years?" In 1954 the district's regulations on new wells set minimum distances from existing wells: four-inch pumps were 200 yards, five-inch 250 yards, six-inch 300 yards, and eight-inch 400 yards. Old wells could not be replaced with larger ones without a permit.[21]

Most important, a unit of government was created to follow environmental lines. It made physical geology primary, in this case the thick underground layer of water-filled gravel and sand. Although political and economic boundaries were not eliminated (three counties overlying the aquifer voted against joining the district), nevertheless the intent of the district was to cross man-made borders to establish a management program suited to a natural resource. All in all, formation of District No. 1 was a remarkable political step to identify and manage an environmental entity. It had been anticipated only by the creation of soil conservation districts by the Soil Conservation Service in the 1930s. The idea of districts along nature's lines was surprising in light of the long tradition of the extremely rigid geometric patterning of the land—sections and quarter sections—by the historic federal land survey and sale since 1785.[22]

Wayne Wyatt has been manager and groundwater hydrologist of District No. 1 for many years, and over the last thirty-five he has seen the best of times and the worst of times as farmer, irrigator, and district manager. "I began my farming career when I was in high school. In the early fifties we were in the most severe drought we had ever seen. Our production was virtually zero. I bought cows for $400 and sold them for $175 after buying alfalfa and feeding them for two years."[23] Family friends staked him to an education at Texas Tech University, where he studied agriculture and ended up in hydrology. He also struggled with bare-bones farming on rented land with his brother, who was two years older. Only years later did he discover that the loans they received for tractors and combines were secretly cosigned by his landlord to help the two young men. In the 1950s, he remembers, "there was no federal support, no deficiency payments, nothing. I was living off mother and dad, living at home. Dad survived but he was a pretty tough gent. I didn't survive."

Out of his own youthful experience, Wyatt agrees with Phil Tooms in Kansas and Roger Trescott in Oklahoma that a young farmer today is even less likely to succeed in the still-harsh Dust Bowl country without friendly cash aid. Wayne Wyatt concludes that the older generation stood their ground for the sake of the farm lifestyle more than for the promise of financial success: "Well, let's squeeze this back to my dad. He's 78 years old now. He was good as a farmer. He didn't worry about making money or not. He made a damn good crop he could be proud of. Finally he got old enough that his energy level was not adequate. He'd still love to go out there today. He's out at my place today, working outside."

Thirty years later, in the 1980s, even with federal supports, the picture is worse because of heavy debts for land and equipment. Said Wyatt: "Ten years ago you could have a crop failure and in two years be out. You could manage to pay off your debt and be back into an opportunity for profits. [Today] you really got to have four out of five good years. Now if you have crop failure or something, it takes you ten years to recover." Despite the recognized virtues of irrigation, farming remains a high-risk, undependable activity. The High Plains region is still one of the toughest places to farm in the

United States. Wyatt observed that "climatic conditions, hail storms, personal management skill, and plain old circumstances—a single isolated bad misjudgment—would get people into a hell of a mess." Despite all the improvements, the 1980s were more troublesome to farmers than the 1970s, and no farmer who was interviewed for this book believed that the 1990s promised better days. The 1990s could be worse.[24]

Love of farming even in thin times, and loyalty to harvesting "a damn good crop" despite dry land and scarce water, make Wayne Wyatt's job at District No. 1 satisfying. Seated in his pleasant air-conditioned office in an unpretentious one-story building on a shady side street near downtown Lubbock, Wyatt does not seek to turn the world upside down solely to protect Ogallala water and save the small farmer. As is true in Oklahoma, where the matter went to the state supreme court, major oil companies in Texas also tap vast amounts of groundwater for secondary and tertiary oil recovery. But Wyatt plays down the impact. "Of the total water used, the oil companies take on the order of 2 to 3 percent or less in a particular county, like ours. So we really don't find any sufficient problem with it. It isn't that big of a deal. Even local people can't seem to get concerned about it. Most of the time the way the oil company does business, they buy the ground, they buy the ground water, and they've got a right to use it. They have to get the permits for the wells just like any irrigator and we issue the permits. As long as they don't infringe on the rights of the adjoining landowners, and we don't see any major pollution problems occurring, we don't interfere. Haven't for years."

While sidestepping the trading-water-for-oil-recovery controversy, the district tries to reassure farmers of their private property rights. A brochure distributed by the district quotes a March 1956 editorial by Allan White in the district's newsletter, *The Cross Section,* to promise suspicious farmers that Hitlerism is not on the way: "The Water District was not created to do away with the rights of the individual but rather . . . to maintain those . . . rights and . . . provide for orderly development and wise use of our own water." The brochure also claims that "the powers that can be exercised by districts under this law supplant and exceed the ground-water regulatory powers of any other unit of government, either State or Federal.''[25] Popular representation also is evident in the district's structure: a five-member board of directors supported by five-member committees from each of the fifteen counties, "a grassroots network of 80 elected officials." According to the brochure, when the district was formed by popular vote in September 1952, financing for it was established by a maximum tax of fifty cents per hundred dollars of county and state valuation. In 1952 the district's net tax revenue was $42,189.31 based on five cents per hundred dollars per acre. In 1973, on the same nickel rate, the district netted $283,453.40, a sevenfold gain in twenty years. In 1984 the actual rate was seven and a quarter mills per hundred dollars of valuation, still a small percentage of the allowable maximum.

The state legislation, Underground Water Districts Act of 1949, provided that districts "make and enforce Funds to provide for conserving, preserving, protection, recharging, and preventing waste of the underground water."[26] From the first it was clear that the mission of a district was not groundwater preservation but its most efficient use, even if that is also its greatest use. This included detailed geological and hydrological surveys "for development, production and use of the water" as well as to "determine limitations which should be made on withdrawing underground water." Recharge is a major agenda, but with little practical progress. The district is also the administrative center for well permits, drillers' logs, and record keeping on drilling, spacing, and production of wells.[27] To this Wayne Wyatt added that the district disseminates scientific data and reports on new technologies to encourage water efficiency and guarantee continued prosperity for regional irrigators.

The line drawn between Ogallala water conservation and Ogallala water development may be a difference of style more than substance. In 1975 the district distributed a policy paper by Frank A. Rayner, who emphasized (Rayner's italics) that

> *there must be groundwater development before there can be groundwater management—groundwater management is groundwater development.* Groundwater management is not prohibiting groundwater development; it is finding equitable means for making reasonable use

of groundwater supplies. . . . *Groundwater management is prohibiting the vested interests of the few from thwarting the best interests of the many.*[28]

In this populist-cum-entrepreneur mode, Rayner opposed closing any groundwater basin to further development or additional well drilling. He fervently argued that such control and regulation hobbles the study of existing water supplies and closes exploration for "new and deeper groundwater supplies by severing the profit incentive expected from the drilling and developing of new and deeper water wells. . . . the ultimate solution of local problems primarily rests with the local unit of government." Rayner concluded:

What is groundwater management? The individual extracting water from a well constitutes groundwater management—whether his use of the groundwater is for a beneficial or wasteful purpose. . . . Since most wells are privately owned, groundwater management is the management of private properties, and the resultant management of individuals—a people management problem.[29]

Despite the attempt to bring the boundaries of the district into convergence with the boundaries of the aquifer, Rayner noted that the creation of the district in 1951 had little to do with environmental protection. Instead, it meant the protection of farmers' groundwater as valuable private property. He was convinced that the pressures of the 1950s drought threatened direct state and federal intervention. As a result, the district's own irrigators had to take control of their own destinies.[30] He argued (the italics are his):

Under the present private ownership of groundwater—the landowner owns all groundwater tarrying beneath his land—there are absolutely no legal constraints preventing . . . local governments from acquiring and developing groundwater, *if* they purchase it from the landowner. However . . . if groundwater was the property of the State, and if the State would issue a groundwater permit to some local authority, it could develop the landowners' groundwater without the present purchase cost. . . . [At issue is] the all American profit motive.[31]

173

By 1978, only three years after Rayner's policy paper for the district, the Texas Supreme Court moved to prevent groundwater waste: withdrawing groundwater could be "negligent" and "willfully wasteful."[32] By 1982 the district's newsletter, *The Cross Section,* reported that wasteful open ditches were a thing of the past. It reported water savings through tailwater recapture, dropped sprinkler heads on center-pivot systems to reduce evaporation loss, control of well spacing, and cost-in-water tax-depletion allowances.[33]

Based on the premise, according to Wayne Wyatt, that "we're going to run out of money [to pay for pumping] before we run out of water," the district provides detailed hydrological atlases for each of its fifteen counties. "If you have 100 feet of saturated thickness, you ought to get 1,000 gallons per minute. If you go down to 50 feet of saturated thickness, you might be able to get 200 gallons per minute. You would have to drill additional wells to maintain" center-pivot irrigation equipment. "Say you're drawn bone dry down to 25 feet. You can figure out well yield is only 50 gallons and 50 gallons would probably not be economical. At that point the irrigator would say no, I'm through irrigating." Since at least 50 percent of land value depends on the capacity to irrigate, the results would be devastating. Wyatt concludes that the high point was reached in 1983, when top-quality irrigated land sold for eight hundred dollars an acre, and prices have fallen 15 to 20 percent since then. Dryland farming is no alternative when it comes to land values.

The district devotes a great deal of attention to irrigation efficiency (water use and cost related to crop prices) to keep the water running, particularly in view of pumping costs that are likely to increase four to ten times. A major goal is to ensure that future crops can be irrigated even when pumping rates drop below fifty gallons per minute. This includes new low-pressure overhead sprinklers, soil moisture monitoring, irrigation scheduling, tailwater and other water reuse systems, recharge through small rainwater-storage lakes called playas, furrow dikes (rediscovered from 1930s conservation practices), low- or no-tillage practices (also practiced since the earliest dryland farming days), and the science of crop water consumption. As elsewhere, when the mature irrigation phase is reached, the trend is away from historic overpumping and toward minimum-water-use conservation.

Even while Ogallala waters showed important declines in District No. 1, irrigators still had mixed feelings about extensive water management because "when you start talking about a man's water, you get into real trouble." According to a 1975 survey, seven of every ten irrigators supported the way the district was doing its job, although one farmer reflected the minority view when he said, "All I want is to be left alone. If I can't make it on my own I'll go out of the farming business. This is the way it ought to be with everything. Survival of the fittest." But most agreed with the irrigator who supported local regulation "because I fear large corporate farming operations . . . that can drill too many wells . . . and would get all the water."[34]

Wayne Wyatt concludes that High Plains irrigation is still flourishing in its own golden age, which began after World War II and will extend into the early 1990s. He says that after 1993 irrigation will begin a gradual but inevitable decline. At that time, Ogallala water will become scarce enough and costly enough that even the best irrigators, now defined as the most water-efficient irrigators, will have to reduce the acres they water. They will be ready, since they have been practicing more efficient sprinkling since gas costs began to climb during the energy crisis of the mid-1970s. But attached to this accomplishment were the high technological costs and capital debts of an industrial enterprise. Virtually all farmers interviewed for this book said success or failure depend less on hands-on farming skills and more on the solid knack for business management described in the next chapter.

The Oklahoma Difference: TCIWRA versus OWRB

America's legal system encourages vast open spaces for profitable maneuvering by individuals and corporations. Despite the recent growth of regulations concerning natural resources, strict water management still constitutes a sketchy web rather than an all-inclusive net.

This sievelike regulatory process is nowhere more evident than in the interaction among three natural resources in the Oklahoma Panhandle. Fuel from the Hugoton-Guymon field is used to pump fresh Ogallala water, the largest and most exploited aquifer in the nation, to recover oil from old oil fields. This process is the result of technological prowess, the profit motive, old-boy politics, and the fastest possible consumption of irreplaceable natural resources.

On December 20, 1984, after fifty-two months of costly litigation, the Oklahoma Supreme Court found against the Oklahoma Water Resources Board. The OWRB had granted a temporary permit that allowed a New York-based company, Mobil Oil Corporation, to pump fresh Ogallala groundwater into an old oil field, the Morrow, to push out some of the remaining oil. The most prominent member of the OWRB is Robert S. Kerr, Jr., of Kerr-McGee Oil. The *Oklahoma Observer* editorialized in its January 10, 1986, issue that "the Oklahoma Water Resources Board has always been a cruel hoax, poorly administered, universally condemned by those who cherish Oklahoma's environment, under constant attack from a handful of rapacious oil operators." It also took a shot at Kerr: "Bob Kerr's father was Mr. Water in Oklahoma. . . . [He] would weep if he could see the crassness of his namesake today."[35]

Secondary or tertiary oil recovery involves the injection of water under pressure into an oil-bearing formation; the oil is pushed by the water toward an existing well. But since oil and water do not normally mix, the water soon bypasses the oil, which in turn is trapped. To overcome this problem, a slug of chemical surfactant (similar to a modern household detergent) is injected, which allows the oil to mix with the passing water and continue on to the well. The surfactants frequently are chemicals—at best carbon dioxide and alcohols but often phenols—that are toxic to plants, livestock, and humans even at very low concentrations. Commonly used polymers, such as polyacrylamide, and aluminum solutions permanently contaminate the water and threaten to contaminate formations through which they pass. The concentration of chemicals in the water is fifteen thousand times greater than the federal Environmental Protection Agency water-quality limit for drinking water.[36]

The process is called waterflood. It was opposed by the Texas County Irrigation and Water Resources Association, a citizens group made up of irrigators dependent on the Ogallala aquifer in the Oklahoma Panhandle. Unlike Texas and Kansas, Oklahoma has no water conservation districts; instead, the Oklahoma Water Resources Board administers a statewide master plan. On paper the plan is exemplary and is intended to favor agriculture, but without local districts, citizen-interest groups have come to play a key role. The association insisted the waterflood illegally wasted fresh water when saltwa-

12. Ownership of land and wells in Texas County, Oklahoma. Section of a privately published county map of Texas County, Oklahoma. According to local farmers and irrigation district officials in the old Dust Bowl region, the most informative maps are these county maps identifying the locations of oil and gas wells and, particularly, the ownership of sections, half sections, quarter sections, and quarter quarter sections. Ownership includes the right to pump water. Mobil Oil and Cities Service are two of the largest landowners in the excerpt shown above. Map reprinted by permission of Kansas Blue Print Company, Inc., Wichita, Kansas.

ter could be pumped from another, deeper aquifer. The association deftly turned the problem into an environmental and moral debate as well as a legal action and an economic quarrel. Quoting the legislation that created the board, including a unambiguous statement about the beneficial use of water for agriculture, the association condemned the permit. It was wasteful of irreplaceable water, caused permanent harm to the environment, was not cost-effective in the long term, and served no beneficial interest except, inappropriately, Mobil's short-term profits.

The temporary permit spanned twenty years, through 1998. Critics were suspicious because the company began its fresh-water use for oil recovery in 1965 with no permit or hearings about waste, pollution, or beneficial use. By 1979 it had consumed almost 25,000 acre-feet, or more than 8 billion gallons. The company began by leasing water rights to 3,442 acres overlying the aquifer. In its temporary permit it sought to take each year an average of 6,375 acre-feet of fresh groundwater and pump it into the oil field. In Texas County alone, Mobil's project soon covered 24,540 acres with ninty-six injection wells. The final result is a thirty-three-year waterflood that began in 1965 and is to end in 1998, consuming more than 24 billion gallons of water to force up 46 million gallons of leftover oil, a ratio of 520 gallons of water consumed on site to produce a gallon of oil.[37]

The association demanded review of the board's ruling because, it argued, Mobil's freshly pumped water, to be effective, had to be blended with chemicals to move the oil. Such used water could not be returned to the natural hydrological cycle. It was "polluted and lost permanently," not available for human, animal, or plant consumption. Mobil Oil countered that its use was beneficial under Oklahoma water law. Mobil merely borrowed the water from the state, used it in the oil field, then pumped it down into storage in a deep shelf of porous rock, the Glorieta formation. The confrontation was between the oil company, which put no cash value on the water because it concluded that technology would eventually find a way to clean the used water of additives and oil residues, and irrigator groups, who claimed the water was "limited, valuable and irreplaceable." Mobil engineer R. A. Irwin argued in 1985 that "there is no waste because it is reused and reused and re-

used. It will [eventually] be recycled seven to ten times."[38] Mobil attorney
Gary Davis pointed out at a December 3, 1985, meeting of the Oklahoma
Water Resources Board that if Mobil's use of fresh water was waste by pollution, other beneficial uses were, too. "Irrigation water is lost down ditches,
to evaporation, and to the Gulf of Mexico; but the water used in the Mobil
process would remain in Oklahoma for future consumption."[39]

The association opposed three specific practices allowed by Mobil Oil's
permit. The first was to take fresh Ogallala water from five hundred feet and
pump it down six thousand feet into the Morrow gas and oil formation,
where it was "permanently removed from nature's water cycle." Saltwater
from the Glorieta aquifer at nine hundred feet was available to Mobil, costing the company $0.52 cents more per barrel, reducing profit from $12.03 to
$11.51 per barrel. The company would save about $24 million over a thirty-
three-year period. Second, the water was moved too many times through the
Ogallala, raising the risk of pollution from leaking pipes. The water would
be raised from the Ogallala to the surface, then pumped down through it to
the oil field, then the used water would be returned to the surface and
pumped down again to storage in the Glorieta, a total of four risky operations. Third, there was the risk of "fracking," in which Ogallala water could
be lost or polluted by geological cracks or crevices that caused mingling of
fresh, salt, and polluted water, particularly with the changing pressures of
forced injections.

The momentum was in Mobil Oil's favor. Legislation in 1972 emphasized
"reasonable" and "beneficial" groundwater use regardless of heavy depletion. In a 1977 case, *Texas County Irrigation* v. *Cities Service Oil Co.*,[40] the
Oklahoma Supreme Court had "stamped its imprimatur on the use of fresh
groundwater in secondary oil recovery." This was called the Texas County
Doctrine. But in its 1984 turnaround decision, the Oklahoma Supreme Court
quoted critically from the 1972 law: "Waste of water means any act permitting or causing the pollution of fresh water or the use of such water in an inefficient manner or any manner that is not beneficial."[41] The court used a definition of pollution—turning fresh water into waste water—from a 1981 law:

Pollution means contamination or other alteration of the physical, chemical or biological properties of any natural waters of the State or such discharge of any liquid, gaseous, or solid substance into any waters of the State as will or is likely to create a nuisance or render such waters harmful or detrimental or injurious to public health, safety, or welfare, or to domestic, commercial industrial, agricultural, recreational, or other legitimate beneficial uses, or to livestock, wild animals, birds, fish, or other aquatic life.[42]

Contamination would occur as the fresh water was used in the oil field; discharge would take place as the used water was removed and stored in the Glorieta saltwater aquifer at six thousand feet.

The court then chided the OWRB: "Mere recitation that the Board finds that waste will not occur is insufficient. A finding of no waste must be supported by evidence in the record." It then noted that the evidence "establishes undisputively that the tertiary [waterflood] process proposed by Mobil is one in which [contaminating] detergent additives and polymers will be mixed with the fresh water to reduce the water's surface tension so that more oil can be recovered from the formation." Not only had Mobil tried to ignore the effects of the additives, it had not yet explained how the contaminated water would be disposed of, only "somehow." Nor had Mobil submitted documentation required by the OWRB's own regulations concerning alternative use of saltwater, total project costs, the expected amount of recovered oil or gas, and why fresh water was desired. Instead, Mobil merely stated the costs of oil recovery as compared with irrigation of certain crops.

The court ordered the board to reexamine Mobil's request in light of its own rules. Justice Evonne Kauger added her concurring opinion:

I am still concerned with the responsibility we share to prevent the unbridled consumption of fresh groundwater and to exercise both the will and the wisdom to conserve the good earth, with the certain knowledge that unless we act, the Ogallala aquifer probably will be exhausted by the year 2020. We cannot wait until tomorrow to worry about this problem. It must be faced today, before the last acre-foot of water is sucked from the breast of the Ogallala, and the Panhandle becomes a desolate desert—a stark and silent monument to our unwillingness responsibly to function, and a place where the price of water exceeds the price of oil. . . . I can think of no commodity which affects and concerns the citizens of this state more than fresh groundwater.

She concluded that "the issuance of the temporary permit [to Mobil Oil] was an invalid exercise of jurisdiction by the Oklahoma Water Resources Board" because it had failed to follow its own fact-finding procedures. In fact, she noted, at the time, January 8, 1980, that the board granted Mobil's temporary permit, it had not yet established its own rules concerning the use of fresh water for oil recovery. It seemed curious, she said, that this was done almost three months later, on March 31, 1980. She then concluded:

Because no rules had been adopted by the Board, it had no authority to conduct a hearing, to take evidence, to make findings of fact, or to issue temporary permits to mine fresh groundwater for use in tertiary oil recovery. The issuance of the permit is void, invalid, and of no effect.

In a paraphrase of the board's own rules and regulations, Justice Kauger also concluded that "reasonable diligence and reasonable intelligence militate against the use of fresh groundwater in enhanced oil recovery operations." The board had encouraged wasteful consumption of fresh groundwater by giving Mobil a twenty-year deadline to consume a water resource at "not less than two acre-feet" per year. "The 'pie' is being divided without a determination of the size of the pie—yet everyone is consuming the pie," she said. She remembered that Mobil was seeking 51,211 acre-feet, or approximately sixteen billion gallons, of water. "If Mobil uses the amount of water it has the *right* to use under the terms of the temporary permit . . . Mobil can fill a family-size swimming pool every minute; it can fill an Olympic-size swimming pool every twenty-three minutes." Keeping the larger picture in mind, Kauger wrote: "While other states implement programs to conserve, protect from pollution, and guard with zeal the diminishing fresh water supplies, Oklahoma has initiated a program which by its very nature encourages complete consumption of its fresh groundwater within a twenty year span. . . . it is not a reasonable exercise of reasonable intelligence and reasonable diligence to sanction a process which causes a loss of unestimated billions of gallons of fresh groundwater. . . . The Dust Bowl was not a mirage." The justice observed that it was problematic enough that irrigation, a well-defined beneficial use, had already dropped the water table one hundred feet in forty years. If the same water source also was applied to enhanced recovery of oil, "no one can predict a twenty-year life-span. . . . The alarming facts are: one flood project by one company will use 16 billion gallons of fresh water; Mobil is not the only oil producer to use, or to desire to use the water; nor is the field to be flooded Mobil's only oil field or the only oil field which will be developed; nor is Oklahoma the only oil producing state that overlies the aquifer."

Nine days after the supreme court decision was issued, a flurry of pro-Mobil activity energized the Oklahoma legislature. Identical legislative bills, Senate Bill 282 and House Bill 1447, created a new state water policy that would no longer require fresh-water use-permit applicants to demonstrate that "waste will not occur."[43]

The Texas County Irrigation and Water Resources Association complained that "this legislation, if enacted, completely repeals and annuls the decision of the Supreme Court. It legalizes waste by pollution and waste by depletion under the guise of 'beneficial use.' " Texas County irrigator Bob Fowler said at a hastily convened hearing that the actions of the Oklahoma Water Resources Board, "the authorized agency to protect and conserve all of the waters of Oklahoma," is instead like "putting Dracula in charge of the Blood Bank."[44] Neighbor Roger Trescott testified that "unless the legislators can name the various tertiary methodologies, identify the chemicals that are allowed to be injected, understand the concentrations of toxicity that can be in the produced water, the potentially serious disposal problem . . . then they should not blindly rubber stamp this dangerous legislation." The TCIWRA attorney, Tom Dalton of Tulsa, reported that "the proposed law *falsely assumes* [his italics] that if groundwater has a 'beneficial' use, waste will not occur through pollution or depletion." State Sen. Tim Leonard opposed the bill because, unlike the supreme court decision, it tried to yoke together the concepts of beneficial and nonwasteful use, which were not identical concepts.

The association complained that the legislation would allow an oil producer to use a thousand barrels of fresh water to produce one barrel of oil and claim that it was a beneficial use of water. Was not fresh water wasted if saltwater could be used instead? Was not fresh water wasted by commingling with harmful chemicals? Would not water be wasted if after two or three decades of pumping, still 80 to 90 percent of the oil remained in the ground?[45] Gerald Hofferber of the association said, "Even in the use of fresh water for the highest and noblest purposes—sustaining life, cleanliness and health, it is possible under certain circumstances to waste it. . . . the same would be [even] true for agricultural purposes. If agriculture is actually polluting, then we too need to clean up our act, because no one has the right to waste our groundwater." But once the legislation removes the safeguard requiring that waste will not occur, it is easy to argue for any number of beneficial uses.

The association noted that Publication 25 of the Oklahoma Water Resources Board had already stated that fresh water should never be used for secondary recovery because it is lost forever. Said attorney Dalton: "This [new] legislation adopts as state policy the notion that you can contaminate and pollute water while using it, and not be required to clean it up. Under no other condition have you ever [before] been able to take and pollute water and leave it dirty for others to use." Another anti-Mobil argument was that the water polluted by the oil-recovery process was then stored in the Glorieta aquifer, an underground formation that Mobil had not purchased or leased. Virgil Higgins of the association wrote in 1975 that "this is not salt water disposal—it is really [polluted] salt water storage."[46] Irrigator Betty Trescott noted that free storage already existed with natural gas. Farmers make contracts with energy companies to pump natural gas from under their ground. The contracts are often "dedicated to perpetuity," or until the gas company wants the gas. "It's like having big gas tanks under ground. We store [the gas] for them, absolutely free," she said.

In October 1985 the Oklahoma Water Resources Board, pressured by the objections of the Texas County Irrigation and Water Resources Association, Save Our Water, Inc., and other groups, ordered an in-house report. The document stunned the board by recommending that Mobil Oil be refused the right to pump water from under the land it owned or leased. The report, compiled by OWRB staff, did accept Mobil's claim that the intended use of the groundwater "is a beneficial use,"[47] but it insisted that Mobil's use was waste by pollution and hence could not be permitted by state law. Mobil's argument took a desperate turn. "Virtually all uses of water, including irrigation and municipal uses, alter to some degree, the physical, chemical, or biological properties of ground water." Hence, argued Mobil, such a narrow reading of the law could prevent anyone from using the water, even the most efficient and virtuous irrigators, because any use of the water would modify the water. On this basis the board could not grant groundwater permits to anyone, yet Oklahoma water law promoted a "policy of utilization." The company claimed that the water left after a thirty-three-year recovery process would be "available in situ for withdrawal and use for further enhanced recovery use [and it] could be withdrawn, treated and used for all beneficial uses." The oil company defended its actions on the grounds that it is theoretically possible to find a technological fix to decontaminate or to reuse contaminated water. In contrast, the report given to OWRB concluded that "there is only a possibility that the water could be used for a beneficial use at some future time, without more [treatment, and] constitutes a loss of the water for beneficial use and therefore is waste by pollution."[48]

In an extraordinary strategy, Robert S. Kerr, Jr., moved that the board adopt only certain portions of the report, which, TCIWRA said, were "favorable to oil companies." The OWRB voted for Kerr's motion and Mobil, instead of a flat rejection based on the report, received another temporary permit to use 25,660 acre-feet of fresh Ogallala water in Texas County between 1985 and 2007.

The combination of a state agency and a powerful corporation were hard to beat. Like Texans, Oklahoma Panhandle irrigators worried about government interference. Now corporate America rifled their cash drawers as well. TCIWRA President Norman Steinle of Hooker wondered: "It is difficult to understand why five of the nine [OWRB members] considered themselves such instant experts as to reverse their own staff's recommendation at a [monthly meeting], lasting a few hours."[49] The association argued: "Someone should do an energy audit on this scheme. . . . no colony in darkest Africa has ever been more exploited than the Oklahoma Panhandle. Our natural gas is 'dedicated' to the industrial northeast. Our surface water is dedicated to Oklahoma City. And with passage of S.282 our valuable Ogallala groundwater will be dedicated to oil companies." Mobil wrote gas-lease holders who were receiving royalties from Mobil in a campaign to support Mobil's controversial application, but when these owners, many of them also irrigators, learned that fresh water would be depleted and polluted, they supported the denial instead. One owner who would receive royalties from the tertiary recovery, Allan Fischer of Hooker, Oklahoma, said, "I would prefer to go broke today farming and have fresh water for my children in the future."[50] TCIWRA worked to raise funds to file an appeal and urged area people to buy back the eight billion gallons of water Mobil sought to consume. Mobil Oil is continuing to use Texas County fresh water for tertiary recovery despite the 1984 Oklahoma Supreme Court decision. The matter is in litigation. There has been no cease-and-desist order.

A David against Goliath is Gene Barby, who operates a thirteen-thousand-acre family ranch on the eastern edge of the Oklahoma Panhandle. He is also a thirty-year veteran petroleum geologist with his own oil business. Barby has been president of the water-advocacy organization Save Our Water, Inc., and spokesman for the Oklahoma Cattlemen's Association. He complains that, with no permit, Mobil Oil had, since 1965, already consumed 8.1 billion gallons of fresh Ogallala water. Gene Barby testified:

The reason is nothing more than greed for corporate profits. It costs more to lift a barrel of brine water from 2700 feet than it costs to lift a barrel of fresh water from 500 feet. Lifting costs using brine water is 61 cents per barrel whereas lifting costs for fresh water is 11 cents per barrel. This amounts to less than 2 percent of the projected net income for the field, calculated over a 20 year life.[51]

Significantly, Mobil profit is tied much more closely to world oil prices. Barby observed that between 1961, when Mobil purchased the oil field, and 1985, the company made an eightfold profit as oil prices escalated from $3.30 a barrel to $27.50. He then reported on his own operation, in which he used saltwater from four thousand feet even when abundant shallow fresh water was available: "Yes, it was more expensive to lift this brine water, but the operators were independent oil men who were concerned with the environment." Later he observed that Mobil's claim "moves us miles backwards in conservation. It is a revolutionary concept that will cause disaster for our children and grandchildren." He was particularly agitated over the Mobil Oil statement that the use of fresh water for irrigation constituted a waste. "Who has ever suggested that using fresh water to grow crops is a waste?" he asked.

The Case of Kansas

Kansas irrigators now face the water scarcities that Lubbock farmers experienced two decades earlier. Garden City hydrologist Andy Erhart tried to make water conservation acceptable to farmers facing higher costs. Protection of Ogallala water would protect agriculture, the farm family, and irreplaceable resources. As early as 1957 in an article written for a special edition of the *Pratt Daily Tribune,* he set down the basic priorities by which he still operates. A well-planned and well-managed irrigation system needs to (1) increase the efficient use of available water supplies, (2) reduce labor requirements, (3) prevent excessive erosion, and (4) permit maximum production.[52] Southwest Kansas Groundwater Management District No. 3 was created in 1976 out of such thinking.

The district is legally dedicated to management and conservation (controlled use) of the groundwater under its jurisdiction. Its management of the Ogallala is widely accepted as the primary means for economic stability in the district. Its 1976 birth was a local initiative— the will of the people is repeatedly affirmed in the documentation—to build democratic bridges between individual freedom and community power. When the district was being planned, a citizens group, the Southwest Kansas Irrigation Association,

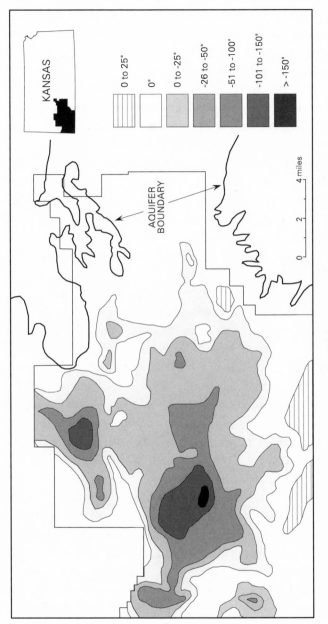

13. The region covered by the Southwest Kansas Groundwater Management District No. 3, showing water-level changes between 1940 and 1980. Redrawn from the May 1, 1986, "Revised Management Program III: Rules and Regulations, and Policies and Standards," Southwest Kansas Groundwater Management District No. 3, Garden City, Kansas.

KANSAS

0 to 25"
0"
0 to -25"
-26 to -50"
-51 to -100"
-101 to -150"
> -150"

AQUIFER
BOUNDARY

0   2   4 miles

held a series of town meetings in the fall of 1973 "to sense the will of the people" concerning the formation of a groundwater management district. A steering committee came out of the meetings to identify and organize a district that included all of eight counties and parts of five others in southwest Kansas. After state approval, Southwest Kansas Groundwater Management District No. 3 was organized in February 1976 by a large five-to-one majority (1,155 in favor, 230 opposed, an 83 percent majority) of the voters. The district exists as a localized corporation managed by a local board of thirteen directors serving staggered three-year terms, with four officers named by the board.

The case of F. Arthur Stone put Kansas water management to an early test. In December 1979, Stone, a Finney County irrigator southwest of Garden City, applied for permits to drill seven wells. In February 1980 his application on two of them was denied because they exceeded the area depletion rate. Stone drilled the two wells anyway. The driller he hired from across the border in Colorado remained silent; he needed the work. But in May 1980, to no one's surprise, Southwest Kansas Groundwater Management District No. 3 got wind of the wells, and in June the chief engineer of the Kansas Division of Water Resources ordered Stone to stop pumping water from the two wells. Stone and the engineer found themselves in an angry personal confrontation on Stone's land and the case went to court. Stone's attorneys argued that Kansas water laws were unconstitutional invasions, takings, and deprivations of private property. State attorneys argued that the regulations were a valid exercise of the police powers of the state to manage groundwater for public benefit. In 1981 the state supreme court upheld the state, and the district began prosecution of Stone on thirty-seven counts. Stone responded by moving, according to district bylaws, to disband the district, or at least to replace existing board members with his own candidates at the annual election. He failed in both attempts, but the Stone case signaled more litigation and conflict over the equitable distribution of water as Ogallala groundwater becomes more scarce.[53]

There is still confusion about who controls the water. Well into the 1940s, Kansans could claim three different water rights. Riparian rights involved ownership of land bordering a stream or natural lake, with equal claims by all owners to the infinitely adjustable reasonable-use policy. Absolute ownership based on traditional common law is the law of capture, or however much one can pump regardless of consequences to the water table or the neighbor's well. Prior appropriation is also known as "first in time, first in right" ownership. No matter how much water, or how little, or how much the supply has changed, the first user can still claim his entire original supply, even if later users run out. This was still beneficial and reasonable use. But one had always to consume his full allotment or forfeit his right: use it or lose it.[54]

For Kansans, the matter of who owned the water came home when in 1944 the Kansas Supreme Court struck down state laws based on the widely supported appropriation theory.[55] With surprising speed, the state legislature passed the 1945 Water Appropriation Act. It "solved" the problem by apparently taking no sides. It declared water a public resource which belonged to all the people of the state. Water was severed from land ownership; the state then took control of the water by controlling the allocation process. The effect of the law was to act according to prior-appropriation principles and continued support of the philosophy that "unused water is waste water."[56] It was said that only by undercutting riparian rights and common law for the sake of prior appropriation could Kansas water be profitably developed. Kansas water-law specialist Earl B. Shurtz wrote in 1967: "Unused water could not wisely be held in perpetuity for a common law owner who may never have use for it, without resulting in underdevelopment, permitting the water to flow out of the state and on toward the ocean, as an economic waste and loss of a valuable natural resource."[57] But according to state planners in 1982, if full use was made of appropriated rights each year, as the law still encourages, then western Kansas would run dry in twenty-five years.[58] The case of F. Arthur Stone demonstrated the classic confrontation between private rights and public interest that has characterized much of American resource history.

The district's 1986 *Management Programs* published the updated rules, regulations, policies, and standards of the district. It set a grass-roots-democracy tone by opening with an 1878 statement by John Wesley Powell:

The people in organized bodies can be trusted. . . . residents should have the right to make their own regulations . . . the entire arid region [should] be organized into natural hydrographic districts, each one to be a commonwealth within itself . . . the plan is to establish local self-government by hydrographic basins.[59]

District No.3 was organized to implement a recognized need to manage and conserve the groundwater supplies of the district. The appropriation of groundwater in Kansas, including specifications and regulations, had been institutionalized in the Kansas Groundwater Management District Act of 1972, which added local groundwater-management districts to the 1945 Kansas Division of Water Resources. The district has policies that control irrigation-well permits and spacing to promote water conservation and efficient water use. The intent is to prevent economic deterioration (for example, a return to dryland farming) and stabilize agriculture. Nevertheless about 18 percent of all the district's groundwater reserves had been consumed by 1990, and in some places it was more than 50 percent. Since 1978 a district also can designate some of its territory to be an "Intensive Groundwater Use Control Area," where levels are declining dramatically, where waste or deterioration exists, or where the "rate of withdrawal equals or exceeds the recharge rate."[60] The last includes almost all of southwest Kansas, and by 1984 four areas already had received the ominous IGUCA designation. In extreme cases, all new water development can be halted in such an area, and existing withdrawal levels face reduction. The IGUCA allows for many different and creative alternatives for enhanced management. Local people complain that such controls are an illegal taking of individual property rights, and the issue may be thrashed out in the courts. District No.3 planned to close down 80 to 90 percent of its district to new development in 1991. It has become clear that Ogallala groundwater depletion was, and still is, inevitable, but it can be carefully managed over several decades to limit harm to irrigators and the larger economy they support.

District planning also admits to a water table that is declining one to five feet each year, but at a decreasing rate with better management and an increasing rate during drought years like 1988. The district emphasizes conservation and efficient use of groundwater, including the use of crops requiring less water, irrigation scheduling, water-saving tillage and cropping practices, water metering, recharge methods, and tailwater reuse. About 20 percent of water is lost by tailwater runoff or deep percolation, which amounts to about 400,000 acre-feet. A complicated formula was established to limit aquifer depletion in district areas where pumping exceeded the planned depletion rate. The formula now covers most of the district[61] and attempts to limit depletion to not more than 40 percent during a twenty-five-year period. By 1977 in Finney County, six out of ten applications for new wells were denied; by May 1987, nearly 90 percent of new well applications were being denied as contrary to depletion-policy guidelines.

The data gathered by the Soil Conservation Service in Haskell County described some recovery under district management but still pointed toward long-term Ogallala water decline. Harold Stapleton's well No.5 at the county's northern border,[62] just east of U.S. 83 between Liberal and Sublette, descended to water 194 feet deep in 1966, 240 feet in 1984, and 237 feet in 1986. Jack Dufield's well No.6 at the eastern border went from 172 feet in 1971 to 212 feet in 1984 and back slightly to 204 feet in 1986. Henry Guttridge's well No.7, at the western border of the county went down to 129 feet in 1970, 169 feet in 1980, and rose to 144 feet in 1986. Once, in 1979, when measurements were taken while the pump was running, Guttridge was in a cone down to 227 feet before he got to his water. One acre of irrigated corn in western Kansas uses at least 90 million gallons of water during a dry year. Another of Jack Dufield's wells in Seward County went down in 1977 to 211 feet to reach water, a drop of more than 18 feet since 1966 and more than 31 feet since 1940.

The district covers more than 5.7 million acres of prime farmland largely in Class I, II, and III soils (the Trescotts' Oklahoma soil was a better grade of Class III), most of which can be irrigated with modern equipment and techniques. Irrigation is identified as the essential instrument "to stabilize and increase crop production" in this predominantly agricultural region. In 1975, about fifteen years after new pumping technologies were readily available, approximately 1.6 million acres were irrigated from about 7,800 large-capacity wells providing 100 to 3,000 gallons per minute. Nine years later, in 1984, at the peak of irrigation, over 1.8 million acres were irrigated from 9,800 wells. In 1975, about 3 million acre-feet of water was consumed and about 3.5 million acre-feet was used in 1984. In the mid-1980s, approximately 75 percent of irrigation was gravity flood and 25 percent by sprinklers, primarily center pivot, but this ratio is being quickly reversed with the rapid spread of more efficient sprinklers. Haskell County, for example, was 79 percent irrigated in 1984 (295,000 of 371,200 acres), using 1,048 wells pumping more than 564,000 acre-feet. Finney County was 41 percent irrigated with 1,662 wells producing more than 506,000 acre-feet irrigating 270,000 acres of a total 662,880. Haskell County, almost three-quarters irrigated, was the twenty-first most-productive county in the nation with $344 million and Finney County was thirty-eighth with $225 million. In sum, of six western Kansas counties in 1982, 963,000 acres were irrigated, or almost 30 percent of the total, with one-third under center-pivot sprinklers and two-thirds under gravity irrigation (mostly gated pipe and some ditch).[63]

According to its statement of purpose, District No.3 is not interested in keeping the water locked in its beds of sand and gravel; its mission is "to provide the greatest total social and economic benefits . . . for the longest period of time."[64] After the state law was passed in 1972 but before local district controls went into effect in 1976, the rush to drill new irrigation wells brought significant declines in groundwater levels, down fourteen feet in Grant County by 1974 and nine feet in Finney County by 1976. The Gigot family's Circle Land and Cattle Company alone drilled over one hundred wells between 1972 and 1974.[65] Only higher energy costs, not conservation principles, prevented a continued rapid slide. Irrigation still consumes up to ten times the recharge, even without a rash of new wells. But if higher market prices covered energy costs, all-out pumping would resume.

No one doubts that the future of southwest Kansas is closely tied to heavy use of water for intensive irrigation. A quarter section of irrigated corn may demand three acre-feet of water in a particularly dry season. Further expansion of groundwater pumping is not mentioned much, economic lasting power (sustainable development) a lot. Some irrigators, such as the Gigots, are moving out of corn, but alfalfa or sugar beets need even more water, so they must turn to less-profitable wheat or milo or an alternative crop yet to find a market. The water, doled out in far smaller quantities, is there to sustain a workable way of life for farmers in southwest Kansas, but the High Plains Ogallala Aquifer Regional Study of 1982 predicted that at present consumption rates, by the year 2020 three-quarters of Kansas's current High Plains irrigated land will be back in dryland acreage.[66]

Kansas District No. 3 goes to a lot of trouble to minimize waste. Waste of water is defined as:

(1) Groundwater that has been diverted or withdrawn from a source of supply, and is not used, managed or reapplied to a beneficial use.

(2) Any act or omission causing the unreasonable deterioration of the quality of water.

(3) Groundwater which an irrigator permits to escape and drain.

(4) Groundwater applied to an authorized beneficial use in excess of the needs for such use.[67]

A public advocacy group, the Kansas Rural Center, does not believe the issue of waste or beneficial use is simple. Mary Fund of the center writes:

The term "beneficial," though, is still rather ambiguous, since what is beneficial to one person may still be seen as wasteful by someone else. For example, lawn watering to the city dweller is an important use of water—beneficial to lifestyles, self esteem, and aesthetics, but open to question by some in arid regions, or during drought. In the same vein, irrigating corn with irreplaceable fossil water when we have record harvests and the price is below the cost of production, is also open to question by some people. Therefore, we suggest that in addition to minimizing waste, conservation also implies recognition of "appropriate use"— the use of water that fits the particular situation, climate, and supply.[68]

Other water-management-district regulations cover tailwater control and waste, well-spacing requirements, measuring devices, and aquifer depletion, limited to no more than 40 percent in twenty-five years within a two-mile radius (8,042 acres) of a proposed well. Violators lose their right to pump water following a formal complaint and thirty-day notice until they comply with the regulations of the district.

Once a well is drilled, there are not yet any rules or regulations to control the scale of pumping. Farmers north of the Arkansas River are atop ground-water that is already 50 percent depleted, and the remaining 50 percent is not all accessible or of good quality. One farmer told Mary Fund of the Kansas Rural Center that his water was being pumped out from underneath him, but hydrologists doubt any declines except from the nearest well.[69] Ogallala wa-ter naturally moves five hundred to one thousand feet a year from northwest to southeast. Fund raises the unexamined question of fair distribution of the remaining water. There were complaints of injustice when Master Land Company of Oklahoma applied for sixteen wells in 1981. At the public hear-ing sponsored by the district, a farmer argued: "It seems that the bigger and more powerful the corporation or individual is, the more influence they have in obtaining well permits." The district approved fifteen of the sixteen wells, and the general manager of the Master Land Company noted that "water rights are administered on a fair and equal basis, regardless of the size of the company."[70]

As a followup, the Kansas legislature in 1986 passed a law that obligates "an applicant for a permit to appropriate water to adopt and implement con-servation plans and practices." These included improved water-use effi-ciency (higher yields for the same water or the same yields with less water). Together with an analysis of traditional flood irrigation and newer sprinkler and trickle alternatives, conservation methods could include water metering, ir-rigation scheduling, tailwater recovery, land shaping and leveling, and better information about soil characteristics, climate conditions, topography, and crop requirements. The objective was to make better use of Ogallala water through more efficient equipment and better management. Goals were set at 5 percent better performance. The Soil Conservation Service cooperated with the pub-lication of a Kansas irrigation guide that offered data on irrigation needs, based on an 80 percent chance of rain, for western Kansas crops.[71] Under these condi-tions, wheat needed an acre-foot, sorghum fourteen inches, corn sixteen inches, and alfalfa more than two acre-feet. Simultaneously, the Kansas State Board of Agriculture, through its Division of Water Resources, announced the requirement of conservation plans for "all new applications to appropriate water for beneficial use" beginning January 1, 1989. The plans were in the name of the public interest, had to be technologically and economically feasible, curtail waste of water, serve reasonable needs of the water user, and "be limited to practices of water use efficiency."[72]

A Special Case: Northwest Kansas Groundwater Management District Four

A radical new development bears watching. In 1990, Northwest Kansas Groundwater Management District Four, established in 1977 and supervising more than thirty-six hundred wells, set a zero-depletion goal to be reached in as little as ten years. To quote a district official, "the declining levels meant zero depletion anyway, so why not opt to reach the same goal earlier while retaining an acceptable quantity of water for future management options."[73] But the district is experiencing much difficulty in matching this Draconian goal with the immediate needs of local farmers to irrigate for their survival.

Nevertheless, District Four sees zero depletion (discussed in chapter 7) as a logical extension of its stated mission for "proper management and conservation practices of the groundwater resource . . . to derive optimum social and economic benefits accruing from the wise development, use, and management of the groundwater reserves." The district covers all or part of ten counties occupying 3,100,000 acres, supplied by more than 40 million acre-feet of Ogallala groundwater that is being depleted over most of the district from six to eighteen inches a year.

Conclusion

All three of the organizations just discussed have a common mission—not always well served—to provide a structured means by which to continue indefinitely the development of Ogallala water for agriculture. The problem with this reasonable goal is that it does not keep in mind that the Ogallala is in truth an environmental resource that is mostly nonrenewable and being used up at a very rapid rate. None of the agencies faces up to the fact that pumping water for irrigation is a mining operation as much as coal, gold, or oil. USGS hydrologist John Bredehoeft stated it clearly (his italics): *"To the extent that we are mining groundwater, we are running out of water."*[74]

However, according to agricultural policy analyst Earl O. Heady, exclusive attention to protecting the Ogallala from water mining ignores other national and international problems, including population growth, food supplies, and extended drought. He concludes that these should overshadow declining Ogallala levels. Unlike more pessimistic analysts, Heady believes that the advent of new, efficient technologies, despite lower water levels, will continue to support current food production and probably surpass it.[75] According to this view, the Ogallala can be sacrificed to serve such higher goals. Heady does admit, however, that the surplus conditions of the 1960s, when sixty million acres were held out of production, are not likely to return in the future, creating more pressure to mine water to irrigate farmland. After all, an irrigated cornfield produces 115 bushels an acre, compared to 89 bushels on an eastern humid-land farm and 48 bushels on a dryland field.[76] "I am optimistic about our ability," despite declining water levels, "to continue growth in agricultural productivity and food production." In a remarkable statement about high farm output, Heady argues for a bullish future at least as productive as the past, based on "our ability to recreate [1960–90 golden age] conditions of the past"[77] instead of an alternative future.

To others, this is perpetuation of a Maginot Line mentality. Societies everywhere have the propensity to prepare for a repeat of their last crisis, as the French did before World War II when they made the Maginot Line a splendid defense for a repeat of World War I. The continued heavy consumption of irreplaceable Ogallala water, no matter how judiciously regulated by state agencies, will make the future of the High Plains different from the past.

6

. . .

Making Irrigation Work
in a Risky World

Irrigation is as old as civilization; it is one of humanity's great historical innovations. The great cities and cultures of the ancient Near East, of India and China, and of Mexico and Peru depended on this sophisticated technological complex of lifts and pumps, canals and laterals, work forces and schedules, and sensitivity to land, water, and climate. It could even be said that cities were created to make irrigation work. On the High Plains today, on a less grand scale, mechanized and powered irrigation guarantees an abundance of food in a hostile environment. Equally important, irrigation also ensures the security of an almost mythic independent farming lifestyle that Americans cherish.

The irrigation farming life of Phil and Linda Tooms in southwest Kansas needs land, water, capital, equipment, and management skill on a larger scale than one finds in the traditional image of the independent family farm, yet it is not agribusiness. The Toomses represent mechanized large-field farming defined by a combination of factors: skill in using soil and water, environmental sensitivity to the nurturing of their land, family ownership, a sense of belonging to a specific place, and loyalty to rural values. They stand midway between the industrial Gigot family and the more traditional Oklahoma Trescotts. Nor are the Toomses participants in the small but growing organic-sustainability farming represented by the Land Institute; they feel it is naïvely idealistic about hard labor, per-acre yields, and markets. Instead, the Toomses seek to be the best mainstream or conventional farmers they can be, since they believe it is still the better road to long-term success. Because they live in semiarid country, their irrigation practices, probably more than any other factor, will determine whether they can perpetuate and even enhance a satisfying and productive farm life. Their experience can be examined as a quest for sustainable agricultural development that emphasizes environmental management, site-specific activity, local decision making, and general well-being.

Phil and Linda Tooms live about a half-mile north of the graded dirt Moscow Road and five miles west of the main road, U.S. 83, which runs between Sublette to the north and Liberal to the south. The drive up to their house is pleasant; their spacious and comfortable ranch house is tree shaded, with a green lawn in front sloping toward a south-looking open vista of gently rolling, buff-colored fields and grassland. Their backyard contains a shaded stone patio and wrought-iron furniture, a garden protected by bushes and trees from the plains sun and wind, and more shade trees before opening up to the flat, dusty plains landscape, "the floor of the sky." The wind blows and the birds sing in the oasis they have created since 1954 from a small cabin, "a little old dinky building unchanged since 1912," the old frame of which is now encased in the modern suburban-style home. Inside are the amenities of middle American consumer society: color TV and VCR in a comfortable family living room, kitchen with convenient appliances, an attached three-car garage. The home office is the center of farm-management operations. Unlike many suburban homes, however, the Toomses' house contains hundreds of books on shelves, not for show, but obviously thumbed and read. Phil Tooms is a history enthusiast who sometimes speaks to groups about southwest Kansas history.

Next to the house on the west side are the buildings of a modern working farm: no barn, but large, plain metal sheds for tractors, field implements, trucks, and storage. Here Phil exercises his jack-of-all-trades know-how. The yard does not have the eastern humid-lands barn smell of straw, manure, and animals, but instead is a mélange of painted steel implements, aluminum machinery housings, the odor of oiled gears, engines of all sorts, and a red gasoline tank on struts. The farmyard, buildings, and equipment are all strangely silent; the machinery is taken elsewhere, into the fields, to do its work. This farmyard is more a parking lot and repair shop than the center of a constant flurry of activity as it might be in Pennsylvania or Illinois. Yet nowhere is it more clear that irrigation farming depends on a vast diversity of large powered equipment and the skills to use it.

Most of the Toomses' land is just west of the Cimarron River. Their most obvious landmark is a shiny natural-gas pipeline that rises to the surface on their land, spans the river on its own metal bridge, then snakes underground on the other side, still on Tooms land. Like most streams in this flat country, the Cimarron is wide and shallow and looks like it has been dry for a long time, with dead cottonwood trees along its edges and scrub bushes in the streambed. Phil and Linda and their two grown children remember when the river flowed year round and even flooded. But as Ogallala aquifer levels declined, the river's surface water seeped underground. Phil Tooms is convinced that upstream irrigation in Colorado also captured much of the river's supply. The riverbed cannot provide water for crops or cattle; hence the Toomses must irrigate from deep groundwater or farm dryland. The natural-gas pipeline, as well as gas wells and and a small oil well, with its praying-mantis-like rig, provides a steady and substantial income. The loss of either gas or Ogallala water would bankrupt them.

At fifty-six, Phil Tooms is a linebacker-size man, as are many plains farmers, at ease working with his equipment and comfortable on High Plains farmland. Today he would be considered a successful businessman anyplace, and he is self-assured as a director of the People's Bank in Liberal and a member of the local businessmen's club. A local boy, son of a used-implement salesman, he did not start out to irrigate; he didn't even start out to be a farmer: he saw his secure future in cattle. But he began to grow some feed for his cattle, then irrigated eighty acres in 1956 for a better yield, and one thing led to another until he got out of cattle and into irrigation farming.[1]

Four generations of family history did not encourage a future in plains farming. Thomas Tooms, a Civil War veteran, had adventuresome sons who in 1887 preceded the railroad into southwest Kansas. They were lured by the heavy rains, which promised a better climate, and cheap land. However, when the rains ended, the family, including Phil's father, "didn't know how to handle their dry land." Like many plains failures, he moved to California briefly in the desperate 1920s, when "there was no government help and you either made it or you left the country." Back in Kansas in time for the 1930s crises, the family survived by trading used farm equipment. Hence the Tooms family was dubious about direct hands-on plains farming.

Nevertheless, Phil and Linda Tooms moved from town to a piece of ranchland in the mid-1950s. Their first year was rainless from September through late May. "We were just desperate to have some sure sort of grain" for cattle feed. Linda observed that they turned to irrigation farming because it obviously offered exceptional security compared to the uncertainty of dryland farming or ranching. In this seemingly simple choice, they dramatically changed the direction of their lives. Irrigation is remarkably different from anything previously known on the plains. They moved away from familiar farm and field practices and instead chose the promise of newfangled irrigation, a form of industrial farming. They found themselves thrown into the novel demands of daily irrigation practices, where their untested skills involved costly new machinery—pumps, engines, gearboxes, pipes, and later sprinklers—set permanently on the fields. They had to learn how to finance and manage their operation as if it were a small industrial factory.

Linda remembered their initial fascination with irrigated water. It was both an agricultural triumph and a symbolic victory over the plains: "This is a semiarid area, you know. Every time it does rain you try to hold on to all that moisture to sustain the crop the next year. With average rainfall twenty bushels of wheat [per acre] is a good deal. You live in that sort of [semiarid] environment and then when you can actually have [irrigation] water when you want to put it down the rows. Your crops flourish and it is just like gardening in the desert and making it blossom." Irrigation water was more than insurance, it was at the center of the new venture to which they had committed their lives. "That small, littlest good" of irrigation on eighty acres was so rewarding that "we put down another well and we gradually got to be bigger and bigger in irrigation."

But Linda also concluded that many farmers were too ready to jump into irrigation as the cure for all the region's woes. It was not a magic bullet. "Too many people state they can put water on any kind of ground, spend the same amount on fertilizer, and think they're going to get the same yield per acre as they would on class A or 1A ground. They'll spend the same amount of money per acre as the man that's going to get, say, 175 or 200 bushels of corn. You can go out here on a piece of poor ground and try to spend the same amount on it, fertilizers and insecticides, and you're going to be lucky to get 100 bushes and you'll go into a hole. If you are a real poor farmer, it'll cost you just as much to raise a poor crop if you don't get it done right." The technological innovation called irrigation does not guarantee success. Amid the complex of land, water, capital, equipment, and management, it was still good management, and an indefinable love of farming, that held the key to success. In the farmer's world, nothing is guaranteed.

Phil and Linda now irrigate over 1,800 acres, mostly in wheat and alfalfa, with some milo and a little corn. Their first well was drilled in 1950 to sufficient water at 300 feet, but Phil did not start large-scale pumping until 1956, when he spent $5,600 for a Peerless pump and a 413 International industrial engine to start flood irrigation. In 1956, $5,600 was considerably more than the cost of a Cadillac or a small farmhouse and worth three tractors. This first well, a moderate six inches in diameter, still produces its original 700 gallons per minute. Since then his pumping level has dropped 37 feet. In 1964, to irrigate another field, he drilled a second well to 486 feet, put in another Peerless pump and a 605 International engine, all for $16,000, together with $14,000 for an early Valley No.1260 center-pivot sprinkler. In 1964, $30,000 would buy a nice three-bedroom suburban house or a Ferrari or set up a young farmer with basic equipment. With these commitments between 1956 and 1964, Phil Tooms broke with his past and risked his future on large-scale flood and center-pivot irrigation. The last of his seven wells went into service in 1975. Now he could not turn back; if he failed he could only go bankrupt and out of farming entirely. Today such a turnkey irrigation system would run at least $70,000 per 160-acre quarter section and could go as high as $200,000. Tooms's 1964 well is already sanded in from 465 to 360 feet, and he had an $18,000 repair bill on that well in 1986. Between 1981 and 1986 alone he discovered that the per-foot cost of drilling a new well had risen from $35 to $50.

Phil Tooms is not a pure irrigator; and few people in the region are. His nonirrigated land consists of 640 acres in dryland wheat and more than 3,500 acres in dryland grass on which he contracts with a feedyard to graze cattle in the summer, 8 acres per head. The remaining 900 acres are in summer fallow. He estimates that most of his soils are Dalhart, with some Ulysses and Richfield. Dryland farming alone is not much of an alternative. Linda wondered: "Sometime I think it would be interesting to figure out how much profit you made in the good year on dryland compared with the profit you made on a good year with a wonderful yield in irrigation and just see where the margin is." But she also noted that if everyone did dryland farming only, "we would probably not have this surplus [to feed the world]. When you can produce three times [dryland yield] under irrigation you can see how you are producing more than is otherwise possible." Plains farmers take tremendous pride in their high productivity.

Phil Tooms concludes that he would not have the financial resources to start irrigating today.[2] In agreement with most of his fellow plains farmers, as well as conservation-district officials, Tooms believes that extensive irrigation from the Ogallala is under severe pressure. While some water will always remain, the combined problems of higher equipment costs, pumping from deeper levels, and increasing energy costs cannot be overcome at the low grain prices that have prevailed for several decades. The high-consumption irrigation era that opened in the 1960s will end, many farmers believe, in the 1990s. Linda said the Toomses' early 1960s success in irrigation added up to "needing bigger machinery and more machinery and more help and it's just a vicious thing where we need to borrow more money to, you know, keep us going. Every well you put down you don't realize it at the time because at that point the prices were good." Low grain prices and heavy debt have always clouded the picture.

In the 1980s, Linda said, the only "successful people are the ones that own their own land paid for already. You either have to inherit it or marry it, and then you've got to be a tremendous manager after you get it." She added: "Or have oil or gas; our salvation has been that we have oil and gas." Linda talked more like a corporate manager than a traditional farm wife. At one point Phil remembered Kansas State (K State) University data that said farmers required eighty-five to ninety bushels of milo per acre to break even. Linda retorted: "To break even, you've got to get it over that. What if you get hailed out? You still got that crop, and your [crop] insurance [only] gets your seed back to you." Phil remembered that in 1974 he took eight hundred head of cattle to market, sold them for less than they cost, and lost $100,000 cash. "Well, you lose that kind of money and it takes years to recover. One might have to triple one's net income to start paying back the debt." Phil and Linda figure they operate about $350,000 worth of equipment to work their land and it costs them $250,000 a year to run the farm. Annual income comes from a mixture of crop sales, cattle grazing, natural-gas leases, and outside business.

They talk like industrial managers, but both Phil and Linda love the rural independence of a farmer's lifestyle; they would not switch to another vocation. Irrigation brought them the enviable (to them) combination of a successful farm life on the plains and a standard of living comparable to metropolitan prosperity. Such balance is the whole point behind the old idea of rural-urban parity that was first set according to 1910–14 standards. Successful irrigation results in immeasurable satisfaction. "We're living in a wonderful age," said Linda, "when you can produce all this food. And there's so much emotion tied to the land. It is a love relationship." But when Wes Jackson, Wendell Berry, or Robert Rodale and organic farming were brought up, Linda sniffed, "Who wants to live that way? We wouldn't be satisfied to live like my mother grew up. You couldn't afford a car. You couldn't afford what's considered normal living in this day and age." One example was criticism of farmers for their use of air-conditioned tractors. "The person saying that works in an air-conditioned office. If he would come out and just spend an hour on a tractor, he would realize that we want [air conditioning] in our work life too. I'm an American citizen and I have these rights too. You can't go back and buy a 1960-style tractor."

Phil Tooms estimates today's startup costs for a successful irrigation farm would total to $1.5 million for land and equipment, requiring at least forty-five hundred acres owned and twenty-five hundred leased. Even as a successful irrigator, Tooms concluded, his best years came erratically in 1968 and 1969, 1974, and 1978, with far less profitability since then. Phil Tooms also observed that irrigation equipment, once thought good for thirty years, can require replacement within ten years. Speaking of his 1956 well, Tooms said, "I don't know how long steel set there in the ground with the pressure of sand and the aquifer pushing in on it, the corrosion, the rust, when is that steel going to give up? Collapse. When that well collapses, I am not spending $50 a foot to drill a new well because it will not pay off. I'm not going to do it."

Although irrigation gave Phil his start toward the brass ring, he sustains himself with gas leases, banking, and land deals as well as spreading groundwater on grain fields. He thinks 60 percent of the usable water in the Ogallala aquifer was consumed before tough regulations were set in place in 1976 with the creation of Southwest Kansas Groundwater Management District No.3.[3] Between 1977 and 1987, even after strict controls, his 1950 well's water level descended 21 feet from 199 feet to 220. Rising energy costs for natural gas, from $0.29 per hundred cubic feet in 1986 to $0.52 in 1987 to $1.40 in 1988, may well end his irrigation before the water runs out. Seeing the handwriting on the wall, Tooms and his fellow farmers are working hard to stretch out their capacity to pump Ogallala water by progressive improvements in water efficiency. Tooms switched from flood irrigation to center-pivot sprinklers, then to low pressure, then to drop sprinklers closer to the ground. His future, he says, includes surge valves and tailwater recovery in order to save water and reduce energy costs.

Not the least, Phil Tooms, like Wayne Wyatt of Texas District No.1 and irrigator Gene Barby in Oklahoma, wonders where the young farmers will be coming from when he and his generation of long-term irrigators retire. His own son is a lawyer in New York City, and his daughter and her new husband wonder about their future on the plains. "This young guy's fuel costs, his machinery costs, his labor costs are going to be worse, and yet his commodity price is no better." Nevertheless, Tooms suggests that while many good irrigators around him are not going to survive the decline of Ogallala water, they should have a try at dryland farming. A well-managed and efficient dryland farming operation could still prevail on two to four times his irrigated land. "People have confidence in the farmer around here. The farmer will keep trying and a lot of them don't know anything else. The farmers are different than any union like the teamsters or steel workers union. Farmers are very independent." He said, "The little guy who has five or six quarters of ground and maybe four or five or six irrigation wells and he's not making it. I think what people resent is that they see this big corporation over here with 50 or 200 or 300 or 400 wells and getting large government payments. You get a load of this bitterness toward the government, too. I think some of these big corporations received $2 million from the PIK program. The little guy looks at that and he says that's too much to give one guy. I think we'll see high food prices if the big corporations take control. Corporations can afford to hang on to their wheat and wait for higher prices. Then the price of bread would get maybe to $2 a loaf. If that happens, some day, in twenty years, then we're going to look back to these days and say, 'Hey, why didn't we help these little farms out so that they can stand in.'"

Phil Tooms wonders: are the little farmers naïvely optimistic, or are there other reasons to farm besides profit alone? Commitment to farming as an entire way of life is difficult to shake off. "It just boggles the mind," he said. "If you owned a chain of stores like Wal-Mart, you follow the law of supply and demand. They're not going to buy a bunch of stuff and let it set; they're buying stuff they can turn over quickly. The farmer absolutely doesn't use that same mentality." Farming is the nation's economic anomaly that doesn't fit into the usual market rules. Tooms sees an entire way of life at stake: "Only one entity in the world can help the farmer and that is the U.S. government. [But] I still think that people in our government feel that we could do with half the [three million] farmers in the United States."

Tooms blamed overproduction and the resulting high irrigation consumption on wrongheaded federal policy: "A lot of grass that was plowed up out there should never have been plowed up. There was a time when [Agriculture Secretary Earl] Butz was saying we'll never be able to keep up with the world, the population will continue to grow, and we must plant fencerow to fencerow. That's when a lot of farmers got into trouble because they said, 'Well, if that's the case, let's get out here and buy some of this land.' Dear God, the land prices started going up and they just kept buying it, and started buying bigger machinery, for three or four years. In Iowa a lot of this land that is selling today for $1,800 or $2,000 [an acre] someone bought it for $4,000 an acre. They invested a lot in machinery. They went broke."

Nothing is more basic to the American agricultural tradition than ownership of land. High plains land prices are linked directly to available water; farmland with a good supply of Ogallala water brings high market prices. As a director of People's Bank in Liberal, Phil Tooms watches carefully over the good and bad fortunes of southwest Kansas land. As is true of most of his fellow farmers, Tooms believes ownership of good farmland is fundamental to his entire identity as a farmer, both personally and professionally. High-quality topsoil should be the first measure of good land, and the second should be whether the tract is dryland or irrigated. But the picture has become complicated. As the water is depleted and irrigation costs go up, he said, "irrigated land has probably taken the biggest punch" from banks that are anticipating tougher times. "Our appraisal officer this year [1987] took off 25% to 30% valuation on irrigated land in our trust department. Land that was selling for $1,200 an acre a few years ago now brings $650. It costs so much to produce an irrigated crop. When a fellow comes in to borrow money, he's got to fill out a cash flow form, to tell how much fertilizer, how much herbicide, how much insecticide, how much his payments are on his land, how high his repair is on his well or sprinkler, how high his taxes are, how much return he's going to make. His cash flow form tells how much he's going to need to operate that year. He needs to project. 'Well, I'm going to raise a hundred and ten bushels of milo and the price of milo this year is only going to be $1.70 a bushel compared with $2.25 in the past two or three years.' So he is going to get a lot less for his return and is it going to float? The banker looks at this and says, you can't do it, there's no way.''

Tooms is not vertically integrated with his own feedlots, as is the nearby Gigot family, but sells his alfalfa to Alfalfa, Inc., feedlots in Sublette, his milo to Supreme Feeders in Liberal, and his wheat to Cargill and Collingworth to be shipped out of the region. In the area, three meatpacking plants consume almost a hundred thousand head of cattle weekly. Phil Tooms noted that a lot of cattle consume a lot of alfalfa and ''it would be impossible to produce the beef without irrigation because with dryland farming we couldn't guarantee the grains that it takes.'' Tooms also remembered he was told recently that Americans were foolish to be so inefficient with grain when starvation is still endemic on the globe. It takes six pounds of grain to put on a pound of beef, but Linda wondered, ''Who would you get to eat six pounds of grain?'' Locally, all sorts of jobs are tied to irrigation. Feedlots put a lock on high levels of irrigation.

Linda also was sensitive to overproduction: irrigation is essential to the economic well-being of the region, yet irrigation farmers in southwest Kansas have joined farmers in the Dakotas and western Canada to produce more grain than can be exported or consumed domestically. The end result is large surpluses and low prices. ''We became expert producers,'' she said, but ''here there's just a few crops that we can really raise successfully: alfalfa, milo, corn, and wheat.'' Linda remembered that when they put in their first well in 1956, farm experts from Kansas State University came and stressed ''push, push, push for more yields.'' So they irrigated their first eighty acres.

How Risky Was Historical Farming on the High Plains?
Bending the Rules

The irrigator's life of Phil and Linda Tooms is a success story thus far. This is not unusual. They, the Trescotts, the Gigots, the Allens (see chapter 7), and many others have the advantage, as earlier generations did not, of successful irrigation. Their success makes it easy to label earlier plains farming a failure, but their heavy dependence on large-scale water consumption casts doubt on the future.

On what grounds can the historic attempts to settle the High Plains be called failures? And can we learn how to reduce hard times by studying historic patterns?[4] The story of plains settlement and farming seems to contain more catastrophe than victory. What long-term forces can still bring on painful and life-threatening collapse?[5] The climate is likely to become worse rather than better. Is the High Plains a region of perpetual risk, or have there always been corrective measures that could have been or can be taken? How well, or poorly, did farmers, politicians, and other boosters understand agricultural expansion into arid grasslands? For example, in our examination of the plains environment, we have seen the contrast between actual climatic conditions as compared with what pioneer farmers hoped would come.[6] How do the attempts of the ill-prepared and undertooled first settlers compare to doomed Dust Bowl farming in the 1930s or to profitable irrigation technologies in the 1960s? Did irrigation change the rules? On the Kansas Sandhills, how was one man, Clarence Gigot, able to make a garden out of another man's desert? What are the future conditions that would promise success or threaten failure?

America's early plains farmer lived under conditions of extremely high risk. He was undertooled, underinformed, and undercapitalized. A single incident of a broken axletree or smashed kneecap, bad seed corn or a rainless June, could put him out of business. This condition is itself a definition of how frontier settlement differs from more stable situations.[7] The early farmer was aware of many risks, but usually not all the risks, involved in settling any new region. He believed that the resources he imported with him, ranging from information to seed corn to a new plow to a little cash, would allow him to exploit opportunities for settlement, growth, and permanence. In today's parlance, he was involved in his own risk-benefit analysis. But it is less clear why the frontier farmer insisted on settling the semiarid lands of the central High Plains, a region already distinguished by shortgrass prairie, temperature extremes, low rainfall, and intense sun and wind, where he should have known he could have little success with his existing resources.

When farmers moved westward into a new region, they had many sources of contradictory information, which sometimes went against their own common sense toward the sunny wind-blown quarter section many of them homesteaded. Many farmers on the shortgrass prairie had been led to believe that the true prairie of the High Plains was once humid land with tall grasses that would return when the rains prevailed. Farmers also assessed the agricultural potential of a new piece of land by the kinds of wild grasses it produced. Water, weather, and the fertility of the soil determined which grasses grew where. Tall grasses, such as prairie cordgrass or sloughgrass, switchgrass, wild rye, and particularly bluestem, promised productive acreage for corn and soybeans. Medium grasses, notably western wheatgrass, June grass, sideoats grama, three-awn, needlegrasses, and various dryland sedges, told the farmer that the land had potential for wheat and grain sorghums. Shortgrass prairie, largely blue grama and buffalo grass, were signs that the land was too arid for anything but cattle grazing—until the revolutionary advent of winter wheat and dryland farming. There are other preconditions for agricultural success, including land ownership, the right tools, transportation to markets, ingenuity, and community infrastructure.

The plains farmer also learned that these so-called rules for cultivation could be bent in his favor by the arrival of new grains, such as hard winter wheat; by new field methods, such as dryland farming; and, much later, by new irrigation technologies. When High Plains conditions became excessively difficult, which was often, his hope rested on changes in the rules. Humid-land responses to a fixed dryland climate had already failed. He looked forward to the moment when the climate changed and agricultural improvements reached him. The climate did not change but was mastered by new irrigation machinery and new agricultural science that bent the rules and transformed extensive pioneer farming into today's intensive commercial farming. Not the least, in the 1930s the New Deal also sought to end high risk on the High Plains when it singled out the independent on-site family farmer for protection, almost at any price. He was not to be allowed to wither away. Sometimes, however, changes in the rules did not favor the farmer: by 1939 the Dust Bowl region offered fewer agricultural supports and buffers, such as good land prices, a sufficient work force, and investment in new equipment, than it had in 1929.[8] But federal intervention continued to challenge the rules by supporting farmers through the little dust bowls of the 1950s and 1970s. The question here is what rules and bent rules created today's High Plains irrigator and might allow him to prevail?

Another important question was whether a single aspect alone, such as a depleted soil or an empty well or drought or prices, could deprive the farmer of his livelihood. For example, after World War II, had the traditional family farmer in reality vanished from southwest Kansas because farming required the high capital investment now associated with agribusiness? Can the farmer successfully respond to one or two critical changes without modifying the entire farming culture? Today, would a dramatic rise in energy costs alone, as high as a not-unlikely ten dollars per hundred cubic feet of natural gas, bring irrigation pumping to a sudden halt in southwest Kansas? A depleted Ogallala aquifer, for example, is already spreading its effects widely, affecting farm size, ownership, land-use patterns, land values, and outside private and public investment.

When in the early 1880s the frontier farmer encountered unexpectedly heavy rains in this formerly unfavorable climate, he concluded that a permanent climate change had taken place, which seemingly opened a new region for farming. In doing this, he committed three errors.

First, he failed to realize the gap between the pragmatic know-how he carried with him and the scale on which new and unexpected environmental conditions could threaten his survival. Earlier successful settlements from eastern farmland into the unexpectedly fertile but treeless midwestern prairie encouraged him to believe that his farming skills and technical resources were likely to conquer any geography. No matter how extraordinary the conditions were, he optimistically believed his resources were superior. To this must also be added his conviction that he was in the vanguard of an irreversible and irresistible Manifest Destiny. The problem was, considering his limited resources and parochial know-how, he did not have the ability or backup resources to respond flexibly to major surprises. He took the unusually severe external conditions too lightly, responded too rigidly, and the High Plains elements mastered him for seventy years.

Second, the frontier farmer could not distinguish between signal and noise. That is, he did not separate useful information (the long history of a permanently arid region) from misleading and useless information (temporarily heavy rains). This limitation was attenuated by his agricultural success in the humid East, government and railroad-company boosterism, and the inherent limits of single-family self-sufficient subsistence farming.

Third, we need to add secondary and tertiary impacts, the so-called ripple effect. If the climate militated against the frontier farmer, would such an event trigger a collapse elsewhere in the system? Society might not support the farmer but might actually hamper him under conditions of a climate change. Does a climate reversal affect farming by offering less access to credit and mortgage money because the farmer becomes a higher risk? It would affect his ability to pay his debts as his yield of wheat or corn or alfalfa declined. Commercial interest in a climate-burdened region would dwindle, or at least shipping rates would go up to cover losses. Pressures on the autonomous on-site farm family would multiply, tending toward increased conflict and possible breakup. Modern agribusiness removed many local environmental and economic risks but created new risks in monoculture and extreme dependence on commodity markets. Society can amplify climate reversals as well as disperse them.

Climate impact could also be dispersed into society. The farmer depended on the ability of social mechanisms, particularly credit institutions, market prices, railroad policies, and government planning, to minimize adverse climate conditions. During the 1890s drought and depression, state agencies in the Dakotas and Nebraska reluctantly provided welfare relief and the United States Army was eventually ordered to make surplus supplies available to destitute farmers. Federal legislation, such as the Timber Culture Act, the Desert Land Act, and the Reclamation Act, while they created tempting opportunities for speculators, were also attempts to reduce farmer risk.[9] But there was little talk of alternative social institutions that could minimize unexpected climate changes; few questions were raised about the essential weaknesses inherent in the on-site family-operated farm. American society had committed itself to private and independent farm ownership since Colonial times, institutionalized in the Land Survey Ordinance of 1785 and not significantly modified for the next 150 years.[10] Apparently, German immigrants who held to their traditions of the extended multifamily community, where support went deeper and longer, were far more effective in keeping people on the land in hard times than the American single-family homestead.[11] It is difficult for farmers to calculate risk when climate, land, and prices are all uncertain.

Changing Loyalties Toward the Family Farm

Whose interests does consumption of the Ogallala serve? What does American agricultural policy protect? In 1980, for example, the U.S. Department of Agriculture, after working through volumes of data and reels of computer tape, identified 575,000 "primary farmers." Primary farms were classified in terms of efficient production, strategic crops, gross sales, large size, and superior geographical location. The 1980 USDA report concluded that "these farms will most likely influence the effectiveness of the commodity programs as now structured, and they will be the largest beneficiaries of the program benefits."[12]

Since the 1930s, at least, government policy had been biased toward protection of the family farm. This reflected society's judgment that the resulting benefits (cheap food, surplus food, highest profits, the farming way of life, historic values) outweighed the unfair cost imbalance. Corporate farming probably reaped more benefits than family farming. Now, a shift away from farmer protection is taking place as the public sees agriculture as a special-interest group rather than a source of traditional values.[13] Rarely has any ecological element, or maintenance of a sustainable physical environment, been factored in. Nevertheless, in the words of Richard Duesterhaus, "the consumer has come to expect food that is plentiful, nutritious, and free from contaminants and/or other ingredients that may cause short- or long-duration health hazards."[14]

What should not have caused surprise was that the USDA's primary farmer in 1980 was not necessarily the historic family farmer, yet the level of public surprise was considerable. The primary farms listed were those operations that produced almost 80 percent of the nation's food and fiber al-

212

though they accounted for less than 20 percent of all farms.[15] There is a tendency to lose sight of the individual farmer in the big picture. Worldwide markets, chemical companies, agribusiness interests, and even environmental protection tend to keep the local producer submerged. Irrigation farming creates enough profits to keep autonomous farm operations on the land, but is it traditional family farming, which may not be sustainable in any recognizable manner?

The USDA then targeted a more select group of 115,000 farms that produced almost three-quarters of all the nation's strategic foods: wheat, corn, and soybeans. These 115,000 farms alone could each year supply the nation's basic grain needs, support overseas exports, and still maintain a surplus. Geographically, we were told that wheat farmers do best in Kansas and North Dakota on 1,500 acres with gross sales of $105,000. Primary corn or soybean farmers fare best in Illinois and Iowa on 640 acres grossing $145,000. Totally discounted by the USDA report were "rural farm residences"—44 percent of all farm households—with sales of less than $5,000 and "small farms"—34 percent of all farms—grossing $5,000 to $40,000. Lack of federal attention to nonprimary farms made them more vulnerable to other forces. On the High Plains, vulnerability means a higher level of climate dependence as farmers become unable to pay the increasing costs of irrigation. In other words, the federal definition of a farm, and its acceptability for federal funds, controls its success on the arid High Plains.

On the High Plains, smaller farmers were pushed out of the way because it was assumed that only industrial farming could afford and manage extensive irrigation. This seemed to be the result of the hectic 1970s.[16] One farm economist called it cannibalism.[17] Compared to 1950, half the number of High Plains farmers worked the same amount of land in 1980, while the regional economy grew. Phil Tooms and other farmers expect the number to be halved again by the year 2000. No one, especially not politically sensitive congressmen and USDA officials, openly advocates abandonment of the family farm. Phil Tooms, the Trescotts, and even the Gigots claim their personal identity is with family farming. But fewer and fewer operations still thriving on the High Plains fit the mold.

In this light the individual farmer is part of the problem rather than part of the solution as long as he or she practices conventional rather than sustainable farming. A New York state farmer spoke for most counterparts when he wrote:

I don't know a farmer who enjoys using chemicals, but faced with a mortgage payment and a crop-threatening pest, the choice is inescapable, and you spray. . . . evidence seems clear that [agricultural chemicals] don't yield safer, healthier food. Farmers know this: They're not being paid enough to produce safe, healthy, life-sustaining foods, nor to be good stewards of the Earth. Society asks them to do this for free, for altruistic reasons. . . . We must ask ourselves, what is the real cost of putting a meal on America's table? . . . the bottom line of our cheap food system . . . isn't on the supermarket tape. We need to factor in the decline of soil fertility, erosion, and related problems, food safety, polluted groundwater, the health troubles of farmers and farm workers, tax money used in commodity payments, and the destruction of our family farms and rural communities.[18]

In an apparent turnaround from the 1980 USDA analysis, the 1990 farm bill, FACTA (Food, Agriculture, Conservation and Trade Act), focused on the family farm as a means to achieve sustainable agriculture. This was based on both economic and human values. FACTA offered support for owner-operated small and moderate-sized farms: "Build on the entrepreneurial skills, self-employment tradition, and the [existing] resource base of rural communities." In terms of agricultural sustainable development, the family farm may persist as the best local on-site choice despite its many serious defects and apparent obsolescence. It alone embraces a complex variety of agricultural, environmental, economic, social, and cultural values. This variety makes it durable because its priorities are multiple. Above all, the family farm does not give sole allegiance to short-term profits that contradict sustainability. It is more likely to accept the initial sacrifices required for a shift to low-input organic agriculture. If short-term profits had been the primary interest, the family farmer would have disappeared long ago. But when FACTA spelled out the details for sustainability, the conventional agenda reappeared: large surpluses from industrial agriculture based on costly technology. The new objective of the 1990 farm bill was to lock in American agriculture as a servant to "competitiveness of food production within the global economy." Sustainability was folded into competitiveness to the extent that only agribusiness provided acceptable levels of scale and efficiency. Critics of the actual outcomes of the 1990 farm bill, despite its promises toward the family farmer, conclude that he or she will again be effectively excluded from federal support.[19]

Agricultural economist John E. Ikerd writes that "many farmers feel special responsibilities to society . . . for providing food, clothing, and shelter for the people. . . . [in return] Society has given special consideration and concessions to farmers reflecting these critical relationships. . . . farmers [have] a set of values that cannot be captured in the dollar-and-cent language of most economic analyses. . . . But farmers cannot live on appreciation from society."[20] Tomorrow's farming must simultaneously be ecologically sound and productive and profitable. But Pierre Crosson of Resources for the Future claims that "alternative [sustainable] agriculture is less profitable because what it saves in fertilizer and pesticide costs is not enough to compensate for the additional labor required and the yield penalty it suffers relative to conventional farming."[21] Nevertheless, low-input farming strategies are attractive because the public demands environmental protection.

Don Paarlberg writes that the individual farmer has a privileged position in American society. He is exempt from labor laws concerning child labor, working conditions, and minimum wages. He receives preferred transportation rates. The farmer's major asset is public goodwill, but Paarlberg wonders whether this is dwindling rapidly.[22] This special status of agriculture in the United States, says ecologist Richard Lowrance, "will mean that the public will hold agriculture, as an industry, to higher standards of environmental quality and safety than other industries."[23] Such expectations from the larger society cannot be escaped; they can only increase. Economic expectations are reflected in higher quality production at lowest possible costs, environmental demands, such as resource conservation and pollution avoidance, and social needs in terms of revived rural communities and the well-being of farm families.[24] Fee Busby, writing from the perspective of a think tank, the Winrock International Institute for Agricultural Development, says environmental protection is the end of Manifest Destiny because soil and water are no longer free goods in the commons, available indefinitely.[25]

The Family Farm: Definitions

The family farm has been long esteemed in the United States as the place where the patriotic frontier and rural virtues of rugged individualism, hardworking industriousness, and personal self-sufficiency were practiced best. In 1986 philosopher Paul B. Thompson restated the historic Jeffersonian yeoman-farmer definition that has shaped both reality and myth about American agriculture:

> The farmer was tied to his land; the good of the land was identical to the farmer's self interest. Since a farmer must stay in one spot, he must learn to get along with his neighbors and take an interest in long term stability. The virtues of honesty, integrity, and charity promote a stable society, and are also the virtues that promote the farmer's own interest.[26]

The family farm has been characterized by on-site ownership, family labor, agrarian values, land stewardship, and generational continuity, where "household members own the land, perform the labor, control the capital, and make the important economic decisions."[27] Willard W. Cochrane called it the "single enterprise farm firm."[28] More important than income off the farm from working at the local plastics factory were ownership of land and lifestyle, remembering that historic frontier farmers also hunted game and collected wild foods away from the place they plowed and harvested. A 1979 Nebraska conference tried to establish modern identifying marks:

Owner-operation, in which the rights and responsibilities of ownership are vested in an individual who works the farm for a living;

Independence, with financing from within its own resources using family labor and management to build the sweat equity and cash flow;

216

Economic dispersion, in which large numbers of efficiently sized farms operate with equal access to competitive markets;

Family centered, in which the family lives its life in harmony with its workplace, the responsibilities shared by all family members;

Commercially diversified, as to commodities produced as an economic precaution to reduce price risks and maximize the use of farm resources to produce production inputs internally;

Innovation and adoption of technology, to reduce family labor or make it more efficient.[29]

The definition concluded: "the family farm carries with it a commitment to certain values which include conservation, frugality, responsibility, honesty, dignity in work, belief in community, caring for future generations, neighborliness, and self-reliance."

In the modern American economy, family farming is a unique enterprise.[30] The labor force, the role of women, the unusual involvement of children, ownership, capitalization, management, and location are all intertwined. A rural sociologist wrote:

Farm family members work together with varying degrees of solidarity, seeking to reach the common goal of a profitable farming operation. . . . Farm families that lost their farm also lost the major basis of their interaction. . . . Farm families are also unique because of their demand for family labor in terms of career planning for farm children. . . . When the family farm is foreclosed and this option is gone, the young adolescents often have a great sense of anger and betrayal. Not only is the present destroyed, but their sense of future as well. . . . The very agrarian values that built farm families and kept them in farming make it difficult to restructure their lives.[31]

The recently passed Kansas corporate farming law sought to distinguish between family farms and corporate farming. A farm corporation was still a family operation when the majority stockholders were related to each other and "at least one of the stockholders is a person residing on the farm or actively engaged in the labor or management of the farming operation." But this left the door open for a wide variety of interpretations, depending on active family participation in each piece of land or farmstead it owned. Did the Gigot operation, despite its very large and profitable scale, fit the definition? Since alternative-crop farmer Keith Allen rented all the land he farmed north of Sublette, would he receive any benefits from the legislation? The matter is not insignificant: more than a third of Finney County's irrigated acres are on corporate farms, but whether much of this or other farmland is still a family operation is far less clear.[32]

But it was abundantly clear by 1980 (and unchanged in the 1985 and 1990 farm bills, despite claims to the contrary) that the USDA's primary farm was identified differently—based on a different paradigm—from the historic family farm.

High Plains Family Farmer as Government Client

Despite the romance, it is historically clear that the family farmer was never heroically independent on the High Plains. Abundant land was his first free good. He survived and enjoyed a false prosperity by mining the land. It eroded and blew away in the 1930s, with even worse damage in the 1950s and 1970s. As land costs rose, Ogallala water became the farmer's free good, as it still is. He prospered (still too rarely and infrequently) because he could exploit abundant, inexpensive water. Commercial agriculture—agribusiness—only intensified exploitation of first land and later water. The on-site American family farmer historically has been the recipient of special privilege that involves large sums of federal money and disproportionate agricultural research and development to protect him from natural disasters and market forces.[33] So insulated, he may always have been an excessively vulnerable workman artificially isolated from harsh reality instead of the free and spirited yeoman widely admired in congressional rhetoric, newspaper editorials, and the public eye.

As a result, the American family farm has persisted for more than a hundred years on the plains (and more than two hundred years nationally) as a decentralized cottage industry in an increasingly industrialized world. It is inherently site specific. There are many historical parallels. The shift from family farm toward large-scale centralized agribusiness operations can be compared to the demise of mom-and-pop neighborhood grocery stores after World War II as supermarkets became commonplace. Similarly, the early American iron industry at first depended on locally produced iron pigs before it moved toward centralized and vertically integrated factory mills. A similar vertical integration, based on mining the land and water, can be seen today at cattle-feedlot operations in the old Dust Bowl.

High Plains farming persists as a high-risk occupation; in this sense it is still flavored by the frontier experience. But over the last fifty years, as the government has attempted to buffer farmers from natural disasters like the Dust Bowl and human mistakes like the Great Depression, it has turned independent farmers into dependent clients. Once having created clients, the federal government may be obligated to protect them as federal wards. Agriculture became "the industry which, on the surface, seems to come closest to the perfectly competitive model [of capitalism] (many firms, undifferentiated products, etc.), [yet] is the one where government intervention is the most extensive."[34] Ironically, on June 30, 1987, Soviet President Mikhail S. Gorbachev called for a sharp increase in "small-scale family farming," and in February 1990 the Supreme Soviet approved a local option to lease small farmland units that could also be inherited. It also approved in principle the private ownership of farmland, but not for speculative resale and with economic benefits "for farmers who take proper ecological care of their land." Gorbachev spoke of letting demoralized farmers once again feel themselves to be "masters of the land" so they might be productive and reduce expensive grain imports.[35]

Federal protection from the risks of drought eventually reintroduced new risks. The family farmer became dependent on costly equipment, chemical pesticides, and heavy energy needs, and all these threw him heavily into debt. He shifted from labor-intensive to capital-intensive farming. Whether intentional or not, federal commodity and credit policies drove virtually all farmers, large and small, into the patterns of high-water-consumption industrialized farming.[36] Hidden costs can rise when easily acquired water becomes debt-producing water by the need for expensive irrigation equipment.

The burden is shifted from the vulnerable natural resource to the vulnerable farmer. An irrigator in Swisher County, Texas, said "it was 1976 when we bit the bullet and decided to go dryland. From 1976 to 1980 I accumulated a quarter of a million dollars in debt. . . . Every time I went to the bank, I had lost more money. . . . You might have one really good year followed by three or four bad ones"—exactly the risk that irrigators worked to avoid. The farmers around Sublette, Kansas, conclude they can pump until the end of the century at best, then go dryland. The *Oklahoma Comprehensive Water Plan* of 1980 concluded that farmers returning to dryland farming—at only one-third the wheat or milo production—will fail.[37] The unknown question is whether existing conservation practices, described in the next chapter, are little more than Band-Aids on the Great Plains. The old assets, fertile land and individual skills, are now masked or even diminished by external inputs like farm chemicals. In addition, no one foresaw global externalities of the 1980s: the high value of the dollar, high interest rates, the decline of inflation, the worldwide commodity surplus of the Green Revolution, increased international competition to market the same commodities, the international debt crisis—all of which came together to cause farm prices to decline markedly and farm land prices to decline at even a faster rate. Alternative-farming advocates like Robert Rodale concluded that high capitalization and debt may do less to protect the family farm from erratic rain and soil depletion than do certain biological approaches.[38]

Despite the brilliant technological feat that High Plains irrigation is, the severity of drought experienced so far may be far surpassed in the future. Some climate forecasters wonder whether the severe drought year of 1988, discussed in chapter 8, is not simply the forerunner of the next dry spell scheduled for the 1990s. It could be the first real taste of the dire greenhouse effect resulting from the accumulation of carbon dioxide in the upper atmosphere caused by the burning of fossil fuels.[39] A gradual rise in world temperatures during the last several decades may now be taking its toll. CO_2 doubling of two to three degrees Celsius would mean Sahel-like or Great Basin–like desertification of the central High Plains. Global computer modeling—the General Circulation Model, or GCM—indicates that some parts of the world will become warmer and drier, others even cooler. But it puts the Gigot, Tooms, and Trescott gardens—the old Dust Bowl—at the center of an utterly waterless and barren wasteland. With their water running out, not even the Gigots could make the desert bloom.

Concluding Cautionary Note: Making the Most of Uncertainty
There are phenomena that never find a steady state, the plains farm system may be one of them. It exists in a state of irregularity, jumps and starts, and big unexpected swings away from center. This is called aperiodicity. This is why American farm policy may be doomed. It seeks to steady agriculture away from its historic oscillations, but American farming on the High Plains will never evolve into a steady state. Instead, it will follow its own rationale of irregular oscillations. In addition, James Gleick reminds us that "nonlinearity means that the act of playing the game has a way of changing the rules."[40] This means that farm policy can never catch up with either the game or its rules. But fault is not with government policy alone. When plains farming is accepted as aperiodic and nonlinear, it becomes clear why the small farmer became a long-term government client. His expectations, were, unfortunately, frozen in time—the parity years of 1911–14—out of sync with the world while the rest of the world changed. Irrigation's golden years, roughly 1960 to 1990, may have been equally misleading. This small farmer, as well as his friends, is prone to be wrapped in his own mythology, unable to cope with the inherent limits of independent farming on the plains and disengaged from the trends of contemporary society. A harsh climate is still more dominant than either farm policy or the independent farmer or, it appears, large-scale irrigation.

The wide chaotic swings that characterized human history in Ogallala country were often seen as useless noise, since scientists, policymakers, and even farmers looked for steady patterns that would ensure continued monoculture. Hence they looked for technological fixes to Ogallala problems that worked to mask the realities behind the noise. But what is noise to one is signal to another. Chaos theory (nonlinear self-organizing systems theory) wonders whether the "solvable, orderly, linear systems were the aberrations," while the irregular oscillations tell the true story.[41] Monoculture and ecology invariably have different values, use data differently, and come up with different conclusions. James Gleick writes, "It would be like looking at the universe through a red filter—you see what is happening at that particular wavelength of light, but you miss everything happening at the wavelengths of other colors, not to mention that vast range of activity at parts of the spectrum corresponding to infrared radiation or radio waves."[42] What is signal and what is noise depend on both the model and the observer.

American farm policy is not the engine that runs our agriculture but is currently a subset in a much larger economic system. In the United States today the engine is usually the marketplace, and that creates social and cultural externalities that are not accounted for. The problem, when seen in environmental terms, is that farm problems are answered using too narrow a source of acceptable information. The result is often unacceptable: escalating insecticides to higher levels of toxicity or encouraging farmers to irrigate more acreage to overcome low grain prices. While seeking to stabilize farming, such actions may force the system into still more extreme oscillations. In place of either the marketplace or environment, American society can apply a holistic agricultural model that it already possesses, but understands badly, in the historic family farm and its effects.

7

. . .

The Future of Plains Irrigation:
Searching for Sustainability

The Eleventh Commandment—Thou shalt inherit the Holy Earth as a faithful stew-ard, conserving its resources and productivity from generation to generation. Thou shalt safeguard the fields from soil erosion, thy living waters from drying up, that thy descendants may have abundance forever.—W. C. Lowdermilk, assistant chief, Soil Conservation Service, 1956

If the efficiency of an irrigation system is increased by 5 percent from 55 to 60 on a 160-acre field of corn, . . . [and] assuming the pumping head was 250 feet and die-sel fuel was $1.25 per gallon, the monetary savings would amount to $1,244 per year.
—Kansas Water Facts sheet, SCS-USDA, mid-1980s

For more than three decades the plains irrigator has been persuaded to plow his fields and water his plants fencerow to fencerow to keep domestic prices low and feed the world. Between 1940 and 1980, agricultural production doubled and tripled through a combination of mechanization and agri-cultural science that was unimagined earlier in the century. This combina-tion produced high yields that kept the plains irrigator in business during de-cades of crop-price declines, but it was rarely intended to save water. Instead it followed the conventional path of pioneerlike exploitation, this time of water, the last free resource to support high yields on the difficult plains. Ac-cording to conventional thinking, the mission of the agricultural enterprise has always been to make the natural environment less hostile to cash crops.

223

Today, as costs go up and soil and water go down, more farmers are shifting their thinking from changing the environment to changing the crops.

Difficult choices between large fields profitably under heavy irrigation and the need for effective water saving cannot be postponed forever. Original irrigators Phil Tooms, Wayne Wyatt, the Gigots, and the Trescotts have come face to face with water scarcity in their own lifetimes. Using conventional thinking, even efficient consumption still can encourage heavy consumption. Based on complicated equations, if the plains irrigator in southwest Kansas or the Texas-Oklahoma Panhandle plants corn on a fifth of his land and applies two and a half acre-feet of water, his well levels are likely to decline three feet a year; if the same farmer plants less-demanding wheat on 40 percent of his land using only three-quarters to one acre-foot of water to maintain the same profit, his well levels would decline a bit more.[1] Now farmers are learning to measure yields and successful farming not by the acre or by market price, but by the cost of an acre-foot of groundwater. Using today's new groundwater conservation methods, if the plains farmer could survive on less than a one-foot water-table decline a year, he would see it as a major accomplishment. Plains irrigators were among the first to use the Conservation Reserve Program of the 1985 farm bill to take their marginal fields out of production, thus reducing their acreage under irrigation.

From Development to Sustainability:
What Are the Chances for Change?

Pessimists say we cannot indefinitely sustain the levels of groundwater use and food production attained during irrigation's golden age, 1960 to 1990. Secured by an abundance of inexpensive water, plains farmers could be insulated from the effects of low commodity prices while they gave American consumers cheap food and their surpluses served world markets. In contrast, today declining water levels alone prevent return to the recent golden age. The greater threat is that Ogallala consumption can soon double or triple because of a blitzkrieg combination of aging, less-efficient equipment, lower government supports, eroding soil, high-consumption vertically integrated agribusiness, and the threat of the next drought (possibly intensified by the greenhouse effect). Very few irrigators believe they can successfully revert to dryland farming; to them the High Plains have a future only in widespread irrigation. Virtually all of the irrigators interviewed for this book do not take seriously the Land Institute's experiments in alternative farming with perennial grains because they cannot sustain profitable farming on the plains. As Linda Tooms complained in the last chapter, they currently offer insufficient yields, poor markets, and a return to frontierlike working conditions.

Optimists seek to reverse the trend toward scarcity by using new water-sustaining techniques that simultaneously guarantee high yields. Optimists believe that plains farmers, and the world, have only begun to explore the capabilities of increased agricultural production with less water from the Ogallala. Above all, optimists say farmers are still using far more water than they need to keep profits and yields at satisfying levels; the real answer is better water management.[2] All in all, a combination of strategies—planting drought-tolerant crops, using surge systems for furrow irrigation or converting to sprinkler systems, heavily managed irrigation scheduling, tailwater reuse, and special tillage procedures—have already increased groundwater efficiency. From 1974 to 1984 in Texas District No. 1, consumption decreased from 8.13 to 5.24 million acre-feet, while irrigated acres decreased only 24 percent and production even less.[3] Another argument is that if the shift from irrigation to dryland farming on the High Plains cuts per-acre production in half, there is still so much land currently held out of production, 127 million acres, that the return of 60 million acres into genetically transformed dryland farming alone would compensate entirely for the loss. Yet it cannot be assumed that the next decades can match the improved production (or bear the costs) of the last fifty years. The argument by the Land Institute is that conventional farming will always be so extremely exploitive of soil and water that it cannot succeed much longer on the difficult plains, thus justifying a drastic move toward perennial crops and more self-sufficiency.

Today's mood in the old Dust Bowl region is cautious. Today's goal is to preserve past achievements and conserve resources to keep the future stable, if not buoyant. No one has devised an alternative to the current irrigation strategy based on expensive equipment, skilled management, and cheap petroleum energy. The efforts directed toward water management are prodigious. Words like "phreatophytes," "albedo," and "evapotranspiration" come into play. Each issue of the Texas District No. 1 newsletter, *The Cross Section,* tells readers of the latest engineering and genetic developments. There is a sense of urgency.

Low Input Sustainable Agriculture on the High Plains:
Federal Programs

If water conservation becomes the rigorous discipline of the plains, irrigation can be stretched out to continue the High Plains in its classic agricultural pattern a while longer.[4] In the old Dust Bowl region we have seen that virtually all irrigators envision a future with far less water; acceptance of this reality and appropriate responses have been central themes in this book. Without radical changes, on-farm water efficiency rose from 53 percent in 1975 to 59 percent in 1982 and continues to rise significantly as more irrigators shift to improved center-pivot and drip-trickle methods. Older flood and furrow irrigation is, conservatively, 15 percent to 20 percent less efficient.[5] The combination of better management and new technologies offers the plains irrigator the capacity to cover three sections instead of two with the same water and still grow his wheat and sorghum. Today's irrigator, committed to efficiency, is thus three to four times more productive than the dryland farmer as compared with a preconservation difference of two to three times.

Plains irrigators can stretch out their farming careers another twenty years only by accepting a multipath, comprehensive approach: the development of production systems "that strike a balance between the goals of high crop yields and protection of the land's productive capacity . . . nondegradation or, preferably, enhancement of the elements and processes in the biosphere that support plant growth."[6] The end result can be a new gospel of efficiency: low-input sustainable agriculture (LISA) is a new name for an old idea—profitable conservation farming—that appeared with the 1985 farm bill. An expanded LISA became SARE (Sustainable Agriculture Research and Education program) in FACTA (Food, Agriculture, Conservation and Trade Act) the 1990 farm bill. Both are belated acknowledgements that soil and water mining is inevitably fatal to both farmers and their farmland and that the trouble is accelerated by expensive equipment and chemicals.[7] But LISA/SARE is difficult to generalize from because farming will always be, in the last resort, a local phenomenon. It is tied to the land and always requires on-site decisions. While irrigators readily accept industrial-farming techniques, "what suits one operator may not suit another. Management prescriptions will likely be worked out farm by farm."[8] As noted in the last chapter, the tendency in the 1990 farm bill to define sustainability in ways that favor large-scale industrial farming and defeat support for the self-employed family farmer suggests that the problem of local survival is not being addressed.

On a federal level, the 1985 Food Security Act, with its Conservation Reserve Program (CRP) mandate, including support for LISA, meant a policy breakthrough for resource conservation.[9] For the first time, conservation was directly linked to price supports, farm credit, and insurance benefits by offering to pay farmers for voluntary long-term cropland retirement. With the CRP, farmers are beginning, on a small scale, to enjoy an economic climate that encourages them to move toward sustainable farming or at least penalizes them less for the attempt. Through the sixth CRP signup in February 1988 already 25.5 million acres (of a possible 45 million) had been enrolled to be put into permanent grass cover.[10] In the 1980s, most environmental action by government was given to protecting highly erodible land and reducing chemical pollution, while groundwater mining was largely ignored. A 1989 study of CRP activity in Colorado's Baca County, which overlies the Ogallala at the Kansas border, gives no attention to groundwater.[11] The county had the most acres (266,851) enrolled in CRP in the nation, yet the effects on groundwater preservation were not addressed. Thus while High Plains erosion received attention, the overdraft of Ogallala water remained an invisible issue. Questions are being raised whether revised CRP policies for the 1990s should, for example, encourage the retirement of 20 million or more currently irrigated acres because the groundwater under them is dropping rapidly.[12] In addition, a modification recommended for CRP would expand its land-retirement program beyond the current 40 to 45 million acres to

50 to 70 million acres and would add groundwater depletion to soil erosion as an environmental standard of measure.[13]

CRP farmers will receive about $3.7 billion over a ten-year period, often exceeding their expected net production income in the same period. Negatively, the more CRP land there is around a given community, the less demand there will be for agricultural services, leading to reduced income and employment with lower agricultural production. This could be fatal on the plains. Private and public services will be reduced or eliminated, and less attention will be given to alternatives to traditional crops. It has already been estimated that the rate of economic decline wherever a plains region comes under CRP would be more than five times the national average.[14] Generally the High Plains have the lowest per-acre benefits from enrolling in the CRP. Texas irrigators, for example, believe they will be sorely pressed to develop adequate soil conservation plans to remain eligible for such support.[15] In its 1988 study, the venerable Great Plains Agricultural Council, established during the 1930s Dust Bowl, recommended that plains farmers receive higher benefits and more initiatives than farmers elsewhere to participate in CRP without risking regional collapse.[16] Nevertheless, CRP signups were higher in the plains than anywhere else; local irrigators and district officials agreed that the 1985 farm bill, despite its defects, has done more to promote soil and water conservation than any national legislation since the 1930s.[17]

CRP or LISA farm policy toward the plains still assumes that irrigators will successfully turn to dryland farming when they cannot pump water any longer.[18] The question is not theoretical, since about 13.8 million of the 39.1 million irrigated western acres are in groundwater decline areas, including Kansas, Oklahoma, and Texas. In addition, drought is still treated by federal policy planners as an anomaly, although admittedly an event with dramatic effects on the farm. It is clear that dryland farming under drought conditions, even with new conservation tillage methods, will fail.[19] Vulnerable irrigators, with low current profits, low crop-price expectations, and significant pumping from declining water levels, may accept CRP enrollment as their only economic option.[20]

New Conservation Technologies for the Irrigator's Farm

Current plans are to stretch out Ogallala groundwater supplies. Based on my numerous on-site interviews which were reinforced by a 1985 High Plains survey by Kansas State University geographers David E. Kromm and Stephen E. White, it is clear that farmers, seeing their well levels decline, are acting ahead of public thinking and the policymakers.[21] The two leading concepts are now mitigation and efficiency, when once the bywords were development and production. Conserving water at the wellhead is a front-end mitigation; higher grain yield per unit of water is a move away from waste toward efficiency.[22]

The shift from changing the environment to changing the crops includes biotechnological modifications: the manipulation of physiological mechanisms that plants use to influence the uptake, use, and loss of water, defined as their water stress or drought tolerance.[23] For most of the twentieth century crop gains from plant breeding averaged 1 to 3 percent each year for High Plains corn, wheat, and sorghums. During the last twenty years alone the proportion of harvestable wheat increased from 35 percent to 50 percent.[24] But, beginning in the 1970s, incremental technological changes did not bring the same levels of improved yields and higher per-acre profits; the 1980s saw only marginal gains. For example, during the 1970s and 1980s, wheat and corn production remained constant after decades of doubling and tripling.[25] It was as if High Plains soils and crops were fully exploited no matter how much water was dumped onto them. The last possible grain or kernel seemingly had been pushed out of wheat and corn and milo. As a result, without some significant improvement, the future involves a less-adaptable farm economy. The old buffers—soil, water, appropriate crops, and efficient equipment, even government cash and credit—have been used up.

Nevertheless the technological-fix mentality remains generally unchanged among many plains irrigators in anticipation of a new leap forward through genetic engineering. In this view, biotechnology offers a wish list of dramatic breakthroughs, including "increasing crop adaptation to stress conditions; . . . hybrid wheat; increased protein content of corn; breaking the yield barrier of soybeans; improving photosynthetic efficiency of plants;

developing nitrogen fixation by nonleguminous plants; . . . improved efficiency of those that now fix nitrogen in the soil; . . . improving the efficiency of nutrient uptake of plants."[26] The genetic potential of corn is said to be nine hundred bushels per acre.

The balance sheet for irrigation plant technology now includes "agronomic WUE" (water-use efficiency). WUE compares the amount of crop or forage produced—the amount of harvestable or economic biomass—for the water consumed by evapotranspiration.[27] Research includes tissue-culture work with protoplast fusion and recombinant DNA technologies to reduce stresses of salinity, drought, flooding ion toxicities, nutrient deficiencies, temperature extremes, and photosynthetic efficiency. Nor is classical plant breeding, such as hand pollination, being ignored. In all cases, there are important trade-offs. According to a 1980 study, "breeding lines [specific plants] that use water efficiently in a dry environment may not do as well as other lines under more favorable water conditions. This is because tradeoffs exist regarding plant responses in different environments. Therefore selecting plants for wide adaptability may be selecting for mediocrity."[28]

Reflectants and *albedo* refer to an identical phenomenon: the more a plant can bounce back the sun's light and heat, the less water it evaporates (evapotranspiration) from its leaves into the atmosphere. Artificial coatings, for example, have been applied to rubber plants indoors and soybeans in the field. One drawback is that photosynthesis also can be reduced, but in the case of soybeans, neither photosynthesis nor yield were reduced. On the other hand, while net photosynthesis in sorghums was reduced by almost a quarter, the total yield went up. Artificial coatings worked best in regions of high temperature and high humidity and less so in the High Plains low-humidity climate. Yet albedo treatment could extend, it is argued, the western range of soybeans into the drier zone.[29]

Some attempts to reduce water needs are exotic. In this era of lean diets, a lot of beef tallow is left in the beef plants around Garden City, Amarillo, and Lubbock after processing to suit public tastes. Beef fat is abundant, cheap, and undesirable, unless it is used as an antitranspirant. A Texas Agricultural Experiment Station research team, not a vegetarian among them, mixed the dense waxy tallow with water at several levels of mixture to test for phytotoxicity, or the tendency of plant leaves to "burn" and wilt and die from a fatty substance sprayed upon them. The best concentration was 2 percent beef fat to water. The first test on a potato crop yielded an increase of more than five hundred dollars per acre over untreated plants, largely because of the better quality of the resulting potatoes. Currently, work is under way on higher concentrations of tallow to water "so farmers won't have to carry around so much water."[30]

Equally sophisticated is the use of electronic meters to measure soil moisture in the fields when and where the crops are growing. Four basic soil types hold water differently, and there are also three categories of soil water. Plant-available water is self-explanatory, while gravity water descends below roots and molecular water is too strongly bound to soil particles to be released to the plants. Moisture blocks and resistance meters identify how much plant-available water is available. A soil moisture block looks like a small soldering iron containing a parallel pair of stainless-steel electrodes attached to wires and cast into a small gypsum block, hence "electrical-resistance gypsum blocks." As any high school chemistry or physics student knows, electrical resistance between the electrodes would indicate soil moisture. The blocks are buried vertically at one foot intervals to a depth of four feet, with the wires exposed at the surface and staked for easy identification. Resistance is measured with a resistance meter and is directly read as soil moisture. The blocks and wires are destroyed at tillage time, but the entire inexpensive device can be replaced annually.

Other devices to measure soil moisture are tensiometers, which measure soil water suction, or "force of attraction" of the soil for water; it is similar to the process by which a plant root gets water. Looking like a shiny cattle prod, it is a water-filled tube with a porous top and a vacuum gauge.[31] A more state-of-the-art instrument is the neutron moisture meter, costly but reliable and accurate. It uses a radioactive source and electronics to meter for moisture. Composed of a gauge and probe, when it is lowered into the soil it emits radioactive "fast" neutrons (6,000 miles per second), which collide with hydrogen atoms, almost exclusively in water in the soil. As they lose energy, the neutrons slow to about 1.7 miles per second and become "slow" neutrons. The probe becomes surrounded by a cloud of slow neutrons. The denser the cloud, the more water is in the soil, and it is this density which is measured by the detector and gauge above ground. But the neutron moisture meter is a health hazard demanding special storage, transportation and handling, and a license from the state department of health. It also is accurate only at depths of eight inches or more, since too many fast neutrons escape through the soil surface at shallower levels. For installation, permanent aluminum tubes, virtually transparent to neutrons, are buried below plow depth and covered with soil, which is removed to make annual measurements. Unfortunately, metering can be skewed if the soil contains boron, cadmium, or iron, as well as forms of soil hydrogen in humus, calcium carbonate, and gypsum.[32]

The widespread droughts of 1988 and 1989 called attention to unusual research in plant water needs. For more than four years USDA scientists have known that drought-stricken plants emit high-pitched noises as their cell structures break down.[33] These are too high-pitched for humans to hear normally, but special electronic gear can listen to the screams for water. Under normal conditions, water and the nutrients it carries flow from the soil into the plant under tension into a plant's water tubes, but if there is not enough water in the soil, the tension builds up and the tubes break and collapse, making ultrasonic noises. By using these sounds as signals of water deprivation, irrigation farmers could know precisely when to release water into the fields or start the center-pivot irrigator. In addition, sound measurement of this plant stress could point to new plant varieties that are better equipped to move water and nutrients from the soil into roots and leaves. It is fortunate, no doubt, that the sounds of the tension fractures are too high for normal human hearing (one hundred kiloherz while human ears range to twenty kiloherz) or fields throughout the High Plains would be noisy indeed. USDA scientists are currently trying to determine whether damaging insects are attracted by the noise of the stricken and vulnerable plants.

Rediscovering Traditional Practices for Water Conservation

Far less exotic and more subjective is the time-tested "feel and appearance" method to estimate soil moisture. The farmer goes to his field with a soil auger or sharpshooter, digs three sets of four-foot holes to find his average, grabs a handful of soil from each, squeezes it in his hand, and tests it by appearance and texture. According to twelve photographs in a full-color brochure offered by Texas High Plains Underground Water Conservation District No. 1, at one extreme is sandy clay loam, which is powdery dry and easily crumbled, indicating 0 to 25 percent available moisture; at the other extreme is silty clay loam, which "forms a soft, sticky, plastic (pliable) ball, easily ribbons out between thumb and forefinger, slicks readily," indicating 75 to 100 percent available moisture.[34] By following a feel-and-appearance chart and knowing his soil type, the farmer can decide when and where to irrigate. "As a good rule of thumb, the irrigator should begin irrigating before the soil moisture level in the upper two feet of the root zone profile falls below fifty percent available moisture. . . . Soil moisture in the three- and four-foot levels could be compared to a savings account."

Other methods range across the large variables of the inexact science called irrigation efficiency. These include analysis of soil structure that holds and transmits moisture and nutrients to plants, the differences among plants in their ability to acquire water from the soil, the differences in plant responses to drought stress, and different needs for water during the growing season. Highest transpiration and crop yields take place when the soil is kept consistently moist. "Plant transpiration is a mandatory cost."[35] The so-called harvest index includes the fraction of the plant that is of economic value to the farmer. The goal is to develop plants that produce more grain with less vegetation, as well as plants less sensitive to brief periods of water stress. To these matters of soil chemistry and plant genetics are added the traditional mechanics of water conservation, such as avoiding waste by controlling runoff at the end of the field, correcting the tendency to overwater, the old problems of evaporation and seepage, and soil erosion.

Waste is particularly evident in flood (furrow) irrigation. The old open, unlined ditches, when they water fine sandy loam, typically lose in a single season five thousand gallons of water per foot of open ditch, or more than twenty-one acre-feet per quarter-mile of ditch. The lost water could have irrigated sixty-five additional acres with a 4-inch application. By late 1989 in Texas District No. 1, open ditches were being replaced by more than ten thousand miles of underground pipeline; with the new pipeline in place, labor costs were cut more than half, fuel efficiency doubled, and water consumption was cut a quarter.[36] Twenty percent of the water flooded onto a field runs off as tailwater because the farmer tries to make certain his entire field gets water. Groundwater management districts made tailwater recycling pits an early priority; in Kansas more than twelve hundred new pits were constructed between 1978 and 1982. Another control is surge irrigation, in which special pumps cycle flow by spurts and delays into furrows in order to spread the wetness in a uniform application while avoiding waste through seepage into the ground. Texas High Plains irrigator Melvin Bentzen was told by the Soil Conservation Service that he needed only 3.5 inches of water to fill his soil to field capacity but he was using 8 inches. Using a surge valve in 1982, he doubled his earlier irrigation area on 4.9 inches of water;[37] a 15 percent increase in water use efficiency paid for his surge valve. Laser-beam land leveling, which reduces water costs by allowing more uniform water distribution and eliminating dry or waterlogged spots, is a public service provided by the Soil Conservation Service, since equipment costs run from twenty-one to fifty thousand dollars.[38] The simple act of leveling a field to a slope of .05 percent allows a farmer 10 percent better water application efficiency than he had before leveling.[39]

When farmers convert from furrow irrigation to center pivot, they find they pump 20 percent less water with little difference in yields. When center-pivot irrigation first appeared, as much as 50 percent of the water was still lost on hot, dry, windy days through evaporation because the sprinklers were high above the soil surface and sprayed upward. But in recent systems sprinkler heads are lowered and point downward, called partial dropline or full dropline center-pivot sprinkler systems. Their spray covers less area but offers better control. Center pivots with partial droplines can reach 80 percent efficiency with only 20 percent water loss because they are also inherently more flexible in applying smaller amounts of water for crop and seasonal differences. Early sprinklers also demanded high pressure because they were water-driven to make their circles. Newer sprinklers have electric drives and water pressure has been reduced four- to tenfold. The new low-energy precision application (LEPA) goes further with the use of drop tubes, allowing efficient and uniform irrigation at less than ten pounds pressure.[40] Less pressure means that irrigators can continue to sprinkle even as their pumping declines.

Alternatives to the popular center pivots, such as trickle or drip microirrigation, offer 90 percent efficiency but are costly, management intensive, and better suited to vegetables and fruits than large grainfields.[41] In an August 1984 interview, James Mitchell on a 317-acre farm near Lubbock, Texas, said he had turned to drip-irrigation devices that measure out drops of water at the base of each plant. The technology was expensive, he said, but it saved water and energy. "You can almost spoon-feed a crop with them. With those old sprinklers, on a windy day you could feel the mist a quarter of a mile away. The amount of water [and pumping costs] they wasted was just tremendous."[42] Mitchell also uses surge pumps that provide water between rows of crops in timed pulses. Wasteful runoff is avoided by machine-made furrow dikes—small mounds of dirt every few feet along irrigation rows. As a result, Mitchell's well levels have remained nearly constant for several years.

State groundwater districts, the Soil Conservation Service, and farmers themselves are seeking better management practices.[43] Wasteful irrigation includes full irrigation, which meant turning on the pumps and letting them run until the farmer judged that the field was well watered. Much of the water escaped below the root zone, but his field was kept constantly wet during the growing season and the farmer felt comfortable about the safety of his crop, no matter whether rain came or not. Open ditches lose up to 30 percent per thousand feet, meaning that an irrigator who needed to add four inches of water per acre to the plant root zone would need to pump six inches of water per acre to get his required four inches. It is still typical that half the water pumped from the Ogallala is lost through evaporation and deep percolation.[44]

The better practice called irrigation scheduling brought more complexity but more savings for the farmer because he learned when to apply the water, how much, and when to shut off the pumps. One farmer reported that with scheduling he needed only two-thirds the water on a field 50 percent larger than on a nearby unscheduled field.[45] Generally, proper timing and the application of sufficient water can increase yields 10 to 30 percent at critical stages of crop growth, such as tasseling and silking, head emergence, or pod and bean development.[46] But most farmers still feel most confident with full (excessive) irrigation.

For further savings, there is also limited irrigation, which provides water only at critical crop stages and pushes plants to their limits of stress and tolerance,[47] but it requires relatively drought-resistant crops, deep-rooted or dense-rooted crops, and crop rotations to rotate growth periods of different crops on a single farm. A further refinement combines limited irrigation and dryland farming: the upper half of a field is fully irrigated, the middle quarter uses furrow-tailwater runoff, and the lower quarter uses natural rainfall together with any remaining runoff. Despite this form of triage, sorghum yields rose a third on the same amount of water. Other management strategies include alternate-furrow irrigation, skip-row planting, and staggered planting dates. Both scheduling and limited irrigation indicate that farmers have been overwatering their crops for the past three decades.[48] Now the managerial ability of the farmer and his willingness to change his work habits provide better results.

As water becomes scarcer, farmers are being told to sacrifice perhaps 10 percent of a field on the theory that overall they will save more than they would lose because of saved energy, capital, labor, maintenance, and other production costs. One such underirrigated wheat field, using so-called deficit irrigation, saved water with a quarter less evapotranspiration, yet net income stayed the same.[49] With the saved water, farmers are told they could irrigate additional land or, in a time of scarcer water, still irrigate. scs guidelines suggest a field provides roughly the same net income when it is seven-eighths irrigated.

Other management skills involve mechanical land treatment: land conservation, including tailwater recovery pits, terracing of sloping land, erosion dams, and other erosion, seepage, and runoff controls. Runoff farming puts crops in widely spaced rows at the base of contour strips treated chemically or mechanically to increase runoff. Runoff farming works well on abandoned irrigated land otherwise prone to dust and tumbleweeds.[50] Other mechanical land treatment shapes the furrows by pitting, land imprinting, terracing and the contour furrowing of the 1930s, and the still-older deep plowing or ripping.

Conservation tillage is new, controversial, and popular.[51] Kansas leads the nation in this stubble-mulch or no-till farming , in which much of the previous crop's residue is left on the field during the planting and growing season. Not only is water erosion reduced remarkably and moisture better held in the fields, but evaporation can be reduced by 30 percent. There are also savings in fuel costs and man-hours when traditional cultivation is bypassed, but there are heavy new costs in weed control and pesticides. In addition, farmers who identify good farming with tidy farming have difficulty with the debris-filled fields of no-till. Clean fields look best but may not be saving water.

The objective of conservation, to use less water, also serves the profit-margin objective (keeping the farm successful) if successful crop yield is measured by net income and acre-foot consumption of water. According to one model, if irrigation costs double, it means a 20 percent reduction in net farm income, forcing closure of low-income farms, large-scale consolidation, and movement toward the deep pockets of vertical agribusiness.[52] It is equally troublesome if higher irrigation costs can push farmers into higher-value new crops, since the changes can require more water, more risk, new machinery, more labor, sophisticated management, and several years of heavy investment before the first returns. Hence most farmers stay with familiar field crops.

Zero-Depletion Irrigation

In 1990 Northwest Kansas Groundwater Management District Four set a zero-depletion goal to be reached in as little as ten years. After reviewing declining levels despite new management strategies, district manager Wayne Bossert concluded that "future consumption (although more efficient) will still translate into heavy consumption. . . . we are planning to define efficiency in terms of less water use."[53] He told a newspaper reporter that "the

237

declining levels meant zero depletion anyway, so why not opt to reach the same goal earlier while retaining an acceptable quantity of water for future management options?"[54] Kansas agricultural economist Orlan Buller said, "The question is not if, but when and how fast are the adjustments within the region going to happen."[55] The district, established in 1977, supervises more than thirty-six hundred wells that were drawing levels down two feet a year. Worst-case wells declined as much as fifty-nine feet between 1966 and 1990.[56] The objective, first conceived in the summer of 1989, was to reach zero depletion in a ten- to twenty-year span, but the district is having much difficulty in matching its Draconian goal with the immediate needs of farmers to irrigate for their survival. Farmers might not accept Bossert's assertion that "any operator who increases efficiency will not have the option of putting the same water on added acres for increased production. He or she will have to sustain the current acreage and production and simply pump less water."[57] Can water rights be set aside without losing them? Bossert in turn wonders how the high costs of more efficient irrigation equipment can pay off if water levels reach zero anyway. "This scenario simply continues the 'overcapitalization' cycle which has caused much of the decline problem in the first place."[58]

District Four's plan requires major decisions to redistribute costs and benefits among irrigators, businesses, taxpayers, and consumers by placing protection of the aquifer above existing economic, social, and political factors. Nevertheless, the long-term goal is also to protect economic stability for today's irrigators who want to stay irrigators in the future. Nonirrigated agriculture is less desirable because it varies greatly from year to year, depending upon rainfall and climate. Between 1985 and 1989 the average value of crop production in northwest Kansas was forty-three dollars higher for an irrigated acre than for a nonirrigated acre.[59]

More than five years earlier Bossert and the district paved the way for rigorous water conservation by requiring "Resource Development Plans" that would deny all new water rights unless they included systems that achieved 80 percent efficiency. Bossert also called for a citizen's committee, in the democratic tradition of plains water management, "for identifying 'hot spots,' places where depletion of the acquifer [*sic*] is too rapid."[60] After the district was divided into appropriate areas, each would have a "management trigger" at a specific water-table level (usually 50 percent of the depletable reservoir) that would put an automatic regulation into effect. According to the *Colby Free Press*, "though this may not mean an end to irrigation, it does herald an end to an age where unrestricted usage endangered the future of water in this portion of the state."[61] A zero-depletion formula applied today would preserve roughly 78 percent of the water now in storage under the district's land, approximately 40.5 million acre-feet; by the time the goal is fulfilled, 31.6 million acre-feet would be left. The newspaper hoped "that the ensuing regulation does not crumble the regions [*sic*] economic structure."

Bossert recommended to the Kansas Department of Commerce that the region move "toward a replacement economy of some kind to compensate for the lost agricultural economy."[62] This implied that even if alternative agriculture were introduced it was unlikely to continue without extensive irrigation. Bossert concluded that "an ag [*sic*] approach might be to promote price supports for less water-intensive crops within the federal farm program," meaning less corn and more grain sorghum, wheat, beans, or sunflowers that use less water. A "non-ag" approach might be to make the Ogallala into a perpetual water supply to attract less-intensive water-use industries that could afford high water prices. By September 1990 the district board recommended that the amount of water that can be withdrawn be limited, a move toward zero depletion. For most areas, withdrawals would be restricted to two-tenths of 1 percent for every foot of water remaining in the ground, but in areas of heavy depletion, farmers would be allowed to take more water to protect their economic well-being.[63] Otherwise, Bossert concluded, "some of these [farmers] would hit it [zero depletion] in three years."[64]

The Privatization of Water: Make the Irrigator Pay His Own Way

Today, although the long-term effects of declining aquifer levels are accepted, the water is not given a dollar value. Most consumers of High Plains groundwater still treat it as a free good, available to the first taker at no cost for the water itself.[65] It takes only fifteen dollars to pump an acre-foot using natural gas and thirty dollars using electricity. Hence this free water has been generously consumed on profligate levels. Waters laws, such as prior appropriation (use it or lose it) also counter sustainability. Pierre R. Crosson and Norman J. Rosenberg of the think tank Resources for the Future write that "markets are not well equipped to protect resources such as water . . . in which it is difficult to establish property rights."[66] An imperfect first step is not to try to change agriculture, but to broaden economic analysis to include environmental costs. One controversial solution, more applicable elsewhere in the West than on the plains, is privatization of water, remembering that in Kansas, Oklahoma, and Texas groundwater is by law a state-controlled public resource.[67] The economic, political, and societal climate of the 1980s has encouraged such efforts.

There is an old irrigationist maxim: "Water flows uphill to money." The privatization argument is that the nation's farmers are wasteful and extravagant with their water consumption because it costs so little. They also have first right to waste it—the policy of prior appropriation. True conservation, it is argued, would take place when water is separated from land ownership and allowed to float on an open market: "Water will start reflecting its true price."[68] On the High Plains there is little competition for Ogallala water from new cities, as in Arizona, although Mobil Oil's use of water for oil recovery is not the only such case in Oklahoma or elsewhere.

The objective of privatization is to measure a water resource entirely according to its price on current markets.[69] In California, Arizona, and central Colorado, for example, water from federal reclamation projects that sells to farmers for ten dollars an acre-foot could be marketed to a growing retirement city for more than one thousand dollars per acre-foot. Regions with extra water—not being currently consumed—could sell and ship it elsewhere. This is the argument behind shipping water from the Great Lakes to the plains or from the water-rich Sandhills of western Nebraska to parched regions elsewhere on the plains. In August 1984 the San Diego (California) County Water Authority paid ten thousand dollars for the option to buy

Yampa (Colorado) River water from the local water conservation district. The option fell through, but San Diego would have picked up the water out of the Colorado River through southern California's system of canals.

Privatization creates enormous pressures to abandon the long history of water's nonmarket function based on a water ethic. As early as 1937 the Oklahoma Supreme Court decided water use must be controlled by beneficial use and greatest need for the sake of agricultural stability set by safe annual yield. In the American West, water costs have been set extremely low to support the farmer, in perpetuity a low-cost, high-consumption consumer. In turn, the farmer's privilege is based on the externality that he sells his crops well below real water cost (particularly if all factors, including an ecological deflator, are included) to guarantee traditionally low food prices for the consumer.[70]

The ability of farmers to pay high prices for water as required by privatization is yet to be demonstrated. Under ideal conditions they can be much more efficient, from less than 40 percent for flood irrigation to more than 75 percent with scheduled sprinkling. Drip irrigation offers as much as 90 percent efficiency, but an underground version being tested on the plains costs at least $15,000 per forty acres. California and Arizona farmers admit that their federally subsidized $5 to $10 an acre-foot is relatively inexpensive water and that they can tolerate new $17 rates, but they would have to shut down at the $55 predicted for 1994. As perennially low-cost users, farmers have little flexibility to absorb higher water prices. A peak agricultural use price of approximately $70 an acre-foot (in 1977 dollars) is often compared to urban pricing as high as $2,500 per acre-foot. The U.S. Army Corps of Engineers claims farmers could afford $120 an acre-foot, yet its own calculations for a major High Plains water-importing project from the Mississippi and Missouri rivers range from $320 to $880 per acre-foot.[71]

Farmers' headroom to absorb high water prices is constrained by food prices acceptable to the American consumer and world markets. When water levels eventually drop below economical pumping levels, one estimate is that grain prices for feed or food would rise 10 percent annually and meat prices 20 percent annually.[72] Would the public pay ten dollars (1977 dollars) for a loaf of bread or forty dollars for a pound of steak to allow the farmer to buy irrigation water at competitive water prices? Cheap water has always buffered other farming costs to keep food prices low. This is water's historic "duty" throughout the nation. No wonder plains farmers have zealously guarded their individual access to water under their land with their own wells, pumps, and irrigation systems.

This argument for water conservation and management on the basis of the efficiency of market prices has been rejected by those who insist that other, different, forces also affect natural resources. Policy analyst Mark Sagoff, for example, believes that the measurement of resources by the marketplace alone—who is willing to pay the most—ignores the historic and powerful American tradition of public interest. Efficiency is not the only guiding force; Americans do not put a dollar value on the Bill of Rights or protecting wilderness or even the 1985 farm bill's aid to private farmers. Americans, Sagoff and others argue, see themselves not only as private consumers but also as members of a larger community that supports environmental protection and public welfare aside from cost-benefit analysis.[73] According to this antiprivatization, antimarketplace argument, the ethical duty of water as a low-cost free good for farmers is not an externality or secondary matter but a direct social or cultural priority reflected in public policy. Water may run uphill to money, but it also flows steadily and strongly toward the national interest. Sagoff concludes that although public policy (government) is expected to stay neutral toward individual freedoms, it is also expected to serve a national good (protecting natural resources, such as air and water) for the sake of the nation's well-being. State water laws and groundwater management districts are based on the protection of public interest. The Stone case in Kansas and the Mobil Oil case in Oklahoma are examples of the privatization debate.

Individual farmers and local conservation boards cannot include the true cost of water in their economic balance sheets without immediately reporting devastating losses. As a result, the free-goods equation is being reversed: groundwater irrigation can be sustained only by increasing the costs of capital (energy costs), equipment (drip irrigation), and management skills (labor). By using more efficient equipment and better management, Texas High Plains farmers reduced their average water use by half (from 1.38 acre-feet per acre in 1977 to 0.68 in 1990) while crop yields rose, a net increase in efficiency.[74] But other forces control the irrigator's future; actual declines of water levels are still inevitable, which means that proportionally higher pumping costs will take a bigger bite out of low farm income. In the 1960s, natural gas cost $6.07 to lift an acre-foot of water 250 feet; by the 1980s the new gas cost was as high as $36.49 per-acre foot. Electricity cost seven times more than it did in the 1960s, as did liquefied petroleum gas, or LPG, while diesel fuel was three to five times more.[75] These rising expenses can be balanced temporarily with successful waste reduction and a better ratio between water use and crop yield. Hence, according to today's equation, conservation of water does not make the farmer's pockets jingle with extra cash.

Importing Outside Water

Why not bring more water to the plains instead of devising costly ways to conserve water? The historical record is not good. Nineteenth-century frontier farmers believed in the myth that rain follows the plow. They chased the unusual rains of 1878–86, and as a result they failed, starved, and lost their farms. Dependence on surface water in the Arkansas River as it ran past Garden City, Kansas, proved wrong, and the underflow proved confusing. In the twentieth century, cloud seeding is more scientific but equally unpromising.[76] Nor have attempts at artificial recharge to rebuild the aquifer brought any significant change in the rate at which the water is running out. Texas District No. 1 is experimenting with air injection, which, like water-infusion secondary recovery in old oil fields, would seek out leftover unpumped water. Where the Ogallala sand and gravel waters have a clay lid, air pressure conceivably could drive water up and out through wells at the cost of fifty dollars per acre-foot. At present, this is too costly.[77] This capillary water (so called because it is held by surface tension on sand and gravel) may be as much as 25 percent of the total; the Texas High Plains might have 840 million acre-feet of capillary water that would otherwise be unreachable. Other water-recovery plans, such as the use of surfactants, heat, vibration, and osmosis, were rejected as costing three thousand dollars an acre-foot or more.

Several projects have been proposed to import outside water from abundant sources, such as the Canadian Rockies or the Great Lakes. The border which divides the plains and the Rockies between Canada and the United States is a political line, not an environmental or geographical border. Vast quantities of surface water in Canada, mostly stored in year-round glaciers and snowfields, together with torrential high-mountain rivers renewed each snowy winter, could meet and surpass all conceivable agricultural needs on the central and southern plains.

This tantalizing resource, a thousand miles distant and in the hands of another albeit friendly nation, tempts the American predilection toward large-scale technological solutions. The first such plan came surprisingly early: Eli Newsom, speaking in 1896 before the newly formed Nebraska State Irrigation Association, outlined an irrigation plan which was ambitious but not outlandish. Everyone knows, he said, of the vast and inexhaustible supply of underground water topped by the Great Plains. This underflow was a massive body of water from the Rocky Mountains, or perhaps from the Arctic, that could instead be channeled to huge underground reservoirs controlled by lateral tunnels. Fed by gravity, discharge tunnels would direct the water to centralized surface outlets from which large agricultural regions could be irrigated. Newsom, a former immigration booster for the Santa Fe Railroad, concluded that the lack of pumping technology could thus be effectively overcome: "Today we find the pump too limited and too expensive, too uncertain and troublesome, to practically serve the increased demand of the practical irrigator. . . . *Throw the old pump away* and substitute nature's forces. Gravity . . . like charity, never faileth."[78] Newsom believed he would become "the Elias Howe of the Irrigation Methods," but he did not have a George Washington Goethals to engineer the project or the backing of a Theodore Roosevelt for the venture; if his geology had not been so wrong, his plan might have been as technologically feasible and as demanding as the Panama Canal.

Seventy years later, two plans stayed within the nation's political borders. The 1968 Texas Water Plan sought to divert 5.8 million acre-feet a year to the

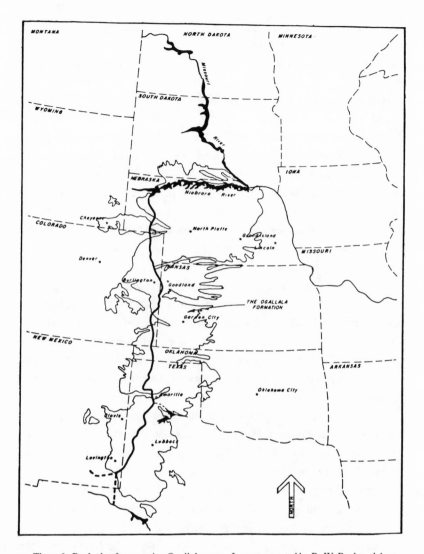

14. The 1967 Beck plan for rerouting Ogallala water. It was presented by R. W. Beck and Associates, consulting engineers, and sought to transfer water internally across the High Plains, most notably by reversing the flow of the Niobrara River in northern Nebraska. But the plan encountered major deterrents, particularly rising energy costs, environmental-impact statements, upper Missouri River navigation problems, political questions, and, above all, construction costs. From Morton W. Bittinger and Elizabeth B. Green, *You Never Miss the Water Till . . . . (The Ogallala Story)* (Littleton, Colo.: Water Resources Publications, 1980), 95, with permission of Resource Consultants, Inc.

water-starved southern High Plains from the abundant supplies of the lower Mississippi River by means of fourteen hundred miles of canals and seventy-one pumping stations. Construction was scheduled for 1977 through 1985, but rising energy costs—more than fifty billion kilowatt-hours of electricity would be needed each year to pump and raise the water—ended this dream.[79] More ambitious was R. W. Beck's 1967 plan to divert water from the upper reaches of the Missouri River in the Dakotas by reversing the course of the Niobrara River in northern Nebraska.[80] Between 9 and 15 million acre-feet would be lifted upstream to the head of a large canal in western Nebraska and the water would be channelized to flow by gravity south into the parched central and southern High Plains. Once again the plan foundered on rising energy costs and environmental impacts, as well as concern for commercial transportation on the lower Missouri.

The 1975 Rocky Mountain plan of consulting engineer William G. Dunn would take water from Canadian mountain rivers—the Peace, Athabasca, Smoky, and Mackenzie—and from upper tributaries of the Columbia River, and run it through Alberta rivers and the upper Yellowstone, Missouri, and Snake rivers. In 1977 the cost of the project, including hydroelectric facilities, was estimated between forty and fifty billion dollars. Several large reservoirs in Montana would hold nearly one hundred million acre-feet of water and distribute twelve to twenty-five million acre-feet a year through 5,850 miles of aqueducts onto the plains.[81] Similar was U.S. Bureau of Reclamation engineer Lewis G. Smith's plan to tap Mackenzie River water rather than the Yukon River.[82] Water intended for the High Plains would be stored in a massive reservoir at seven thousand feet in the Centennial Valley of southwestern Montana. In 1968 cost estimates were twelve billion dollars for delivery of forty million acre-feet annually.

The most remarkable plan appeared in the 1960s: the North American Water and Power Alliance (NAWAPA) project to import "excess" water from western Canada not only to the central and southern plains but to other chronically parched regions of the United States. Another project of engineering consultants, the massive plan was attractive to a citizenry that also supported a successful multibillion dollar National Aeronautics and Space Administration moon-landing program, nationwide Great Society bureau-

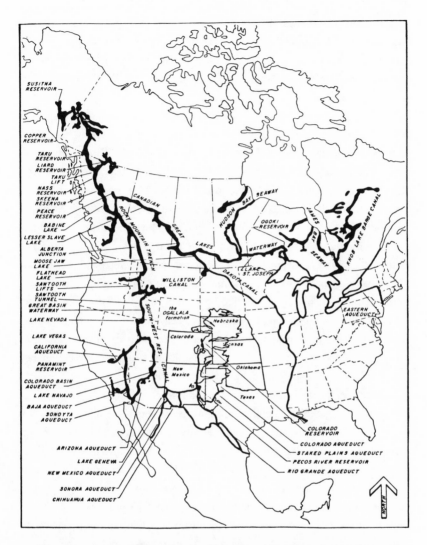

15. The 1965 NAWAPA water-transfer plan. The most ambitious water-import plan was the North American Water and Power Alliance proposal from a California-based international consulting engineering firm, the Ralph M. Parsons Company, to bring water across the entire continent from Canada into the United States and down to Mexico. NAWAPA ran into grave environmental, political, diplomatic, and economic problems. Costs doubled and tripled from the original estimate of one hundred billion dollars in 1964. From Bittinger and Green, *You Never Miss the Water,* 98, with permission of Resource Consultants, Inc.

cracies, and assurances of both guns and butter during the Vietnam War. Senator Frank Church of Idaho expressed the opinion of many regional advocates: "We must not be deterred by its size. To perform the task before us, we may well need a program as far-sighted as was the Louisiana Purchase."[83] Under the plan, 158 million acre-feet of water would be diverted south each year from water-rich western Canada (estimated to provide 633 million acre-feet to rivers that flow to the oceans) primarily through canals in the reconstructed valleys of the Rocky Mountains (the Rocky Mountain Trench, combining the upper reaches of the Peace, Fraser, Columbia, and Kootenay river valleys). This is the equivalent, said Colorado water resource expert Morton W. Bittinger, of 125 percent of the annual flow of the Mississippi River at St. Louis. At least 80 million acre-feet (the rest going to Canada and Mexico) would go to the western United States, including the High Plains, by way of new aqueducts: the Colorado and the Staked Plains. Opponents were dismayed by the environmental, economic, and political problems. Estimated costs rose from $100 billion in 1964 to $200 billion in 1977 to $300 billion in 1982, roughly equivalent in each case to the annual defense budget of the United States but presumably spread over thirty years. The pressures of drought in the early 1970s encouraged support, but the energy crisis and rising fuel costs after 1973 dampened interest.

These spectacular plans ran aground on rising energy costs, growing environmental concern, and changing public sentiment toward large reclamation projects. All of them beggared the three-billion-dollar Central Arizona Project, which was belatedly completed in 1990 despite high costs, delays, and protests. USDA water policy official Herman Bouwer observed that when "water runs uphill to money . . [it] does not bode well for agriculture, which traditionally is accustomed to inexpensive water for irrigation."[84] He noted that all large water transfer schemes involve capital costs of several thousand dollars per acre-foot per year. An existing project like the Central Arizona Project is costing $2,000 per acre-foot per year, discounted by subsidies that give farmers $52 per acre-foot; the California Aqueduct runs about $100 per acre-foot. Bouwer argued instead for better conservation of existing water.

A changing national mood, weary of costly pork-barrel projects and sus-

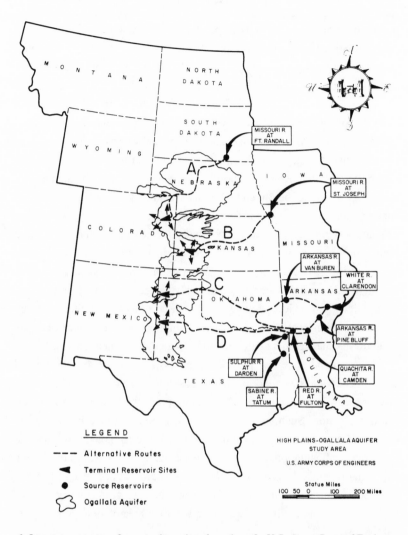

LEGEND

− − − Alternative Routes

◄ Terminal Reservoir Sites

● Source Reservoirs

⌘ Ogallala Aquifer

HIGH PLAINS-OGALLALA AQUIFER
STUDY AREA

U.S. ARMY CORPS OF ENGINEERS

Statue Miles
100 50   0   100   200 Miles

16. Interstate water-transfer route alternatives from the 1982 U.S. Army Corps of Engineers plan. A primary mission of the *Six-States High Plains–Ogallala Aquifer Regional Resources Study,* written in 1982 by three consulting firms for the U.S. Department of Commerce and the High Plains Study Council, was to identify new sources of water to replace the depleted Ogallala Aquifer. The map identifies potential alternate routes of supply from the Mississippi River. Serious difficulties included financing, environmental effects, politics, and the cost to High Plains irrigators. From *Summary Report: Six-State High Plains–Ogallala Aquifer Regional Resources Study* (Austin, Tex.: High Plains Associates, 1982), 71.

picious of a ballooning federal deficit, did not prohibit the six-million-dollar 1982 Six-State High Plains Ogallala Aquifer Regional Resource Study ordered by Congress and sublet by the United States Department of Commerce to private consultants. It was not the first federal water study, of course, but it was the first to pay significant attention to the long-ignored Ogallala. In 1950, President Truman's Water Resources Policy Commission barely recognized the High Plains when it considered groundwater in only ten pages of a two-thousand-page report.[85] In 1955, President Eisenhower's Advisory Committee on Water Resources briefly reported that regulation and management of groundwater belonged to the states; acknowledging wastefully high consumption, it recommended further study.[86] This was followed in 1959 by a Senate committee that held twenty-five public hearings (none on the High Plains) and barely mentioned Ogallala aquifer draindown. Much more ambitious was the 1968 National Water Commission, which conducted a five-year, five-million-dollar study but gave only 5 pages to groundwater mining on the High Plains in its 537-page report. The commission admitted that major consumption problems had national implications but concluded that groundwater management belonged to the states and local agencies.

A background paper for the 1968 commission forecast that the federal government could be called upon for "costly rescue projects" when water levels ran low in critical regions. The author proposed legislation to encourage conservation. Such a costly rescue was used as a threat in 1977 when President Carter's secretary of the interior, Cecil Andrus, noted that "groundwater overdraft situations [based on] unwise resource practice" could bring unpopular federal interventions. The states, Andrus argued, need "to bring laws, rules, and institutions governing water into the 20th century [or] the Federal government will . . . step in and another area of state prerogatives will be lost."[87]

A Carter task force concluded in 1978 that federal farm supports "may be contributing directly to shortages of underground water reserves." An editorial in the *Southwest Kansas Irrigator* (Ulysses) quickly headlined: "Carter Task Force Fears Farming May Be Too Profitable."[88] A 1979 Carter task force recommended: reduce federal actions contributing to groundwater depletion, provide federal remedies for groundwater depletion, and work with the states to develop consistent groundwater management programs. A March 1979 editorial in the Texas High Plains Underground Water Conservation District No. 1 newsletter, *The Cross Section,* quickly retorted that "the National Water Policy with respect to groundwater appears to be tied to some mystique of conservation, translated to mean 'cut back,' 'control pumping,' 'regulate.' "[89]

It was in this suspicious climate, based on apprehension over Ogallala water losses and fears of heavy-handed federal intervention, that the Department of Commerce study started. It also began in an era that feared for American and world food supplies based on a widespread belief that most of the nation's and the world's agricultural lands were already under full production.[90] An outside water resource to relieve depletion (and avoid a return to less-productive dryland farming) on the High Plains seemed to be an appropriate response to the perceived crisis (which faded away in the 1980s). Water-policy analyst Morton W. Bittinger concluded in 1980 that "if a large importation project is going to be tackled, it is time to get started. The time required even to design and construct a N A W A P A or Smith project could be 10 or 20 years [akin to the construction history of a typical U.S. nuclear power plant]. Adding in the time required to solve the financial, political, social, and environmental problems could mean 30 to 50 years before delivery of water."[91]

The six-million-dollar High Plains Study (as it was commonly called) began in 1978 and was published in 1982 under contract from the Department of Commerce to the consulting firms of Camp Dresser; McKee, Black and Veatch; and Arthur D. Little. It was the first to set High Plains agriculture (and Ogallala groundwater) into a broader economic and political framework. The congressional legislation creating the High Plains Study (Public Law 94–587, Section 193) stated: "In order to assure an adequate supply of food to the Nation, and to promote economic vitality of the High Plains Region, the Secretary of Commerce . . . is authorized and directed to study the depletion of the natural resources of those regions . . . presently utilizing the declining water resources of the Ogallala aquifer, and to develop plans, to increase water supplies in the area and report thereon to Congress."[92] Using 1974 data, it reported that on the High Plains 1 percent of the nation's people living on 6 percent of the nation's land area produced over 15 percent of the nation's wheat, corn, sorghum, and (in Texas) cotton and 38 percent of its livestock. It identified 150,000 irrigation wells that served 14.3 million acres in 1980, compared to 3.5 million acres in 1950. Another 18.3 million acres were in dryland farming and another 18 million acres in dryland grazing and fallow land. It estimated that Ogallala groundwater totaled 3.05 billion acre-feet in 1974, 77 percent of it in Nebraska. Eight percent was in Kansas, 2 percent in Oklahoma, and 9 percent in Texas. This water was being consumed at the rate of 22.14 million acre-feet annually despite better efficiency that had reduced per-acre water use 30 percent, from 2 acre-feet to 1.4 acre feet. The report optimistically concluded that about 23 percent of the existing aquifer water would not be consumed until 2020, but the remaining water would be largely inaccessible or too costly to pump.

The study seemed predisposed, with little supporting evidence, to portray the agricultural future of the High Plains in the most favorable terms possible, including the creation of 350,000 new jobs by 2020 on top of the 1,000,000 jobs of 1977.[93] The study asserted that the High Plains deserved priority attention over other regions. It had "large quantities of flat, productive agricultural land which is amenable to mechanized production of fiber, grain, and livestock commodities of significant importance in national and international markets. The area has deposits of oil and gas, which are finite in quantity, and deposits of ground water which receive . . . very little recharge in the southern parts of the Region."[94] The report noted that rainfall is inadequate in both quantity and seasonal reliability "to realize the potential productive capacity of the area's land resources." Acceptable levels of food production depend on irrigation; without irrigation it would fall to a third or quarter that of irrigated yields. Considerably more than half of the southwest Kansas and Oklahoma-Texas Panhandle water would be consumed, the rest of lower quality and less accessible at deeper levels.[95] Yet the study predicted that by 2020 an additional 3,800,000 acres would come under irrigation in the region served by the aquifer. Contrarily, it stated that "even with the most effective water conservation program possible, over five million acres currently irrigated will be returned to dryland production or native vegetation by the year 2020 because of declining water supplies."

The study is flawed. Its basic division between northern Ogallala and southern Ogallala at the Kansas-Oklahoma line does not make geohydrological, agricultural, or economic sense. A 1977 USGS Ogallala study plan was more appropriate:

> The High Plains is divided into four roughly equal segments by the valleys of the major rivers that cross the High Plains from the Rocky Mountains. The streams that divide the Ogallala Formation into major segments are the Platte and the South Platte Rivers, the Arkansas River, and the Canadian River. These rivers flow through valleys 1 to 10 miles wide. The Platte and Arkansas Rivers are incised 100 to 300 feet below the High Plains. In contrast, the Canadian River has incised its valley nearly 1,000 feet. These major streams act as lines along which natural discharge from the Ogallala aquifer occurs.[96]

The report is wildly optimistic about increased irrigation potential, future grain yields, energy alternatives, agribusiness fixes, and outside water sources, among other factors. Corn production is projected to double between 1977 and 2020; instead, corn is declining as a major crop on the High Plains because of its heavy water demands. In Kansas alone, wheat production is projected nearly double between 1977 and 2020.[97] Donald Worster has also observed that the study concluded that a return to dryland farming would be supported by significantly higher commodity prices on world markets. "Yet," Worster states, "the bushel price of wheat *today* (1991) is no higher than it was in the 1950s!"[98] The study also favors large-scale expansion of vertically integrated cattle-feedlot operations; these are extremely sensitive to water supplies. The study pays little attention to a still-declining number of farms or to the inevitable rise in the cost of irrigation retrofitting and the burdensome debt left over from the more prosperous 1970s.[99]

The study makes an innovative contribution by recognizing the connections linking High Plains water resources to commodity prices, energy costs, interest rates, inflation rates, and export markets. "A collapse in the export market would have a more significant effect on the economy of the High Plains Region than likely variations from the projected levels of energy price, agricultural productivity, or domestic economic growth." Its recommendations cover four major interacting forces affecting food production on the High Plains: water resources, market forces, production technology, and societal institutions. Particular attention is given to which forces are prone to change, which forces can be reasonably managed, and which forces are beyond reasonable control. Emphasis is placed on the "production enterprise management" of agribusiness, including the supply of capital, technological fixes, and the role of regulatory agencies.[100] The study also recognizes the all-important connections with local oil and gas production and feedlot and meat-processing operations.

Predisposed to the continued growth of High Plains agriculture along its current high-yield, high-water-consumption pattern, the study breaks no new ground in the answers it offers.[101] It supports current thinking that irrigation will continue into the known future as the only workable substitute for the water-poor High Plains climate. The plan identifies four basic methods to achieve the goals ordered by Congress: improving irrigation efficiency, restricting groundwater use, increasing the region's water supply, and a broader economic base for the region.[102] "For the near term, it appears that a major commitment to water conservation should be made, since many desirable results of water conservation can be realized relatively quickly and at relatively low cost. Both public and private activities are needed." The study gives considerable attention to voluntary or mandatory conservation methods, most of which are already providing significant improvements in water-use efficiency. The study warned that continued high Ogallala water withdrawals "could result in economic failure of irrigation in the near future, with devastating results to the region." It also stated that "regulation of ground water withdrawal is a state responsibility."[103]

The most controversial recommendation of the High Plains Study supported future imports of water from outside the region. While the study ignores the grandiose N A W A P A plan, it does explore the feasibility of importing water in four possible ways from the Missouri or Mississippi rivers. But the study acknowledged that water costs would be prohibitively high. If farmers can ill afford $70 to $120 per acre-foot in 1977 dollars, then the transfer costs of Route B (from the lower Missouri at Saint Joseph to west-central Kansas) from $226 per acre-foot to $569 per acre-foot and of Route C (from the Mississippi River in Arkansas to the Texas High Plains) make outside-water costs prohibitive. These costs do not include distributing water to individual farms from the pipeline terminals. A 1978 Bureau of Reclamation study for Oklahoma estimated that recovery of construction costs (capital costs) alone to move water from the Mississippi directly to individual farms (farm headgates) would require a total of $2,150 per acre supplied.[104] The study does not include expensive subsidies (as in existing reclamation projects west of the Rockies) or substantially higher consumer food prices as a means to pay for imported water. Construction time was estimated optimistically at ten to fifteen years. Its final recommendations in December 1982 were not optimistic: "It was not possible to conclude that major multistate conveyance systems will be financially feasible in the foreseeable future; importation costs would be quite high in relation to ability of water users to pay for imported water."[105]

New Dryland Farming: Better Than Abandoning the Land

Caught in an iron triangle between declining Ogallala water levels, low commodity prices, and rising costs, a few plains irrigators have already become plains dryland farmers. Forced into retreat they felt defeat, but it is not the dryland farming their grandfathers knew. It is a more sophisticated, more complex enterprise using new methods combined with hard labor and the intuitive experience of mature farmers.[106] Nevertheless, the dryland farmer reverts back from dependable irrigation to luck with the weather: the right rain at the right time. If the prospects are not favorable, no crop is planted and the field is left fallow for better water conditions. One newer dryland management practice is flexible cropping, in which a crop is planted only if carefully measured stored soil water and expected rainfall promise a satisfactory yield.[107] Winter wheat, for example, is difficult for flexible cropping because it is planted in the fall before most water is accumulated. Dryland farming is daunting, but the alternative may be abandonment of the plains.

New dryland farming can also involve altering the microclimate conditions of growing plants. Microclimate technology is often simply a modern way of describing the windbreaks and shelterbelts successfully advocated and installed in the late 1930s. Cold winds in spring and fall can physically damage plants, while freezing damages plant tissues. Arid winds put plants under severe moisture stress that brings wilting, desiccation, and poor production. The same winds erode the soil and sandblast young plants. Postwar fencerow-to-fencerow planting brought down the successful tree windbreaks planted in the 1930s. Since then, farmers have begrudged field space to windbreaks. Shelterbelts also interfered with the mechanical operation of large center-pivot sprinkling systems.[108] Successful in-field windbreak experiments have included double rows of corn sheltering irrigated sugar beets or, with irrigated sorghum, ryegrass.[109]

Most new dryland farmers do practice some limited irrigation. As plains farmers move away from water-sensitive crops, such as corn and soybeans, and toward more sorghums and wheat, crop rotation can involve the cycle of irrigation-fallow-dryland. One management practice is the above-mentioned limited irrigation-dryland system, in which the upper half of a field is fully irrigated, the next one-quarter is a tailwater-runoff section using runoff from the fully irrigated section, and the lower quarter is managed as a dryland section dependent on rainfall only for its water. On the Texas High Plains this system offers high water-use efficiency compared to full or conventional irrigation.[110]

One proven practice rubs the good farmer wrong; he takes pride in his weed-free and stubble-free clean fields, the historic sign of his industry and virtue. Conservation tillage, also mentioned earlier, uses crop residues as soil cover; whatever is not worth harvesting is not cleaned away but left on the fields. This no-till or low-till farming leaves the field surface rough, holds water in place, reduces evaporation, controls wind and water erosion, and increases organic matter in the soil. The goal is to capture rainfall and hold it in storage in the soil;[111] in addition, soil erosion is reduced—cut to one-third in Nebraska tests. Energy costs and the work put into cultivation also go down. Results are enviable. In dryland wheat, conventional tillage in the 1930s and 1940s yielded no more than seventeen bushels per acre while stubble mulch and minimum tillage in the 1960s and 1970s produced over thirty-two bushes an acre, and there are predictions with improved no-till yielding forty bushels per acre. Sorghums rose 50 percent from 2,190 pounds per acre to 3,150 pounds.[112]

No-till production has its costs. No-till wheat yields change enormously from year to year, depending on annual rainfall. Yields are much higher in good years and much lower in bad years than conventionally tilled and irrigated wheat. It is also harder to seed crops into heavy stubble, with 10 to 30 percent less production than on conventional fields. Most controversial is the abundance of weeds, insects, and the harboring of potential plant disease in crop residues. This paradoxically demands heavy herbicide and pesticide application on low-till or no-till fields, which Wes Jackson vividly has called "chemotherapy on the land."[113] His view is reinforced by agricultural scientist David Pimentel, who notes that insects' ability to develop resistance to every new pesticide has meant an actual rise in crop losses because of the risks of monoculture. If farmers cut their use of chemical pesticides in half and rotated their crops with biological pest control, food prices would rise less than 1 percent.[114] Intensive use of herbicides not only raises costs significantly but in too many cases makes fine-textured soils under chemical fallow (weed control with herbicides) too hard to seed.[115] Unsolved problems include uneven seed germination, low soil temperature in spring, and environmental pollution by the heavy use of chemicals. Nevertheless, no-till is one of the few regional substitutes when the water disappears.

Arguments against dryland farming may still be persuasive. According to a cautious 1982 federal study, if the high point of irrigation was the late 1970s and early 1980s, the gradual transition to dryland farming since then could reduce gross farm income to half the irrigated levels.[116] Part of a decline is also psychological, since family farms and small towns, still admired as the bearers of basic American values but sensitive to agricultural decline, would be first to weaken and disappear. A region's institutions and communities can only go so far in adapting to water scarcity.[117] Rural communities would experience the ripple effect of weakness in farming. Banks would quickly be affected by defaults by farm borrowers. Lack of credit for less-efficient or more highly leveraged farms would force them to cease operations. Support businesses, from equipment suppliers to the local Wal-Mart discount store to doctors and lawyers to filling stations and local newspapers, would lose their "critical mass" for successful operation.[118] Without competition, prices go up before the lone remaining business shuts down. Schools, government, churches, and services weaken and roads and bridges and utilities suffer. Younger community leaders leave farm and town, and for the older leaders, malaise and defeatism often defeat efforts at stabilization or recovery. Farmer know-how, including the subtle and arcane skills of successfully planting, cultivating, and harvesting 640 acres of High Plains crops, can disappear forever when it skips a farm-family generation. First the satisfaction of a skill is lost, then a career, and finally work as meaning for life. Texas sociologists Albert and Ruth Schaffer conclude: "If a drought should persist for several years, many farm communities will cease to exist."[119]

Alternative Crops: Keith Allen's Experiment

With the threat of failure, whether from declining groundwater, dryland farming, or the swath of social effects, the farmers' search for high-value alternative crops may accelerate. Wheat and sorghums have never been truly adapted to extended dryness and prosper best under irrigation, while corn and alfalfa have always been unlikely crops for the High Plains. Those scientists and farmers who work under the conventional wisdom of highest possible productivity search for new plants, mostly native to arid regions in the United States and Mexico, that can be adapted to environmental stress and provide a marketable product. In 1978 the National Science Foundation identified fifty-four such potential crops.[120]

One farmer who is trying alternative crops lives in Haskell County, Kansas where farmers are reputed to be more risk taking, innovative, and less committed to a single piece of worn-down land on short water rations.[121] Keith Allen is in his early thirties, of medium height, has a wiry build, and sports a sandy mustache. Like every farmer in the area, he wears the ubiquitous adjustable cloth cap with a slogan or seed or implement company name in front above the bill. The cap is worn indoors and out, sitting or standing or riding. He farms seventeen miles north of Sublette.[122] Meeting with him for a double-cheeseburger lunch in the town's Pheasant Inn (it also offers a small salad bar), Allen gives a double impression: the idealistic farmer-irrigator who sees a bountiful future in profitable alternative crops and the wary entrepreneur who is already a product-testing consultant to feed companies to guarantee that he gets in on the ground floor of any new food-production developments in the region. His fields are test acreages for alternative crops. He rents his farmland, but his father and uncle own considerable acreage and he hopes to follow in their stead.

The difference is that Keith Allen has a degree in agronomy from Kansas State University and has chosen to specialize in alternative crops. He is still rare, but not alone. Kansans already have advocacy in alternative crops at the nationally known Land Institute, led by Wes Jackson, and the Kansas Rural Center, a broad-based public-interest group. Keith Allen himself established the aggressive High Plains Growers Association. As energy costs to pump the Ogallala went higher, he concluded that he needed to generate three times the cash per acre compared to the region's conventional crops. If natural gas rose to $1.70, he would shift from water-intensive corn to milo. If it went up to $2.80, he would use half the water for a limited milo crop. If natural gas went up to $10.00, he would have to abandon existing production and turn to alternative crops, such as canola (rapeseed), provided that a market had developed.

Other alternative crops are guar, which is similar to soybeans but produces a resin, and sunflowers, which can yield 80 percent more in Kansas than in the better-known sunflower region of North Dakota. But Gary Baker of District No. 3 in Garden City observed that farmers would need to get twenty cents a pound for sunflowers instead of today's ten to twelve cents. Nevertheless, Jeff Schmidt of the Soil Conservation Service in Liberal noted that while in 1987 there were only four hundred acres of sunflowers in his region, this doubled in 1988 and he was bullish about the future.[123] As for new, improved versions of existing crops, wheat can yield more valuable gluten, and grain sorghums (milo) are more profitable as a source of ethanol. In the past southwest Kansas farmers also have raised sugar beets (around heavily irrigated Garden City), highly profitable popcorn, and even watermelons and tomatoes. Baker also wondered about the introduction of beans—pinto, lima, great northern—but Schmidt noted that a drip irrigation installation for vegetables costs fifteen thousand dollars for 40 acres. Keith Allen and others have not yet felt the pressure to turn to gopher weed, kenaf, or Jerusalem artichokes, which require little or no irrigation water. With efficient and intensive drip irrigation for a variety of vegetables, he has concluded that farmer cooperatives can succeed where individual farmers could not, either on extensive dryland farming or with costly irrigation. There are successful historic precedents among cooperatives in Colorado and Nebraska.

As water costs rise and water supplies become scarcer, there will be more Keith Allens, not only among the adventuresome farmers of Haskell County but throughout the old Dust Bowl region. They cannot change the water and land, nor do they have the power to raise grain prices. The future of generous government supports is in doubt, so their options are limited. One answer is several new field crops that are less water intensive, but the right crop must include a combination of successful production, the creation of a marketing infrastructure, and willing consumers. On the farm, alternative crops would demand reeducation for weed, insect, and disease control, appropriate tillage, fertilizer and irrigation practices, use of pesticides, and new investment in equipment. New management would require new understanding of yield levels, per-acre net returns, and marketing to buyers and processors.[124]

High Plains farmers have historically produced food for humans or animals. They speak of their positive service to society: feeding the nation and the world. But this may be disrupted when they feel compelled to grow nonfood crops as the only means of survival. Guayule is a native perennial plant of the southwest United States and north-central Mexico; it produces rubber and does it best when less than twenty-five inches of water is applied. An advantage for the plains climate is that guayule prospers in a wide temperature range up to 120 degrees Fahrenheit, but a major disadvantage lies in its failure and death at the freezing temperatures that also hit the plains. As is true with most new plants, processing operations and commercial guayule production do not exist. Another connection with rubber is in the annual plant crambe, which produces plant oil with a high erucic acid content; it can be used for rubber additives. Crambe is a cool-season crop requiring significant irrigation, but profit per acre could be much higher than it is for today's High Plains crops. Today's harvesting technologies, however, still damage mature seeds and the rubber-additive market is very competitive. The combination of guayule and crambe might see a tire factory outside Garden City instead of IBP.

Slightly better known is jojoba, a perennial shrub from the same region. It produces oilseeds about the size of an olive with 50 percent oil by weight. It requires as little as five inches of water a year for survival, but irrigation allows faster growth with bigger plants. Again, jojoba is not a food; the oil can go into detergents and is the only known source of unsaturated liquid wax other than sperm-whale oil. The same commercial-production questions remain. Only vertically integrated operations are likely to succeed, linking growing crops through seed-crushing facilities to marketing. If plains farmers find it necessary to grow an alternative food, the seeds of buffalo gourd yield a protein oil similar to corn oil, and the meal product can be used as an animal feed. It is another perennial plant, in this case a spreading fruit vine from the North American West needing only twelve inches of rain. Year-round cattle forage—sainfoin, a perennial legume; alfalfa; and some wheat grasses—is being investigated by Texas researchers.[125]

Wes Jackson's Land Institute at Salina

The introduction of perennials instead of annuals has attracted the interest of the innovative Land Institute at Salina; it has experimental test fields for alternative crops. One is leymus, a ubiquitous temperate-zone grain-producing grass long known by gathering peoples since the Vikings, American Indians, and Russians. Once used for roof thatch and basket making, it can be woven into mats and natural rope; it is also a forage crop and can be harvested for hay or silage. Historically, leymus also served as human food in

Central Asia in times of drought when conventional crops withered and died. It has received more attention recently because its protein content rivals that of red beans and its fatty-acid percentage surpasses all other seed grains, including amaranth, wheat, high-protein corn, rice, and oats. In fields its perennialism reduces erosion and reduces cultivation efforts, and it works in a polycultural system. On a Land Institute field, it yielded over eight hundred pounds per acre, about half of a wheat yield on the same plot.[126]

The institute is also experimenting with native prairie vegetation, such as the common animal forage eastern gama grass, which produces the same per-acre yield as did early corn five thousand years ago. The primary goal of the institute is "to develop an agroecosystem that reflects more the attributes of climax prairie than do conventional agricultural systems based on annual grain crops"[127] in order to identify crops for sustainable agriculture. "Our work flows from a philosophical basis that regards nature, that is the patterns and processes within the native prairie ecosystem, as the most appropriate standard for sustainable agriculture on the Great Plains."[128] In the drought summer of 1988, institute researchers discovered that while the drought reduced seed yields on most of its monoculture plots, yields of eastern gama grass and leymus rose on polyculture plots. In a mission statement for the institute, Wes Jackson and Marty Bender wrote: "We believe that the best agriculture for any region is the one that mimics the region's natural ecosystems. . . . our goal is . . . to create prairielike grain fields." Jackson wrote elsewhere that "the agricultural human's pull historically has been toward the monoculture of annuals. Nature's pull is toward a polyculture of perennials."[129] According to Jackson, perennials offer less soil loss, reduced energy needs compared to monoculture cultivation, and less pesticide and fertilizer dependency, and they would reverse the decline of genetic diversity.[130] Not the least, perennial agriculture, because it draws on existing plains plants, would require little or no irrigation, thus achieving the ideal Ogallala groundwater zero-depletion goal.

The Land Institute is taking a broad-based look at grain sorghums, the current standby of both irrigators and feedlot suppliers, long harvested as an annual monoculture. Sorghums are among the world's staples, along with maize, wheat, barley, and rice. Researchers at the institute note that the sorghums are taxonomically related (the same tribe, *Andropogoneae,* of the grass family, *Gramineae*) to two plains grasses, big bluestem, a major Kansas tallgrass, and eastern gama grass. Of African origin, sorghums did not appear in the United States until 1857. By the 1960s, with the advent of irrigation, Kansas became the center of the "milo belt" as production multiplied tenfold. It is grown almost exclusively as a feed-grain crop, second only to corn in importance. New hybrid grains, true yellow milos, are more digestible with higher nutrition than before. The vegetative biomass (the plant aside from its grain) is fed to livestock as forage, silage, green chop, and hay. In India and Central America, sorghums are human food in breads and tortillas, and are not converted into meat. Africans make the grain into a porridge, including a sorghum couscous.

On the plains, sorghums are attractive because their root systems are more efficient in extracting soil water than corn and they require less water for growth than corn, barley, or wheat. Hence they have better drought tolerance. Maize requires weekly irrigation and heavy pesticide application. A sorghum field needs as few as three irrigations per growing season and attracts fewer pests. Land Institute researchers also see sorghum as a natural herbicide, since it prevents the spread of certain grasses and broadleaf weeds. A hybrid of milo, sudan grass, and sordan grass is also apparently a soil desalinator and can play a role in soil reclamation while simultaneously serving as livestock food.[131] Among several experiments, Land Institute researchers chose so-called long-season sorghums (entire growing season) to intercrop with early maturing millet and tropical maize and with late-season cowpeas and certain beans. Total yield is 50 percent better than sole cropping. Grain sorghum is perennial in its native tropical and subtropical environments but cannot survive temperate winters. The institute's goal is to develop a winter-hardy perennial grain sorghum by cross-cultivating it with Johnsongrass, a winter-hardy perennial sorghum better known as a particularly distasteful weed. If it is successful, Ogallala farmers in the old Dust Bowl would have a familiar crop and commodity that would need planting only two or three times a decade. The institute notes, however, that seed companies might be loath to market it. In addition, sorghum prices are a sixth less than corn, and livestock is supposed to do better on corn than milo. A long-term, integrated, whole-system approach to sorghum will have to take more into account than prices and animal feed. A positive outcome to the Land Institute's research, however, would help to fulfill its long-term goal of making perennial polyculture the agricultural wave of the future on the High Plains. This would assist the farmer by reducing his costs and his labor and help the regional environment by reducing water consumption and limiting chemical use.

Other crops mentioned are mung beans, kochia, fourwing saltbrush, pearl millet, amaranth, and guar, some of which are ancient low-yield crops associated with the agricultural revolution in the Middle East ten thousand years ago. Alternatives to new high-value crops include the use of known field crops with improved yields, decreased costs, and new technologies and new management—the combination known as LISA.

Conclusion

It is widely acknowledged that access to sufficient water for high-yield production is limited and will gradually change High Plains farming. In 1970, farmers around Sublette, Kansas, concluded they had three hundred years of water left in the aquifer. By 1980 their estimate had fallen to seventy years and by 1990 it was less than thirty years. Today, using current techniques, irrigators say they will be happy to last until the end of the century. More than half of the usable water is gone and levels continue to drop as much as two feet a year.[132] In a 1976 study of Ogallala supplies in Texas's Parmer County, midway along the New Mexico border, a well that had 110 feet of saturated thickness (storing 15 acre-feet and allowing pumping rates of one thousand gallons per minute) in 1974 would have been down to 74 feet of saturation (11 acre-feet, allowing eight hundred gpm) in 1984, to a limited-use 52 feet (7.5 acre-feet, allowing five hundred gpm) in 1994, and an uneconomic 37 feet (5 acre-feet, allowing three hundred gpm) in 2004.[133]

Answers to declining water supplies are also sought in more-profitable alternative crops, like canola, sunflowers, or popcorn, more efficient technologies like drip irrigation, better management like irrigation scheduling, and water-holding techniques like no-till farming. Other answers include horizontal drilling and the use of vertical turbines, greater well and pumping efficiency, reduction of center-pivot pressures by half, improved on-farm conveyance systems and tailwater recovery, alternative furrow irrigation, and more know-how concerning plant growth and water stress. Efficiency can rise significantly under ideal conditions, from the miserable 45 percent in furrow irrigation to 75 percent with scheduled sprinkling from groundwater. Drip irrigation applied directly to the roots of plants claims 90 percent efficiency. But extremely high equipment costs skew these advantages. The end of extensive irrigation for intensive farming can also mean the end of family farming on the High Plains.

The arid climate of the High Plains may once again have the direct effect it has not had for fifty years. With yields three times higher today, together with unprecedented capital investment, the stakes are far higher than they were in the 1930s. Intensive agriculture is vulnerable to changes in its environmental base. Not only would grain production be ended by desertification, but today's all-important cattle-feedlot operations would be halted by sun, wind, and temperature extremes. Frontier conditions on the High Plains can still control its future. As water levels decline, High Plains agriculture is subject once again to unpredictable interruptions from its old enemy, climate.

Farm economist Willard W. Cochrane sees a pattern: the period 1930–37 was one of uncertainty and instability. A technological payoff began in 1937 and continued for an extraordinary fifty years. Cochrane concludes that as long as government intervention continues, it prevents a return to the chaos of the 1930s, but the last fifty years of abundance cannot be repeated.[134] In addition, the last fifty years have given rise to new technologies that have increased the power of large-scale industrial farming while weakening the smaller family operation that did not have access to the latest technological fix. The problem is that such fixes are often isolated and narrow solutions that can produce unintended social and environmental disruption. The family farmer is driven away, while the soil and water are still weakened. Many of the individual responses to declining groundwater I have described are under attack because they merely support prevailing bad habits or ignore their wider effects. A natural resource, such as water, is treated in isolation from larger chronic problems and the answers are piecemeal, disengaged from any longer plan. Critics from the Land Institute in Kansas or Nebraska's Center for Rural Affairs, say preoccupation with technological (and managerial) fixes will fail, since the root of the problem lies in the plains farm system itself because it is not sustainable.

8

. . .

The Move toward a Drier World:
The Summer of 1988

The great drought of 1988 was most severe on the northern plains in the Dakotas and Montana; it was less severe in the old Dust Bowl heartland of southwest Kansas and the Oklahoma-Texas Panhandle. As the summer progressed, however, the awful combination of sun, wind, and lack of rain once again began to hammer the Dust Bowl, the region best prepared to protect itself from lack of rain. Not only had lessons been learned the hard way from the 1930s, but farmers, suppliers, bankers, and extension agents had been tested by the droughts of the 1950s and 1970s.[1] Most important, the south-central High Plains enjoyed their climate substitute: heavy irrigation from large groundwater supplies. The waters were receding, but no doubt they could carry farmers through one more time. The next time around, however, would the new threat of a man-induced global warming—the CO_2 or greenhouse effect—overwhelm the substitute? On the plains a newsman called the spring of 1988 "this eerie spring—a spring without thunder, a spring without rain. . . . some rangeland barely turned green this spring. . . . Many fields of spring wheat, pathetically trying to head out on plants only four inches high, would be almost too short to harvest." The lack of rain had a finality about it: "Rain—even in torrents, even tomorrow—would come too late."[2]

Once more it is clear that the plains cannot be understood in isolation. The

267

jet stream, Earth's high-altitude climate maker, spent the spring and summer of 1988 flowing off course far to the north, responding to below-average ocean surface temperatures along the equator in the Pacific.[3] As a result, a vast stretch of the United States, from Montana through Georgia and most of the East, suffered through record stretches of ninety-degree-plus temperatures. Forty-five days and nights of pounding heat were contrasted with Noah's flood of forty days and forty nights. Francis Bretherton of the National Center for Atmospheric Research (NCAR) in Boulder, Colo., frightened people when in October 1987, well before the drought, he spoke prophetically to *Time* magazine of the greenhouse-effect consequences of a doubled atmospheric concentration of CO_2: "Suppose it's August in New York City. The temperature is 95 degrees; the humidity is 95%. The heat wave started on July 4 and will continue through Labor Day," a span of fifty-five days.[4] In reality, the 1988 New York heat wave lasted forty-four continuous days, started well before July 4, with the temperature and humidity in the nineties, and continued through August 18.

On the plains, the first to be hard hit were ranchers; their cattle demanded daily water and access to grazing. Nineteen eighty-eight was already their second or third year of drought. As early as the middle of May, Texas ranchers were burning thorns off prickly-pear cactus with gas torches. In Minnesota a Soil Conservation Service official said, "There are drifts of dirt like snowdrifts in the ditches and lots of dirt in the air and lots of dirt in the houses." In a modern twist, a farmer near Minton, South Dakota, pulled out his snowblower. "It worked. I created a mini-dust storm blowing the soil back onto my wheat field."[5] Farmers used the 1930s term "black blizzards" to describe murky conditions that reached from the old bonanza country of the Red River Valley of the North in the eastern Dakotas down into eastern Colorado and the Texas Panhandle. In the Southeast, an Atlanta water bureau official summed up farmers' feelings nationally: "There's a double drought, a drought of reality and a drought of anticipation." This reflected the fears of plains farmers while they waited uneasily to see if 1988 was the beginning of the next Dust Bowl, expected by the early 1990s.[6] LaVerne G. Ausman, longtime Wisconsin farmer and USDA official in charge of the federal response to the drought, spoke of the sense of impotence and despair brought on by day after day of no rain. "There isn't anything more disheartening. You're totally helpless. You just watch your crops wither away."[7]

By mid-August the U.S. Department of Agriculture made front-page news when it predicted a 37 percent plunge in the nation's corn crop, a 23 percent drop in soybeans, a 13 percent drop in wheat, and a 31 percent overall drop in all grains. In early August, President Reagan belatedly signed a $3.9 billion disaster-relief bill, the costliest ever: "This bill isn't as good as rain, but it will tide you [farmers] over until normal [*sic*] weather" returns. The president's comments mimicked the old hope for better weather that farmers had laid to rest in the 1930s. Said a plains insurance agent: "Farmers aren't buying anything but crop insurance." A *New York Times* editorial on August 26, 1988, proposed that crop insurance be required of any farmer who benefited from federal income supports. In Draconian language, it concluded, "Perhaps the only way to persuade individual farmers to take charge of their fate will be to deny them special relief the next time disaster strikes." The editorial may have signaled exasperation with federal farm support during endlessly cycling crises and the end of the nation's loyalty to the myth of the independent farmer. Ultimately, this drought consumed twenty billion dollars of disaster-relief for nine million acres of farmland.[8]

Some people profited from the drought. At the Chicago Board of Trade, where much of the nation's supply of wheat, corn, and soybeans is traded in the volatile futures market, the volume of trading soared to 170 percent of normal as big grain users, food-processing companies, tried to lock in prices from grain-elevator operators. At the beginning of May, wheat futures hovered around $3.30 a bushel and reached $4.20 in early July. Corn stood at $2.30 in early May and neared $3.60 in early July. One market journalist claimed that "bullish traders . . . gleefully detail the damage that the drought has already wrought. . . . one would think that the entire corn crop will consist of nothing but cocktail party-size baby ears. . . . Predictably, the price action has been galvanic."[9] Another bullish soybean trader said, with more passion than sense, that "it will never rain again in your or my lifetime. Climatic changes are in the process of transforming Illinois and

Iowa into the Gobi Desert. . . . since we're repeating the weather conditions of the Dust Bowl years, it stands to reason that the corn crop is doomed to come in with yields 65% or so of normal like it did in 1936."[10]

Some midwestern and plains farmers, having already speculated and lost on the right climate for their stunted fields, decided they could survive only by gambling a second time on the futures markets. Critics called it a highly volatile "de facto insurance policy on at least a portion of their crops to lock in prices before the harvest."[11] Prices soared in June, but scattered midwestern showers in July caused prices to collapse to their daily permitted limits. Wheat highs of $4.20 in early July were down to $3.70 by the end of the month, while corn futures fell from $3.60 to $2.75.[12] Shortages of durum wheat for pasta, corn oil for margarine, soybeans for mayonnaise, soybean meal for chickens, and feed corn for cattle pushed consumer prices up 5 to 7 percent, the highest rise since 1980. A fifteen-ounce box of Cheerios that cost $1.98 in October 1987 sold for $2.14 in June 1988.[13] A one-pound loaf of white bread rose 10 percent between April 1987 and June 1988. A 6 percent increase in food prices would cost a typical American family of four more than $300.00 a year. Nevertheless, food costs still accounted for only 17 percent of the American consumer's pocketbook, less than half that of Europeans. Despite the swings, it was clear that consumer food prices would not soar because low consumer prices are one of the USDA's sacred tenets.

With drought damage in Canada, China, and the United States, the globe had only a fifty-four-day supply of stockpiled grain, down from eighty-nine days earlier in 1988 and below the sixty-day global minimum set by the United Nations Food and Agriculture Organization.[14] It was the lowest figure since the food crisis of 1972 and 1973, when wheat prices doubled and corn prices tripled. The drought laid waste Canada's farm belt and ravaged China's central and southern grain belts.[15] In this fourth drought since 1980, Canada's prairie grain crop fell to about thirty-three million tons, down a third from 1987 levels. "We've had people up here who've walked away from their crops." In China, 65 million acres of grain from 196 million acres of farmland had been hit by a heat wave and two-thirds of the country's peanut and soybean crops were lost for the year. Chinese meteorologists be-

270

lieved the drought to be global, the result of an increase in sunspot activity or the greenhouse effect. There were fears that if the United States, which produces a fifth of the world's grain, abandoned export subsidies because of short supplies, it would bring more famine to poorer nations. Two and a half billion dollars had been spent in the Export Enhancement Program to encourage foreign nations to buy American wheat, and build their need for it, at twenty-five dollars to thirty-three dollars a ton less than in the United States. In December 1987 the Soviet Union's dependence was ensured when it bought wheat for forty-two dollars a metric ton less than the domestic going price in the United States, a subsidy of more than a dollar a bushel.[16]

The green revolution had been widely expected to overcome global food scarcity by the early 1960s. Historic importing nations, such as India, China, Brazil, and Mexico, became major exporters.[17] But if a worldwide drought hit for several consecutive years, the United Nations Food and Agriculture Organization in Rome concluded that it would collapse food surpluses and threaten widespread hunger on a global basis; the green revolution was running out of steam. A USDA report in early August noted that the 1988 American grain harvest was the smallest since 1970 and even smaller than the Soviet harvest. Lester Brown of the environmentally oriented Worldwatch Institute argued that even if the fifty-four million fallow acres in the United States were put back into production, the cumulative effects of loss of farmland to erosion and development, depletion of water for irrigation, and higher costs for farm equipment globally meant less agricultural resiliency. Between 1965 and 1983, for example, India more than tripled its wheat harvest but has hardly raised its output since.[18] Virtually everyone agreed that another global drought year in 1989 would be catastrophic.

Ghost of the Dust Bowl

The drought that drove half a million people off the land in the 1930s would not be repeated in the 1980s.[19] As many as sixty-four million acres of land had been abandoned fifty years earlier, compared to only fourteen million acres in 1988. The dry spell was severe, even more severe for some plains farmers than it was in the 1930s, but when a young farmer could raise three times more wheat per acre than his father or grandfather, or five times more corn, he had a greater capacity to recover in the next wetter season. Hence his borrowing power was better and could tide him over. In 1984, following the bad drought of 1983, harvests had nearly doubled. Farmers also were protected by government subsidies and drought relief born out of the sufferings of the 1930s. After the 1930s experience, over fourteen million acres on the High Plains—grassland, fallow land, conservation reserve—had been set aside as unsuited for farming. In the 1980s, at considerable taxpayer cost (but willingly offered to support the family farmer), government agencies prevented wild swings in prices, supplies, and production.[20] Up to two years' worth of wheat and corn prudently could be set aside to stabilize supplies and prices.

Not the least, better farming skills meant that the 1988 winter wheat crop came through virtually unscathed compared to the minuscule wheat harvests of the 1930s. Genetically superior seed varieties were available now, together with better fertilizer and pesticide know-how. Following the creation of the USDA's Soil Conservation Service in the 1930s and the widespread creation of soil conservation districts throughout the High Plains, farmers learned to contour and terrace the land, practice minimum tillage, plant grain in strips, and graze cattle more carefully. A combination of higher wheat prices (because of the drought), standard subsidies, emergency drought relief (from the federal government), and crop insurance (farmer good sense) pulled farmers through.

Soil erosion was severe in 1988 and dust storms caused heavy environmental damage. Plains farmers lost a year's crops and permanently damaged their land. A North Dakota state conservationist observed, "Landowners aren't only concerned about losing their crops this year; they're also concerned about losing their soil, because that's their livelihood." Damage was measured by a formula: an acre that lost about fifteen tons of topsoil, or three times what the land can regenerate in a year, was a damaged acre that could receive federal attention. In such a case, nutrient loss—nitrogen, phosphates, potassium—runs $576 per inch of topsoil. Kansas State University researchers say that wheat yields drop 5.3 percent for every inch of topsoil lost to erosion, with corn declining more and grain sorghum a bit less.[21] In 1988, 1.5 million Kansas acres were vulnerable, 200,000 in the Oklahoma Panhandle, and 3.8 million in West Texas, or four times normal.[22] Across the entire plains, almost 12 million acres were damaged by erosion and 19.5 million acres lacked cover and were at risk, ready to blow.

Drought in the 1980s and the 1990s would have a more global effect than in the 1930s because of the intensive high-yield farming that now prevails on the plains. Together with irrigation, the combination of superior genetic strains, intensive use of fertilizers and pesticides, and better on-farm management transformed American agriculture in the 1970s and 1980s. But widely predicted claims of future yields of five times as much corn per acre and three times as much wheat as fifty years earlier actually resulted only from precisely defined conditions rarely experienced in the field. Farmers had unrealistically fine-tuned their crops to match ideal climate patterns instead of a generalized drought. The high yields of modern industrial farming, with its reliance upon a small number of basic plains crops—wheat, milo, alfalfa, and corn—matched to specific chemicals and irrigation methods, would be extremely vulnerable to both drought and limited irrigation. The discovery and application of underused but more adaptable crops could take a decade. If the greenhouse effect took hold tomorrow or a no-rain climate anomaly appeared in the 1990s (the opposite of the decade of extraordinary rain from 1876 to 1885), a spell of hotter, drier conditions would find farmers once again vulnerable to any extreme.[23] Climate still mattered.

Amaranth is a heat- and drought-tolerant grain, but Keith Allen north of Sublette, Kansas, had learned that alternative crops require public acceptance and markets before they become profitable. The Land Institute is exploring means to improve the cattle forage characteristics of naturally occurring plants, such as Illinois bundleflower and leymus. The institute also urges a move away from today's industrialized monoculture, no matter how productive, to the more flexible diversity field (polyculture) planting, which would mix grain crops with legumes, sunflowers, and perennial grasses. In this way farmers could mimic the historic prairie, which survived under all weather conditions, but it is unlikely that this alternative would offer the high-yield productivity on which the agricultural economy depends. Plant physiologists are also pushing to determine why plants fail at times of extreme stress, such as heat or drought. Can proteins be inserted to protect crops? Such research for alternative or sustainable agriculture, long a stepchild in the nation's federally financed research and development programs, has grown little since 1980.[24]

Unlike traders in the Chicago pit, who profited handsomely, and unlike America's consumers, whose pocketbooks were not rifled, drought-stricken farmers took the brunt of the collapse. Reduction of wheat storage from a two-year supply to a one-year supply and of soybeans from a year to six months drove commodity prices to their highest prices in a decade at a time when plains farmers had little to sell. Farmers had looked forward to the beginnings of a recovery from a six-year-long debt-ridden agricultural recession; it had already forced the largest number of farm and bank failures since the 1930s. One in every six farmers in one Minnesota county had fallen behind on his debt payments. Commodity prices stayed high, but the ability of farmers to cover the inevitable lean years by taking advantage of a fat year or two slipped away with the drought. Echoing his predecessors of the mid-1930s, a farmer said: "High prices don't help if you go into town with an empty truck."

In 1988 farming was once more between a rock and a hard place. An eighty-eight-year-old Montana rancher who had weathered the 1930s told a reporter: "Back then, things cost less and everybody had a little money to get by. That's all you needed was a little income. Our expenses today are 10 times higher, maybe 20 times higher. So even if you make a little money, you're still going to be short. You can't pay for the equipment. This drought is going to put a lot of ranches out of business."[25] By June 1988 land prices, upon which loan equity is often based, stopped climbing and started slipping. As the drought continued into early 1989, a Kansan from Hays wrote the *Wall Street Journal* that "our little patch of wheat is dead. The evergreen shelter belt is more brown than green. The creek is barely running and most of the migrating water fowl are bypassing our country because the ponds are dry. The weather that scares the birds and animals has us worried too. But that's nothing new to Kansans. . . . [Your statement that] 'the name Kansas became a byword for the impossible and ridiculous' doesn't bother Kansans more. . . . Wall Street looks to a lot of us to be a hell of a lot less predictable than Kansas weather. . . . while Kansas weather may be ridiculous, Kansans are sublime."[26]

The Case for Irrigation . . . and Its Limits

One well-established regional alternative was to ignore the drought. Whoever irrigated his land could still proceed as if the drought of 1988 had never come. Larris Hollis, a hands-on Wisconsin farmer with over three hundred acres in corn and hay and also a Milwaukee stockbroker who watched farm production trends, observed in June that the driest Wisconsin spring in a century meant that his crops came nowhere near their moisture requirements. By contrast, he noted, the irrigated High Plains were "in pretty decent shape" no matter the absence of rain.[27] Established High Plains irrigators could be envied for their ability to ignore the drought. They could schedule irrigation and not wait for rain. If, for a field of corn, more water was needed to support day 40 through day 50 of the growth cycle, when the plants begin to grow substantially, then so be it at the flick of a pump switch. But without irrigation, said Hollis, "what we need is several days of nice gentle rain . . . a good soaking" of the kind that center-pivot irrigation provides by flipping a switch on the normally rainless Kansas Sandhills of the Gigot family. "[Irrigators] can pick and choose."[28]

Because of 1988's delayed rains, farmers' irrigation engines worked harder than before pumping water; by May they had recorded approximately 50 percent more pumping time. Gary Baker, manager of Southwest Kansas Groundwater Management District No. 3, noted that farmers around Garden City had planted 10 percent more corn (wheat was a swing crop for them) in 1988 than in 1987. In the drought, their rate of groundwater declined almost 3 feet in 1988 alone compared to a twenty-year average of 1.8 feet. This was all the more disappointing because in recent years irrigators using conservation methods had reduced their annual decline to a foot or less.[29] Like an evil portent, dust storms swirled through all of Kansas west of Wichita. scs offi-

275

cial Jeff Schmidt went out to check on crops damaged by sand and static electricity. He called for emergency tillage as serious soil erosion hit fields emptied of their crops.[30]

Throughout the United States during the 1980s, over 270,000 farmers—more than 11 percent of all U.S. farmers—abandoned their fields. Most High Plains farmers, now heavily insulated by irrigation, efficient machinery, sophisticated plant science, and federal prices and credit supports, survived the drought of 1988. As commodity prices were kept high and grain surpluses hit their lowest levels in a decade, farmland prices began to rise by the fall of 1988. Hugoton, Kansas, grain farmer James Kramer concluded that "we could see two or three years of a relatively stable farm economy, if the weather is fairly normal."[31] In Hugoton's Seward County, where pick-and-choose irrigators were plentiful, the 1982 National Resources Inventory recorded, probably at the peak of plains irrigation, that 113,600 of the county's 263,800 cropland acres were irrigated. In Finney County, 244,400 acres, almost 30 percent of the farmland, were irrigated from 2,267 wells, largely with sprinklers. In Haskell County it was 263,900 acres, more than 71 percent, from 988 wells and 90 percent sprinkled.[32]

On the central and southern High Plains, any long-term drought, such as from global warming from the greenhouse effect, would reduce crop acreage as much as 25 percent.[33] Some of farmers worst fears materialized as drought continued into 1989 on the central High Plains, with little snow in the winter and belated rains in the spring.[34] In February, farmers around Liberal, Kansas, did their regular tests of soil moisture. Instead of the four-foot moisture depth needed to plant their milo, they found two feet. Instead of forty-eight inches needed to plant their wheat, they found thirty inches of moisture. At Hays in the middle of Kansas it was reported that gravediggers were not hitting moisture at six feet. Those who planted wheat in the hope of fall rain and winter snow (neither appeared) were compelled to destroy their crops because yields were so low it was too costly to harvest. Furthermore, the crop had been unprotected by snow and left exposed to sandblasting winter winds. The result was winter kill of 20 percent of the crop, and by May the USDA projected total loss on fourteen million of fifty-five million acres planted in the fall. With no leaves, young wheat plants must start all over again from the top of their root systems, but, farmer Larry Kern near Salina said, "the wheat's just not rooting down . . . to the subsoil because there's no moisture down there for it to get."

A year earlier, in the spring of 1988, the winter wheat crop had ripened before it was hit by intense drought in May and June, but in the spring of 1989 little rain or snow meant no ripening. In March the wheat plants were a shriveled brown instead of greening up. Since bare land might blow, the Soil Conservation Service recommended "ghost crops" (no profit) of wheat for ground cover.[35] U.S. wheat stockpiles fell close to a seventeen-year low, only a third of the previous year's mark. Kansas farmers abandoned a fifth of their winter wheat acreage, and the fields that were harvested dropped by 10 bushels an acre. Kansas, the biggest wheat-producing state with one-quarter of the nation's output and a third of its hard red winter wheat, faced the worst harvest in thirty-two years, with its one-billion-dollar crop down more than a third. Heavy rains, up to seventeen inches, made up for deficits from late April to mid-June, but it was too late for wheat, although just right for another try at milo.

In late December 1989, after six more months of drought, Kansas farmers once again worried about lost wheat crops and more severe damage from erosion. Little rain had fallen since September in wheat-growing regions, and lack of snow cover in southwest Kansas and the Oklahoma-Texas Panhandle region, together with double-digit below-zero temperatures, meant failure. In 1989 a central Kansas winter wheat farmer harvested only seven bushels an acre instead of his usual thirty-five, his net worth down to twelve thousand dollars after paying off the interest and part of the principal on last year's operating loan. A Kansas crop specialist worried: "Many farmers had operating loans last year that they couldn't repay because of crop failures. Now they are facing the threat of two in a row. . . . we're looking at a rising number of distressed farms."[36]

Thinking the Unthinkable: The Greenhouse Effect

High Plains drought reflected global climate events. It also was worse because of human influences, not just one of nature's capricious shifts. Not since 1936 had a dry April and May been followed by a very dry June and July as occurred in 1988. According to the standard measure, the Palmer Drought Index, the 1988 drought was the fourth worst on record based on effects on cropland; the other truly bad years were 1934, 1936, and 1954.[37] Average global temperatures in the 1980s were the highest measured in the last 130 years, when reliable records were first kept. Seven of the last twelve years—1980, 1981, 1983, 1987, 1988, 1990, and 1991—had been the warmest on record. Temperatures had been rising very gradually and steadily for the last hundred years, but the sharper rise detected in the 1980s may be, according to some scientists, the beginning of more extreme cycles yet to come during the next two decades. Since the nineteenth century, global temperatures have risen nearly half a degree Celsius, 28 percent of the warming (1.8 degrees Celsius) expected by the year 2030.[38] Federal climate program director Alan Hecht noted recently that the recent warming is unlikely to be part of a natural trend because the Earth is now the later stages of a period between ice ages, meaning that temperatures should be growing cooler with an approaching ice age.[39] What may temporarily protect our children and grandchildren from unbearable heat may be the world's oceans, which have heat-absorbing capacity more than forty times that of the atmosphere.

The cause could be a full-scale global greenhouse effect because industrial carbon dioxide, methane, nitrous oxide, and other gases are trapping heat in the atmosphere.[40] Signs of global warming are evident in temperature patterns, increased atmospheric water vapor, rising sea surface temperatures, and dramatic seasonal fluctuations.[41] Some greenhouse effect is natural; the earth would be frozen and lifeless without it. If rising man-made greenhouse gas emissions are unrestrained and the climate is highly sensitive to a worst-case scenario, temperatures could rise 0.8 degrees Celsius each decade, sixteen times faster than the average rate of warming during the past industrialized one hundred years. As it is, the world's oceans soak up heat and chemicals (half the carbon dioxide humans produce) and do much to delay rising temperatures.

Geologist Dewey M. McLean of Virginia Polytechnic University testified at a congressional hearing: "If humans were not present on Earth, the climate would likely cool into a new ice age as it has done many times in the past." This may be a fine outcome, but "we may be moving through an entire geological epoch in a single century," an unacceptable pace, said John S. Hoffman of the global atmosphere program at the federal Environmental Protection Agency.[42] Geochemist Wallace Broecker at the Lamont-Doherty Geological Observatory spoke of a number of extreme climate "jumps" millions of years ago, and wondered whether the unusual temperature increase in the 1980s might "provoke the system into another mode of operation," as *Science* put it, "one not at all to the liking of humans and other living things." Human societies are remarkably resilient to climate changes that reach known extremes, but there is no history of human ability to respond to extreme and repeated swings in temperature and moisture.[43] Stephen Schneider of the National Center for Atmospheric Research (NCAR) reminded *Science* readers that the planet Venus, with its dense carbon-dioxide atmosphere and temperatures of seven hundred degrees Kelvin, and frigid Mars, with a thin CO_2 atmosphere, are both examples of "runaway greenhouse."[44]

Climate is one of the globe's most turbulent and unpredictable phenomena. Schneider, looking over NCAR's batteries of computers modeling tomorrow's trends from yesterday's data, concluded that any prediction more than six hours into the future is like sorcery.[45] Depending on small changes, any given climate can have several natural behaviors or outcomes. Like most climatologists watching for greenhouse trends, Schneider is concerned that "a kick from outside" (industrial gasses) can force climate to change states, from the unusual narrow-temperature-range steadiness of the last hundred years to oscillating extremes in the twenty-first century. Then the oscillations could become the new steady pattern of irregular wide swings that would send humanity (and the rest of life on Earth) into a new existence. Climate extremes could rapidly overtake humanity's best abilities merely to ensure ordinary survival. Schneider would probably agree with research meteorologist Edward Lorenz, who said, "We might have trouble forecasting the temperature of [a cup of hot coffee] one minute in advance, but we should have little difficulty in forecasting it an hour ahead."[46] Despite their short-term uncertainty, nonlinear systems shape themselves toward identifiable long-term outcomes.

A single year's heat wave, as in the summer of 1988, made commodity prices first skyrocket and then fluctuate wildly. It tied up transport in shrunken rivers, decimated the world's food reserves, brought record smog levels to cities, terminated any last remaining hope for helpless populations in Africa's Sahel, intensified long-term water wars, and profoundly affected humanity's psychological security. Climate scientist Michael Oppenheimer of the Environmental Defense Fund noted that the new warmer world would be a place with no stability, only change.[47] Oppenheimer also noted that the world is already one degree Fahrenheit warmer than it was a century ago and "within the lives of our grandchildren, it could become a blistering 8 degrees hotter. . . . remember that small temperature changes can remake the face of the earth: The planet was [only] 8 degrees cooler during the glacial age."[48] With far greater extremes in regional climates, the unpleasantness of the spread of a Sahel-like desert onto the High Plains or the equivalent of a Bangladesh monsoon in Chicago twenty years from now would have devastating effects on population, food, and a nation's well-being and security.[49] While a U.S. Weather Service official played down permanent effect ("This is a tough summer well within the normal range of variability"), the normally cautious James E. Hansen, a National Aeronautics and Space Administration research scientist, shook up a lot of people when he told a worried Senate subcommittee in June that he was 99 percent certain of a permanent man-induced greenhouse warming.[50] If this were so, the measures devised during the last fifty years to protect farmers against drought, such as irrigation, crop insurance, and emergency efforts like the multibillion-dollar federal drought bill of August 1988, would be like pitching money into a black hole.

The great food belt of middle America would probably move northward into central Canada, but with lower productivity because of poorer soils and a much shorter growing season. NASA and NOAA global climate modeling, despite its recognized coarseness, almost invariably placed the central and southern High Plains in harm's way if a CO_2 doubling took place, with hot, dry, cloudless weather. The High Plains would experience a perpetual Dust Bowl far more severe than anything seen in the 1930s.[51] Soil moisture levels would drop 40 to 50 percent, levels which Gary Baker in Garden City, Kansas, reported destroyed wheat crops in the spring of 1989. Multiple studies correlated by Stephen Schneider indicated that the old Dust Bowl region (Arkansas-White-Red River Basin) is the fourth most vulnerable to greenhouse effects in the nation after the Great Basin, the Missouri Basin, and California because of extreme groundwater loss.[52] Although the greenhouse effect would not be uniform around the globe, the United States would have specific winners and losers, and the old Dust Bowl region is always listed as a loser. James Hansen argues that while natural forces bring on droughts and other climate changes, the greenhouse effect acts on these natural forces to make weather extremes even more likely.[53] Modern society has no comparable historic past experience with the temperature swings of a CO_2 doubling, other than distant ice-age data.[54] Irrigation was an exceptionally successful response to Dust Bowl conditions, but how long can it support the High Plains under the pressure of both CO_2 doubling and aquifer depletion? Dryland crop yields could drop by 18 percent and irrigation yields by 21 percent. In compensation, using the example of Texas alone, thirty thousand more acres would have to be irrigated.[55]

Ironically, in geologic time the plains region contributed to global cooling. Over the last sixty-seven million years, its grasses increased the breakdown of soil minerals. When the vast inland seas covered the region, the resulting potassium, calcium, and magnesium ions were captured by marine organisms, which, together with carbon dioxide, formed the carbonate skeletons that made up layers of limestone. This systematic removal of carbon dioxide may have contributed to the overall global cooling during the so-called Tertiary period.[56]

Today the threat to the High Plains is desertification, "a self-accelerating process, feeding on itself, and as it advances, rehabilitation costs rise exponentially."[57] Michael H. Glantz, climate and social-impact analyst at NCAR, observed that when they are intensified by drought, physical pressures on a region resulting from highly mechanized technologies to force high food yields lead to desertification, which is always damaging to humans and the environment. He quotes the 1977 United Nations Nairobi Conference on Desertification:

The deterioration of productive ecosystems is an obvious and serious threat to human progress. In general, the quest for ever greater productivity has intensified exploitation and has carried disturbance by man into less productive and more fragile lands. Overexploitation gives rise to degradation of vegetation, soil and water, the three elements which serve as the natural foundation for human existence. In exceptionally fragile ecosystems, such as those on the desert margins, the loss of biological productivity through the degradation of plant, animal, soil and water resources can easily become irreversible, and permanently reduce their capacity to support human life.[58]

The difference between the High Plains and Ethiopia's Sahel is one of degree.

One desperate response is abandonment of the region as recommended and legislated in the 1930s. There are no new solutions like the irrigation technologies that transformed the Dust Bowl into a 1960s garden. The high-efficiency water-management practices promoted today to stretch supplies for longer-term farming will inevitably run into the wall of depletion. Up to 60 percent of Ogallala water is currently consumed in flood irrigation, not by plants, but lost to evapotranspiration and soil seepage. A spring 1989 Texas water resources study reported a 5 to 25 percent increase in groundwater consumption to raise identical crops.[59] Water importation is unlikely, despite recommendations in 1982 Department of Commerce and Corps of Engineers reports. The cost of transporting water from the Canadian Rockies in the NAWAPA plan was estimated in the mid-1970s at three hundred billion dollars. Importation from the Great Lakes would mean high energy costs (water weighs sixteen pounds per gallon and would have to be lifted more than twenty-five hundred feet from Lake Michigan to southwest Kansas because of altitude differences), and Great Lakes governors have already gone on record opposing sale of their resource.

Stephen Schneider of NCAR warns: "What is new [in the greenhouse threat as compared with the Dust Bowl] is the potential irreversibility of the changes that are now taking place."[60] Swedish scientist Bert Bolin has stressed the severity and universality of the subject: "Climatic problems will be part of people's lives over the next century."[61] Americans have much difficulty thinking and acting in a long-term framework larger than four-year presidential terms and annual reports of corporations. Climate thinking in this case must span more than eighteen thousand years (since the last ice age), or twenty-five thousand years (the estimated age of some of the Ogallala water). As University of Chicago atmospheric scientist V. Ramanathan noted, "by the time we know our theory is correct, it will be too late to stop the heating that has already occurred" and is only temporarily trapped in today's oceans.[62] Ramanathan labeled the current warming as a test of the greenhouse effect by "an inadvertent global experiment" that has now reached "the crucial stage of verification."[63]

Uncertainty makes planners, policymakers, scientists, and politicians uneasy. The problem with the potential effects of drought on the Ogallala aquifer is that this uncertainty is multiplied by inherent murkiness and contingency of both the hydrological cycle and the climate.[64] The *New York Times* editorialized on January 27, 1989:

> Climatologists will argue for many years whether the greenhouse warming has started. But there's every reason to take action immediately, and not wait until that debate is concluded. Once warming begins, its momentum will continue—even if gas emissions could be stopped immediately—for the three decades or so that it takes to heat the oceans. At that point the planet will again be in equilibrium, but at a much higher temperature than that of the initial warming signal.

Writing in *Science,* Schneider concluded, "Whether the uncertainties are large enough to suggest delaying policy responses is not a scientific question per se, but a value judgment."[65] It is a matter of decision making with imperfect information. Decisions are not in the hands of scientists but those of politicians.

283

Conclusion: Think Globally; Act Locally

As recently as the 1930s, there was no significant groundwater irrigation of crops on the High Plains. As irrigation became practicable in the 1940s and 1950s, farmers first used it as extra water that supplemented the marginal twenty inches of regional rainfall. But when wells and pumps and unmuffled engines became commonplace, and as a flood of water coursed through aluminum pipes and center pivots made their circles, irrigation became a necessity. It was the means—water on demand—to provide high crop yields (intensive farming) on ever-increasing acreages (extensive farming). What was once extra water became necessary water.

If the greenhouse effect turned southwest Kansas and the Oklahoma-Texas Panhandle into an arid desert climate, as is predicted, then Ogallala water consumption would be doubled or tripled, not only to compensate for the lack of rain but also because hotter winds and the scorching sun would speed evaporation on irrigation-flooded fields and the growing plants would transpire their moisture more rapidly. In the summer of 1988, Ogallala pumping deficits sometimes went from the usual two feet a year, serious as that was, to up to five feet a year.[66]

One of the principles of irrigation is that it not only can grow reliable crops but also offers yields three times those of dryland farming. As the Ogallala goes dry or becomes unpumpable, the United States would find its overall crop yields reduced as much as 21 percent. A solution to water scarcity then might be a turnabout from Mobil Oil's use of it in Oklahoma: natural gas could be forced into used aquifers for secondary and tertiary pumping of the water field. Alternatively, talk has again started about importing Canadian water.[67] Canada has, it is noted, 9 percent of the world's fresh water with only twenty-five million people to use it. The NAWAPA plan mentioned in the previous chapter, despite costs ranging into the hundreds of billions of dollars and the potential environmental havoc, seems less bizarre after the droughts of 1988 and 1989. Already Canada's opposition Liberal party has publicly wondered, during U.S.-Canadian free-trade talks, "Why are certain commodities like beer spelled out as excluded from the agreement, but not water?"

On the High Plains the appropriate question is what the future would look like with sunnier, hotter, rainless, and longer summers, turning it into an American Sahara or Gobi or Sinai desert. Many conservation regulations, policies, and institutions are already in place on the state and local levels. The debate in Oklahoma over waste and beneficial use takes on new and more critical levels of importance. A national agenda to promote water efficiency belongs nowhere more than on the plains. Regulations on the books in Kansas, Oklahoma, and Texas are good when enforced and could offer a solid response to the forthcoming crisis, but the tendency toward lax enforcement, along with generous exceptions, very often bypass the intent of the various state water laws. In her 1984 Mobil Oil opinion, Oklahoma Supreme Court Justice Evonne Kauger quoted Adam Smith's *The Wealth of Nations:* "How is it that water, which is so very useful that life is impossible without it, has such a low price—while diamonds, which are quite unnecessary, have such a high price?"

9

. . .

A One-Time Experiment

By the time we know whether today's conventional plains farmers can live with less groundwater, it may be too late to save enough to keep them on the land. Pumping the Ogallala is still a one-time experiment, unrepeatable and irreversible. Reasons to tap the aquifer abounded. American farmers suffered and failed during the 1930s because they did not have the technology to reach it. After its initial failure to move farmers elsewhere, the New Deal committed the federal government, and society, to take drastic steps to keep farmers on the plains. The miracle of new irrigation technologies did much to protect farmers from the harshness of drought during the Filthy Fifties, in the early 1970s, and in the late 1980s. In addition it helped create today's highly productive industrial farming and feedlots on the plains. A Faustian bargain with the water is now coming due; it created a prosperous irrigation economy based on levels declining ten times faster than any recharge. But we have no historical experience from which to predict the future of high-production industrial agriculture or the small-time farmer on the High Plains without continuous massive infusions of groundwater. Nor have pragmatic alternatives been devised, much less tested. Pumping the Ogallala remains a one-time experiment.

The Sustainability Ethic
High Plains irrigation in the old Dust Bowl region is undoubtedly an actual and moral victory over drought. The victory is short lived, but it did allow a

generation or two of irrigators to prosper. Negatively, it propped up the kind of farming that consumes soil, water, energy, capital, and human labor. Alternative sustainable farming may be able to keep the farmer on the land longer at less cost, reduce environmental damage, revive a popular rural way of life, and hold on to more water for future generations, but it will have to be a plains farming that can prosper on much less water.

Ethical imperatives are at the heart of decisions about Ogallala aquifer use. Even when conventional farming and environmental protection are as obviously at odds as they are in this book, each serves its own public interest. This book is not a morality tale or tragic history that seeks to tar capitalists and consumers and whitewash conservationists and organic farmers. Embracing the good is interwoven throughout this book on the Ogallala; no one was intentionally evil. The conflicting economic, agricultural, and environmental interests that are compared in this chapter involve difficult ethical compromises and moral decisions that affect the lives of tens of thousands of people in the old Dust Bowl region alone. Debate concerning High Plains agriculture invariably involves fulfilling the public good despite risk and uncertainty.

It is worthwhile noting that the ethically laden phrase "duty of water" was used in 1896 by Frederick H. Newell, chief hydrographer of the United States Geological Survey, to describe the physical application of water to a field. This usage of the word "duty" described "the relation between the quantity of water and the area which can be irrigated. . . . It depends upon the climate, the amount of rainfall, the variations of temperature, the character of the soil and subsoil, the methods of cultivation, the kinds of crops, and perhaps more than all upon the skill of the irrigator."[1] Newell aggressively advocated small-scale irrigation as both virtuous and efficient. A farm family could prosper even on as little as five acres. Irrigation produced bountiful crops that encouraged farmers to settle in otherwise barren regions, one-eighth of the American West, including large parts of Kansas, Oklahoma, and Texas. It avoided "bitter disappointment" for "unfortunate settlers" who "if not driven from the country, alternate between short periods of prosperity and long intervals of depression."[2] In addition, the alternative, dryland farming, went against the then-new American "gospel of efficiency" because it consumed vast acreage with low production. The proper application of water was also, according to Newell, "a businesslike investment." As a result, the duty of water created the capacity to grow healthy, productive plants, uplift farmers who irrigated, and serve the virtue of economic prosperity.

An ethical dimension is also part of the modern environmental movement. Pioneering ecologist Eugene P. Odum would agree with historian Donald Worster's argument that environmental analysis is "born out of a moral purpose."[3] Odum finds that environmental science, in its comprehensiveness, offers society something of greater value than traditional reductionist science:

> There is much to be said for a procedure that combines a few carefully selected systems-level properties that monitor the performance of the whole, with selected "red flag" components such as [water,] a game species or a toxic substance that, in themselves, have direct importance to the general public.[4]

In this context, irreplaceable water is unique and distinct from other agricultural needs like equipment or pesticides. Policy analysts Arthur Maass and Raymond L. Anderson write that

> farmers typically refuse to treat water as a regular economic good, like fertilizer, for example. It is, they say, a special product and should be removed from ordinary market transactions so that farmers can control conflict, maintain popular influence and control, and realize equity and social justice.[5]

Just as Odum finds energy a particularly useful common denominator between man and nature, water for food can become the meeting point—the focus for a holistic strategy—between an ethical imperative (saving the farmer) and environmental protection (saving the water).

If water can be given value that keeps it outside the economic marketplace, the debate over the ethical duty of water can take place more in the world of law and public interest. Since the days of the founding fathers, the nation's mission had been to create the good society, not merely an indifferent government.[6] Ethical priorities—doing good things—go far beyond prices, markets, and efficiency. A more inclusive agricultural paradigm includes ethical judgments about both farmers and water. Philosopher and policy analyst Mark Sagoff writes of "important shared values" to which the public will sacrifice prices and efficiency.[7] As long as the public remains sympathetic to the needs and services of the family farm, it will subsidize it. Social regulation expresses not simply individual self-interest but public values we choose collectively. The role of government is not merely to correct market errors but to reflect a sense of national well-being. In American history, so-called benevolent goals, such as the antislavery movement, women's rights, the Marshall Plan, open immigration, urban welfare, and environmental protection, accurately reflect, Sagoff claims, not primarily self-interest and market efficiency but widely held national values. Americans are willing to support policies not tied to the profit motive. Short-term maximum profits and the good society may not be the same.

The Marginal Plains:
The History of a Stubborn and Confusing Place

It is significant that European settlement of what would become the eastern United States took place on an Atlantic coastline that was covered by a temperate forest familiar to Europeans instead of a desert or equally suspect low-rain grassland.[8] It is equally significant that the settlers who migrated westward were dismayed by the treeless prairie that began roughly at today's Indiana-Illinois border. Three hundred miles to the west, the first explorers of the High Plains damned the region as the Great American Desert. Pioneer settlers and respected scientists concluded the plains could never support farming or settlement and would remain permanently uninhabitable.[9]

The image of the central High Plains as marginal land would never be entirely erased. Migration into the highly suspect semiarid shortgrass country ranging from the 97th to 102d meridians would come only after its soil proved extraordinarily fertile.[10] The High Plains frontier was historically the last American frontier of the lower forty-eight states; it was deliberately skipped by settlers who found California and Oregon far more attractive. Nevertheless, by the 1870s and 1880s hardy and determined men and women invaded the windswept low-rain grasslands.[11] But farming was so harsh that some parts of southwest Kansas and the Texas-Oklahoma Panhandle were not homesteaded until the early 1900s. The first deed to the Trescott's land was not until 1911.

By chance, when plains settlers first struggled with the tough sod, they were deluged with several seasons of heavy eastern-style rains. These and settler muscle made believeable the bewitching slogan "Rain follows the plow." The Great American Desert became the Great American Garden. Wrote a hopeful farmer in 1880: "This is the sole remaining section of paradise in the western world." The land was level, free from stones and stumps, highly fertile, and its aridity had been apparently overcome by a man-induced climate change. To the nineteenth-century American, the conquest of nature was a moral good linked to Manifest Destiny; settlement of the High Plains as the last empty quarter of the agricultural West would complete the nation's mission to domesticate the continent. Thus the High Plains was first populated under a boomer psychology that often denied geographical realities and led to extraordinary hardships and wholesale failures.

What the settler did not know was that he or she entered the region simultaneously with the temporary rainfall anomaly of 1878–87.[12] When drought returned in the 1890s, as many as two hundred thousand settlers felt fortunate to escape the region, now trailing a new slogan: "In God we trusted, in Kansas we busted." Habitual dryness was not generally admitted until the 1930s, when the still-struggling farmer was whipsawed by a devastating climate change that really was no climate change at all. Severe drought returned like clockwork, some said on a twenty-two-year cycle linked to sunspot patterns. Drought appeared not only in the 1930s Dust Bowl but in the Little Dust Bowl of the 1950s, the record-setting aridity of the early 1970s, and, presumably, another cycle in the 1990s, probably foreshadowed by the rainless season of 1988. The trend toward CO_2 greenhouse warming may intensify High Plains drought into extreme desertification. There have always been stubborn climate limits to traditional farming on the harsh High Plains. No wonder farmers dreamed of the constant flow of irrigation water.

The traditional farmer had neither the tools nor the experience to survive in the true climate of the region. Useful intelligence about rainfall and tough sod, the right tools and machines, and dryland crops was virtually nonexistent. Pioneer farmers carried limited supplies of food, equipment, and cash in their wagons as they rattled onto the plains. (In my house sits a mantlepiece clock that went by wagon to Kansas in 1883 and was back in Illinois by 1891.) Back in the fertile and humid East, failure might come in three years if the settler lacked one essential factor, capital, to secure his home and barn, a water well, tools, and livestock. Plains settlers faced additional crippling hardships, notably drought, hail, prairie fires, grasshoppers, and the maddening wind. They lacked wood for fences and buildings and water for fields, yet they were willing to risk themselves, their families, and their fortunes on the notorious High Plains because of technological breakthroughs like John Deere's steel shear plow, Cyrus McCormick's mechanical reaper, Halladay's economical windmills to tap water, and Joseph Glidden's barbed wire. These new inventions and new crops, such as Ukranian winter wheat, promised successful farming in a difficult region.[13] Before the plains experience, the inherent weaknesses of the family farm did not combine to bring its downfall. But on the Plains, a combination of problems—the isolated farmstead (instead of village community), accelerated exploitation of soil, distance from markets, and lack of capital—defeated many farmers in the face of the additional threats of little rain, weather extremes, no wood, geographical isolation, fire, and wind. It was difficult to alter an established farm way of life that in spite of its defects had been so successful elsewhere.

The independent farmer had become idealized into a mythic undefeated hero early in the Republic's history. Since Colonial times American society had committed itself to private and independent farm ownership. This commitment was institutionalized in the Land Survey Ordinance of 1785, passed by the Confederation Congress two years before the Constitution and not significantly modified for the next one hundred fifty years.[14] Back East the 160 acres of a quarter section provided a bountiful life; in the Kansas Sandhills the 640 acres of a full section might only graze a few cattle. Americans found it difficult to admit that Jefferson's yeoman farmer might not prosper everywhere. On the plains the traditional farm family, prideful of its independence, could barely survive, much less thrive. Instead of the abandonment advised by some, by the mid-1930s, New Deal farm assistance offered farm subsidies, credit programs, agricultural extension and the Soil Conservation Service.[15]

The inability of settlers to comprehend climate conditions, the limited resources they brought with them, and their patriotic zeal to deny reality held the central High Plains in the thrall of a long-term frontier: "America's Seventy-Year Mistake."[16] It was a self-inflicted wound on the settlers and on the American psyche. Eventually farmers would progress from frontier subsistence life into a settled rural society for a time, but not as the result of a better climate.

The Comforts of Irrigation

Irrigation was the climate beater, but it did not start well enough. Windmills in the late nineteenth and early twentieth centuries did not have the efficiency, energy, or deep-pumping technology to flood more than ten acres when sixteen times that was needed. In one growing season a single acre of alfalfa or corn needs up to thirty inches of water, equivalent to two and a half acre-feet or more than nine hundred thousand gallons.[17] Except in southeast Colorado, cooperative systems of irrigation canals and peripheral ditches did not take hold on the High Plains. The influence of the Reclamation Act of 1902, so important elsewhere in the West, would not be felt in the Dust Bowl region. For a time early in the century, entrepreneurs around Garden City, Kansas, laboriously dug canals and ditches that ran from the Arkansas River to their fields and later to a sugar-beet factory; the operations were private and underfinanced. Very soon the Arkansas River was running mostly dry by the time it reached Kansas because upstream around Lamar in southeast Colorado irrigators were taking its water. This is still true today. The only current product for Kansans from the Arkansas River is extended litigation with Coloradans. Money, not water, flows between two sets of lawyers.

Nationwide, irrigation was treated as a farmer panacea almost beyond credibility. During the Irrigation Crusade at the turn of the century, "Forty Million Forty Acre Farms" became a national slogan. Irrigation booster William E. Smythe, despite his High Plains origins, claimed that the California farmer who worked compact irrigated fields was morally superior to midcontinent farmers, who tilled large fields "promiscuously and carelessly." Bonanza farmers along the Red River of the North were condemned for "skimming the fertility" from hundreds of square miles. In contrast, said Smythe, the virtuous irrigator "farms a few acres and farms them well." Reclamation engineer Frederick N. Newell wondered whether ten acres were excessive.[18] Smythe claimed that a hard-working family could generate $490.95 (1910 dollars) a year from one acre of land, equal to an average working man's annual income.

Not until after World War II did the combination of efficient deep-well pumps, low-cost energy to run gasoline or natural-gas engines, inexpensive aluminum piping, center-pivot sprinklers and other watering technologies, new management skills, an increased scale of operation, and, not least, the existence of the vast water-filled gravel beds of the Ogallala aquifer allow farmers to ignore the lack of rain.[19] The emotional and economic power of irrigation cannot be overemphasized. First, it offered a long-sought and effective climate substitute. The lack of water was so severe a problem that there were repeated attempts to declare the region submarginal and redundant, off limits to further attempts at farming. Much of the land, like the Sandhills of southwest Kansas, seemed more suited to light cattle grazing than wheat production. By the 1950s and 1960s, water was being pumped from each of hundreds of wells at the rate of a thousand cubic feet a minute to water quarter sections of wheat, alfalfa, grain sorghum, and corn. Irrigation on the High Plains was not merely a response to climate, but its replacement. When the plains farmer irrigates, it means he does not have to wait for the ever-elusive rain. Today's problem is that all these technological and management skills will count for nothing unless a solution is found for declining water levels.

Second, irrigation became as indispensable as the land and sunshine. At first the farmer tapped the groundwater only as a last resort when rains failed, and often he applied the water when it was too late. By the 1960s irrigation was integrated into the farming routine as the single most important activity to guarantee big yields. The farmer could schedule irrigation into his cropping plans by starting a pump. The noisy engines, running day and night, changed farming from a pastoral and seasonal life into a form of machine-dominated labor.[20] Cutting off the water meant shutting down the farm. The old alternative, dryland farming, became a doubtful last resort.

Third, irrigation made possible top yields that matched or surpassed corn or sorghum production in Iowa or Illinois or California. The effect of this on plains farming cannot be overstated. Before irrigation the plains farmer had to work very large dryland fields to keep himself in shoes or a plow. Now he believed he had the advantage of high yields on large fields.[21] As late as the 1850s all American commercial farming relied on large tracts of cheap land. High Plains agriculture seemed destined to remain such a big-acreage, low-yield region until Ogallala irrigation took hold. In 1950 the Ogallala irrigated 3.5 million acres of farmland; today it is 16 million acres.[22] The plains seem capable of matching grain production with any other part of the nation. High-yield irrigation farming is also virtuous; farmers believe they are no longer misusing large tracts of land as the irrigation crusaders had complained.

As a result, High Plains irrigators for thirty years have been consuming aquifer water at a rate conservatively estimated to be ten times the rate of natural recharge, and energetic attempts at artificial renewal have made no significant difference. Phil and Linda Tooms in Kansas expect their irrigation operation to retrench in the next decade; they are not encouraging the next generation of Toomses to stay in farming. The Gigots in the nearby Sandhills will no doubt squeeze the last drop of water onto their sorghum fields before moving into 100 percent cattle processing. Wayne Wyatt down at Texas District No. 1 in Lubbock is optimistically looking into high-pressure groundwater recharge, but with little success thus far. Oklahoma's Betty and Roger Trescott are looking forward to retirement, with no one to succeed them in their irrigation operation. This is the case with many of the original 1960s irrigators. There are far fewer farmers and irrigators in the next generation.

The Persistence of "Pioneer Farming"

The Toomses, Gigots, Wayne Wyatt, the Trescotts, and other thoughtful farmers say that copious amounts of water are still wastefully pumped from the Ogallala. On this basis, Americans are still at the pioneer stage of groundwater use. Historically, the pioneer farmers who settled on the virgin plains in the last century were not efficient stewards of the land, and sadly their habit persists. They practiced a diminishing kind of farming in which the land was mined for a single purpose: crop after crop of corn or wheat. Land exploitation was accepted as necessary for their survival. Today it is land and water exploitation. (Energy use deepens the problem.)

The pioneer stage is also called extensive farming, the planting of all possible acreage. It is still widely practiced on the High Plains. When the pioneers were replaced by permanent settlers, commercial markets institutionalized extensive farming. Agricultural economist Willard W. Cochrane observed that "this behavior was not irrational" but was done "with reckless abandon."[23] American farmers needed to turn a profit; the way to keep production costs down was to expand on the cheapest resource, which was land. For most of American farm history, labor was scarce, capital was expensive, and land was cheap.

During the last thirty years groundwater has become another disposable resource to stretch extensive farming practices. The new pumps, gear heads, and engines (fueled by cheap energy), together with aluminum pipe and automatic sprinklers, made available a low-cost expendable supply. Or so it seemed. Groundwater depletion is the underground equivalent of topsoil erosion. Once the pumping and sprinkling machinery put it within easy reach, water allowed the plains farmer to continue to prosper even as land became more costly, labor became scarce, and capital became the heaviest burden of all, all this as grain prices stayed too low for survival without federal supports. Hence High Plains irrigation, despite its technological sophistication, is a version of extensive farming on a pioneer level. This is rarely the path toward sustainable development.

The pioneer analogy does break down. In today's high-production scenario, yield is not low as it was on the early wheat fields. Instead, High

Plains irrigation is also intensive farming. It is both extensive, (very large farms) and intensive (highest possible yields per acre). To serve this practice, the vast supply of groundwater from the Ogallala plays the role of a nearly free good that is doubly exploited for extensive and intensive reasons. True replacement cost is not figured in. As long as no price is attached to the Ogallala resource, water for irrigation appears to offer a double benefit that is a dangerous masking of reality: water is being ignored as a real farming cost, and water increases yields dramatically. But cheap resources tend to be squandered. Under current marketplace pressures, resources are conserved only when they become scarce and expensive.

In sum, the new intensive-extensive farming of the modern High Plains depends largely on the mining of Ogallala groundwater.[24] This will end when the "lagging cost line" on Ogallala groundwater rises to the levels already reached by other agricultural resources, such as land, machinery, energy, and labor.[25] The Gigots, Toomses, and Trescotts acknowledge that their good irrigation times are nearly over. What is surprising is that groundwater has yet to be added to the plains agricultural balance sheet, both short term and long term. Inescapably, the last thirty years of consumption mean a long-term price is due in the future. It involves the probable failure of both local farmers and high-yield grain production. Groundwater always was a phantom or hidden cost.

Different Approaches to Ogallala Irrigation

For more than thirty years the irrigated High Plains have provided food for world markets, helped overcome the trade deficit with grain exports, produced the surpluses that allowed foreign policy flexibility in sales to the former Soviet Union, benefited both the independent family farmer and agribusiness, and sustained historically low American food prices. But can Ogallala water serve all these masters? Should it be used to maximize profits, which is the "American way"? Should it maximize yield "to feed the world"? Should it minimize risk to shield the family farmer and keep him on the land? The difficulty is that each of these objectives, worthy as it may be, can distort and subvert the integrity of a larger inclusive agricultural paradigm described below. Ogallala water, if it is not to be entirely preserved like a scenic wonder, is now dedicated by law and by an ethical imperative to support continuous farming on the difficult High Plains. Profits, yields, and the family farm are not final goals and can only be understood as ingredients of a larger picture.

The beneficial use of irrigation depends on specific and sometimes conflicting approaches to farming.[26] By unpacking these approaches we can understand how the farm lobby or special-interest groups or federal planners influence Ogallala pumping and what answers each offers for the problem of less water. Back in the 1930s Dust Bowl days, government intervention began to protect the independent farmer. This attention has changed between the 1930s and the 1980s to favor agribusiness. Stormy debates over the 1985 and 1990 federal farm bills were criticized because they apparently gave lip service to the traditional family farm but in truth produced farm policy that was more likely to serve agribusiness.[27]

For the first time in history, the 1985 farm bill, particularly its Conservation Reserve Program, added environmental protection and resource conservation policies to traditional production- and market-oriented farm commodity programs. The 1990 farm bill committed the nation to integrate environmental protection and family farming with international competitiveness. But the new connections have turned out to be a shotgun wedding, since they force contradictory worldviews, forcibly linked by "cross compliance," into bed together.[28] Farmers are receiving contradictory (hence self-defeating) messages from the government. Minnesota senator Rudy Boschwitz noted that, "when farmers are required to reduce the number of acres they have in production, they usually compensate by farming the rest of their land more intensively, using additional fertilizers, herbicides, and insecticides. Year after year, acreage limitations have failed to achieve intended reductions in total production of program crops."[29] Best management practices (BMPs) can be at odds: an environmental-protection BMP is not likely to be identical with an agricultural-productivity BMP.[30] As two congressional researchers wrote in 1989, "a farm manager views pollution and how to control it from the perspective of farm productivity; the environmentalist views the problem and its control from the perspective of environmental quality." Despite crosscurrents and overlappings evident in USDA definitions, public opinion, farm-bloc interests, and ecological goals, there are nevertheless distinguishable models of agricultural productivity and sustainability.

CONVENTIONAL AGRICULTURE

Conventional agriculture slips too easily into a subset of economics. In brief, this is historic American farming that over time gradually dedicated itself to the highest possible productivity, using industrial equipment, heavy agrichemical applications, risky monoculture, and few soil-building crops. This approach has been institutionalized for the last century by federal legislation and, particularly since the 1930s, by costly farm-support policies financed willingly by the American taxpayer. Massive industrialization is attractive because it has produced remarkable yields. On the plains, using the strategy of maximum consumption of resources, it accepted soil erosion and water (and energy) exploitation to produce a large surplus of a narrow range of commodities.[31] The original goals, going back to the late eighteenth century, were to support the on-site family farmer, build commercial markets, and preserve low food costs for the nonfarmer.

However, conventional agriculture was never practiced purely after railroads became major agricultural landholders in the nineteenth century and found market monopolies profitable, nor has it been the case since the rise of large-scale agribusiness in the twentieth century. According to a pair of congressional researchers, conventional agriculture "is losing its special status as the bastion of traditional values as the public recognizes that the small-scale family farm no longer dominates agriculture. People now view agriculture as just another large business that should not be excepted from the environmental quality requirements placed on other businesses. People also realize that agriculture is an important source of environmental problems."[32]

In addition, for the past two decades the traditional farmer has not been served well by the conventional agriculture model. Crop prices fell and stayed low, while costs of machinery, land, chemicals, and interest rates went up. Conventional agriculture only remotely factored outside political and economic forces into its equation, nor did it heed most environmental constraints.

THE ENVIRONMENTAL WORLDVIEW
ITS AGRICULTURAL DIMENSIONS

Environmental debates today tend to range over the problems of industrial pollution, urban blight, population growth, wilderness protection, and global climate warming. Now agriculture's large-scale land and water consumption is receiving long-overdue attention.[33]

There is also a far broader general environmental paradigm, biocentrism, that gives nature much autonomy and argues that humanity is best understood if it is seen as part of nature. This turns on its head the historic Western view that nature is humanity's raw material, which is the way nature is usually treated in most studies of the agricultural revolution and today's industrial agriculture. To accept the general environmental worldview requires a new understanding of the function of agriculture. Agriculture's traditional attachment to marketplace values would expand into an entire lifestyle, be given a global framework, and be broadened into an overall humanity-nature philosophy.

Environmentalists believe that disturbingly exploitive levels of farm productivity, exemplified by high-chemical-use monoculture, will not sustain the levels of environmental quality that are essential to human well-being. They also argue that there are large areas of marginal land that ought never to have been farmed and are overdue for retirement, even at the risk of putting farmers out of work. The environmental stance concludes that farmers are locked into an economic and technological system that rewards waste, pollution, and inefficiency.[34] Existing modes of agricultural production result in major environmental risks, including land erosion, contamination of water, and destruction of wetlands and grasslands.[35] When all of this is added to the realization that agriculture consumes over 80 percent of the nation's fresh water supplies, probably half of which is wasted, attention to the agriculture-environment linkage is overdue. The leading question is what degree of environmental degradation is a necessary price for a healthy farm society and whether a clean, safe natural environment is compatible with profitable agriculture. Instead of sacrificing land, water, and energy to serve market value alone, this strategy seeks to make the best use of resources according to an appropriate range of human values that are themselves subordinated to environmental goals. Emphasis is laid upon the drastic reduction of soil erosion, nonpoint pollution, and improved water quality.

Environmentalists have contributed to the larger farm debate by insisting that more attention be given to effects beyond the fenceline or beneath the soil. These effects, it is argued, remain unrecognized otherwise, give inappropriate subsidies to farmers, and raise costs to society. A major flaw in the current official environmental strategy is that neither the farm bills of 1985 and 1990, as they shape USDA actions, nor the mission of the Environmental Protection Agency (EPA) devote attention to sustainable development, nor does either make sustainability a priority goal. The protection of Ogallala groundwater for thoughtful and long-term consumption is largely ignored on the federal level.

Several versions of the agricultural approach are mostly indifferent to sustainability interests, while others are responsive to sustainable development:

Food Sufficiency (Food Security). This appears to be the dominant viewpoint in American agriculture today. Fostered in the 1970s and 1980s by the U.S. Department of Agriculture (but hardly limited to USDA), this viewpoint emphasizes expansion of agriculture to serve rapidly expanding global food needs. Its claimed social good is to minimize human misery by establishing high food-surplus levels. It seeks to prove the Malthusian formula wrong. Fundamental daily human need is measured as subsistence at 180 kilograms and carryover or reserve stocks of grains at fifty to eighty days.[36] Paradoxically, however, this high-production model is dominated by worldwide market forces and macroeconomic conditions that in fact prevent appropriate distribution for social good.

This model also serves nonagricutural or external interests, including

U.S. foreign policy (for example, toward the former Soviet Union), the balance of payments (U.S. food exports substantially reduce the deficit), and historically low U.S. food prices (a sacred tenet of the USDA and Congress). To serve these nonfarm ends as well as sufficiency-security, this narrow-based approach is used to justify the fastest possible expansion of cropland through intensive use of irrigation, chemical fertilizers, mechanized equipment, and energy consumption. Farming is seen as another form of industrialization.

Conservation and protection of the resource base, including land and water, are downplayed and excluded from cost-efficiency calculations. Emphasis is placed on neoclassical concepts of production and efficiency and the laws of supply and demand, which it is believed will serve the general good. It is believed that scientific discoveries and technological fixes will consistently compensate for current and future environmental problems. This approach also ignores negative effects on the labor force and the wider culture.

Stewardship or Sustainability. This position emerged in recent years primarily as a critique of the food sufficiency–security approach. It concludes that the goals of high-yield production are the source of needless soil depletion, pollution, and disruption of natural and human resources. Proponents argue that the agribusiness pattern deceptively offers levels of food production that are ultimately unsustainable.

Sustainability gives priority to preservation and improvement of fertile soils, maintenance and expansion of supplies of clean water, and protection and regeneration of a satisfying quality of life for the work force. Admittedly, according to this view, the food-sufficiency model can be applauded for its attention to the elimination of starvation. This is virtuous. Nevertheless, its scope is too narrow, separates agriculture from other human and natural forces, and as a result, according to Paul B. Thompson, isolates humanity "from the feedback mechanisms that inform us when we are increasing our vulnerability to a breakdown in the environmental system that supports agricultural practices."[37]

Sustainability includes Lester Brown's Worldwatch Institute "ecological deflator" to take into account soil and water mining, nonpoint pollution, exploitation of human groups, and intergenerational needs, all of which would significantly lower real production levels. Emphasis is instead placed on the on-site balance between agriculture and nature, in Congressman George Brown's words, using "stable, self-maintaining ecological systems [of farming] tailored to suit local variations in knowledge, climate, soils, and biological diversity." Critics of the sustainability approach argue that its production levels would not match global population growth.

Variations of the two primary agricultural paradigms are Profit Motive or Marketplace, which detaches itself entirely from agricultural values and treats food production primarily as a business operation in which success is measured solely by quarterly and annual profits, and Organic Farming–Jeffersonian Yeoman, which gives primary attention to farming as a way of life producing both the best citizens (civic virtue) and sufficient crops.[38] The profit-motive view can be criticized for ignoring issues unique to farming, while the organic-farming view is criticized for low production and antiquarianism (at this writing, criticism is changing rapidly into a wider public acceptance of organic farming, including guidelines in the 1990 farm bill, as a valid balance of conservation and production).

Still another model, Third World, is inappropriate to American agriculture but stands as a global generic model by which other types are measured. It centers on small family, tribal, or community operations that have limited access to equipment, fertilizers, and pesticides and suffer from low productivity, intensive manual labor, and heavy environmental degradation despite the goal of achieving a self-sustainable rural society based on appropriate technology.

None of these approaches is neutral in its effects on the wider society; each has specific social, technological, and economic repercussions.[39] Obversely, none stands independent of effects from nonagricultural forces. The food-sufficiency model tends toward corporate agribusiness; it leads to fewer and larger farms; more mechanization; greater need for entrepreneurial skills; more farm-site specialization (monoculture); higher debt;

more external inputs from government, science, and industry; and higher environmental costs, such as soil erosion and chemical pollution. It probably means the collapse of traditional rural economics and the end of the family-farm lifestyle. The stewardship model receives favorable attention because of the historic American reformist or populist critique of corporate power, growing public dedication to environmental protection, and the surprisingly durable American myth of the independent family farm. The related organic farming model offers an alternative lifestyle based on self-reliance and long-term farmland preservation.

The above viewpoints and their implications offer opportunities to clarify the interconnections between Ogallala water and social needs. Researchers at the Kansas Rural Center, a private advocacy group, use the example of a 1976 agribusiness failure that caused profound problems in Edwards County.[40] First National Investment Company bought 9,664 acres of sandy pastureland and got rights to put down forty-eight wells for irrigation. But as an absentee nonfarm investor, the company apparently was more heavily committed elsewhere. Despite exclusive access to water on its property, it let the newly plowed sandy soil, vulnerable to wind erosion, blow away as its farm managers lackadaisically came and went. In 1982 more than 3,000 acres were foreclosed and went into the hands of Connecticut General Life Insurance Company. Fortunately, the land is now under local management and planted to low-value alfalfa and grasses, but in the process various businesses, including the county co-op, were saddled with unpaid bills and contracts. There is high risk in corporate speculation, not only for the corporation, but also for unprotected businesses without the corporation's deep pockets. When the marketplace is the only measure for action on the High Plains, the larger farm picture becomes distorted and severe damage quickly occurs.

What Is Required:
A Shift into Sustainable Development

Sustainable development gained currency in the 1980s. It is commonly defined as "development that meets the needs of the present without compromising the ability of future generations to meet their own needs."[41] The practice of sustainable development may date back to the ancient Greeks, whose laws avoided exploitation of resources and sought environmental balance to sustain the polis indefinitely.[42] The modern discussion opened in 1972 when the United Nations Environment Program stressed the importance for Third World nations to build a balance between natural resources and economic development. This emphasis on the maintenance of essential ecological processes continued to receive fresh momentum with the publication in 1987 of *Our Common Future* by the World Commission on Environment and Development. This still-emerging concept of sustainable development is particularly appropriate to High Plains farming as Ogallala water levels decline to inaccessibility in today's uncontrolled experiment.

Sustainable development seeks a balance between the conflicting interests of environment and economics. Emphasis is given to protecting life-support systems and biotic diversity because they sustain human existence. Control of pollution and waste can help degraded ecosystems to recover. A purely economic orientation that assumes unlimited natural resources and gives no consideration to externalities is rejected; it only creates "transitional unsustainability." Environmental costs do not disappear and inevitably will become economic costs. It is clear that vast food surpluses are being created at huge cost not passed on to the consumer, grain trader, or foreign buyer. More recently, attention is being given not only to environment and economics but also to the societal context of resource management and development. Canadians Scott Slocombe and Caroline Van Bers, for example, are shifting their attention to the sustainability of current societies on the grounds that true sustainable development requires more fundamental changes than improved government policies alone. "We should be thinking in terms of sustainable societies, not sustainable development."[43] A sustainable society, they argue, is attentive to personal rights, family stability, health and safety, and respect for nature. In this sense it includes the cultural dimension of the agricultural paradigm.

On the High Plains, such a comprehensive response to the combined effects of less groundwater, low commodity prices, farmer removal, and environmental degradation requires a major shift in thinking. A changed perspective may be revolutionary, since today's successful conventional farming is so deeply committed to flawed practices that now appear to guarantee wholesale failure.[44] Not only are water levels declining at ten times recharge, but we are losing five feet of topsoil each year when it takes centuries to replace a foot. Common sense (and high fuel prices) calls for better energy efficiency as well. Nor are farming skills in unlimited supply. A skipped generation, if farmers fail, means the loss of accumulated knowledge. Almost universally, the farmers I interviewed spoke of the inability of a new generation of farmers to accumulate enough capital to continue irrigation as water levels decline. This is attenuated by the reality of aging wells, pumps, engines, and sprinklers that will have to be replaced in the next decade. Surpluses have in turn promoted on the High Plains an expanding beef industry, in which six pounds of grain produce one pound of beef. Cattle feedlots that run tens of thousands of cattle through their pens every year demand a minimum of eight to ten gallons of water per head per day. Historically, meat consumption grows as living standards and social expectations rise; this is true globally. Today the plains are locked into high water consumption to grow the wheat and water the beef. In today's jargon, the paradigm shift covers the entire farming infrastructure.

One objective of sustainable development is to track soil and water consumption as real environmental costs as compared to the historic treatment of natural resources as a free commons.[45] A second priority is to produce more wheat (and alternative crops) while using less water, chemicals, soil, fuel, and capital. Third, sustainable development does not support fixing resources in place as an extreme environmental paradigm might; it argues for a shift that would still allow humanity to live comfortably, but within the world's ecological means. Fourth, sustainable development seeks to integrate the rival interests of environment and economics.[46]

Finding broad-based definitions in the world of economics, agriculture, and environment is akin to priests' reading entrails, but definitions can point out the salient features of an inclusive agro-ecological model. The abuse of the Ogallala aquifer for the last thirty years together with wasteful depletion of soil symbolized by the Dust Bowl, matched by the decline of America's historic independent farmer, signals that today's conventional farming, now dominated by agribusiness, cannot continue indefinitely into the future. The need is to identify a workable farm model or paradigm that avoids both environmental and human (social, economic, political) pitfalls, such as the ones American farming has already fallen into. Characteristics of a farmer-oriented SESA (socially and environmentally sustainable agriculture)[47] include:

1. Support to make small- to moderate-size farms economically viable because they can ensure social, economic, and environmental diversity (for example, the family farm).

2. Ensure rural community and institutional viability because it provides a working social "surround" of goods and services as well as an extended lifestyle.

3. Make farming attractive (for example, reduce the escape to the cities) by supporting self-employment, training for hands-on management, minimizing farm debt, improving farm safety, and encouraging low-input self-sufficiency (for example, farm resiliency).

4. Promote long-term environmental integrity together with long-term productivity: conserve soil and water; reduce dependence on capital-intensive equipment and chemicals; create new crops and markets; promote individualized on-site response to climate and geography; encourage diversity of crops (for example, good environmental stewardship based on locally specific knowledge).

5. Commit society at large to farming as an essential and central enterprise for the well-being of civilization, including citizen participation and government supports. Because of its fundamental role in human affairs, farming should be seen as special and unique, deserving extraordinary attention from the society it supports (for example, make farming meaningful).

6. Shift the wider economic picture from a limited agribusiness marketplace structure to "secure the economic basis of a sound democracy through widespread ownership of productive resources by those who work on farms" (Elizabeth Ann R. Bird). This would be the most difficult shift because of its widespread implications for society at large.

Much of this book has been dedicated to understanding Ogallala groundwater as part of a larger agricultural system that is situated on the High Plains and is extremely sensitive to external marketplace forces. In most instances today, when the larger agricultural system is conventional, it is heavily committed to agribusiness and an exploitive world economy and has been extremely abusive of plains water, soil, and people. An all-too-brief attempt is made here to identify the features of a better system that has come to be known variously as sustainable, alternative, regenerative, low-input, and agro-ecological agriculture. The greatest challenges are to identify the ways in which the place of the independent family farmer is shown to be essential to SESA, to incorporate successful existing farm policies and procedures into the new paradigm, and to position the new paradigm within the existing global marketplace, since the latter is unlikely to change without a major world upheaval.

The Autonomous Farm: Toward a Site-Specific or Microenvironmental Paradigm

One key to sustainability is recognition of the essential on-site localism of agriculture. Agriculture is local everywhere in the world; it succeeds or fails depending on the ability of a tract of land, minuscule in global terms, to produce a crop. The forces that shape the crop may have different magnitudes of water, wind, and sunshine or markets, technologies, government policies, and national eating habits, but their influence is ultimately focused on a single tract of farmland. This site-specific situation is strengthened in the United States by historic land policies that mostly required farmers to have their homes on their land (e.g., the Homestead Act of 1862) and have recognized that farmland is private property purchased and separated from the federal public domain. On the plains this is represented not only by efforts to identify and protect the family farm, but is brought into sharper focus by water self-sufficiency from the Ogallala aquifer through on-site wells, pumps, energy (natural gas), and water-application (center-pivot) devices. It is reinforced by the democratic process of home rule in the Soil Conservation Service and regional water districts in Kansas and Texas.

Ultimately, the farmer's decisions are local:[48] what crop to plant in a quarter of a quarter section, when to fertilize, and how to exercise weed control. What will be the response to the application of nitrogen? Add to this detailed planning of irrigation scheduling. How to prevent soil erosion and avoid wasting water. The choices of tractors, plows, spreaders, and harvesters depend on the piece of land, its crops, and the resources and skills of the farmer who plows in the shadow of his own home. Irrigation farming, like all farming, above all involves continuous interaction with the basic physical and organic mechanisms on a specific piece of land: the biochemical, genetic, and molecular mechanisms of what happens when plants take up water; the mechanisms of plant responses to environmental signals; the intrusions of chemical fertilizers, herbicides, and pesticides; the complex yet fundamental mechanisms underlying photosynthesis and regulation of the plant life cycle; the molecular and cellular mechanisms of disease. As Elizabeth Bird quoted a researcher, while science can create tricks and fool biological systems, Mother Nature endures the trickster only for a time, and it is the on-site farmer who is left with the messy results.[49]

Natural-resources stewardship and environmental ethics also begin at home. Agro-ecology is merely a concept until it is applied to soil resources, water quality and quantity, biological and genetic diversity, pest and disease control, and waste management. Guidance for sustainability comes from the application of scientific principles of ecosystems and biodiversity. The farmer combines these into the ecosystem and its constantly changing dynamic functions. What farming system will be the most resilient in the face of changing weather patterns? How is quality of the soil related to water retention? To what extent does more efficient irrigation equipment, which is costly, allow the farmer to stretch out his ability to water conventional crops or even new alternative crops that do not have a well-established market? Or is it better to introduce genetically engineered drought-resistant versions of conventional crops?

National policies, international trade agreements, global environmental debates, and even a holistic ecological science are irrelevant or possibly harmful unless they can be applied directly to sustain the individual tract of farmland.[50] Nitrogen fertilizer, for example, is costly and energy intensive and is affected by tillage, irrigation, crop rotation, the level of residual soil-nitrate nitrogen, the yield goals of the farmer, and the level of threatened pollution. Effective use of groundwater to irrigate a piece of farmland depends on a specific pumping rate; the benefits and limitations of a sprinkler system; chemical inputs; the rate of evaporation in the flood, from the soil, and from the plants; the water scheduling needs of corn versus alfalfa; the personal management ability of the individual farmer; and, not least, what the weather is like. If only generic information is available or the farmer's work is controlled by impersonal marketplace forces, it may be wrong for the land and its crop. Sustainable agriculture is incomprehensible except as it is site specific. The slogan still holds: think globally, act locally.

Successful agricultural localism, intensified by private-property rights in the United States, is at the heart of economic, political, and environmental sustainability. North Dakota farmer-philosopher Fred Kirschenmann concludes that when local needs are lost to macroforces, the result is destructive to sustainable agriculture. Industrial farming is at risk because of its centralized decisions; the lack of field experience by managment; overwhelming and unnecessary technological and capital inputs; vertical integration that plays down land, water, and people; and less on-the-job training in farming as a total way of life.[51] In this light, sustainable agriculture cannot be separated from the skilled, pragmatic self-employed, owner-operator family farmer who is dedicated to an esteemed lifestyle as well as profits in the marketplace. On-farm access to Ogallala groundwater has merely intensified this commitment to independence.

Choices: Is There Already a Move toward Sustainable Development?
In Ogallala country, as this book shows, agricultural models are inevitably local. They must be applied to groundwater being pumped at individual farms. Some environmental degradation—water mining and soil erosion—is accepted as a legitimate cost of maintaining productivity and farm income. Contrarily, some productivity may have to be sacrificed, such as limiting water use through irrigation scheduling, to protect the environmental

resources. The question is whether this widely acknowledged conflict contains impossible contradictions or instead looks to convergence of two paradigms, economic and environmental, into the larger agricultural SESA model.

The current trend is toward recognizing a larger role for the ecological viewpoint. In the past, alternative agriculture was marginalized. The National Environmental Policy Act of 1969 (NEPA) set federal policy by requiring detailed environmental-impact statements from all federal agencies. NEPA has had significant effects on the development of irrigation projects, but mostly in the Far West.[52] The Soil and Water Resources Conservation Act (RCA) of 1977, reinstituted in 1982, established objectives and guidelines for new soil- and water-conservation programs of the Soil Conservation Service and their continuous long-term review. The National Farmland Protection Policy Act of 1982, another long-term approach using the SCS, sought to maintain both quantity and quality of the nation's agricultural land base for future generations. The Conservation Reserve Program of the Food Security Act of 1985 seeks to reduce soil erosion and overproduction for at least ten years.[53] The debates of the 1990 farm bill tended to be proenvironmentalist and seek to toughen and stretch out farmland protection. Alternative agriculture is now credited with profitabiliy as well as environmental protection and healthy products.[54]

Kenneth A. Cook of the Center for Resource Economics proposes "a new social contract between farmers and society. For its part, society will have to recognize the enormous cost farmers already bear to conserve natural resources and protect the environment. Taxpayers will have to be willing to share more of that burden—probably a great deal more—as external costs of agricultural production becomes internalized."[55] But instead of compliance across conflicting paradigms, it is argued that Congress should "decouple" support payments from the usual commodity programs and "recouple" them to environmental recovery.[56] In this way, agriculture's environmental externalities—free water and off-site problems—could be internalized. "Congress must restructure the nation's farm policy, placing conservation at the core—not just at the periphery."[57]

The 1990s are likely to become a time of radical reconfiguration for plains farming in the old Dust Bowl region. At present, maximum economic yield (M E Y), urging the highest fencerow-to-fencerow production, is still the controlling viewpoint. The pace at which Ogallala water is consumed could even rise. A potential shift from M E Y to M S Y (maximum sustainable yield)[58] would conserve Ogallala water for another generation or indefinitely, but it might not make enough net profit to keep today's farmers on their land. The decline of the Ogallala may be only the last stage of a long series of events that will once again test survivability in this submarginal agricultural environment.

Final Note

The High Plains environment was and is easily harmed. Since the first settlers, farming there has created dangerous dependencies on scarce resources and fragile processes many times. Repeated depopulations and inescapable drought, together with the accelerated and wasteful overconsumption of Ogallala groundwater, continue to make the region so vulnerable that farming prevails only with heavy government infusions of cash and credit. The livelihood of hundreds of thousands of people depends on this flimsy infrastructure. In turn, it is not inconceivable that the decline of the Ogallala would weaken national security and the stability of world civilization.[59]

Sustainable agriculture is a key ingredient for a sustainable society. Jake Vail of the Land Institute finds it worthwhile to read between the lines of Eugene P. Odum's 1969 paper "The Strategy of Ecosystem Development."[60] In it Vail finds parallels between the complex dynamics of maturing natural ecosystems and human society. Odum's ecological goal of maximum biomass is readily translated into the category of high information content in an established and developing society: "Cultural information may be seen to increase just as biological information does, and as it does we find symbiosis—cooperation—easier, and, indeed, necessary." As Scott Slocombe observed,

> feedbacks and cycles, nonlinear dynamics are what produce the mysterious random amplification of microscopic fluctuations [for example, a light winter snow forces plains farmer bankruptcy]. Think of

ideas as alternatives, proposals and thoughts as microscopic fluctuations, and communication and consensus as amplification and you will have the key to management of self-organizing human systems. Such an approach puts the lie to "rational comprehensive planning"—the process is really creative, non-rational, and inherently unpredictable.[61]

Knowledge is a nutrient in a larger process, a better concept, says Vail, than knowledge as power. "Mature systems have a greater capacity to entrap and hold on to nutrients/knowledge; internal quality and feedback control are also trademarks of a mature system."[62]

Like environmental systems, human institutions also change with time. Modern society is moving from isolated cultures to an interconnected global situation in which complementarity is as important as diversity. To comprehend society in the framework of Odum's model, Vail argues, will better inform us about approaching global issues, such as carrying capacity and restraint in resource exploitation. The goals are "cooperation, knowledge conservation, resistance to perturbations, a decrease in disorder and unpredictability, and an increase in cultural information."[63] The more information we have on the attainment of ecostability, the more society can understand how to reach global stability.

· · ·

Appendix: Puzzling Out the Plains

The early struggle of frontiersmen on the High Plains did not lead to comfortable settlement, only to more struggle. Unlike successful earlier settlement across the Appalachians and through the Midwest, the vaunted yeoman farmer seemed unable to conquer the drought-prone plains. Instead farmers endured decades of hardship. The problem attracted the attention of a galaxy of scientists, geographers, and historians who sought to comprehend the unexpectedly tough region. The High Plains became the battleground over an American identity and raised doubts about the settlement myth, Manifest Destiny, that was forged from the eastern and midwestern frontiers. The successive failures to turn the High Plains quickly into still another permanent cornucopia suggested that the American Dream had its limits and thus defined that dream. In 1878, John Wesley Powell, government scientist and explorer, published his grave warning about lands beyond the ninety-eighth meridian: the semiarid climate of the High Plains would not sustain American development. But Frederick Jackson Turner, a Wisconsin historian, gave a popular shape to America's passionate westering. His 1893 frontier thesis, which never took the plains experience into account, enthusiastically claimed that a truly American character was forged out of the frontier struggle.[1] Turner insisted that conquest of the Old West (crossing the Appalachians) was replicated in settlement patterns across the entire continent. In the twentieth century the writers Walter Prescott Webb, Frederic E. Clements, James C. Malin, Paul B. Sears, Carl Ortwin Sauer, Martyn J. Bowden, and Donald Worster are among the multifold and multidisciplinary examiners of nature and settlement, space and time on the High Plains. They have striven to explain what happened to Manifest Destiny when Americans, like marathon runners, hit the wall of drought on the High Plains.

Walter Prescott Webb

Native Texan, teacher, and writer Walter Prescott Webb hated the plains but loved them more. He virtually created for Americans the great presence of western space and time when he published *The Great Plains* in 1931. According to Webb, who wrote before technology tapped the Ogallala, insufficient water would perpetually limit settlement on the plains and those who attempted it would always find life a trial. He believed vaunted American technological acuity had found its master. Webb did not anticipate the irrigation revolution of the 1960s and 1970s, but he did insist that the High Plains climate would necessarily exert environmental limits on human well-being. In a lesser-known and more philosophical work in 1951–52, *The Great Frontier*, he anticipated the "limits to growth" debate of the early 1970s, "The passing of free land should be registered by the passing of cheap food," and predicted that the end of the four-hundred-year European expansion boom would also signal the decline of rampant capitalism.[2] "In the Age of the Frontier western European society lived on the returns from its capital; today the capital is being consumed."[3] Again Webb did not anticipate the energetic durability of capitalism, although his futurist vision worried about the high consumption of limited resources that supported worldwide economic growth. What would the United States and the world be like without four hundred years of frontier expansionism into new regions? Webb was unusual among historians of his day in that he anticipated the study of environmental history in the 1970s and 1980s: "We always deal with man in an environment, and we believe that the two are reciprocal factors which complement and adjust themselves to each other."[4]

Webb emphasized climate factors usually ignored by historians. He was one of the first to acknowledge the problems of the plains: unfriendly and un-conquerable climate extremes characterized by insufficient rain, intense heat and cold, and the steady, strong, maddening wind. He quoted a 1925 United States climate report that plains wind velocities averaged fourteen or fifteen miles an hour in the Panhandle country, "winds which are ocean-like in character, as vast stretches of the Plains are themselves ocean-like in their monotony and in their unbroken sweep to the far-away horizon."[5] The im-pact of plains wind, Webb concluded, "offers an alluring study for the stu-dent of social institutions and for the psychologist." Intensified by blistering heat and extreme dryness, the furnace blasts from June through September invite economic disaster: "Over ten million bushels of corn were destroyed in Kansas in one season. It is not uncommon for fine fields of dark-green corn to be destroyed in two days."[6] Winter northers and blizzards (the "griz-zly of the plains") are equally devastating and maddening. Webb told the story of an eastern visitor. "Does the wind blow this way here all the time?" the visitor asked a cowboy. "No, Mister. It'll maybe blow this way for a week or ten days, and then it'll take a change and blow like hell for a while."[7]

Benefiting from his own lifelong experience, Webb contrasted the know-how of American farming in his day with the environmental pressures of the High Plains to explain the baleful history of failed settlement. It was not enough to say the rainfall was too low. What was its seasonal distribution in April through June? How much did hot, sunny weather evaporate away what little rain did fall? What combination of environmental factors and farming capacity made settlement in southwest Kansas and the Texas-Oklahoma Pan-handle particularly vulnerable? Webb wrote before the 1930s Dust Bowl, but he could have foretold its impact.[8]

Webb took care to note that plains conditions were measured improperly with the benchmark of a wetter East: "It has been customary to speak of the rainfall in the West as deficient. The term is relative, coined or adopted by a people from a wetter region. Had the Great Plains been taken over by a peo-ple from a desert, another term, expressing the opposite meaning, would no doubt have been applied. The Spaniards, for example, said less about the aridity of this region than the Anglo-Americans."[9] And: "The distinguishing climatic characteristic of the Great Plains environment from the ninety-eight meridian to the Pacific slope is a deficiency in the most essential climatic element—water. . . . This deficiency . . . conditions plant life, animal life, and human life and institutions. In this deficiency is found the key to what may be called the Plains civilization. It is the feature that makes the whole aspect of life west of the ninety-eight meridian such a contrast to life east of that line."[10]

Paul B. Sears and Frederic E. Clements

Stormily received when it was first published in 1935, *Deserts on the March* by biologist-turned-historian Paul Sears has rarely been out of print and reached its fourth edition in 1980.[11] Sears turned upside down the popular textbook version of America's benevolent westward expansion. While Webb had emphasized harsh environmental conditions, Sears blasted destructive human exploitation that severely damaged a fragile and difficult environment. When settlement reached the High Plains, the nation's vaunted combination of "mechanical invention," "exuberant vitality" and "unparalleled speed" destroyed the plains as a sustainable agricultural heartland. Wrongheaded human intervention helped intensify the drought and dust storms that came back to haunt Americans and drove half a million people away in the 1930s.[12] Americans may have squandered their agricultural future. Sears introduced a global perspective. Had not China and India, Greece and Rome, brought about their own downfall by overexploitation of the land? Were not all civilizations built on the borrowed capital of diminishing soil fertility?[13] On the plains, modern profit-oriented, high-production, mechanized agribusiness mined the soil at unexpected speed. This had disastrous effects, largely because of the refusal to acknowledge the limits the region's climate places on intensive farming. Using the emerging science of ecology, Sears emphasized the fragile balance between soil and humus, water and climate. "It is not too far off to say that when life enters new territory, environment dictates the terms."[14] Instead, Americans blindly tried to make the High Plains into another ideal agricultural region like southeast Pennsylvania or the humid tallgrass prairie of Illinois and Iowa. The native grasses are durable, but the single-crop farming that replaced them was not. Overplowing and overgrazing made the fine plains soil vulnerable to wind and water erosion.

According to Sears, the settlers' blind push on the plains meant they did violent harm to an ecological balance and consequently to themselves. Biologist Frederic E. Clements, a Nebraska native, studied the native plains grasses and in his conclusions did much to invent American environmental science. Donald Worster's important 1977 study, *Nature's Economy: The Roots of Ecology,*[15] cites Clements's emphasis on the delicate and nervous interplay between plains ecology and its settlement: "From Clements' plant studies emerged a coherent and elaborate system of ecological theory that was not only preeminently influential in the new science, but also had important things to say about the pioneers' relation to the American grassland."[16]

Clements emphasized that a natural landscape was "not an aimless wandering to and fro" in some kind of a meaningless chaos, but "a steady flow toward stability that can be exactly plotted by the scientist" into the ecological "climax." In the long run, the intertwined variables of heat and cold, rainfall, and wind become the forces that control plains soil and vegetation. Clements's climax condition "is a unified mechanism in which the whole is greater than a sum of its parts and hence it constitutes a new kind of organic being with novel properties."[17] If on the plains "only one kind of community deserves to be called the mature stage," then human intervention, which diverts this community to its own purpose, brings on a fatal chaos. What does human invasion tear apart, and can anything satisfactory be built in its place? In Clements's words: "There is good and even conclusive evidence . . . that the prairie climax has been in existence for several millions of years at least."[18] According to Clements, writes Worster, "it was not possible to have both a climax state of vegetation and a highly developed human culture on the same territory. . . . the pioneers and homesteaders unwittingly prepared the soil for a social and ecological disaster: the Dust Bowl of the 1930s."[19] Americans could not comprehend the full extent of the opportunities and pitfalls of their westward expansion until ecology and history had been wedded.

James C. Malin

Kansas-born James C. Malin wedded climate and history to build a holistic ecological approach toward grassland settlement.[20] Writing in the 1940s and 1950s, Malin took issue with Clements's permanent-climax view that the plains had been irremediably harmed. Rather, he joined Henry Chandler Cowles at the University of Chicago in his conviction that the grassland was an open ecological system. A stable final environmental statis is a myth. By locating humanity's place within a seamless ecological web of past, present, and future, Malin saw the Dust Bowl as merely the most recent phase of the cycles of drought and erosion that began long before human arrival on the plains. "Man's turning over of the sod with the plow is only a more complete process of cultivation of the soil that took place continuously in nature." The Dust Bowl, nevertheless, was surely intensified by pioneer settlers, who were still farming in an early exploitive stage as the drought struck.[21] While settlement did change the land, the climate is perpetually in flux, soil and vegetation in constant turmoil.

Successful plains settlement by people accustomed to forest culture should have involved the slow adaptation of human technologies and institutions to new conditions instead of fastest-possible soil mining and water exploitation. In this light, Malin unknowingly paralleled the work of the French *annales* historians Marc Bloch and Fernand Braudel.[22] Malin's synthesizing approach remained largely unknown except to a small group of loyal students at the University of Kansas because he published his typescripts privately, among them the 1947 *Grasslands of North America*. Even Malin admitted his style was convoluted and cumbersome. But he went further than his predecessors (and virtually all who wrote later) in building a unified picture which covered the geological underground, surface topography, climate, soil dynamics, plants and animals, even effects of insects and fire, in order satisfactorily to identify human opportunities and pitfalls as the plains were settled. Human responses remained the creative center, and humans were expected to be opportunistic. The grasslands, Malin believed, were so unlike earlier American settlement experiences that they offered a real test for American innovation and ingenuity. The dynamic environment of the plains does not tell the entire story unless human possibilities were taken into account. "New skills acquired by man create new natural resources and new opportunities. The process is indeterminate."[23]

Carl Ortwin Sauer

Geographer Carl Ortwin Sauer focused on the destructive power of human greed and cupidity more than did Malin in his open-ended acceptance of human opportunism. Sauer did equal justice to the web of physical environmental conditions and their role in human settlement, but Sauer was far less optimistic than Malin about the potential for farming the plains. Humans can quickly and irreparably damage the natural productivity of the plains and as a result harm themselves.[24]

Born in Missouri and raised in the Black Forest country of Germany, Sauer studied geography at the University of Chicago and came under the influence of plant ecologist Henry Chandler Cowles. Like so many plains interpreters, Sauer sought to find a workable balance between the vicissitudes of grassland conditions and the virtuous industry of "homefolks," but he was bearish about the future.[25] In the tradition of George Perkins Marsh and Aldo Leopold, he elaborated a land ethic. In a 1956 essay, "The Education of a Geographer,"[26] he insisted on reverence for land as humanity's living tether, in part to compensate for historic exploitation. Sauer did much to support a landmark 1955 conference titled "Man's Role in Changing the Face of the Earth," in which High Plains studies played an important role.[27]

Sauer used the early settlement of American grasslands as a typical example of unthinking human intervention. The actions of pioneers on the High Plains frontier when they broke the prairie sod, burned off the grasses, and aggressively worked to adapt to local conditions caused Sauer to emphasize the power that humans had to damage frontier environment. When the "forest society" unexpectedly encountered the flat, open, fertile midwestern prairie, it was a particularly vivid man-environment encounter.

Sauer also emphasized the power of settlers' "psycho-milieu," their preconceived picture of "barrens," no matter whether in Kentucky, the Midwest, or the plains. He argued that the emotion-laden set of mental expectations was as powerful a force as the physical reality.[28] A specific and identifiable geography is out there, a combination of landforms, climate, and vegetation. Humans, however, highlight certain features and ignore others, based on their cultural baggage. In sharp contrast to Turner's thesis, it is the cultural baggage carried to the frontier that is ultimately the shaping force of settlement. No wonder plains settlers held out so long in hope of rain and struggled in vain to force their eastern humid-land farmways upon the drylands.

Sauer's influential 1925 paper "The Morphology of Landscape" broke with the environmental determinism of his day. Earth was "the scene on which the activity of man unfolds itself." The scene is itself a living whole, made up of a series of moving points on a variety of moving lines. Sauer saw too much of civilizations' power to exploit nature to be an environmental determinist; instead he actively promoted "the humane use of the earth." He looked backward nostalgically to a plains "golden age" in the early 1900s, where a simpler farm culture was less destructive than modern consumption-oriented technology. This era did suggest to him that harmony can be achieved between a sustainable environment and the satisfaction of human needs if humans can control their greed. If attention is paid to the lessons taught by the golden age, Carl Sauer believed, the past experiences of settlement can offer guidelines for a better balance between the capacity of land and the requirements of modern society than is in effect today.

Martyn J. Bowden

Contemporary historical geographer Martyn J. Bowden follows another course to identify the real situation on the High Plains. He assumes that drought is the primary controlling factor determining whether successful settlement and long-term prosperity can happen on the plains. Since denials of drought harmed historic settlement and because there are recurrent fears that the devastating 1930s Dust Bowl could be repeated, Bowden sorted through dubious myths and anecdotes to collect climate data that identified the real occurrence of drought on the High Plains.[29] He concluded that American attitudes toward the High Plains repeatedly shifted between the Great American Desert and the Great American Garden. Politicians, literary romantics, explorers, farmers, land promoters, and boomers all participated in creating

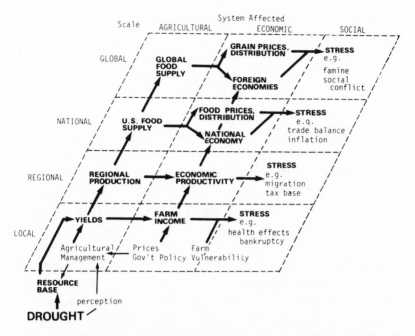

Scale

System Affected

AGRICULTURAL ECONOMIC SOCIAL

GLOBAL — GLOBAL FOOD SUPPLY — GRAIN PRICES, DISTRIBUTION → STRESS e.g. famine social conflict — FOREIGN ECONOMIES

NATIONAL — U.S. FOOD SUPPLY — FOOD PRICES, DISTRIBUTION → STRESS e.g. trade balance inflation — NATIONAL ECONOMY

REGIONAL — REGIONAL PRODUCTION → ECONOMIC PRODUCTIVITY → STRESS e.g. migration tax base

LOCAL — YIELDS → FARM INCOME → STRESS e.g. health effects bankruptcy

Agricultural Management — Prices Gov't Policy — Farm Vulnerability

RESOURCE BASE

perception

DROUGHT

17. Drought impact pathways. This diagram identifies the widespread and complex effects of High Plains drought as its impact spreads regionally, nationally, and internationally, and influences farmers and communities, consumer prices, and international trade, even causing a global threat of famine. From Richard A. Warrick and Martyn J. Bowden, "The Changing Impacts of Droughts in the Great Plains," in Merlin P. Lawson and Maurice E. Baker, eds., *The Great Plains: Perspectives and Prospects* (Lincoln: University of Nebraska Press, 1981), 113.

the eastern public image of the plains.[30] This mythical image included false information on rainfall, soil quality, heat, wind, cold, and the capacity of the region to grow corn, since corn symbolized agricultural prosperity. Bowden notes the historic irony that the myth of the garden did coincide with data on unusually heavy rains in the 1860s (said to be the result of wartime cannon fire) and again in the early 1880s (rain follows the plow). The contrasting myth of the desert reflected early nineteenth-century antipathy by a forest society toward grassland settlement, and it was reinforced by drought and depopulation in the 1890s and 1930s.

How to separate reality from myth? Bowden and his colleague Richard A. Warrick integrated dendroclimatological (tree ring) and sunspot cycles, tracked down direct nineteenth-century climate data that had been gathered, for example, by medical doctors attached to army forts on the plains, and made inferences from data on wheat yield declines, population migration, farm transfers, and federal relief programs. This data was then collated with the historic memory of climate's effects on society. Bowden and Warrick arrived at two conclusions. First, their "lessening" hypothesis suggests that technology and societal infrastructure can reduce the impact of climate change, as is demonstrated in the minimized effects of the drought of the 1970s compared to that of the 1930s. Second, however, this protection received by farmers creates a "partially closed livelihood system." Farmers become less self-sufficient and depend all the more on the external supports of world markets, federal aid, and new machinery. They are less able to fend for themselves in a crisis: debts cannot be paid off. In the face of severe drought on a local level, the larger society can feel a ripple effect more than it did when farmers alone bore the brunt of hardship. The vaunted self-sufficiency of the independent farmer had been lost, and so had his identity.

Although Bowden and Warrick do not discuss it, the real victim of the 1930s Dust Bowl on the High Plains may have been the small farmer, who never recovered. By clearly identifying "pathways of drought impact" through regional, national, and global society, Bowden and Warrick provided a systems analysis structure of the man-environment interaction described by Webb, Malin, Worster, and others. They argue that environmental problems like drought (and presumably global warming), when identified soon enough, can be influenced by public policy and crisis management. But in all his writings, Bowden did not identify a clear role for Ogallala water.

Donald Worster

With the fervor of a latter-day Paul Sears, historian Donald Worster found that the combination of aggressive human intervention and an unexpectedly vulnerable environment guaranteed trouble for both the white European invaders and the environment on the High Plains. In his 1979 *Dust Bowl: The Southern Plains in the 1930s*, Worster argued that the 1930s Dust Bowl combined the worst drought cycle in 360 years with major human error to raise the scale of the disaster to catastrophic proportions.[31] Worster moved beyond strict historical analysis to offer a cautionary and reformist statement.[32] High Plains troubles resulted not only from a misunderstood climate, but even more from mechanized, single-crop, exploitive farming.[33] The results will not be easy to overcome even with the best resources and intentions. Unlike historic Chinese deforestation or Mediterranean soil destruction, each of which happened over hundreds of years, "the Dust bowl took only 50 years to accomplish. It cannot be blamed on illiteracy or overpopulation or social disorder. It came about because the [capitalist] culture was operating in precisely the way it was supposed to. . . . the inevitable outcome of a culture that deliberately, self-consciously, set itself that task of dominating and exploiting the land for all it was worth."[34] When a fragile environment was invaded by such narrow-minded settlers, the result was "tragic, revealing, and paradigmatic" for American civilization. As Paul Sears did for the grim 1930s, Worster does for today's era of environmental breakdown. Can a humane society really be founded on "a highly mechanized system of cropping plants and animals, making the earth a vast food factory, controlled by a very small number of multinational corporations"? Worster concluded that the tragedy of the Dust Bowl, and society's responses to it, was a judgment on the nature of the twentieth century.

• • •

A Paradigm Shift: The Environment-Agriculture Connection
The contributions of historians, geographers, and scientists from Webb to Worster go far beyond the traditional explanation of the High Plains represented by Frederick Jackson Turner and his frontier thesis.[35] Today, any comprehensive study must play fair with both environmental sustainability and economic development. The historic fate of the groundwater of the Ogallala formation, in service to specific agricultural needs, is a particularly appropriate subject for agro-ecology.

Water and farming on the High Plains is a thin slice of the continuing Agricultural Revolution. We humans have now enjoyed over ten thousand years of domesticated plants and animals and a subdued soil from whence they spring. Farming is probably the only place left where humans continuously and directly experience the nonhuman world. Despite mechanization and chemicals, agriculture is still humanity's most direct and intimate living tether to the natural world, a direct and continuous use of the physical earth, organic and inorganic. Farming remains our most rudimentary and profound form of environmental management. Humans use nature in a surprisingly narrow vein (a handful of different grains) that industrial agriculture narrows still further (monoculture). When compared to the vast array and diversity of nature's species, the variety of resources that humanity farms is a thin sliver indeed.

Farming is also invariably tied to a specific place (the lingo is "site specific"). Farmland is a once-natural place entered, cut back, and rearranged into a domesticated landscape. Nevertheless, the physical setting, natural or modified, is still the primary agent controlling agricultural success. Nature's bounty allows farming. Its failure has meant the fall of civilizations, and nowhere else in American history have stronger environmental and agricultural extremes been experienced than in the old Dust Bowl region.

The study of agriculture is different from other subjects for the environmental historian. Most environmental history first gave its primary attention to an understanding of wilderness. But unlike agriculture, wilderness is said to function without human activity and does not inform humanity except as a contrast. Environmental historians also have devoted their attention to industrial and urban waste and pollution, where the remains of nature are hard to find in the fumes and the concrete. Here humanity is dominant and dangerously isolated. In agriculture, however, the farmer, though distanced from elementary nature by his reconfigured soil, reshaped plants, and his chemical additives, must still deal with the basic stuff of his physical surroundings: climate, soil, organic matter, and water, all moving in long-term processes with far-reaching consequences. Agriculture is the least prone of all fundamental human activities to be permanently transformed—truly domesticated—into an environment of artifacts, "the clusters of things that people have made." Even a genetically altered ear of corn is still closer to the soil than a steel bar is to iron ore. Agriculture is least likely to join fully the heavily controlled "Second Nature" that men have fought to create since the Renaissance, the Age of Reason, and the Industrial Revolution. Nature always interrupts the farmer's best-sown plans, as in the Dust Bowl drought of the 1930s. The limits discovered in the 1980s concerning overconsumption of groundwater foretell another, different Dust Bowl. Continued success in the old Dust Bowl region may inevitably depend on external inputs, particularly government subsidies and incentives. Dust Bowl farming of any kind is arguably not self-sufficient nor self-sustaining.

The Butterfly Effect

A 1952 tale by Ray Bradbury, "A Sound of Thunder," is the story of a game-hunting safari by time machine from the late twenty-first century into the prehistoric era of dinosaurs. The only reptiles that are shot (from a floating walkway) are those that would have died of natural causes—a falling tree or drowning in a tar pit—two minutes later, and the only trophies are photographs, so as not to violate the future. One hunter is told:

> Crushing certain plants could add up infinitesimally. A little error here would multiply in sixty million years, all out of proportion. . . . A dead mouse here makes an insect imbalance there, a population disproportion later, a bad harvest further on, a depression, mass starvation, and, finally, a change in *social* temperament in far-flung countries.[36]

Panicked by a tyrannosaurus, one of the hunters stumbles momentarily in some swampy muck before clambering back onto the walkway. At the end of the safari, participants find their home world subtly and frighteningly changed: "year" is "yeer," "name" is "naim," and "time" is "tyme." Before their expedition left, the recent presidential campaign victor had been a humane and generous man; they now returned to a newly elected fascistic president. The stumble in the muck had killed a butterfly, still stuck on the hunter's boot:

> Embedded in the mud, glistening green and gold and black, was a butterfly, very beautiful and very dead. . . . It fell to the floor, an exqui-

325

site thing, a small thing that could upset balances and knock down a line of small dominoes and then big dominoes and then gigantic dominoes, all down the years across Time.[37]

In his 1987 study of chaos theory, James Gleick revived Bradbury's 1952 butterfly-effect concept: "Tiny differences in input could quickly become overwhelming differences in output. . . . Errors and uncertainties multiply, cascading upward through a chain of turbulent features" that are both unpredictable and certain. The butterfly effect acquired its own technical language: sensitive dependence on initial conditions. "In science as well as in life, it is well known that a chain of events can have a point of crisis that could magnify small changes. . . . chaos meant that such points were everywhere."[38]

North Dakota farmer Frederick Kirschenmann, who is also an academically trained philosopher, gives an added twist to this small input–large output approach. He says society is now faced with choosing between an agriculture based on the accelerating force of industry that is narrowly focused on profits or an agriculture based on nature.[39] The factory-type farm, which considers fields and animals as production units and where economic performance is based on the year-end bottom line, is quickly becoming so dominant that there may be no return. The nature-type farm treats itself like a complex interrelated organism that has biological limits and where economic performance is "judged by the long-term health and achievement of the total organism within a larger bioregion." Kirschenmann is concerned that the days are limited to put this organic model into effect because of three common fallacies. The fallacy of misplaced concreteness says soil is measured by its "maximum yield" instead of its organic health. The fallacy of reductionism involves the dollar "economic threshold" for insecticide application rather than whether we are killing off beneficial insects and natural predators. The fallacy of unlimited growth ignores the reality, according to William E. Reed, that "a dependent part cannot grow indefinitely within a limited whole."[40]

The more elaborate a technical system is, the better it can insulate us from the cycles of drought we have come to expect, but this is at the price of greater vulnerability to a major catastrophe. It is the surprise or nonlinear event that brings failure to a highly rational but limited factory society. The fear is that today's conventional factory farming is, in Jesse Ausubel's words, too brittle in the face of long-term climate change.[41] As was true of ancient farming, modern farming can creatively perpetuate itself only when it is primarily grounded in complexity, variety, and openness rather than the predetermined world of monoculture and marketplaces.

Ecology and the Ogallala

The science attached to this book is ecology. Attention has also been given to geology and hydrology, soil chemistry and plant science, physical geography, and climatology. But our particular interest here is the interactions among the physical environment of landscape, soil, and water, the organisms that spring from them, and their treatment by human beings as resources for subsistence and the good life. Water, particularly the disappearing groundwater of the Ogallala, rarely enters the domain of historians; they are a notoriously traditional lot. But the subject is urgent. Water in a dry place like the Dust Bowl region cannot exist merely as the historian's background noise. Rather, it is the first and essential signal to come out of the cosmic roar.

Eugene P. Odum, who has given textbook shape and direction to ecology for the past thirty-five years, writes:

A human being, for example, is not only a hierarchal system composed of organs, cells, enzyme systems, and genes as subsystems, but is also a component of supraindividual hierarchal systems such as populations, cultural systems, and ecosystems. . . . It is in the properties of the large-scale, integrated systems that hold solutions to most of the long-range problems of society.[42]

Modern scientific activity tends toward reductionism to explain the world by its smallest component parts and often loses a sense of the whole. Odum complains that "today we have only half a science of man" and urges large-system corrective links between ecology and economics, ecology and political science, and ecology and social benefits.

Gene Odum aids the environmental historian by reminding his fellow scientists of "wrong-level applied science." Environmental-impact statements, for example, give attention to an individual species or waste problem instead of addressing the problem at the ecosystem level, where policy questions should be raised, legislative decisions made, money spent, and where people's lives are likely to be put in harm's way. Similarly, in agricultural economics, when attention is devoted primarily to profitable production, it may subvert the means toward sustainable farming. Historians, too, "should move from mere component analysis" to "more holistic approaches wherein interactive, integrative, and emergent properties are also included." Most analysts—from federal scientists to local farmers—treat Ogallala decline as a one-problem, one-solution subject. Fortunately, some public-policy thinking is moving away from the "quick fix," the "tyranny of small technologies," and the "tyranny of small decisions."[43] Admittedly, this suggests a hybrid procedure involving hard and soft science, but it ensures attention to the multidimensional aspects of groundwater use in the old Dust Bowl. As ecologists might say, "it is the secondary impacts that will get you if you do not consider the whole."

An ecological systems approach takes the environmental historian beyond the hybrid. Surely the complexity of problems requires a multifold response. The first step is to remeasure the geography of farming according to aquifer or river basin instead of section or county or state. With the response of (1) sustaining long-term use of Ogallala groundwater (the resource base) (2) by appropriate conventional and emerging technologies, (3) institutional mechanisms can be created (4) to provide a decision-making process (5) to formulate public policy (6) linking public interest with the private sector (7) to ensure equity and fairness.[44] Thus groundwater use, seen in its necessary context, is a valid measure of and tool for social justice. The system must be both vertical—physical, chemical, biological, economic, legal, sociopolitical, and ethical—and horizontal: a long-term time line to identify the rehabilitation of a region from what it once was, what it had become under human intervention, and what it should become to sustain itself and the humans dependent upon it.

A systems approach is rewarding because it identifies and links a large array of different elements, in this case the forces that created the Ogallala aquifer and the forces that manipulate it today. Historically, for more than one hundred years, the goal of the American farmer has been to improve the results of his labor (output or yield per person-hour) through mechanical aids (harvesters, tractors, etc.), chemicals (pesticides, herbicides, fertilizers), and genetic engineering (plant breeding). He was so successful that he is today overwhelmed by overproduction. Systems analysis takes into account, as he did not, larger and larger circles of effects that led to a gradual but steady loss of control of his destiny. Control of farm production moved away from the individual farm into the hands of agribusiness, food processors, government, and especially the worldwide grain and food markets. The farmer, on which the entire system depended, became a distant nonparticipant in global agricultural decisions while he should be at the heart of policy choices. He has felt helpless during the last few decades when global conditions and the new technologies of the green revolution raised world food supplies and lowered commodity prices. At the same time, the costs of the farmer's inputs, especially chemicals, fossil fuels, machinery, and credit, rose significantly. The newest input is environmental protection, already institutionalized by the farm bills of 1985 and 1990. A systems view also can offer solutions that can satisfy many system pathways. One current possibility is that the adoption of alternative, low-input, more ecologically oriented farming can give the farmer more control over his destiny by reducing his dependence on the forces revealed by systems analysis.[45] Fewer chemicals, less fossil fuel, lower credit demands, and diversified crops all would make the farmer less dependent.

A Complementary Approach: Plains Agriculture as a Nonlinear Self-Organizing System

An approach suggested by this book is to treat Ogallala groundwater as a prominent part of a nonlinear self-organizing system, in this case plains agri-

Decision Model for a Grain Farmer

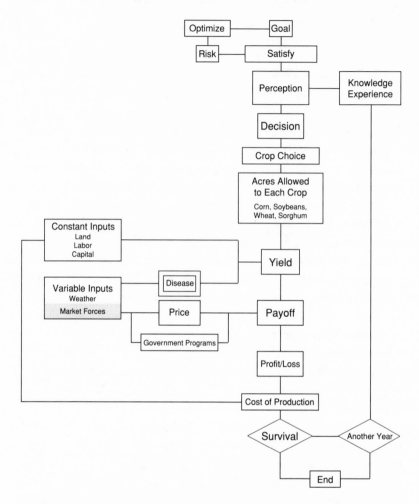

18. A decision model for a grain farmer. The modern High Plains farmer who is a commercial grain producer, works like a corporate manager as much as a hands-on farmer. This diagram outlines the complex factors that such a farmer must keep in mind to be successful. Some High Plains farmers have computerized their activities, following this model. Redrawn from Kent McGregor, "Effect of Climate Change on Cropping Structure of Shawnee County, Kansas: A Bayesian Model," *Agricultural History* 63, no.2 (Spring 1989): 206, with permission of the Agricultural History Society.

culture.[46] It is not enough for a system to emphasize connectedness. The old atomism "A thing consists of the sum of its parts, no more and no less" is wrongheaded and socially and environmentally dangerous. The classic three-dimensional material world—longitude, latitude, altitude—needs to be integrated with the additional dimensions of time (duration), energy (dynamic change), shape or form (metabolism), and multifold human actions.

In the thinking of most economists and government planners (and even most farmers), the money economy is the single dominant force controlling Ogallala farming. But capital creates a false notion of an infinitely expanding environment. Neither economic growth nor natural resources can continue infinitely. The Ogallala was treated as if it would water the fields forever. Unlimited expansion, intellectually justified since the wondrous anthropocentrism of the Renaissance era and locked into Western practices by the economic theory of laissez faire, is still the platform upon which politicians run and win. The search for wealth or mastery characterizes every aspect of industrial society. This single-minded linear movement is addictive. When only marketplace rules are applied, monoculture farming runs without a governor: "The system is constantly slipping into runaway." There is no limiter applied by another priority, such as public values or environmental degradation, to slow the engine down. James Gleick, in his provocative study of the science of chaos, writes: "A linear process, given a slight nudge, tends to remain slightly off track. A nonlinear process, given the same nudge, tends to return to its starting point."[47] Philosopher Morris Berman adds,

> In a self-corrective system, the results of past actions are fed back into the system, and this new bit of information then travels around the circuit, enabling the system to maintain something near to its ideal, or optimal state. A runaway system, on the other hand, becomes increasingly distorted over time, because the feedback is positive, rather than negative or self-corrective.[48]

Under the circumstances of declining water levels, a shrinking family farm, and persistently low crop prices, the policy goal should not be to maximize grain production at all costs, but to optimize Ogallala pumping to save the water, revive the farmer, and limit the influence of prices. In a telling comparison, Berman writes, "The human body, for example, needs only so much calcium. We do not say, 'the more calcium I have in my body, the better.' . . . [We seem to think we cannot have] too gross a Gross National Product."[49]

If we are to reflect the real world of the Ogallala, we need to accept the fact that it is a complex natural force that involves abrupt discontinuous change, far-from-equilibrium states, and irreversible but nondeterministic evolution. Internal interactions and external inputs will swing with constantly changing variables. The result is, in the words of systems scientist Scott Slocombe, a dynamic sociobiophysical system.[50]

Slocombe argues that this approach is particularly appropriate for the exploration, understanding, and reconstruction of "environmental messes,"[51] of which the Ogallala problem is certainly a fine example. Environmental analysis, according to a nonlinear self-organizing systems approach, has similarities with Eugene P. Odum's holistic and ecological procedure. Odum writes:

> One first delimits an area, a system, or a problem as a sort of "black box." Then, energy, material, and organism inputs and outputs, and major functional processes (primary production, for example) of the system as a whole are examined. Following this principle, one then examines those components and processes (populations, internal cycles and feedbacks, and food webs) that are operationally significant by observing, modeling, or perturbing the system.[52]

New structures and functions in a self-organizing system may not be predictable. One of the great benefits (though often seen as a hazard) of the Ogallala as an agricultural phenomenon is its incompleteness or indeterminacy. If an environment is to avoid harmful distortion because of the introduction of large unpredictable input from outside—for example, capital and technology inserted into the natural plains grasslands environment—the system must have a means of dissipating the input. A small-scale fluctuation, (declining wheat prices) may instead be amplified by the nonlinear dynamics and result in a macro effect (depopulation). Gregory Bateson wrote, "No variation, however small, can occur in any part without other variation occurring in correlation to it in all other parts."[53] The incremental changes, unexpected abrupt changes, chronic cumulative and synergistic interactions, should not go unnoticed.

This dominant uncertainty should be obvious but often is not: open systems always exchange material with their surroundings. Openness can allow the spontaneous creation of new and more complex elements, in human terms a surprise. For example, in the late 1970s land prices were high, interest rates low, international food demand high, and farmers prospered. But few anticipated the crisis of the late 1980s and its multiple causes that fed on each other in a systems interaction: high value of the dollar, high interest rates, the decline of inflation, the worldwide commodity glut, the international debt crisis—all combining to drive grain prices down markedly and the farmer's borrowing equity, farmland prices, down even further. Unfortunately, most High Plains farmers often still seek a single solution: "Give us a better price, and we will not have a farm problem."[54]

The complexity, interconnectedness, and highly dynamic nature of a self-organizing system cannot be described in traditional scientific terms alone; there is a sociology, politics, economics, history, and ethics in the process, together with a combination and recombination of geology, hydrology, plant and soil science, and climate. The nonhuman environment, because it is nonlinear, runs in unpredictable ways and is unwilling to settle down into the patterns of classic scientific law. Western society is much more comfortable when it finds pattern in its raw data in order to tame, utilize, and exploit nature. Pattern is signal; randomness is noise. A nonlinear approach that creatively opens up the range of questions asked about nature can discover a whole new set of problems to solve. The difficult concept is that pattern or form, not substance, is at the heart of this approach, whether it is called tendency, drift, disposition, or even strategy. It is not being, but becoming.

Without making too much of the organic metaphor, successful farming in Ogallala country is like the question of metabolism: how does a complex phenomenon stay in healthy motion? What are the invisible templates that give it its creative flowing shape? James Gleick echoed philosopher Hans Jonas when he said, "When you reach an equilibrium in biology, you're dead."[55] The balance-of-nature theory may be more poetry than science. There is no perfect state, not even the pristine plains or Wes Jackson's productive polyculture, and obviously not today's extractive agriculture. An environment, like metabolism, is continuously variable, and the variations continuously modify the future. Morris Berman concluded, "If you fight the ecology of a system, you lose—especially when you 'win.' "[56]

The goal of any ecosystem is always continuous and dynamic self-organization, "the spontaneous origin of structure in far-from-equilibrium systems." Any system that manages to maintain itself, says Berman, "whether a society, culture, organism, or ecosystem . . . is rational from its own point of view; even insanity obeys a 'logic' of self-preservation."[57] There is no violating a system's logic without suffering painful consequences. Using the example of plains irrigation, a new technology (the impeller pump), the introduction or eradication of a common species (wheat replacing native grasses), new economic linkages (global markets opened in the 1970s), and new policies or laws (1985 CRP legislation) have had telling effects that have not always been credited. Odum notes that although information is gathered about a specific subsystem, decisions must be made in the larger holistic framework.[58]

In this light, self-organizing systems analysis can bring more appropriate policy responses to extreme crises, such as the severe long-term drought projected with the greenhouse effect or the extreme swings of environmental and agricultural well-being, the boom-and-bust history of the High Plains. When stress (drought) happens, the self-organizing ecosystem should respond in multiple healthy ways—increased energy dissipation, more nutrient turnover, changes in lifestyle strategies, species diversity, and functional properties—to stave off irreversible changes and eventual breakdown of the existing system. If the engine begins running too fast, it will burn out, with some of the parts destructing before the others. There must be the presence of adjustment mechanisms within the system itself, including information.

Writes Odum: "These thermodynamically nonequilibrium systems require strong inflows of high quality energy [for example, information] and a means [policy] of dissipating disorder if they are to survive, evolve, and improve."[59]

Components from the old settlement patterns can recombine in unforeseen ways, pushed by radical economic forces (Worster's capitalism), to produce an agricultural zone (the old Dust Bowl) that is neither economically nor ecologically sustainable.[60] Stephane Castonguay writes, "Any rigid agricultural policy which seeks to be sustainable is condemned from the outset by time: changes in the ecosystem or the identification of new needs will demand strategic adjustment."[61] A major contribution of self-organizing systems analysis is recognition that political institutions, economic policies, and land-use patterns that shape any ecosystem often become obsolete under stress, unable to adjust to new conditions. Their obsolescence (answering the old questions) will drag the ecosystem down, or at least make it a very lumpy and distorted and unhappy structure.

Philosopher Paul B. Thompson, drawing on the views of William Aiken, E. F. Schumacher, Wendell Berry, and Aldo Leopold, attaches a multipath ethic to agriculture as a self-regulating system: the values attached to "economic goals need to be moderated by values that state clearly our society's dependence upon natural systems."[62] Seen in the light of such analysis, agriculture does have a moral purpose beyond the economic goals of production and efficiency. Odum's attention to ethics is as central as his attention to energy. "Going beyond reduction to (ecological) holism is now mandated if science and society are to mesh for mutual benefit."[63] The Ogallala can only be properly identified as a dynamic renewable natural resource only if it is also accepted as a fundamental social good of widespread public interest.

335

· · ·

Notes

Preface

1 Panel on Societal and Institutional Responses, Workshop on Consequences of a Possible CO_2-Induced Climate Change, American Association for the Advancement of Science/United States Department of Energy, Annapolis, Md., May 1979.

2 *History of Kearny County Kansas* (Garden City: Kearny County Historical Society, 1964), 364–65.

3 Donald E. Green, *Land of the Underground Rain: Irrigation on the Texas High Plains, 1919–1970* (Austin: University of Texas Press, 1973).

4 Morton W. Bittinger and Elizabeth B. Green, *You Never Miss the Water Till . . . . (The Ogallala Story)* (Littleton, Colo.: Water Resources Publications, 1980).

5 "The segment north of the Platte and South Platte Rivers is unlike the other three segments. A large part of this northern segment is the Sand Hills of Nebraska, where a thick section of windblown sand overlies the Ogallala Formation. The permeable nature of the Sand Hills permits rapid infiltration of precipitation. It has been estimated that as much as 25 percent of the precipitation is recharged to the water table. As a result, there is little or no surface runoff, the water table is near the land surface, and streams draining the Sand Hills are fed by ground water." John B. Weeks, "Proposed Plan of Study for the High Plains Regional Aquifer-System Analysis," working paper for February 2–3, 1978, staff meeting, Water Resources Division, Geological Survey, U.S. Department of the Interior, Denver Federal Center, 6.

6 See Philip Slater, *Earthwalk* (New York: Bantam Books, 1975), 233.

7 Quoted by William D. Ruckelshaus, "Toward a Sustainable World," *Scientific American* 261, no.3 (September 1989): 169.

8 Analysis according to nonlinear self-organizing systems theory offers "a framework for addressing the complex, interdisciplinary problems of 'managing' and understanding the natural and human environments and particularly the interface between the two," Morris Berman, *The Reenchantment of the World* (Ithaca, N.Y.: Cornell University Press, 1981), 257. Examples are Erich Jantsch, *The Self-Organizing Universe* (New York: Pergamon Press, 1980); G. Nicolis and I. Prigogine, *Self-Organization in Non-Equilibrium Systems* (New York: John Wiley, 1977); D. N. Parkes and N. J. Thrift, *Times, Spaces, and Places: A Chronogeographic Perspective* (New York: John Wiley, 1980); H. Ulrich and G.J.B. Probst, eds., *Self-Organization and Management of Social Systems* (Berlin: Springer, Verlag, 1984); unpublished paper by D. Scott Slocombe and Alex Grzybowski, "Self-Organization Theories and Sociobiophysical Systems: The Case of South Moresby," presented at the annual conference of the North American Association for Environmental Education, University of Oregon, Eugene, 16 September 1986; Eugene P. Odum, "Input Management of Production Systems," *Science* 243 (13 January 1989): 177–81. More popular discussions are in Berman, *The Reenchantment of the World*, and James Gleick, *Chaos: Making of a New Science* (New York: Penguin Books, 1987).

9 Gleick, *Chaos*, 18–19.

10 Ibid., 23–24.

11 Slocombe and Grzybowski, "Self-Organization Theories and Sociobiophysical Systems," 14–16.

12 1972 interview quoted in Berman, *The Reenchantment of the World*, 235.

Introduction

1 See Jesse H. Ausubel, "Does Climate Still Matter?" *Nature* 350 (25 April 1991): 649–52, and a reader response by Nick Sundt, "Proof Negative," *Nature* 352 (18 July 1991): 187.

2 Interview with Michael H. Glantz, head, Environmental and Social Impacts Group, National Center for Atmospheric Research, Boulder, Colorado, 25 May 1988. See H. H. Lamb, *Climate History and the Modern World* (London: Methuen and Company, 1982); Reid A. Bryson and Thomas J. Murray, *Climates of*

Hunger: Mankind and the World's Changing Weather (Madison: University of Wisconsin Press, 1977); Fernand Braudel, *Civilization and Capitalism, 15th–18th Century,* vol. 1, *The Structures of Everyday Life: The Limits of the Possible* (New York: Harper and Row, 1981), chaps. 1, 2, 5, 6; and William Woodruff, *Impact of Western Man on the Global Economy, 1650–1960* (New York: St. Martin's Press, 1964).

3 See Edwin D. Gutentag, David H. Lobmeyer, and Steven E. Slagle, *Geohydrology of Southwestern Kansas* (Lawrence: Kansas Geological Survey Irrigation Series 7, 1981), and Edwin D. Gutentag et al., *Geohydrology of the High Plains Aquifer in Parts of Colorado, Kansas, Nebraska, New Mexico, Oklahoma, South Dakota, Texas, and Wyoming (High Plains RASA Project)* (Washington: U.S. Geological Survey Professional Paper 1400-B, 1984).

4 Data studies and predictions of this sort are gathered from many sources. See, for example, William F. Hughes and Wyatee L. Harman, *Projected Economic Life of Water Resources, Subdivision Number 1, High Plains Underground Water Reservoir* (College Station: Technical Monograph 6, Texas Agricultural Experiment Station, Texas A&M University, December 1969); Oklahoma Water Resources Board, *Appraisal of the Water and Related Land Resources of Oklahoma* (Oklahoma City: Publication 44, Region 12, Oklahoma Water Resources Board, 1973); Gail P. Thelin, Federick J. Heimes, and James R. Wray, "Irrigated Cropland: The High Plains, 1980," Plate 1, Professional Paper 1400-C (Washington: United States Geological Survey, 1987); and High Plains Study Council, *A Summary of Results of the Ogallala Aquifer Regional Study, with Recommendations to the Secretary of Commerce and Congress* (Washington Economic Development Administration, U.S. Department of Commerce, December 13, 1982), and May 1992 correspondence with Edwin D. Gutentag concerning recharge rates. There will be many other references to similar federal, state, local, and independent studies throughout this book, all documented appropriately.

5 Data based on interviews, May 5, 1988, with Andy Erhart, agricultural adviser, and Al Rauhut, sales manager, Henkle Drilling and Supply Company, Garden City, Kansas, and confirmed by data from Kenny Ochs, Gigot Irrigation Company, Garden City, and from the USDA Soil Conservation Service office in Garden City.

6 Pierre R. Crosson and Norman J. Rosenberg, "Strategies for Agriculture," *Scientific American* 261, no. 3 (September 1989): 128.

7 World Commission on Environment and Development, *Our Common Future* (New York: Oxford University Press, 1987), 122–23.

8 Jim MacNeill, "Strategies for Sustainable Economic Development," *Scientific American,* 261, no.3 (September 1989): 158–59, 163–64.

9 *Our Common Future,* 125.

10 The following discussion of global sustainable development is based largely on *Our Common Future,* especially 43–66, and a special issue, "Managing Planet Earth," of *Scientific American,* 261, no.3 (September 1989).

11 See, for example, *Our Common Future,* 8–9; the editorial in the special issue, "The Promise of Low-Input Agriculture: A Search for Sustainability and Profitability," *Journal of Soil and Water Conservation* 45, no.1 (January–February 1990): 4; "Principles of Sustainability," Sustainability Society Project, Department of Environmental and Resource Studies, University of Waterloo, Canada; and the proceedings of the conference of the Agriculture, Food, and Human Values Society, "Varieties of Sustainability: Reflecting on Ethics, Environment, and Economic Equity," Pacific Grove, California, May 10–12, 1991.

12 Quoted in Neill Schaller, "Mainstreaming low-input agriculture," *Journal of Soil and Water Conservation* 45, no.1 (January–February 1990): 10. Schaller is director of the Low-Input Sustainable Agriculture Research and Education Program of the USDA.

13 *Report to Ministers of Agriculture* (Ottawa: Federal-provincial Agricultural Committee on Environmental Sustainability, 1990); see also the useful policy analysis by Stephane Castonguay, "The Technological Function of the Environment in a Sustainable Agriculture," paper presented at the conference "The Environment and the Mechanized World," American Society for Environmental History, University of Houston, February 28–March 3, 1991.

14 Frederick Kirschenmann, "Fundamental fallacies of building agricultural sustainability," *Journal of Soil and Water Conservation* 46, no.3 (May–June 1991): 167.

15 Ibid.

16 Quoted in ibid., 166.

17 Reported in Pierre Crosson and Janet Ekey Ostrov, "Sorting out the environmental benefits of alternative agriculture," *Journal of Soil and Water Conservation* 45, no.1 (January–February 1990): 34–35.

18 See Linda Schroeder, "Low-input agriculture: Overcoming the impediments," *Journal of Soil and Water Conservation* 45, no.1 (January–February 1990): 40.

19 Interview with Wayne Wyatt, manager of the district, in Lubbock, Texas, May
1987. See also *Rules of Texas High Plains Underground Water Conservation
District No.1, 1954;* Frank A. Rayner, *Government and Groundwater Management* (Lubbock, Tex.: High Plains Underground Water Conservation District
No 1, 1975), 1–4, 10; "The Case for Local Regulation," *The Cross Section* 28,
no.12 (December 1982): 1–4; and Frank L. Baird, *District Groundwater Planning and Management Policies on the Texas High Plains: The Views of the People* (Lubbock, Tex.: High Plains Underground Water Conservation District
No.1, July 1976), pp.4–5.

20 See John Opie, *The Law of the Land: 200 Years of American Farmland Policy*
(Lincoln: University of Nebraska Press, 1987), esp. chap. 5.

21 Data provided by the Liberal, Kansas, office of the Soil Conservation Service,
USDA, May 1987. See also "Groundwater Supply Problems," in *Revised Management Program III: Rules and Regulations, and Policies and Standards* (Garden City, Kans.: Southwest Kansas Groundwater Management District No.3,
1986), 6–7; Kansas Water Office, *Agricultural Water Conservation: Irrigation
Plan Guidelines* (enclosed in letter to "Fellow Kansans" from the Kansas Water Office, Topeka, dated December 18, 1986); Kansas State Board of Agriculture, Division of Water Resources, "Administrative Policy No.88-3" (attached
to letter dated December 12, 1988, addressed to "All County Conservation Districts"); Earl B. Shurtz, *Kansas Water Law* (Wichita: Kansas Water Resources
Board, 1967); and see Mary Rule and Elise Watkins Clement, *Distribution of
Land and Water Ownership in Southwest Kansas* (Whiting: Kansas Rural Center, 1982).

22 Quoted in Kip Lowe, "Groundwater future a continuing concern," *Colby*
(Kans.) *Free Press,* June 15, 1990; see also "Groundwater district halts water
rights," *Atwood* (Kans.) *Citizen-Patriot,* February 22, 1990; reports and publications by Northwest Kansas Groundwater Management District Four; and
the author's interviews of the district's manager, Wayne Bossert, in April 1991.

23 Charles W. Stenholm and Daniel B. Waggoner, "Low-input sustainable agri-
culture: Myth or method?" *Journal of Soil and Water Conservation,* 45, no.2
(January–February 1990): 13ff.; see also the critique by Elizabeth Ann R. Bird,
*Research for Sustainability? The National Research Initiative's Social Plan for
Agriculture* (Walthill, Nebr.: Center for Rural Affairs, August 1991).

24 Schaller, "Mainstreaming low-input agriculture," 9.

341

25 Stenholm and Waggoner, "Low-input sustainable agriculture: Myth or method?" 13.

26 Robert Rodale, "A Brief History of Sustainable Agriculture," *Journal of Soil and Water Conservation* 45, no. 1 (January–February 1990): 15.

27 Donald Worster, "A sense of soil: Agricultural conservation and American culture," *Agriculture and Human Values* 2, no. 4 (Winter 1985): 30.

28 Schaller, "Mainstreaming low-input agriculture," 10.

29 Stenhold and Waggoner, "Low-input sustainable agriculture: Myth or method?" 14.

30 Stenhold and Waggoner, "Low-input sustainable agriculture: Myth or method?" 14, who also refer to testimony by D. L. Kleckner, "Statement presented before the U.S. House Agriculture Subcommittee on Department Operations, Research, and Foreign Agriculture, July 19, 1989," Washington, 1989.

31 Robert Rodale, "Conservation is dead," *The New Farm* 2 (1989): 10–13.

32 Quoted in Stenhold and Waggoner, "Low-input sustainable agriculture: Myth or method?" 14.

33 National Research Council, *Alternative Agriculture* (Washington: National Academy Press, 1989).

34 *Our Common Future,* 52–53; see also Constance M. McCorkle, "Toward a knowledge of local knowledge and its importance for agricultural RD&E," *Agriculture and Human Values* 6 (1989): 4–12.

35 See, for example, the discussion in Rod MacRae, "Policies, Programs and Regulations to Support the Transition from Conventional to Sustainable Agriculture," by the Ecological Agricultural Project at Sainte-Anne de Bellevue, Quebec, Canada, 1989.

36 See John E. Ikerd, "Agriculture's search for sustainability and profitability," *Journal of Soil and Water Conservation* 45, no. 1 (January–February 1990): 19–20.

37 Sandra Postel, *Water for Agriculture: Facing the Limits* (Washington: Worldwatch Institute, World Watch Paper 93, 1989), 12, 40.

38 The fatal flaw of the 1900 farm bill may have been turning it into a servant of global competitiveness in which answers are seen only through the expansion of agribusiness. See the discussion in Bird, *Research for Sustainability?* 20–24.

39 William C. Clark, "Managing Planet Earth," *Scientific American,* 261, no. 3 (September 1989): 54.

40 Quoted by William D. Ruckelshaus, "Toward a Sustainable World," *Scientific American* 261, no. 3 (September 1989): 174.

41 MacNeill, "Strategies for Sustainable Economic Development," 156.

42 Ibid., 157.

43 Ruckelshaus, "Toward a Sustainable World," 16.

44 *Our Common Future*, 123–24, 130–35.

45 I regret that I fell into this common trap in two recent articles, "100 Years of Climate Risk Assessment on the High Plains: Which Farm Paradigm Does Irrigation Serve?" *Agricultural History* 63, no.2 (Spring 1989), and "The Precarious Balance: Matching Market Dollars and Human Values in American Agriculture," *The Environmental Professional* (Spring 1988).

46 See William Lockeretz, "Major issues confronting sustainable agriculture," in C. A. Francis et al., eds., *Sustainable Agriculture in Temperate Zones* (New York: John Wiley and Sons, 1990), 423–38.

47 Castonguay, "The Technological Function of the Environment in a Sustainable Agriculture."

Chapter 1

1 See the overall viewpoint of John A. Harrington, Jr., and Jay R. Harmen, "Climate and Vegetation in Central North America: Natural Patterns and Human Alterations," *Great Plains Quarterly* 11 (Spring 1991): 103–12.

2 See the classic report by Willard D. Johnson, "The High Plains and Their Utilization," *Twenty-First Annual Report of the United States Geological Survey* (Washington: Government Printing Office, 1901), 4:657–59, and the analysis in Conner Sorensen, "A History of Irrigation in the Arkansas River Valley in Western Kansas, 1880–1910" (M.A. thesis, Wichita State University, 1965), 8–10.

3 *Oklahoma Comprehensive Water Plan* (Oklahoma City: Oklahoma Water Resources Board Publication 94, 1980), 22–25.

4 "Oil, Gas Applications," *Oklahoma Oil Reporter, Weekly Edition* 4, no.20 (20 May 1985): F-5.

5 Correspondence from Edwin D. Gutentag of the USGS, Denver Federal Center, January 1989.

6 Curtis Marbut, "Soils of the Great Plains," *Annals of the Association of American Geographers*, 13 (March 1923): 41–66.

7 See the summary in *Appraisal of the Water and Related Land Resources of Oklahoma: Region Twelve* (Oklahoma City: Oklahoma Water Resources Board, 1973), 19–27.

8 Nevin M. Fenneman, *Physiography of Western United States* (New York: McGraw-Hill Book Company, 1931), 11–12.

9 See R. F. Diffendal, Jr., "Plate Tectonics, Space, Geologic Time, and the Great Plains," *Great Plains Quarterly* 11 (Spring 1991): 83–102.

10 Edwin D. Gutentag et al., *Geohydrology of the High Plains Aquifer in Parts of Colorado, Kansas, Nebraska, New Mexico, Oklahoma, South Dakota, Texas, and Wyoming. (High Plains RASA Project) (Washington: U.S. Geological Survey Professional Paper* 1400-B, 1984), table 7, 33.

11 Wayne Bossert of Kansas District No.4 considers the inch-a-year recharge generous: "Our data indicates closer to .5 inches/year natural recharge." Correspondence, January 19, 1991.

12 Bruce F. Latta, *Geology and Ground-Water Resources of Finney and Gray Counties, Kansas: Bulletin 55 of the State Geological Survey of Kansas* (Lawrence: University of Kansas Publications, August 1944), 19–23, and O. St. John, "Notes on the Geology of Southwest Kansas," *Fifth Biennial Report of the Kansas State Board of Agriculture* (1885–1886), 135.

13 Southwest Kansas geology and hydrology have been served well. See Latta, *Geology and Ground-Water Resources of Finney and Gray Counties, Kansas,* 46–119; Thad G. McLaughlin, *Geology and Ground-Water Resources of Grant, Haskell, and Stevens Counties, Kansas: Bulletin 61 of the State Geological Survey of Kansas* (Lawrence: University of Kansas Publications, July 1946), 37–86; V. C. Fishel and Betty J. Mason, *Ground-Water Levels in Observation Wells in Kansas, 1965: Bulletin 125 of the State Geological Survey of Kansas* (Lawrence: State Geological Survey of Kansas, June 1957); Margaret E. Broeker and John D. Winslow, *Ground-Water Levels in Observation Wells in Kansas, 1965: Bulletin 184, State Geological Survey of Kansas* (Lawrence: University of Kansas Publications, August 1966), 16–17, 26–27; Barbara J. Dague, *January 1987 Water Levels, and Data Related to Water-Level Changes, Western and South-Central Kansas* (Lawrence: U.S. Geological Survey Open-File Report 87-241, 1987), 21–23, 55–56, 120–22.

14 See Gutentag, *Geohydrology,* 12–13; R. T. Coupland, "The Effects of Fluctuations in Weather Upon the Grasslands of the Great Plains," *Botanical Review* 24 (1958): 273–317; J. R. Borchert, "The Climate of the Central North American Grassland," *Annals of the Association of American Geographers* 40 (1950): 1–39; D. D. Collins, "Macroclimate and the Grassland System," in R. L. Dix, ed., *The Grassland Ecosystem: A Preliminary Synthesis* (Fort Collins, Colo.: Range Science Department Science Series, No.2, 1969), 29–39.

15 William A. Albrecht, "Physical, Chemical, and Biochemical Changes in the Soil Community," in William L. Thomas, Jr., ed., *Man's Role in Changing the Face of the Earth* (Chicago: University of Chicago Press, 1956), 648–49.

16 Edward Hyams, *Soil and Civilization* (New York: Harper Colophon Books, 1976; reprinted from the original 1952 edition), 230–72.

17 Hyams, *Soil and Civilization,* 138–50.

18 Peter Farb, *Living Earth* (New York: Harper and Row, 1959), 103; see also Firman E. Bear, *Earth: The Stuff of Life,* 2d ed. (Norman: University of Oklahoma Press, 1990).

19 The basic soil handbook used by farmers and the local offices of state and federal agencies is, in Texas County, by Hadley C. Meinders, Maurice Mitchell, Edward S. Grover, and Jimmie W. Frie, *Soil Survey of Texas County, Oklahoma* (Washington: SCS, USDA, and Oklahoma Agricultural Experiment Station, 1961, 1984). Most of the following information is based on this handbook, which offers a general survey of soil science, soil maps, and aerial photographs. A farmer is readily able to identify the soil types on his land and plant and irrigate accordingly. For Kansas, see George N. Coffey and Thomas D. Rice, "Reconnaissance Soil Survey of Western Kansas," *Field Operations of the Bureau of Soils* (Washington: USDA, 1910); James L. Burgess and George N. Coffey, "Soil Survey of the Garden City Area," *Field Operations of the Bureau of Soils* (Washington: USDA, 1904), *Soil Survey of Finney County, Kansas* (Washington: SCS, USDA, 1965).

20 Meinders et al., *Soil Survey of Texas County, Oklahoma,* 26–27.

21 Ibid., 19.

22 Ibid., 23. See also 27–33.

23 Perhaps the only book ever published in Bartlesville, Oklahoma, by Phillips Petroleum Company, appeared in 1963 with the unlikely title (for an oil company's publication) *Pasture and Range Plants.* Phillips fertilizer salesmen gave them as premiums to their clients, but the well-researched book, unique in content, has acquired a nationwide life of its own. It is a treasure trove of colored drawings and descriptions of seventy-seven varieties of grasses, forty-four kinds of legumes, fifty-five forbs, three woody plants, and three miscellaneous plants. The last six—Texas buckeye, common chokecherry, Gambel oak, ergot, common horsetail, and arrowgrass—are listed because they are poisonous, as are twenty-three of the forbs and five of the legumes. None of the grasses is listed as poisonous. The book's grasses, legumes, and forbs are not exhaustive, but W.

345

F. Martin, Phillips chairman and chief executive officer, said he hoped the book would "prove a worthwhile, lasting contribution to the nation's health, growth, and prosperity." See also W. Rydberg, *Flora of the Prairies and Plains of Central North America* (New York: New York Botanical Garden, 1932); Great Plains Flora Association, T. M. Barkley, ed., *Atlas of the Flora of the Great Plains* (Lawrence: University Press of Kansas, 1977); Great Plains Flora Association, introduction by T. M. Barkley, *Flora of the Great Plains* (Lawrence: University Press of Kansas, 1986).

24 See Harrington and Harman, "Climate and Vegetation in Central North America: Natural Patterns and Human Alterations," 103–12.

25 See the discussion of early perceptions in David F. Costello, *The Prairie World* (New York: Thomas Y. Crowell Company, 1969), 5–10; J. C. Frémont, *Report of the Exploring Expedition to the Rocky Mountains in the Year 1842, and to Oregon and California in the Years 1843–1844* (Washington: H. Ex. Doc. 166, 28th Cong., 2d sess.).

26 John Madson, *Where the Sky Began: Land of the Tallgrass Prairie* (Boston: Houghton Mifflin Company, 1982), 9–10; see also F. Gerhard, *Illinois As It Is* (Chicago: Keen and Lee, 1857).

27 Quoted in Costello, *The Prairie World,* 40.

28 See J. E. Weaver and F. W. Albertson, *Grasslands of the Great Plains: Their Nature and Use* (Lincoln: Johnsen Publishing Company, 1956); J. E. Weaver, *North American Prairie* (Lincoln: Johnsen Publishing Company, 1954); N. French, ed., *Perspectives in Grassland Ecology* (New York: Springer-Verlag Ecological Studies 32, 1979), 135–55; and T. R. Vale, *Plants and People: Vegetation Change in North America* (Washington: Association of American Geographers, 1982).

29 Still unmatched is H. L. Shantz, *Natural Vegetation as an Indicator of the Capabilities of Lands for Crop Production in the Great Plains Area,* USDA Bureau of Plant Industry, Bulletin 201 (Washington, 1911).

30 See Charles B. Heiser, Jr., *Seeds to Civilization: The Story of Food* (Cambridge, Mass.: Harvard University Press, 1990, earlier editions, 1973, 1981), 61 ff.

31 James C. Malin, "The Grasslands of North America: Its Occupation and the Challenge of Continuous Reappraisals," in William L. Thomas, ed., *Man's Role in Changing the Face of the Earth* (Chicago: University of Chicago Press, 1956) 1:359–60.

32 Jon Piper, "Prairie Patterns and Their Relevance to Sustainable Agriculture," *The Land Report* 33 (Summer 1988): 23.

33 Ibid.

34 Wes Jackson, *New Roots for Agriculture* (San Francisco: Friends of the Earth, 1980), 114.

35 This is the dominant thesis in Jackson's *New Roots for Agriculture*, 2–3 and passim.

36 Keith Schneider, "Science Academy Recommends Resumption of Natural Farming," *New York Times*, September 8, 1989; see also "Academy of Sciences Endorses Low-Input Farming," *Rural Papers*, no.78 (October 1989).

Chapter 2

1 John C. Hudson, "Who was 'Forest Man?' Sources of Migration to the Plains," *Great Plains Quarterly* 6, no.2 (Spring 1986): 69–83.

2 George P. Hammond and Agapito Rey, *Narratives of the Colorado Expedition* (Aubuquerque: University of New Mexico, 1940), 2:186ff. For early European images of the Great Plains as a barren zone, see Waldo R. Wedel, "Some Early Euro-American Perceptions of the Great Plains and Their Influence on Anthropological Thinking," in Brian W. Blouet and Merlin P. Lawson, eds., *Images of the Plains: The Role of Human Nature in Settlement* (Lincoln: University of Nebraska Press, 1975), 13–20; David M. Emmons, "The Influence of Ideology on Changing Environmental Images," in Blouet and Lawson, *Images of the Plains*, 125–36; John Kirtland Wright, "Terra incognitae: The place of the imagination in geography," *Annals of the Association of American Geographers* 37 (1947): 1–5; and the broader studies by W. Eugene Hollon, *The Great American Desert, Then and Now* (New York: Oxford University Press, 1966), esp. 9–20 and 33–52, and the classic statement of Walter Prescott Webb, *The Great Plains* (Boston: Ginn and Company, 1931), esp. 94–114, 141–59, and 486–89.

3 Quoted in Carl Ortwin Sauer, "Conditions of Pioneer Life in the Upper Illinois Valley," in John Leighly, ed., *Land and Life: A Selection from the Writings of Carl Ortwin Sauer* (Berkeley: University of California Press, 1967), 12; see also Martyn J. Bowden, "The Great American Desert and the American Frontier, 1800–1882: Popular Images of the Plains," in T. K. Mareven, ed., *Anonymous Americans: Explorations in Nineteenth Century Social History* (Englewood Cliffs, N.J.: Prentice-Hall, 1971), 48–79.

4 Quoted in John L. Allen, "Exploration and the Creation of Geographical Images of the Great Plains. Comments on the Role of Subjectivity," in Blouet and Lawson, *Images of the Plains,* 3–12.

5 Quoted in Robert G. Athearn, *High Country Empire: The High Plains and Rockies* (Lincoln: University of Nebraska Press, 1962), 19; W. Eugene Hollon's *The Great American Desert, Then and Now,* remains the most comprehensive study of the concept.

6 Washington Irving, *A Tour of the Prairies* (Norman: University of Oklahoma Press, 1956 reprint).

7 Quoted in John Madson, *Where the Sky Began: Land of the Tallgrass Prairie* (Boston: Houghton Mifflin, 1982), 17; see also John F. Davis, "Constructing the British View of the Great Plains," in Blouet and Lawson, *Images of the Plains,* 181–85.

8 Quoted in Wedel, "Some Early Euro-American Percepts of the Great Plains and Their Influence on Anthropological Thinking," 15.

9 Quoted in Athearn, *High Country Empire,* 57.

10 Quoted by Bradbury's traveling companion, Henry M Brackenridge, *Travels in the Interior of America* (Cleveland: Arthur H. Clark Co., 1904 reprint of 1819 original), 267.

11 Quoted in Athearn, *High Country Empire,* 59.

12 Joshua Pilcher, *Remarks to the U.S. Senate* (Washington: S. Ex. Doc. 39, 21st Cong., 2d sess., 1831), 19.

13 Quoted in Athearn, *High Country Empire,* 60.

14 "Speech of Senator G. S. Orth of Indiana," in *Proceedings of Meeting of Excursionists—1867—Fort Harker, Kansas* (Saint Louis, Mo.: S. Levison, 1967), 49.

15 See David M. Emmons, "The Influence of Ideology on Changing Environmental Images. The Case of Six Gazetteers," in Blouet and Lawson, *Images of the Plains,* 125–36.

16 Carl O. Sauer, "Homestead and Community on the Middle Border," *Landscape* 12, no. 1 (1962): 3–7.

17 Athearn, *High Country Empire,* 183–84.

18 See Paul Bonnifield, *The Dust Bowl: Men, Dirt, and Depression* (Albuquerque: University of New Mexico Press, 1979), 15, 27–29.

19 Much of Malin's work was privately published in limited editions or appeared in regional journals. Of the literature still in print, see the excellent collection of

Malin's writings in Robert P. Swierenga, ed., *History and Ecology: Studies of the Grassland* (Lincoln: University of Nebraska Press, 1984); see also the important discussion by Donald Worster in "The Dirty Thirties: A Study in Agricultural Capitalism," *Great Plains Quarterly* 6 (Spring 1986): 107–10.

20 James. C. Malin, "Dust Storms: Part Three, 1881–1890," *Kansas Historical Quarterly* 14 (November 1946): 391–413.

21 See Kenneth S. Davis, *Kansas: A History* (New York: W. W. Norton and Company, 1976, 1984), 74, 121–22.

22 John Wesley Powell, *Report on the Lands of the Arid Region of the United States,* reprint edition (Boston: Harvard Common Press, 1983; originally published 1879), 1; see also Wallace Stegner, *Beyond the Hundredth Meridian: John Wesley Powell and the Second Opening of the West* (Boston: Houghton Mifflin, 1953).

23 Powell, *Lands of the Arid Region,* 38–39.

24 Ibid., 37–38.

25 Quoted in Paul Horgan, *Josiah Gregg and His Vision of the Early West* (New York: Farrar, Straus & Giroux, 1979), 48.

26 This was the thesis about "increase of streams" and "rise of Great Salt Lake" and "theory of human agencies" by Grove Karl Gilbert in the chapter that was inserted in Powell's arid-lands book to counter Powell's pessimistic conclusions. G. K. Gilbert, "Water Supply," in Powell, *Lands of the Arid Region,* 57–77.

27 Samuel Aughey and C. D. Wilbur, *Agriculture Beyond the 100th Meridian* (Lincoln, Nebr.: n.p., 1880).

28 See the discussion of the different viewpoints in Gilbert C. Fite, *The Farmer's Frontier, 1865–1900* (New York: Holt, Rinehart and Winston, 1966), 114.

29 See David W. Craft, "A History of the Garden City, Kansas, Land Office, 1883–1894" (M.A. thesis, University of Kansas, 1981[?]).

30 Quoted in Fite, *The Farmer's Frontier,* 117.

31 Quoted in Athearn, *High Country Empire,* 191.

32 Quoted in Fite, *The Farmer's Frontier,* 117, 118.

33 Craft, "A History of the Garden City Land Office," 31.

34 Quoted in Fite, *The Farmer's Frontier,* 127.

35 Quoted in Athearn, *High Country Empire,* 196.

36 Webb, *The Great Plains,* 423–27, 431.

37 Ibid., 375.

38 Frederick H. Newell, "Irrigation on the Great Plains," *Yearbook of the United States Department of Agriculture 1896* (Washington: USDA, 1896), 168–69.

39 Willard D. Johnson, "The High Plains and Their Utilization," *Twenty-First Annual Report of the United States Geological Survey* (Washington: Government Printing Office, 1901), 4:681.

40 Webb's classic narrative is "The Cattle Kingdom" in *The Great Plains,* 205–69; compare with Athearn, *High Country Empire,* 127–51, Hollon, *The Great American Desert,* 120–40, and Robert G. Athearn, *The Mythic West in Twentieth-Century America* (Lawrence: University Press of Kansas, 1986), 25–37.

41 Quoted in Athearn, *High Country Empire,* 227; see also 207–26.

42 See the folksy but informative essays by old-time Kearny County resident Foster Eskelund in *History of Kearny County Kansas* (Garden City: Kearny County Historical Society, 1964), 363–67.

43 See another local biographical history by Leola Howard Blanchard, *Conquest of Southwest Kansas* (Wichita: n.p., 1931), 151–52.

44 Reported in Eskelund, 364–65.

45 See Webb, *The Great Plains,* 334–35.

46 Eskelund, 365.

47 See James Earl Sherow, *Watering the Valley: Development along the High Plains Arkansas River, 1870–1950* (Lawrence: University Press of Kansas, 1990), esp. 3–7, 79–119.

48 Charles S. Slichter, "The Underflow in Arkansas Valley in Western Kansas," *Water Supply and Irrigation Paper No.153* (Washington: USGS, 1906), and Erasmus Haworth, "Physiography of Western Kansas," *University Geological Survey of Kansas* (1897), 2:12–13.

49 Quoted in Blanchard, *Conquest of Southwest Kansas,* 87; see also 1883 and 1889 correspondence and files in the Kansas Room of the Finney County Library in Garden City.

50 Sherow, *Watering the Valley,* 83–84.

51 See the detailed study in Conner Sorensen, "A History of Irrigation in the Arkansas River Valley in Western Kansas, 1880–1910" (M.A. thesis, Wichita State University, 1965).

52 See correspondence by irrigation-ditch pioneer James Craig quoted in Blanchard, *Conquest of Southwest Kansas,* 89–94.

53 Sherow, *Watering the Valley,* 84–86.

54 See Eskelund, 358–60.

55 See Sorensen, "A History of Irrigation," 37–41.

56 Quoted in ibid., 43.

57 Eskelund, 356.

58 Quoted in Sorensen, "A History of Irrigation," 60.

59 *Climatic Summary of the United States: From the Establishment of Stations to 1830, Section 40-Western Kansas* (Washington: Government Printing Office, 1930), 11–18.

60 Sherow, *Watering the Valley,* 6–7, 101–19.

61 See Sorensen, "A History of Irrigation," 22–27.

62 Ibid., 66.

63 From 81,279 in 1889 to 49,850 in 1895, according to Gerald Aistrup, "An Investigation of the Relationship Between Climatic Conditions & Population Changes in Western Kansas, 1865–1900," (M.A. thesis, Fort Hays Kansas State Teachers College, 1956), 4, 41 and 55.

64 *The Earth* (April 1904), 3.

65 Quoted in Donald E. Green, *Land of the Underground Rain: Irrigation on the Texas High Plains, 1910–1970* (Austin: University of Texas Press, 1973), 166.

66 Ibid., 168.

67 See Richard J. Hinton, *Irrigation in the United States,* S. Misc. Doc. 15, 49th Cong., 2d sess., 1887, Serial No.2450, 42, and *Irrigation: The Final Report of the Artesian and Underflow Investigation and of the Irrigation Inquiry,* S. Ex. Doc. 41, 52d Cong., 1st sess., 1892, Serial No.2899, 303. In 1970, USGS hydrologist Charles N. Gould rejected the Rockies theory in *The Geology and Water Resources of the Western Portion of the Panhandle of Texas,* United States Geological Survey Water Supply and Irrigation Paper No.191, 40.

68 Erasmus Haworth, "The Geology of Underground Water in Western Kansas," *Report of the Kansas Board of Irrigation Survey and Experiment* (1895–96), 44.

69 Sorensen, "A History of Irrigation," 103.

70 Ibid., 152–53.

71 See the discussion in Sorensen, "A History of Irrigation," 107–8, and in Sherow, *Watering the Valley,* 91–94.

72 Quoted in Sorensen, "A History of Irrigation," 114–15.

73 Specifications of the project are reported by Andy Erhart, "Early Kansas Irrigation," *Irrigation Age* (February 1969): 20-CN1–4.

74 See Sorensen, "A History of Irrigation," 119–20.

75 Quoted in ibid., 123.

76 Quoted in ibid., 123.

77 See ibid., 123–24.

78 Sherow, *Watering the Valley,* 88–91.

79 Sorensen, "A History of Irrigation," 129.

80 Ibid., 132–33.

81 Mary Fund and Elise Watkins Clement, *Distribution of Land and Water Ownership in Southwest Kansas* (Whiting: Kansas Rural Center, 1982), 38–39.

82 Sorensen, "A History of Irrigation," 179.

83 Ibid., 177.

84 See Lawrence B. Lee, "William Ellsworth Smythe and the Irrigation Movement: A Reconsideration," *Pacific Historical Review* 41 (Spring 1972): 289–311.

85 *Proceedings, Second Annual Convention, Kansas Irrigation Association, Hutchinson, November 23 and 24, 1894* (Hutchinson: News Publishing Company, 1894), 34–38.

86 Washington: Government Printing Office, 1897, 167–96.

87 Newell, "Irrigation on the Great Plains," 167.

88 Ibid., 169–70.

89 Ibid., 170.

90 Ibid., 173.

91 Ibid.

92 Pamela Riney-Kehrberg, "From the Horse's Mouth: Dust Bowl Farmers and Their Solutions to the Problem of Aridity," paper presented at the Symposium on Agriculture and the Environment, USDA and Agricultural History Society, June 19–22, 1991, Washington, D.C., 2–3.

93 Hinton, *Irrigation in the United States.*

94 Quoted in Walter Rusinek, "Western Reclamation's Forgotten Forces: Richard J. Hinton and Groundwater Development," *Agricultural History* 61, no.3 (Summer 1987): 23.

95 See Sorensen, "A History of Irrigation," 109.

96 Richard J. Hinton, "A Report on the Irrigation and Cultivation of the Soil Thereby," *Irrigation: The Final Report of the Artesian and Underflow Investigation of the Irrigation Inquiry,* S. Ex. Doc. 41, 52d Cong., 1st sess., Serial No.2899, 10.

97 See the discussion in Rusinek, "Western Reclamation's Forgotten Forces," 28–31.

98 Ibid., 34.

99 Ibid., 35.
100 Charles I. Zirkle and Company promotional brochure, Kansas Room, Finney County Library, Garden City.
101 Quoted in Vernon E. Bundy, "Kansas Irrigation is Successful as Local Proposition," *Topeka Daily Capital,* August 10, 1924; see also "Irrigation is a Big Success in Arkansas Valley," *Topeka Daily Capital,* December 20, 1925.
102 Donald Worster, *Dust Bowl: The Southern Plains in the 1930s* (New York: Oxford University Press, 1979), 129.

Chapter 3

1 Walter Prescott Webb, *The Great Plains* (Boston: Ginn and Company, 1931), 366–67.
2 Mary W. M. Hargreaves, "The Dry-Farming Movement in Retrospect," in Thomas R. Wessel, ed., *Agriculture in the Great Plains, 1876–1936* (Washington: Agriculture History Society, 1977), 152.
3 James C. Malin, *Winter Wheat in the Golden Belt of Kansas: A Study in Adaptation to Subhumid Geographical Environment* (Lawrence: University Press of Kansas, 1944), 187, and "The Adaptation of the Agricultural System to Sub-Humid Environment," *Agricultural History* 10, no.2 (July 1936): 131.
4 John J. Widtsoe, *Dry-Farming: A System of Agriculture for Countries under a Low Rainfall* (New York: Macmillan Company, 1911), 301.
5 Webb, *The Great Plains,* 366ff.; see also pp.348ff. and Robert G. Athearn, *High Country Empire: The High Plains and Rockies* (Lincoln: University of Nebraska Press, 1960), 259–62. Webb depended on William McDonald, *Dry-Farming: Its Principles and Practice* (New York: Century Company, 1910), and Widtsoe, *Dry-Farming.* For a more recent analysis, see Hargreaves, "The Dry-Farming Movement in Retrospect," 149–65; "Land-Use Planning in Response to Drought—The Experience of the Thirties, *Agricultural History* 50, no.3 (October 1976); and *Dry Farming in the Northern Great Plains, 1900–1925,* Harvard Economic Studies 101 (Cambridge: Harvard University Press, 1957).
6 Quoted in Donald E. Green, *Land of the Underground Rain: Irrigation on the Texas High Plains, 1910–1970* (Austin: University of Texas Press, 1973), 103.
7 "Changes in Technology and Labor Requirements in Crop Production: Wheat and Oats" (Washington: WPA National Research Project A-10, 1939); R. S. Kifer, B. H. Hurt, and Albert Thornbrough, "The Influence of Technical Progress on Agricultural Production," *Farmers in a Changing World: 1940 Year-*

book of Agriculture (Washington: USDA, 1940), 509–32; Wayne Rasmussen, "The Impact of Technological Change on American Agriculture, 1862–1962," *Journal of Economic History* 22 (December 1962): 578–91.

8 Morrow May quoted in Donald Worster, *Dust Bowl: The Southern Plains in the 1930s* (New York: Oxford University Press, 1979), 91; and see Robert C. Williams, *Fordson, Farmall, and Poppin' Johnny: A History of the Farm Tractor and Its Impact on America* (Urbana: University of Illinois Press, 1987).

9 Worster, *Dust Bowl*, 94.

10 Paul Bonnifield, *The Dust Bowl: Men, Dirt, and Depression* (Albuquerque: University of New Mexico Press, 1979), 47–50.

11 Worster, *Dust Bowl*, 92.

12 See A. B. Genung, "Agriculture in the World War Period," *Farmers in a Changing World: 1940 Yearbook of Agriculture,* and Lloyd Jorgenson, "Agricultural Expansion into the Semiarid Lands of the West North Central States during the First World War," *Agricultural History* 23, no. 1 (January 1949): 30–40; see also Gilbert Fite, "Plains Farming: A Century of Change," *Agricultural History* 51, no. 1 (January 1977): 254, and James H. Shideler, *Farm Crisis, 1919–1923* (Berkeley: University of California Press, 1957).

13 Donald Worster, "The Dirty Thirties: A Study in Agricultural Capitalism," *Great Plains Quarterly* 6 (Spring 1986): 109, 111–13; see also Vance Johnson, *Heaven's Tableland: The Dust Bowl Story* (New York: Farrar, Straus and Company, 1947).

14 Worster, "The Dirty Thirties," 112.

15 Ibid.

16 Webb, *The Great Plains*, 319 and passim.

17 Ibid., 328.

18 Ibid., 330–31.

19 Worster, *Dust Bowl*, 6–7, 44–45, 48, 56–59, 94–97 and passim. The long-term quest to hold to the Jeffersonian ideal is a major thesis in John Opie, *The Law of the Land: 200 Years of American Farmland Policy* (Lincoln: University of Nebraska Press, 1987).

20 Bonnifield, *The Dust Bowl*, 64.

21 See ibid., 70–72.

22 1940 Interview with Woody Guthrie by Alan Lomax, *Woody Guthrie Library of Congress Recordings* (New York: Elektra Records EKI 271/272, n.d.).

23 See Bonnifield, *The Dust Bowl*, 74–75.

24 Woody Guthrie, *Dust Bowl Ballads* (New York: RCA Victor LPV-502, 1964 re-issue of April 26, 1940, recording).

25 See the statistics in Bonnifield, *The Dust Bowl*, 58–59.

26 See ibid., 123–26.

27 Robert Lambert, "The Drought Cattle Purchase, 1934–35: Problems and Complaints," *Agricultural History* 45 (April 1971): 85–93, and see the discussion in Worster, *The Dust Bowl*, 110–17.

28 This is the argument developed in the second half of Bonnifield's *The Dust Bowl*, 91 and passim; see also the critique of Bonnifield in Harry C. McDean, "Dust Bowl Historiography," *Great Plains Quarterly* 6 (Spring 1986): 120–21.

29 Quoted in Bonnifield, *The Dust Bowl*, 117.

30 The treatment of farmland as unrestricted private property is analyzed in Opie, *Law of the Land*, esp. chaps. 2 and 11. Bonnifield claimed that the economic collapse of the Great Depression—bank closings, unemployment, bankruptcies and equipment forfeitures, bare land and empty towns, the decline of implement sales and land values—did not overwhelm the Dust Bowl region as profoundly as it did the rest of the nation. He argued that "the region had two frontier settlement and development patterns occurring simultaneously" that were mistakenly identified as part of the national failure in the 1930s (Bonnifield, *The Dust Bowl*, 97–105). One, the discovery of the world's second-largest reservoir of natural gas, the Hugoton-Guymon field, brought on the speedy capitalization and industrialization of the region and large reductions in dependence on difficult farming conditions; large numbers of people began to prosper from natural-gas production. Second, the mechanization of farming, with the rapid infusion of tractors, combines, trucks, specialized plows, and other field equipment made agricultural production more efficient, reduced labor needs, and offered production security even in dry times. Large-scale mechanized dryland farming, not small-plot irrigation, would offer plains farmers long-term stability. According to Bonnifield, these technological advances limited the effects of the Great Depression. The region was already well into its own readjustment, admittedly a difficult one, of its work force. A population decline, increased mechanization, and farm consolidations were expected and were merely accelerated by the 1930s drought. Bonnifield concludes that "the region did not plunge into the depression until nearly two years after it struck the East." He admitted that "southwestern Kansas [would] suffer the largest reverses of the eighteen dust bowl counties. Nevertheless, during the twenty-

355

four-month period [of 1937–1938], southwestern Kansas had only six months when business conditions were below the national average." Bonnifield, *The Dust Bowl*, 105.

31 Quoted in Richard Lowitt, *The New Deal and the West* (Bloomington: Indiana University Press, 1984), 42–46, 55–63.

32 *Report of the Great Plains Drought Area Committee* (Washington: Government Printing Office, 1936), 4.

33 *The Future of the Great Plains: Report of the Great Plains Committee to the House of Representatives* (Washington: H. Doc. 144, 75th Cong., 1st sess., 1937).

34 See the discussion in Harry C. McDean, "Dust Bowl Historiography," *Great Plains Quarterly* 6 (Spring 1986): 123.

35 Quoted in Worster, *The Dust Bowl*, 184.

36 See Albert Z. Guttenberg, "The Land Utilization Movement of the 1920s," *Agricultural History* 50 (July 1976): 477–90.

37 *Yearbook of Agriculture 1930* (Washington: USDA, 1930), 36.

38 See Worster, *The Dust Bowl*, 184–97; for federal responses, see also Mary W. M. Hargreaves, "Land-Use Planning in Response to Drought: The Experience of the Thirties," *Agricultural History* 50 (October 1976): 561–82, and Theodore Saloutos, "The New Deal and Farm Policy in the Great Plains," *Agricultural History* 43 (July 1979): 345–55.

39 Worster, *The Dust Bowl*, 188.

40 Quoted in Bonnifield, *The Dust Bowl*, 114.

41 *Yearbook of Agriculture 1935* (Washington: USDA, 1935), 46.

42 Pamela Riney-Kehrberg, "From the Horse's Mouth: Dust Bowl Farmers and Their Solutions to the Problem of Aridity," paper presented at the Symposium on Agriculture and the Environment, USDA and Agricultural History Society, Washington, June 19–22, 1991, 7–12.

43 *The Future of the Great Plains*, 175, 182.

44 Ibid., 63.

45 Ibid., 105.

46 Bonnifield, *The Dust Bowl*, 107–9.

47 See Bonnifield, *The Dust Bowl*, 148–49. Relocation itself seemed deceptive. In one case the government placed farmers on inadequate 30- to 60-acre subsistence homesteads at Los Lunas, New Mexico. Resettled farm families were compelled to support themselves by nonfarm employment, and the resettlement

farms themselves were on submarginal land according to the government's own test. In the New Mexico case, no water rights for irrigation were included, which left the relocated farmers helpless. The government seemed intent in getting farmers off the land and into the general labor force. The resettlement of Cimarron County, Oklahoma, farmers onto undeveloped mesquite land in southwest Texas led to complaints that the farmers were being coerced into bare-bones homesteading under worse conditions than the old frontier days. Nor would they gain title until they purchased the land they themselves were developing for twenty to thirty-five dollars an acre. Bonnifield concludes that "the Resettlement Administration was simply a real estate developer who operated at an advantage and kept control of vital aspects of the farm operation."

48 See R. Douglas Hurt, "The National Grasslands: Origin and Development in the Dust Bowl," in Douglas Helms and Susan L. Flader, eds., *The History of Soil and Water Conservation* (Washington: Agricultural History Society, 1985), 144–57, and Hurt's "Federal Land Reclamation in the Dust Bowl, *Great Plains Quarterly* 6 (Spring 1986): 94–106.

49 Bonnifield, *The Dust Bowl*, 173–84.

50 *Report of the Secretary of Agriculture 1894* (Washington, 1895), 22.

51 Wayne D. Rasmussen, *History of Soil Conservation: Institutions and Incentives* (Washington: USDA, 1981), 7.

52 Quoted in Wes Jackson, *New Roots for Agriculture* (San Francisco: Friends of the Earth, 1980), 55.

53 *Spearman* (Tex.) *Reporter,* April 22, 1937.

54 *Farmers in a Changing World: Yearbook of Agriculture 1940,* 413–14.

55 This subject is given particular attention in Pamela Riney-Kehrberg, "From the Horse's Mouth: Dust Bowl Farmers and Their Solutions to the Problem of Aridity."

56 *Report of the Great Plains Drought Area Committee,* 5.

57 See Bonnifield, *The Dust Bowl,* 156.

58 See the analysis in Vance Johnson, *Heaven's Tableland: The Dust Bowl Story* (New York: Farrar, Straus and Company, 1947), 274–75.

59 Worster, *The Dust Bowl,* 223; see also Murray R. Benedict, *Farm Policies of the United States, 1790–1950: A Study of Their Origins and Development* (New York: Octagon Books, 1966), 449–90.

60 See Leslie Hewes, *The Suitcase Farming Frontier: A Study in the Historical Geography of the Central High Plains* (Lincoln: University of Nebraska Press, 1973).

61 John Bird, "The Great Plains Hit the Jackpot," *Saturday Evening Post* (August 30, 1947: 16, 90.

62 Worster, *The Dust Bowl,* 225.

63 *Country Gentleman* 117 (September 1947): 85.

64 Quoted in Worster, *The Dust Bowl,* 226.

65 See R. Douglas Hurt, *The Dust Bowl: An Agricultural and Social History* (Chicago: Nelson-Hall, 1981), 141.

66 Hurt, *The Dust Bowl,* 140–44.

67 See Philip J. Thair, *Meeting the Impact of Crop-Yield Risks in Great Plains Farming,* NDAES Bulletin 392 (Fargo, N.D., 1954), and Great Plains Council, *Research Conference on Risk and Uncertainty in Agriculture* (Proceedings, Bozeman, Montana, August 10–15, 1953), NDAES Bulletin 400 (Fargo, N.D., 1955).

68 Hurt, *The Dust Bowl,* 151–52.

69 Lloyd E. Dunlap, Edwin D. Gutentag, and James G. Thomas, "Use of Ground Water During Drought Conditions in West-Central Kansas," report prepared for USGS 1979 spring meeting, Garden City, Kansas.

70 Edwin Kessler et al., "Duststorms from the U.S. High Plains in Late Winter 1977: Search for Cause and Implications," *Proceedings of the Oklahoma Academy of Science* 58 (1978): 116–28.

71 John Borchert, "The Dust Bowl in the 1970s," *Annals of the Association of American Geographers* 61 (March 1971): 13.

72 *Another Revolution in U.S. Farming?* (Washington: Agricultural Economic Report No.441, ESCS, USDA, 1979), 42–75.

73 Worster, *The Dust Bowl,* 223–24.

74 Quoted in ibid., 225.

75 Mary Rule, *Water in Kansas: A Primer* (Whiting: Kansas Rural Center, 1984), 7.

76 Office of Technology Assessment, *Water-Related Technologies for Sustainable Agriculture in U.S. Arid/Semiarid Lands* (Washington: U.S. Congress, Office of Technology Assessment, OTA-F-212, October 1983), 41–43; see also William Franklin Langrone, "The Great Plains," in *Another Revolution in U.S. Farming?,* 335–61.

77 OTA, *Water-Related Technologies,* 24.

78 Ibid.; see also 343–44.

79 Ibid., 343–44.

80 Ibid., 35, 165.

81 Ibid., 42.

82 Personal interview and correspondence with Deborah Epstein Popper and Frank J. Popper in August 1990; see also "The Fate of the Plains," in Ed Marston, ed., *Reopening the Western Frontier* (Washington: Island Press, 1989), 98–113; "Saving the Plains: The Bison Gambit," *Washington Post,* August 6, 1989; and "The Strange Case of the Contemporary American Frontier," *Yale Review* (Fall 1986): 101–21.

83 Quoted in Andrew Cassel, "Grasslands plan urged for Plains," *Philadelphia Inquirer,* June 19, 1989, 2a.

84 See the discussion by James W. O'Leary in Ernest A. Engelbert and Ann Foley Scheuring, eds., *Water Scarcity: Impacts on Western Agriculture* (Berkeley: University of California Press, 1984), 175–77.

85 See the discussion by Estevan T. Flores in Engelbert and Scheuring, *Water Scarcity,* 327.

86 See the discussion by Charles V. Moore in ibid., see also pp.122 and 277.

87 OTA, *Water-Related Technologies,* 3, 5.

88 See the extended discussion of these different positions in the Appendix, "Puzzling Out the Plains."

Chapter 4

1 See T. Lindsay Baker, "Irrigating with Windmills on the Great Plains," *Great Plains Quarterly* 9 (Fall 1989): 216–30; Volta Torrey, "Catching the Western Winds: Windmills through the years," *American West* 20, no.2 (March–April 1983): 45–51; and the detailed study by Anne M. Marvin, "The Fertile Domain: Irrigation as Adaptation in the Garden City, Kansas Area, 1880–1910" (Ph.D. dissertation, University of Kansas, 1975).

2 See Walter Prescott Webb's fine summarization in chap. 8, "The Frontier as a Modifier of Institutions," in *The Great Frontier* (Austin: University of Texas Press, 1951–52), 239–79.

3 Walter Prescott Webb, *The Great Plains* (Boston: Ginn and Company, 1931), 336; see also Frederick H. Newell, *Irrigation in the United States* (New York: Thomas Y. Crowell and Company, 1902).

4 See Kenneth D. McCall, "Growth of Irrigation in Scott County, Kansas," *Report of the Kansas State Board of Agriculture* 63 (August 1944): 10–12.

5 See Webb, *The Great Plains,* 337.

6 Correspondence dated July 15, 1927, from Fairbanks, Morse and Company, received by Walter Prescott Webb, quoted in Webb, *The Great Plains,* 340.

7 Conner Sorensen, "A History of Irrigation in the Arkansas River Valley in Western Kansas, 1880–1910" (M.A. thesis, Wichita State University, 1965), 83–84.

8 Philip Eastman, "Windmill Irrigation in Kansas," *Review of Reviews,* 29 (February 1904): 183–87, and "Irrigation by Windmills," *Scientific American Supplement* 41 (11 April 1896): 16981.

9 Sorensen, "A History of Irrigation," 78.

10 Henry Worral, "Irrigation in Southwestern Kansas," *Harper's Weekly* 38 (September 29, 1894): 931, quoted in Sorensen, "A History of Irrigation," 81.

11 Ibid., 85–86.

12 Quoted in Webb, *The Great Plains,* 346.

13 See Andy Erhart, "Early Kansas Irrigation," *Irrigation Age* (February 1969): 20-CN2.

14 McCall, "Growth of Irrigation in Scott County," 14–15.

15 Webb, *The Great Plains,* 346.

16 Ibid., 348.

17 Willard D. Johnson, "The High Plains and Their Utilization," *Twenty-First Annual Report of the United States Geological Survey,* quoted in Webb, *The Great Plains,* 342.

18 Quoted in Webb, *The Great Plains,* 343.

19 Ibid.

20 Sorensen, "A History of Irrigation," 90.

21 William E. Smythe, *The Conquest of Arid America,* 2d ed. (New York: Macmillan Company, 1905), 118.

22 The *Yankton* (S. Dak.) *Press and Dakotan* of November 12, 1896, quoted in Donald E. Green, *Land of the Underground Rain: Irrigation on the Texas High Plains, 1910–1970* (Austin: University of Texas Press, 1973), 28.

23 See E. W. Bennison, *Ground Water: Its Development, Uses, and Conservation* (Saint Paul, Minn.: Edward E. Johnson, 1947), 197, 373–76, and B. A. Etcheverry, *Irrigation Practice and Engineering* (New York: McGraw-Hill, 1915), 1:182.

24 Quoted in Green, *Land of the Underground Rain,* 51.

25 See ibid., 43–46.

26 Newell, *Irrigation in the United States,* 271.

27 See the discussion of other unsuccessful attempts in Green, *Land of the Underground Rain,* 47–53.

28 Quoted in ibid., 106.

29 Quoted in ibid., 53.

30 Sorensen, "A History of Irrigation," 88.

31 Ray Palmer Teele, "Review of Ten Years of Irrigation Investigations," *Annual Report of the Office of Experiment Stations 1908,* 386.

32 See the excellent discussion by Green, *Land of the Underground Rain,* 53–60.

33 Sorensen, "A History of Irrigation," 88.

34 Ibid., 89.

35 Green, *Land of the Underground Rain,* 60.

36 According to Green, *Land of the Underground Rain,* 116–17, the company sold a typical 160-acre irrigated farm for $18,400, with a down payment of $2,300, a first installment of $3,200, and annual payments of about $2,000. This compared with an unimproved 160 acres for $4,000, on which the farmer could install his own irrigation plant for another $10,500, about half the cost of turnkey irrigation farming.

37 Green, *Land of the Underground Rain,* 113–15.

38 Ibid., 115–16.

39 See George Soule, *Prosperity Decade, from War to Depression: 1917–1929,* vol.8 in *The Economic History of the United States* (New York: Holt, Rinehart and Winston, 1947), 229–30; and Gilbert C. Fite, "The Farmers' Dilemma, 1919–1929," in John Braeman, ed., *Change and Continuity in Twentieth Century America, the 1920s* (Columbus: Ohio State University Press, 1968), 67–102.

40 Green, *Land of the Underground Rain,* 120.

41 Ibid., 125–30.

42 Quoted by Pamela Riney-Kehrberg, "From the Horse's Mouth: Dust Bowl Farmers and Their Solutions to the Problem of Aridity," Symposium on Agriculture and the Environment, USDA and Agricultural History Society, Washington, June 19–22, 1991, 17.

43 Excellent details on costs and equipment are in Green, *Land of the Underground Rain,* 129.

44 Ibid., 125.

45 See the discussion in Roy E. Huffman, *Irrigation Development and Public Water Policy* (New York: Ronald Press, 1953).

46 *The Future of the Great Plains: Report of the Great Plains Committee to the House of Representatives* (Washington: H. Doc. 144, 75th Cong. 1st sess., 1937), 76–77.

47 Green, *Land of the Underground Rain,* 136–39.

48 Quoted in ibid., 139–40.

49 Ibid., 141–43.

50 *Water in Kansas, 1955: A Report to the Kansas State Legislature* (Lawrence: Kansas Water Resources Fact Finding and Research Committee, 1955), 53–55.

51 Information based on interviews in May 1988 at Gigot Irrigation, the major regional supplier of center-pivot equipment, and Gigot Feeders, a feedlot operation with a capacity of thirty-five thousand cattle. Additional data on Gigot enterprises came from interviews with other irrigators, SCS officials, and the critical study conducted by the Kansas Rural Center: Mary Fund and Elsie Watkins Clement, *Distribution of Land and Water Ownership in Southwest Kansas* (Whiting: Kansas Rural Center, 1982), 33–37.

52 See the chart and discussion in Fund and Clement, *Distribution of Land and Water Ownership,* 23.

53 Jim Toyayko, "Garden City: 'the centre and inspiration' of irrigation," *Garden City Times,* June 29, 1979.

54 "Dean Gigot: He Turns the Sandhills Green," *Wichita Eagle-Beacon,* May 30, 1982, 5H.

55 Quoted in "An Odyssey Through Kansas," *U & I,* no.2 (1986[?]), 5.

56 Ibid., 4–5.

57 C. A. Bonnen et al., *Use of Irrigation Water on the High Plains* (College Station: Texas Agricultural Experiment Station Bulletin No.756, 1952); Green, *Land of the Underground Rain,* 153–55.

58 Green, *Land of the Underground Rain,* 153, 160.

59 Typescript, dated January 1957, by Andrew B. Erhart, "Conservation Irrigation," for a special edition of the *Pratt* (Kans.) *Daily Tribune,* 2–3.

60 William E. Splinter, "Center-Pivot Irrigation," *Scientific American* (June 1976, from reprint); see also "Center pivot development reviewed," *The Cross Section,* 34, no.5 (May 1988): 1, 4.

61 Erhart, "Conservation Irrigation," 3–4.

62 *Finney County Soil Survey, Series 1961* (Wichita: SCS, USDA, 1965), 1–89, esp. 22.

63 See the discussion in Green, *Land of the Underground Rain,* 149.

64 Splinter, "Center Pivot Irrigation," 8, and "Modeling of Plant Growth for Yield Prediction," in John F. Stone, ed., *Plant Modification for More Efficient Water Use* (Netherlands: Elsevier Scientific Publishing Company, 1975).

65 M. E. Jensen, "Water Consumption by Agricultural Plants," in T. T. Kozlowski, ed., *Water Deficits and Plant Growth,* vol.2, *Plant Water Consumption and Response* (New York: Academic Press, 1968).

66 This, of course, is an oversimplification. "Growing degree days" or "heat units" are only cumulatively added while within a range of sixty to eighty degrees Fahrenheit. Correspondence with Wayne Bossert, manager, Northwest Kansas Groundwater Management District Four, January 19, 1991.

67 Interview with Kenny Ochs, sales manager of Gigot Irrigation Company, Garden City, May 18, 1988; data corroborated by Ron Crocker, manager, Gigot Feeders, Garden City, May 18, 1988.

68 Green, *Land of the Underground Rain,* 156–57.

69 Splinter, "Center Pivot Irrigation," 5.

70 See the articles in *The Cross Section,* the newsletter of Texas High Plains Underground Water Conservation District No.1, Lubbock, Texas: "Income-Tax Deduction Sought for Depletion of Ground Water" 7, no.1 (June 1960); "Underground Water Depletion Suit Filed" 7, no.9 (February 1961); "Depletion Case Won" 9, no.8 (January 1963); and "Water Depletion Claim Upheld by High Court" 12, no.1 (June 1965).

71 Wayne Bossert writes (January 19, 1991) that "the tax relief under the water depletion ruling is not as simple as a $2,400 deduction for a Kansas quarter of land. It depends entirely on the price paid for the land versus the base rate for dryland [hence one's 'cost in water'], the rate of depletion, the monitoring used to claim the allowance, and probably a few other items the IRS has tacked on to discourage the process."

72 See the detailed analysis in Fund and Clement, *Distribution of Land and Water Ownership,* 34–37.

73 USDA figures quoted in the *Chicago Tribune,* July 10, 1988, sec. 4, p.5; as fears rose about food price increases, the media paid attention to the ripple effect of the drought of 1988, as in Barbara Rudolph, "The Drought's Food-Chain Reaction," *Time,* July 11, 1988, 40.

74 Water quality may be affected by chloride contamination from the IBP plant according to Wayne Bossert in correspondence dated January 19, 1991.

75 "An Odyssey Through Kansas," 6–7.

76 See Douglas Constance and William Heffernan, "IBP's Dominance in the Meat Packing Industry: Boxed Beef and Busted Unions," paper presented at the No-

vember 1989 conference of the Food, Agriculture, and Human Values Society, Little Rock, Arkansas.

77 Quoted in Constance and Heffernan, "IBP's Dominance," 13.

78 See the critical account in Fund and Clement, *Distribution of Land and Water Ownership*, 48–53; quote from p.50.

79 Constance and Heffernan, "IBP's Dominance," 3.

80 Donald E. Worster, *Dust Bowl: The Southern Plains in the 1930s* (New York: Oxford University press, 1979), 228, 269.

81 Green, *Land of the Underground Rain*, 160.

82 See the case study of "Farmer K" in eastern Colorado described in Morton W. Bittinger and Elizabeth B. Green, *You Never Miss the Water Till . . . . (The Ogallala Story)* (Littleton, Colo.: Water Resources Publications, 1980), 19–22.

83 William F. Hughes and Joe R. Motheral, *Irrigated Agriculture in Texas* (College Station: Texas Agricultural Experiment Station Bulletin No.59, 1950).

84 Leon New, *1977 High Plains Irrigation Survey* (Lubbock: Texas Agricultural Extension Service, 1978); see also Green, *Land of the Underground Rain*, 146–48.

85 Green, *Land of the Underground Rain*, 151–53.

86 See note 1.

87 Green, *Land of the Underground Rain*, 161; see also A. C. Magee et al., *Production Practices for Irrigated Crops on the High Plains* (College Station: Texas Agricultural Experiment Station Bulletin No.763, 1953).

88 Green, *Land of the Underground Rain*, 159–60.

89 William F. Hughes and A. C. Magee, *Water and Associated Costs in the Production of Cotton and Grain Sorghum, Texas High Plains* (College Station: Texas Agricultural Experiment Station Bulletin No.851, 1957).

90 *United States Census of Agriculture 1959* (Washington: Bureau of the Census, U.S. Department of Commerce, 1961), vol.1, pt. 37, 154–73.

Chapter 5

1 P. Barkley, "The Sustainability of Rural Non-Farm Economics in Water Dependent Agricultural Areas," Office of Technology Assessment commissioned paper, 1983, excerpted in OTA, *Water-Related Technologies for Sustainable Agriculture in U.S. Arid/Semiarid Lands* (Washington: U.S. Congress, Office of Technology Assessment, OTA-F-212, October 1983), 137.

2 See Roderick Nash, *Wilderness and the American Mind*, 3d ed. (New Haven: Yale University Press, 1967, 1982), 96–104 and passim; Joseph M. Petulla,

American Environmental History: The Exploitation and Conservation of Natural Resources (San Francisco: Boyd and Fraser, 1977), 217ff. and passim.

3 Commentary by Frank J. Trelease in Ernest A. Engelbert and Ann Foley Scheuring, eds., *Water Scarcity: Impacts on Western Agriculture* (Berkeley: University of California Press, 1984), 78.

4 *Ground Water: An Overview* (Washington: General Accounting Office, June 21, 1977), 9–14; see also "West Texas and Eastern New Mexico Import Project," *Critical Water Problems Facing the Eleven Western States* (Washington: USDI, April 1975); and *Projected Economic Life of Water Resources, Subdivision Number 1, High Plains Underground Water Reservoir* (College Station: Technical Monograph 6, Texas Agricultural Experiment Station, Texas A&M University, December 1969).

5 R. Young, "Allocating the Water Resource: Market Systems and the Economic Value of Water," OTA commissioned paper, 1982, excerpted in OTA, *Water-Related Technologies for Sustainable Agriculture in U.S. Arid/Semiarid Lands*, 388ff.

6 Donald E. Green, *Land of the Underground Rain* (Austin: University of Texas Press, 1973), 165–69.

7 Quoted in ibid., 167.

8 Ibid., 168.

9 See the discussion in ibid., 169–70.

10 See the discussion by Henry P. Caulfield, Jr., in Engelbert and Scheuring, *Water Scarcity*, 462–63; see also J. David Aiken, "Development of the Appropriation Doctrine: Adapting Water Allocation Policies to Semiarid Environs," *Great Plains Quarterly* 8 (Winter 1988): 38–44.

11 This is a major thesis in Mark Sagoff, *The Economy of the Earth: Philosophy, Law, and the Environment*, (New York: Cambridge University Press, 1988); see also F. Lee Brown et al., "Water Reallocation, Market Proficiency, and Conflicting Social Values," in Gary D. Weatherford et al., *Western Water Institutions in a Changing Environment* (Boulder, Colo.: Westview Press, 1980).

12 Oklahoma Supreme Court, *Canada v. Shawnee*, 179 OKL. 53, 64 P. 2d 694 (1936, 1937).

13 This is a variant on the social goals of irrigation communities described by F. Lee Brown and Charles T. DuMars, "Water Rights and Market Transfers," in Engelbert and Scheuring, *Water Scarcity*, 411–13. See also A. Maass and R. L. Anderson, *And the Desert Shall Rejoice: Conflict, Growth and Justice in Arid*

Environments (Cambridge, Mass.: MIT Press, 1978), Kenneth Boulding, *Western Water Resources: Coming Problems and the Policy Alternatives* (Boulder, Colo.: Westview Press, 1980), and Brown et al., "Water Reallocation, Market Proficiency, and Conflicting Social Values."

14 A recent example that links sustainable development with local decision making is the study by the World Commission on Environment and Development, *Our Common Future* (New York: Oxford University Press, 1987).

15 Robert A. Young, "Local and Regional Economics Impacts," in Engelbert and Scheuring, *Water Scarcity*, 244–45.

16 See, for example, the data and conclusions in Edwin D. Gutentag et al., *Geohydrology of the High Plains Aquifer in Parts of Colorado, Kansas, Nebraska, New Mexico, Oklahoma, South Dakota, Texas, and Wyoming* (Washington: U.S. Geological Survey Professional Paper 1400-B, USGPO, 1984); also based on USGS data in the personal papers of Edwin G. Gutentag, U.S. Geological Survey, Department of the Interior, Denver Federal Center.

17 Green, *Land of the Underground Rain*, 172–87.

18 All quoted in ibid., 179–83.

19 Ibid., 177.

20 Ibid., 188, 189.

21 *Rules of Texas High Plains Underground Water Conservation District No.1, 1954.*

22 See John Opie, *The Law of the Land: 200 Years of American Farmland Policy* (Lincoln: University of Nebraska Press, 1987).

23 Interview with Wayne Wyatt in Lubbock, Texas, in May 1987.

24 See also Neville P. Clarke, *Texas Agriculture in the 80's: The Critical Decade* (College Station: Texas Agricultural Experiment Station Report B-1341, Texas A&M University, 1980).

25 Abstracted in High Plains Underground Water Conservation District No.1 brochure received May 1986.

26 Chap. 52, Vernon's Civil Statutes of Texas.

27 Abstracted in High Plains Underground Water Conservation District No.1 brochure received May 1986.

28 Frank A. Rayner, *Government and Groundwater Management* (Lubbock: Texas High Plains Underground Water Conservation District No.1, 1975), 2.

29 Ibid., 1, 2.

30 Ibid., 3–4. Texas water law states: "The water of the ordinary flow, under-flow, and tides of every flowing river, natural stream, and lake, and of every bay or arm of the gulf of Mexico, and the storm water, floodwater, and rainwater of every river, natural stream, canyon, ravine, depression, and watershed in the state is the property of the state." Chap. 5.021, Vernon's Texas Codes Annotated.

31 Rayner, *Government and Groundwater Management*, 10.

32 *Friendswood Development Company* v. *Smith-Southwest Industries, Inc.*, 576 S.W.2d 21 (Texas Supreme Court, 1978).

33 "The Case for Local Regulation," *The Cross Section*, 28, no.12 (December 1982): 1–4.

34 Frank L. Baird, *District Groundwater Planning and Management Policies on the Texas High Plains: The Views of the People* (Lubbock: Texas High Plains Underground Water Conservation District No.1, July 1976), 4–5.

35 *Oklahoma Water Resources Board and Mobil Oil Corporation* v. *Texas County Irrigation and Water Resources Association*, Supreme Court of the State of Oklahoma, 56,355, December 20, 1984.

36 "Chemicals of Potential Use in Surfactant/Polymer Flooding, Appendix L," *Cumulative Production/Consumption Effects of the Crude Oil Price Incentive Rulemakings: Final Environmental Impact Statement* (Washington: U.S. Department of Energy, 1978), IV-71, 76.

37 Data received from Bonita Hoeme of the Texas County Irrigation and Water Resources Association, May 1987.

38 Quoted by Esther Groves, "Area Water, Oil Interests Battle," *Liberal Daily Times,* April 8, 1985.

39 Minutes, Oklahoma Water Resources Board, December 3, 1985, 7.

40 570 p.2d 49 (Okla. 1977).

41 82 O.S. Supp. 1972, para 1020.15.

42 82 O.S. 1981, para 926.1.

43 The issues are outlined in an April 1, 1985, news release from the Texas County Irrigation and Water Resources Association in Guymon, Oklahoma.

44 Records of hearings in archives of Texas County Irrigation and Water Resources Association, Guymon, Oklahoma.

45 In a 1982 report, of the 460 billion barrels of known U.S. oil reserves, 120 billion can be obtained by primary drilling. Enhanced oil recovery can capture 18 to 50 billion, leaving 300 billion barrels to be gotten "using technology not yet discovered." This leaves 83 to 94 percent of the remaining oil still in the ground.

See Gregory Seay, "Enhanced recovery gets big play," *Sunday Oklahoman,*
April 4, 1982.

46 In records of TCIWRA.

47 "Finding of Fact, Conclusions of Law and Board Order on Application No. 85–
581," Oklahoma Water Resources Board, December 3, 1985.

48 Ibid.

49 Quoted by Esther Groves, "Panhandle Irrigators File to Save Water Resources," *Liberal Daily Times,* December 29, 1985.

50 Quoted by Esther Groves, "Irrigators Plan Appeal," *Liberal Daily Times,* December 11, 1985.

51 Copy of testimony to Oklahoma House Natural Resources Committee, May 13,
1985, from Gene Barby; interview with Barby in May 1986.

52 Typescript, dated January 1957, by Andrew B. Erhart, "Conservation Irrigation," for a special edition of the *Pratt* (Kans.) *Daily Tribune.*

53 Interviews (May 1986, September 1987) with Rick Illgner and Gary Baker, for-
mer and current managers of Southwest Kansas Groundwater Management
District No. 3; see the excellent analysis of the issues of the Stone case and Kan-
sas groundwater policies in general in Mary Fund and Elsie Watkins Clement,
Distribution of Land and Water Ownership in Southwest Kansas (Whiting:
Kansas Rural Center, 1982), 40–48, and also *Water Marker Update* 1, no. 5
(May 1987): 2.

54 See Mary Fund, *Water in Kansas: A Primer* (Whiting: Kansas Rural Center,
1984), 8–11, and Robert G. Dunbar, *Forging New Rights in Western Water* (Lincoln: University of Nebraska Press, 1983), chaps. 6–10.

55 Wayne Bossert writes (January 19, 1991): "The Kansas Water Appropriate Act
states that for three consecutive years of non-use *without due and sufficient cause*
the state can determine the right abandoned. However, the state has provided for a
series of 'due and sufficient causes' whereby non-use does not necessarily mean
abandonment. This wording in Kansas is an attempt to move away from the 'use it
or lose it' concept while still recognizing that one cannot sit indefinitely on a water
right to the exclusion of others who may want to use the resource."

56 See Earl B. Shurtz, *Kansas Water Law* (Wichita: Kansas Water Resources
Board, 1967).

57 Ibid., 20.

58 Fund, *Water in Kansas,* 32–34.

59 John Wesley Powell, *Water for the West,* quoted in *Management Programs* frontispiece.

60 Fund, *Water in Kansas,* 62.

61 *Management Programs,* 15–16.

62 According to the common United States Geological Survey location notation that provides precise identification for the Soil Conservation Service and Southwest Kansas Groundwater Management District No.3, Stapleton's well was NE1/4-31-31-33, Dufield's was SW1/4-25-31-31, and Guttridge's was NW 1/4-32-33-34. Dufield's Seward County well was at 32-32W-14BBB.

63 Data provided by the Liberal, Kansas, office of the Soil Conservation Service, USDA, May 1987. See also "Ground-water Supply Problems," in *Revised Management Program III: Rules and Regulations, and Policies and Standards* (Garden City, Kans.: Southwest Kansas Groundwater Management District No.3, 1986), 6–7.

64 *Management Programs,* 1.

65 Fund and Clement, *Distribution of Land and Water Ownership in Southwest Kansas,* 17–19, 33–34.

66 Kansas Water Office, *Summary: Ogallala Aquifer Study in Kansas,* 11.

67 *Management Programs,* 20.

68 Fund, *Water in Kansas,* 43–44.

69 Fund and Clement, *Distribution of Land and Water Ownership,* 45–46.

70 Ibid., 46.

71 Kansas Water Office, *Agricultural Water Conservation: Irrigation Plan Guidelines* (enclosed in letter to "Fellow Kansans" from the Kansas Water Office, Topeka, dated December 18, 1986).

72 Kansas State Board of Agriculture, Division of Water Resources, "Administrative Policy No.88-3 (attached to letter dated December 12, 1988, addressed to "All County Conservation Districts").

73 Quoted in Kip Lowe, "Groundwater future a continuing concern," in the *Colby* (Kans.) *Free Press,* June 15, 1990; see also "Groundwater district halts water rights," *Atwood* (Kans.) *Citizen-Patriot,* February 22, 1990; reports and publications by Northwest Kansas Groundwater Management District Four; and the author's interviews of the district's manager, Wayne Bossert, in April 1991.

74 John Bredehoeft, "Physical Limitations of Water Resources," in Engelbert and Scheuring, *Water Scarcity,* 43.

75 Earl O. Heady, "National and International Commodity Price Impacts," in Engelbert and Scheuring, *Water Scarcity,* 277–78.

76 OTA, *Water-Related Technologies,* 39.

77 Heady, "National and International Commodity Price Impacts," 274, 277–78.

Chapter 6

1 Interviews with Phil Tooms at his home in southwest Kansas in May 1986, 1987, and 1988, backed up by data on his operation collected at the Garden City office of the Soil Conservation Service, USDA.

2 Most of Tooms's conclusions about the current state and future of irrigation from the Ogallala were corroborated by interviews in May 1986 and 1987 with Roger and Betty Trescott, irrigators for forty years in Texas County, Oklahoma, about eighteen miles north of Guymon in the Oklahoma Panhandle.

3 See also Mary Fund and Elsie Watkins Clement, *Distribution of Land and Water Ownership in Southwest Kansas* (Whiting: Kansas Rural Center, 1982), 41–48; and Mary Fund, *Water in Kansas: A Primer* (Whiting: Kansas Rural Center, 1984), 56–73.

4 See the discussion of the uses of historical analogies and comparisons to understand future climate change in Michael H. Glantz and Jesse H. Ausubel, "The Ogallala Aquifer and Carbon Dioxide: Comparison and Convergence," *Environmental Conservation* 11, no. 2 (Summer 1984): 123–31.

5 The literature is vast and diverse. See, for example, Baruch Fischhoff, "For those Condemned to Study the Past: Reflections on Historical Judgment," in R. A. Shweder and D. W. Fiske, eds., *New Directions for Methodology of Behavioral Science: Fallible Judgment in Behavioral Research* (San Francisco: Jossey-Bass, 1980); Mary Douglas and Aaron Wildavsky, *Risk and Culture: An Essay on the Selection of Technological and Environmental Dangers* (Berkeley: University of California Press, 1982); Board on Atmospheric Sciences and Climate, National Research Council, *Current Issues in Atmospheric Change* (Washington: National Academy Press, 1987); Thomas R. Stewart and Michael H. Glantz, "Expert Judgment and Climate Forecasting: A Methodological Critique of "Climate Change to the Year 2000," in *Climate Change* 7 (1985): 159–83; Donald A. Wilhite and Michael H. Glantz, "Understanding the Drought Phenomenon: The Role of Definitions," *Water International* 10 (1985): 111–20; Willard W. Cochrane, "A Conceptual Model of Agricultural Development: 1950–1977," Chap. 4 in *The Development of American Agriculture: A Histori-*

cal Analysis (Minneapolis: University of Minnesota Press, 1979), 355–428; Water Firey, *Man, Mind, and Land* (Glencoe, Ill.: Free Press, 1960); Erich Jantsch, *The Self-Organizing Universe* (Oxford: Pergamon Press, 1980); Ervin Laszlo, *The Systems View of the World* (New York: George Braziller, 1972); Immanuel Wallerstein, *The Modern World-System* (New York: Academic Press, 1974).

6 See the excellent discussion by William E. Riebsame, "The Dust Bowl: Historical Image, Psychological Anchor, and Ecological Taboo," *Great Plains Quarterly* 6 (Spring 1986): 127–36.

7 See Carl O. Sauer, "Homestead and Community on the Middle Border," "Historical Geography and the Western Frontier," and "Theme of Plant and Animal Destruction in Economic History," in John Leighly, ed., *Land and Life* (Berkeley: University of California Press, 1963) 32–41, 45–52, and 145–54, respectively. Wes Jackson of the Land Institute suggests that the situation has been made worse, not better, by contemporary mechanization when he writes of "The $5,000 Flat Tire" in *New Roots for Agriculture* (San Francisco: Friends of the Earth, 1980), 32–36.

8 Cochrane, *The Development of American Agriculture*, 122–23.

9 Nor can differences between time frames be ignored. The typical frontier farmer required three extremely good years for stability; otherwise he experienced failure in three to five years. In contradiction, the political planning process to aid the farmer ranged from two to ten years. Hence the ability of a society to respond to climate change took at least ten years, while the farmer needed a quick response. In addition, climatologists today argue that a climate pattern takes a minimum of thirty years to clarify, and climatological planning is accomplished on a scale of fifty to one hundred years or more.

10 This is a major thesis in John Opie, *The Law of the Land: Two Hundred Years of American Farmland Policy* (Lincoln: University of Nebraska Press, 1987).

11 See Frederick C. Luebke, *Ethnicity on the Great Plains* (Lincoln: University of Nebraska Press, 1980), and *Immigrants and Politics: The Germans of Nebraska, 1880–1900* (Lincoln: University of Nebraska Press, 1969). Irrigation communities like historic Greeley and modern Lamar in Colorado appear to have been equally long lasting.

12 J. B. Penn, "The Changing Farm Sector and Future Public Policy: An Economic Perspective," *Agricultural Food Policy Review: Perspectives for the 1980s* (Washington: USDA, ESS AFPR-4, 1980), 48ff.; see also Wesley F. Peter-

son, "Agricultural Structure and Economic Adjustment," *Agriculture and Human Values* 3, no.4 (Fall 1986): 7.

13 Unpublished paper by Patrick Madden and Paul B. Thompson, "Ethical Perspectives on Changing Agricultural Technology in the United States," quoted in Peterson, "Agricultural Structure and Economic Adjustment," 13.

14 "Sustainability's promise," *Journal of Soil and Water Conservation* 45, no.1 (January–February 1990): 4.

15 Penn, "The Changing Farm Sector and Future Public Policy," 48 ff.

16 Cochrane, *The Development of American Agriculture,* 150 ff.

17 Ibid., 398–99.

18 Letter by David Stern, "On chemical dependence," *Journal of Soil and Water Conservation* (January–February 1990): 6.

19 See, for example, the critical analyses by Elizabeth Ann R. Bird, *Research for Sustainability? The National Research Initiative's Social Plan for Agriculture* (Walthill, Nebr.: Center for Rural Affairs, August 1991), and *Sustainable Agriculture in the National Research Initiative: Recommendations of a Panel* (Walthill, Nebr.: Center for Rural Affairs, October 1991).

20 John E. Ikerd, "Agriculture's search for sustainability and profitability," *Journal of Social and Water Conservation* (January–February 1990): 21.

21 Pierre Crosson and Janet Ekey Ostrov, "Sorting out the environmental benefits of alternative agriculture," *Journal of Soil and Water Conservation* (January–February 1990): 34.

22 Don Paarlberg, "The changing policy environment for the 1900 farm bill," *Journal of Soil and Water Conservation* (January–February 1990): 8.

23 Richard Lowrance, "Research approaches for ecological sustainability," *Journal of Soil and Water Conservation* (January–February 1990): 52.

24 Charles W. Stenholm and Daniel B. Waggoner, "Low-input, sustainable agriculture: Myth or method?" *Journal of Soil and Water Conservation* (January–February 1990): 16.

25 Fee Busby, "Sustainable agriculture; Who will lead?" *Journal of Soil and Water Conservation* (January–February 1990): 89–91.

26 Paul B. Thompson, "The Social Goals of Agriculture," *Agriculture and Human Values* 3 (Fall 1986): 37.

27 See John Lemons, "Structural Trends in Agriculture and Preservation of Family Farms," *Environmental Management* 10, no.1 (1986): 75–88; David M. Kendall et al., *Tomorrow's Harvest: A Study Guide* (Lawrence: University

Press of Kansas, 1982); see also the essays in Michael Chibnik, ed., *Farm Work and Fieldwork: American Agriculture in Anthropological Perspective* (Ithaca: Cornell University Press, 1987); Gary Comstock, ed., *Is There a Moral Obligation to Save the Family Farm?* (Ames: Iowa State University Press, 1988); and Marty Strange, *Family Farming: A New Economic Vision* (Lincoln: University of Nebraska Press, 1988).

28 See Cochrane, *The Development of American Agriculture,* 355–78.

29 Center for Rural Affairs, Walthill, Nebraska, "Center's Dialogue on Farm Structure," *New Land Review* (Winter 1979–80): 8; see also the discussion of absentee, corporate, and family-farm land ownership in Fund and Clement, *Distribution of Land and Water Ownership,* 24–32.

30 Cornelia Butler Flora, "Values and the Agricultural Crisis: Differential Problems, Solutions, and Value Constraints," *Agriculture and Human Values* 3, no.4 (Fall 1986): 16–23.

31 Flora, "Values and the Agricultural Crisis," 19.

32 See particularly Fund and Clement, *Distribution of Land and Water Ownership,* 30–32.

33 "The History of Soil and Water Conservation: A Symposium," *Agricultural History* 59 (April 1985): 2.

34 Petersen, "Agricultural Structure and Economic Adjustment," 7.

35 "News of the Week in Review," *New York Times,* July 1, 1987; *Newark* (N.J.) *Star-Ledger,* February 21, 1990; Francis X. Clines, "Gorbachev Plan for Family Farms Is Approved by Soviet Lawmakers," *New York Times,* March 1, 1990.

36 Joel Sokloff, *The Policies of Food* (San Francisco: Sierra Club Books, 1985), 32–36.

37 *Oklahoma Comprehensive Water Plan* (Oklahoma City, Oklahoma Water Resources Board Publication 94, 1980), 15, 39, 150, and passim.

38 Robert Rodale, "International Resources and External Inputs—The Two Sources of All Production Needs," *Regenerative Farming Systems* (Emmaus, Pa.: Rodale Institute, 1985).

39 The literature has become voluminous; see particularly William W. Kellogg and Robert Schware, *Climate Change and Society: Consequences of Increasing Atmospheric Carbon Dioxide* (Boulder, Colo.: Westview Press, 1981); Lloyd E. Slater and Susan K. Levin, eds., *Climate's Impact on Food Supplies: Strategies and Technologies for Climate-Defensive Food Production* (Boulder, Colo.: A A A S and Westview Press, 1981); Norman J. Rosenberg, ed., *Drought in the*

Great Plains: Research on Impacts and Strategies (Littleton, Colo.: Water Resources Publications, 1980); Norman J. Rosenberg, ed., *North American Droughts* (Boulder, Colo.: AAAS and Westview Press, 1978); Donald A. Wilhite et al. eds., *Planning for Drought: Toward a Reduction of Societal Vulnerability* (Boulder, Colo.: UNEP and Westview Press, 1987); and Ernest A. Engelbert and Ann Foley Scheuring, *Water Scarcity: Impacts on Western Agriculture* (University of California Press, 1984).

40 James Gleick, *Chaos: Making a New Science* (New York: Penguin Books, 1987), 24.

41 Ibid., 67–68, 85.

42 Ibid., 105.

Chapter 7

1 Based on 2.5 acre-feet for corn and 1.5 acre-feet for wheat. In southwest Kansas's Seward County, irrigated wheat might produce 45 to 60 bushels per acre, while irrigated corn offers 100 to 150 bushels per acre. Data received in May 1986 from the Liberal, Kansas, office of the Soil Conservation Service.

2 Earl O. Heady and Roger W. Hexem, *Water Production Functions in Irrigated Agriculture* (Ames: Iowa State University Press, 1978).

3 "Irrigators Save Water and Improve Efficiencies," *The Cross Section* 32, no.10 (October 1986): 4.

4 "LISA Offers Farmers Alternatives," *Rural Papers* 79 (November 1989): 1–2; David R. Cressman, "The promise of low-input agriculture," *Journal of Soil and Water Conservation* 44, no.2 (March–April 1989): 98.

5 *Review Draft: The Second RCA Appraisal. Soil, Water, and Related Resources on Nonfederal Land in the United States* (Washington: USDA, 1987), 2–6, 7–15.

6 Cressman, "The promise of low-input agriculture," 98.

7 William Lockeretz, *Issues in Sustainable Agriculture* (Washington: Rural Economic Policy Program, Aspen Institute, 1988).

8 Kenneth A. Cook, "The environmental era of U.S. agricultural policy," *Journal of Soil and Water Conservation* 44, no.5 (September–October 1989): 366; see also Christine A. Ervin, "Implementing the Conservation Title," *Journal of Soil and Water Conservation* 44, no.5 (September–October 1989): 367; and Cressman, "The promise of low-input agriculture," 98.

9 Charles M. Benbrook, "The environment and the 1900 farm bill," *Journal of Soil and Water Conservation* 43, no.6 (November–December 1988): 440–43; Tony Vrana, "Building constructively on the Conservation Title," *Journal of*

Soil and Water Conservation 44, no.5 (September–October 1989): 360; Kenneth A. Cook, "Consider the Source: Environmental Reform of U.S. Agricultural Policy in the 1990s and Beyond," *American Journal of Alternative Agriculture* 4, nos.3 and 4; U.S. Senator Rudy Boschwitz et al., "Building a conservation-centered farm policy," *Journal of Soil and Water Conservation* 44, no.5 (September–October 1989): 451.

10 C. Edwin Young and C. Tim Osborn, "Costs and benefits of the Conservation Reserve Program," *Journal of Soil and Water Conservation* 45, no.3 (May–June 1990): 370.

11 Stephen O. Myers and P. Lorenz Sutherland, "CRP: A Baca County, Colorado Perspective," *Journal of Soil and Water Conservation* 44, no.5 (September–October 1989): 431–36; by contrast, see P. Lorenz Sutherland and J. A. Knapp, "The impacts of limited water: A Colorado cost study," *Journal of Soil and Water Conservation* 43, no.4 (July–August 1988): 294–98.

12 Charles M. Benbrook, "The environment and the 1990 farm bill," *Journal of Soil and Water Conservation* 43, no.6 (November–December 1988): 440–43.

13 Stephen R. Crutchfield, "Federal farm policy and water quality," *Journal of Soil and Water Conservation* 44, no.5 (September–October 1989): 377.

14 B. L. Harris, J. N. Habiger, and Z. L. Carpenter, "The Conservation Title: Concerns and recommendations from the Great Plains," *Journal of Soil and Water Conservation* 44, no.5 (September–October 1989): 373.

15 "Consider 'Sodbuster' and 'Conservation Compliance' Effects Now," *The Cross Section,* 32, no.9 (September 1986): 1–2.

16 Harris, et al., "The Conservation Title," 375.

17 "New Conservation Rules Will Affect High Plains Farmers," *The Cross Section* 32, no.10 (October 1986): 1–3.

18 Marc O. Ribaudo et al., "CRP: What economic benefits?" *Journal of Soil and Water Conservation* 44, no.5 (September–October 1989): 421; see also Marc O. Ribaudo et al., *The Economic Impacts of the Conservation Reserve Program on Natural Resources* (Washington: Economic Research Service, USDA, 1989).

19 Elbert E. Dickey et al., "To till or not to till during drought," *Journal of Soil and Water Conservation* 44, no.2 (March–April 1989): 117–20. Jeffrey R. Williams, Richard V. Llewelyn, and Chris L. Mikesell, "An economic risk analysis of conservation tillage systems for wheat, grain sorghum, and soybeans in the Great Plains," *Journal of Soil and Water Conservation* 44, no.3 (May–June 1989): 234–39.

20 Ribaudo et al., "CRP: What economic benefits?" 423; see also G. Sloggett and C. Dickason, *Groundwater Mining in the United States* (Washington: AER-555, Economic Research Service, USDA, 1986).

21 David E. Kromm and Stephen E. White, *Conserving the Ogallala: What Next?* (Manhattan: Kansas State University, 1985).

22 Kenneth D. Frederick and Allen V. Kneese, "Competition for Water," in Ernest A. Engelbert and Ann Foley Scheuring, eds., *Water Scarcity: Impacts on Western Architecture* (Berkeley: University of California Press, 1984), 81–108.

23 See, for example, James R. Ehleringer, "Photosynthesis and Photorespiration: Biochemistry, Physiology and Ecological Implications," *Hortscience* 14, no. 3 (1979): 217–22; R. B. Austin et al., "Genetic Improvements in Winter Wheat Yields Since 1900 and Associated Physiological Changes," *Journal of Agricultural Science* 94 (1980): 576–89; J. S. Boyer, "Plant Productivity and the Environment," *Science* 218 (1983): 361–405.

24 See Gary L. Laklig and J. W. Twigg, "Historical Crop Studies," in E. G. Knox and A. A. Theison, eds., *Feasibility of Introducing New Crops: Production, Marketing, Consumption (PMC) Systems* (Emmaus, Pa.: Rodale Press, 1981), 174–91; E. D. Putt, "History and Present World Status," in J. F. Carter, ed., *Sunflower Science and Technology* (Madison, Wis.: American Society of Agronomy, 1978), 1–28.

25 See Willard W. Cochrane, *The Development of American Agriculture: A Historical Analysis* (Minneapolis: University of Minnesota Press, 1979), 156–57.

26 Earl O. Heady, "National and International Commodity Price Impacts," in Engelbert and Scheuring, *Water Scarcity*, 277, and see S. H. Wittwer, "New Technology, Agricultural Productivity and Conservation," in Earl O. Heady et al., eds., *Soil Conservation Policies, Institutions and Incentives* (Ankeny, Ia.: Soil Conservation Society of America, 1982), esp. chap. 9; Yoo-Chi Loo, Philip Cline, and Leroy Quance, *Prospects for Productivity Growth in U.S. Agriculture* (Washington: USDA, ESCS Agricultural Economic Report 435, 1979); and *Soil, Water, and Related Resources in the United States: Status, Condition, and Trends, 1980 Appraisal, Part 1* (Washington: USDA, 1981).

27 Office of Technology Assessment, *Water-Related Technologies for Sustainable Agriculture in U.S. Arid/Semiarid Lands* (Washington: U.S. Congress, Office of Technology Assessment, OTA-F-21, October 1983), 244–56.

28 N. C. Turner and P. F. Kramer, eds., *Adaptation of Plants to Water and High Temperature Stress* (New York: John Wiley, 1980) 179–85.

29 See the documented discussion in Norman J. Rosenberg, "Improving Land and Water Use Practices," in Engelbert and Scheuring, *Water Scarcity*, 212–14.

30 *Thirty Years: A Tradition of Service: 1951–1981* (Lubbock: Texas High Plains Underground Water Conservation District No. 1, 1952), 71.

31 Mike Rising and Ken Carver, "Soil Moisture Monitoring: An Overview of Monitoring Methods and Devices," *Water Management Note* (Lubbock: Texas High Plains Underground Water Conservation District No. 1, n.d.); see also OTA *Water-Related Technologies*, 214.

32 Mike Risinger and Ken Carver, "Neutron Moisture Meters: The Scientific Approach to Monitoring Soil Moisture," *Water Management Notes* (Lubbock: Texas High Plains Underground Water Conservation District No. 1, n.d.).

33 As reported in "Scientists Listen to Noises of Plants in Drought," *New York Times*, September 4, 1988.

34 Mike Risinger, A. Wayne Wyatt, and Ken Carver, "Estimating Soil Moisture by Feel and Appearance," *Water Management Note* (Lubbock: Texas High Plains Underground Water Conservation District No. 1, n.d.).

35 Comment by Wilford R. Gardner in Engelbert and Scheuring, *Water Scarcity*, 241–42.

36 "District salutes water savings by area irrigators: You've come a long way, baby!" *The Cross Section* 35, no. 11 (November 1989): 1–3; see also "Irrigation systems upgraded through Pilot Ag Loan Program have cumulatively saved 25,000 acre-feet of groundwater," *The Cross Section* 35, no. 10 (October 1989): 4.

37 See the paper by Larry J. Kuder et al., "Surge Irrigation in Southwestern Kansas," by the Soil Conservation Service Area Target Team of Garden City, Kansas, undated, but probably in the early 1980s; see also "Lubbock County producers praise surge irrigation benefits." *The Cross Section* 35, no. 5 (May 1989): 4.

38 See C. G. Karasov, "Irrigation Efficiency in Water Delivery," *Technology* 3 (1982): 62–74.

39 Based on interviews of local USDA officials by Marvin E. Jensen reported in "Improving Irrigation Systems," in Engelbert and Scheuring, *Water Scarcity*, 232–33.

40 Robert D. Lacewell and Glenn S. Collins, "Improving Crop Management," in Engelbert and Scheuring, *Water Scarcity*, 194–95; "New improved irrigation spray nozzles, *The Cross Section* 34, no. 6 (June 1988): 1,3.

41 OTA, *Water-Related Technologies*, 234–35.

42 Interview in *Dallas Morning News*, August 19, 1984.

43 USDI, USDA, EPA, *Irrigation Water Use and Management* (Washington: Inter-agency Task Force Report, 1979).

44 "Drier than normal conditions revealed in soil moisture survey," *The Cross Section* 35, no.2 (February 1989): 2.

45 Based on interviews of local USDA officials by Marvin E. Jensen, reported in "Improving Irrigation Systems," in Engelbert and Scheuring, *Water Scarcity*, 232–33.

46 See B. A. Stewart and J. T. Musick, "Conjunctive Use of Rainfall and Irriga-tion in Semi-Arid Regions," in Dan Hillel, ed., *Advances in Irrigation Science*, vol. 1 (New York: Academic Press, 1983); see also *Better Federal Coordination Needed to Promote More Efficient Farm Irrigation* (Washington: General Ac-counting Office, June 22, 1976), 23–30.

47 "Shut Off the Water—The Root Zone is Full," (Washington: U.S. Bureau of Reclamation, March 1973).

48 Barry Flinchbaugh et al., *Who Will Control Our Water Supply?* (Manhattan: Kansas State University Cooperative Extension Service, 1984), 48–49.

49 Comment by Marshall J. English in Engelbert and Scheuring, *Water Scarcity*, 237–39.

50 Based on the discussion by Herman Bouwer in Engelbert and Scheuring, *Water Scarcity*, 128; see also OTA, *Water-Related Technologies*, 216–19.

51 See the useful discussion in Mary Fund, *Water in Kansas: A Primer* (Whiting, Kans.: Kansas Rural Center, 1984), 53–55; see also OTA, *Water-Related Tech-nologies*, 219–23.

52 See Ronald D. Lacewell and Glenn S. Collins, "Improving Crop Manage-ment," in Engelbert and Scheuring, *Water Scarcity*, 180ff.

53 Correspondence from Wayne Bossert, January 19, 1991.

54 Quoted in Kip Lowe, "Groundwater future a continuing concern," *Colby* (Kans.) *Free Press*, June 15, 1990; see also "Groundwater district halts water rights," *Atwood* (Kans.) *Citizen-Patriot*, February 22, 1990; reports and pub-lications by Northwest Kansas Groundwater Management District Four; and my interviews of the district manager, Wayne Bossert, in April 1991.

55 Orlan Buller, "Potential Economic Effects of a Zero Depletion Policy in North-west Kansas," paper presented at the Symposium on the Effects of a Zero De-pletion Policy on the Ogallala Aquifer of the Great Plains, Fort Hays State Uni-versity, Hays, Kansas, April 16, 1991, 13.

56 Data provided by Northwest Kansas Groundwater Management District Four, January 1991.

57 Correspondence from Wayne Bossert, January 19, 1991.

58 Wayne Bossert letter to Division of Water Resources, October 8, 1990.

59 Buller, "Potential Economic Effects of a Zero Depletion Policy in Northwest Kansas," 13.

60 Conrad Easterday, "District seeks input on new water policies," *Colby* (Kans.) *Free Press,* March 14, 1990; see also "Special Bulletin," Northwest Kansas Groundwater Management District Four, March 22, April 10, June 1, and October 8, 1990, and "Water Rights Moratorium Established," *The Water Table* 13, no.2 (March–April 1990), special supplement (March 1990), and 13, no.4 (July–August 1990).

61 Lowe, "Groundwater future a continuing concern."

62 Letter from Wayne Bossert to Kansas Department of Commerce, May 4, 1990.

63 "Draft Ogallala Decline Committee Recommendations to Northwest Kansas Groundwater Management District No.4," October 4, 1990; Wayne Bossert letter to Division of Water Resources, October 8, 1990; "Declines Committee Makes Recommendation," *The Water Table* 13, no.6 (November–December 1990).

64 Mike Corn, "Groundwater district endorses zero depletion recommendations," *Hays* (Kans.) *Daily News,* October 5, 1990.

65 Wayne Bossert of Kansas District Four estimates that pumpage in northwest Kansas ranges from fifteen dollars an acre-foot for natural gas to thirty dollars an acre-foot for electricity, alongside capital costs.

66 Pierre R. Crosson and Norman J. Rosenberg, "Strategies for Agriculture," *Scientific American* 261, no.3 (September 1989): 128.

67 The privatization argument is clearly established in a series of essays edited by Terry L. Anderson, *Water Rights: Scarce Resource Allocation, Bureaucracy, and the Environment* (Cambridge, Mass.: Pacific Institute for Public Policy Research/Ballinger, 1983). A stance critical of privatization is in Robert G. Dunbar, *Forging New Rights in Western Waters* (Lincoln: University of Nebraska Press, 1983).

68 New Mexico law professor Charles DuMars, quoted in *Wall Street Journal,* November 19, 1984; see also Kenneth Frederick and James C. Hanson, *Water for Western Agriculture* (Washington: Resources for the Future, 1982).

69 Lawrence Mosher, "Will the real leaders in national water policy please stand up?" *Journal of Soil and Water Conservation* 44, no.2 (March–April 1989s): 135.

70 K. W. Easter, J. A. Leitch, and D. F. Scott, "Competition for Water, a Capricious Resource," in Ted L. Napier et al., eds., *Water Resources Research* (Ankeny, Ia.: Soil and Water Conservation Service, 1983), 135–53; Kenneth D. Frederick, "Water Supplies," in Paul Portney, ed., *Current Issues in Natural Resource Policy* (Washington: Resources for the Future, 1982), 216ff., and Kenneth D. Frederick and James C. Hanson, *Water for Western Agriculture* (Washington: Resources for the Future, 1982), 165–84.

71 *Six-State High Plains-Ogallala Aquifer Regional Resources Study* (Washington: Department of Commerce, 1982), 6–77; Easter, Leitch, and Scott, "Competition for Water," 135–53.

72 Heady, "National and International Commodity Price Impacts," 280. In the National Water Assessment of 1976, at the same time that water supplies declined from 86.7 acre-feet to 64.6 acre-feet per year, wheat prices rose from $3.84 to $8.82 (in 1972 dollars).

73 This is the central argument in Mark Sagoff, *The Economy of the Earth* (New York: Cambridge University Press, 1988).

74 Frederick and Kneese, "Competition for Water," 99.

75 OTA, *Water-Related Technologies*, 141; see the data in Frederick and Hanson, *Water for Western Agriculture*.

76 See the analysis in OTA, *Water-Related Technologies*, 154–59.

77 See *Investigation of Secondary Recovery of Ground Water from the Ogallala Formation, High Plains of Texas* (Lubbock: Texas High Plains Underground Water Conservation District No. 1, 1982), 2–4, 6–7, 13–20, 25–30, 55–57.

78 A copy of the address is with the XIT Ranch Papers, Panhandle-Plains Historical Museum, Canyon, Texas, 4.

79 *The Texas Water Plan* (Austin: Texas Water Development Board, 1968); see the excellent discussion of the various water-import projects in Morton W. Bittinger and Elizabeth B. Green, *You Never Miss The Water Till . . . . (The Ogallala Story)* (Littleton, Colo.: Water Resources Publications, 1980), 90ff.

80 R. E. Bathen, P. R. Cunningham, and W. R. Mayben, "A New Water Resource Plan for the Great Plains," paper presented at the annual meeting of the Midwest Electric Consumers Association, Omaha, Nebraska, December 8, 1967. The authors were employees of R. W. Beck and Associates, an engineering consulting firm, which also published the plan.

81 See the discussion in Harvey O. Banks, Jean O. Williams, and Joe B. Harris, "Developing New Water Supplies," in Engelbert and Scheuring, *Water Scarcity*, 111–12.

82 Lewis Gordy Smith, "Toward a National Water Plan," *Irrigation Age* (April 1969).

83 Quoted in Bittinger and Green, *You Never Miss the Water*, 96.

84 In Engelbert and Scheuring, *Water Scarcity*, 126.

85 *A Water Policy for the American People*, 3 vols. (Washington: President's Water Resources Policy Commission, 1950, 1951).

86 *Water Resources Policy* (Washington: Presidential Advisory Committee on Water Resources Policy, 1955).

87 *Water Policies for the Future* (Washington: National Water Commission, 1973); see also Charles E. Corker, "Ground Water Law, Management, and Administration," Report prepared for the National Water Commission, 1971.

88 *Southwest Kansas Irrigator*, December 25, 1978, quoted in Bittinger and Green, *You Never Miss The Water*, 106.

89 Quoted in Bittinger and Green, *You Never Miss The Water*, 107.

90 See the discussion in John Opie, *The Law of the Land: 200 Years of American Farmland Policy* (Lincoln: University of Nebraska Press, 1987), xiii–xvi; see also n. 115.

91 Bittinger and Green, *You Never Miss The Water*, 109.

92 The results of the study and its recommendations were summarized in a review draft dated April 23, 1982: *A Summary of the Results of the Ogallala Aquifer Regional Study, with Recommendations to the Secretary of Commerce and Congress: Colorado, Kansas, Nebraska, New Mexico, Oklahoma, Texas* (n.p.: High Plains Study Council, 1982). Many versions of the study appeared in short and long forms, divided according to states and topics. See, for example, *Six-State High Plains Ogallala Aquifer Regional Resources Study: Summary* (Austin, Tex.: High Plains Associates, 1982), and *A Summary of Results of the Ogallala Aquifer Regional Study, with Recommendations to the Secretary of Commerce and Congress* (Austin, Tex.: High Plains Study Council, December 13, 1982).

93 *Summary of Results*, 13–16.

94 Ibid., 1.

95 Ibid., 16.

96 John B. Weeks, "Proposed Plan of Study for the High Plains Regional Aquifer-System Analysis," working paper for February 2–3, 1978, staff meeting. Water Resources Division, Geological Survey, U S D I, Denver Federal Center, 6.

97 *Summary of Results*, 5, 8.

98 Communication from Donald Worster, November 1991.

99 "Review Draft," *Summary of Results*, 4–5.

100 Ibid., 14.

101 See also the analysis in Raymond J. Supalla, Robert R. Landsford, and Noel R. Gollehon, "Is the Ogallala going dry? A review of the High Plains study and its land and water policy implications," *Journal of Soil and Water Conservation* (November–December 1982): 311–14.

102 "Review Draft," *Summary of Results*, 5–8.

103 Ibid., 15, 16.

104 Ibid., 8–10; *Summary of Results*, 22–23.

105 *Summary of Results*, opening abstract summary letter.

106 See K. G. Brengle, *Principles and Practices of Dryland Farming* (Boulder, Colo.: Associated University Press, 1982), and Hayden Ferguson et al., "Dryland Agriculture," O T A commissioned paper, excerpted in O T A, *Water-Related Technologies*, 21 ff.; C. Robert Taylor, Duane R. Reneau, Richard Trimble, "Economics of Conservation Tillage Systems," in B. L. Harris and A. E. Colburn, eds., *Conservation Tillage in Texas* (College Station: Texas Agricultural Extension Service Bulletin B-1290, 1979); see also the discussion by Norman J. Rosenberg, "Improving Land and Water Use Practice," in Engelbert and Scheuring, *Water Scarcity*, 204–17, and the essays in Norman J. Rosenberg, ed., *Drought in the Great Plains: Research on Impacts and Strategies* (Littleton, Colo.: Water Resources Publications, 1980); J. Grace, *Plant Response to Wind* (New York: Academic Press, 1977).

107 See O T A, *Water-Related Technologies*, 300–302.

108 General Accounting Office Report to Congress, *Action Neded to Discourage Removal of Trees that Shelter Cropland on the Great Plains* (Washington: G A O publications R E D-75-375, 1975).

109 Rosenberg, "Improving Land and Water Use Practices," 211–12.

110 J. R. Gilley and E. Fereres-Castiel, "Efficient Use of Water on the Farm," O T A commissioned paper, excerpted in O T A, *Water-Related Technologies*, 237.

111 See Office of Technology Assessment, *Impacts of Technology on U.S. Cropland and Rangeland Productivity* (Washington: U.S. Congress, O T A-F-166, 1982).

112 See B. W. Greb, *Reducing Drought Effects on Croplands in the West Central Great Plains,* (Washington: USDA Information Bulletin 420, 1979).

113 Wes Jackson, *New Roots for Agriculture* (San Francisco: Friends of the Earth, 1980), 24–29.

114 "The Case Against Crop Chemicals," *Science* 251 (1 February 1991): 517.

115 Lacewell and Collins, "Improving Crop Management," 193.

116 See the commentary by Kenneth R. Farrell in Engelbert and Scheuring, *Water Scarcity,* 293–94.

117 See W. G. Matlock, *Realistic Planning for Arid Lands: Natural Resources Limitations to Agricultural Development* (London: Harwood Academic Publishers, 1981), 4; T. W. Box, *The Arid Lands Revisited—One Hundred Years Since John Wesley Powell* (Logan: Utah State University, n.d.), 4–7; Carle Hodge, ed., *Aridity and Man: The Challenge of the Arid Lands in the United States* (Washington: AAAS, 1963).

118 Albert Schaffer and Ruth C. Schaffer, "Social Impacts on Rural Communities," in Engelbert and Scheuring, *Water Scarcity,* 312–15.

119 Schaffer and Schaffer, "Social Impacts on Rural Communities," 322.

120 A. A. Theisen, E. G. Knox, and F. L. Mann, eds., *Feasibility of Introducing Food Crops Better Adapted to Environmental Stress,* vol. 1 (Washington: Government Printing Office, NSF/RA/780289, 1978).

121 See the observations of Donald Worster, *Dust Bowl: The Southern Plains in the 1930s* (New York: Oxford University Press, 1979), 146 passim.

122 Interviews with Keith Allen were conducted at his farm in May 1987 and at the Pheasant Inn in Sublette, Kansas, in May 1988.

123 Interviews with Baker and Schmidt on June 27, 1989.

124 See Lacewell and Collins, "Improving Crop Management," 190–91, and Ellis G. Knox and Arthur A. Theisen, "Feasibility of Introducing New Crops: Production-Marketing-Consumption Systems," a report to the National Science Foundation by Soil and Land Use Technology, Inc., 1981, and the analysis in OTA, *Water-Related Technologies,* 256–64.

125 "Researchers Investigate Year-Round Forage System," *The Cross Section* 32, no. 9 (September 1986): 3.

126 Brad Burritt, "Leymus: A Plant with a History of Human Use," *The Land Report* 28 (1986): 10–12.

127 Jon K. Piper, "The Prairie as a Model for Sustainable Agriculture: A Preliminary Study," in *The Land Report Research Supplement* 3 (1986): 1–4; see also

Mark Gernes and Jon Piper, "Vegetation Patterns in Tallgrass Prairie and Their Implications for Sustainable Agriculture"; Amy Kullenberg, "Survey of Insects in Native Prairie and Agricultural Plots"; Doug Dittman, "Soil Moisture and Nutrient Patterns in Agricultural Plots and Native Prairie"; and Randolph Kempa, "Seed Systems," all in *The Land Report Research Supplement* 4 (1987).

128 *The Land Institute Research Report* 5 (1988), i and passim.

129 Quoted in *The Land Report* 32 (Spring 1988): 9.

130 Drawn from Wes Jackson's influential 1980 classic, *New Roots for Agriculture,* esp. 114–36.

131 Dennis Rinehart, "Sorghum: A Perennial Future?" *The Land Report* 28 (1986): 12–14; see also "Paul Bramel-Cox: Sorghum Breeder," *The Land Report* 34 (Fall 1988): 12–15, and Jennifer M. Delisle, "Perennial Sorghum Breeding: 1988 Progress Report," *The Land Institute Research Report* 5 (1988): 30.

132 Interviews in 1986 and 1987 with irrigators Keith Allen and Paul Boles, corroborated by Jeff Schmidt of the Liberal, Kansas, office of the Soil Conservation Service; see also Edwin D. Gutentag, David H. Lobmeyer, and Steven E. Slagle, *Geohydrology of Southwestern Kansas,* Kansas Geological Survey Irrigation Series 7 (Lawrence: University of Kansas Publications, 1981), 59–64.

133 A. Wayne Wyatt, Ann E. Bell, and Shelly Morrison, *Analytical Study of the Ogallala Aquifer in Parmer County, Texas* (Austin: Texas Water Development Board Report 205, 1976), 5–9.

134 Cochrane, *The Development of American Agriculture,* 324–27.

Chapter 8

1 W. E. Riebsame, S. A. Changnon, and T. R. Karl, *Drought and Natural Resources Management in the United States: Impacts and Implications of the 1987–1989 Drought* (Boulder, Colo.: Westview Press, 1990).

2 Dennis Farney and Bruce Ingersoll, "Drought Damages Bush's Chances in Farm Belt; Rain Now Would Be Too Late for Many Victims," *Wall Street Journal,* June 27, 1988.

3 Kevin E. Trenberth, Grant W. Branstator, Phillip A. Arkin, "Origins of the 1988 North American Drought," *Science* 242 (23 December 1988): 1640–45.

4 Quoted in "The Heat is On," *Time,* October 19, 1987, 63.

5 Bruce Ingersoll, "Extensive Erosion in Great Plains Tied to Dust Storm Is at Worst Level Since 1955," *Wall Street Journal,* June 27, 1988.

6 B. Drummond Ayres, Jr., "Vast Parched Stretches of U.S. Await Hot Summer," *New York Times,* May 15, 1988.

7 Mobilizing to Help Farmers Through the Drought," *New York Times,* June 27, 1988.

8 Letter from Leland B. Taylor to *Journal of Soil and Water Conservation* 45, no.3 (May–June 1990): 357.

9 Jonathan R. Laing, "Greenhouse Effect," *Barrons,* June 27, 1988.

10 Quoted in ibid.

11 Julia Flynn Siler, "Losses Bring Gains For Farmer in Futures," *New York Times,* August 4, 1988; see also Siler, "Drought Means Deluge in Grain Pit," and Keith Schneider, "World Grain Supplies Are Dropping," *New York Times,* August 4, 1988.

12 Laing, "Greenhouse Effect."

13 Scott Kilman and Richard Gibson, "Killing Drought Raises Food Prices, Portends Worsening of Inflation," *Wall Street Journal,* June 14, 1988; Barbara Rudolph, "The Drought's Food-Chain Reaction," *Time,* July 11, 1988.

14 "Worldwide effects of the drought," *Newark* (N.J.) *Star-Ledger,* June 27, 1988.

15 John F. Burns, "Drought Also Lays Waste to Canada's Farm Belt," and Edward A. Gargan, "Flash Floods and Drought Ravage China," *New York Times,* August 3, 1988.

16 Keith Schneider, "Drought Stirs Debate on Wheat Export Subsidies," *New York Times,* June 29, 1988.

17 Keith Schneider, "The Green Revolution: How Much Farther Can It Go?" *New York Times,* August 21, 1988.

18 Lester Brown et al., *State of the World 1989* (New York: W. W. Norton and Company, 1989), 3–58.

19 But it made front-page news almost daily in national newspapers. See, for example, Keith Schneider, "1988 Drought Evokes Ghost of Dust Bowl," *New York Times,* July 7, 1988.

20 William Robbins, "On the Farm, A Disaster That Wasn't," *New York Times,* October 16, 1988.

21 Ingersoll, "Extensive Erosion in Great Plains Tied To Dust Storm Is at Worst Level Since 1955."

22 William Robbins, "Dry Soil Blows Away, Carrying Hope With It," *New York Times,* August 7, 1988.

23 The efforts received front-page attention nationally; see Keith Schneider, "Scientists Trying to Give Crops An Edge Over Nature's Forces," *New York Times,* August 1, 1988.

24 Conversation with John Perkins, Evergreen State College, on his forthcoming NSF-financed study of the politics of agricultural research, November 1990.

25 Quoted in Schneider, "1988 Drought Evokes Ghost of Dust Bowl."

26 Letter from John T. Bird, Hays, Kansas, "Kansan on Kansas," *Wall Street Journal,* April 17, 1989.

27 "Bitter Harvest: A Seasoned Farm-Belt Watcher Assesses the Damage of the Drought," *Barrons,* June 27, 1988.

28 Kilman and Gibson, "Killing Drought Raises Food Prices."

29 Andrew Cassel, "As water level sinks, concerns rise," *Philadelphia Enquirer,* May 29, 1989, and telephone interview with Gary Baker on June 27, 1989; see also "Water Table Drop in Parts of Kansas," *Southwest Daily Times,* June 8, 1989.

30 Interview on June 27, 1989.

31 Quoted in Sue Shellenbarger, "U.S. Farmers Face an Easier Row to Hoe," *Wall Street Journal,* October 25, 1988.

32 Data received in May 1986 and May 1987 from the Garden City and Liberal, Kansas, offices of the Soil Conservation Service.

33 Robbins, "On the Farm, A Disaster That Wasn't"; Philip Shabecoff, "Draft Report on Global Warming Foresees Environmental Havoc in U.S.," *New York Times,* October 20, 1988; "Worldwide effects of the drought," *Newark* (N.J.) *Star-Ledger,* June 27, 1988.

34 See the sequence of articles in the *Wall Street Journal:* Bruce Ingersoll, "Drought Likely to Bring Down Acreage of Harvest to Record Low This Century," September 27, 1988; Carlee R. Scott, "Drought Lingers as Threat to Winter Wheat Crop," December 12, 1988; Sue Shellenbarger, "Unforgiving Climate of Kansas Is Punishing Winter Wheat Again," March 14, 1989; Bruce Ingersoll, "U.S. Sees Wheat Stocks at 17-Year Low Unless Rains Temper Drought's Effect," April 7, 1989; and Sue Shellenbarger and Bruce Ingersoll, "Second Drought in a Row Is Threatening 40% of Farm Belt, Some Western States," and "Wheat Futures in Kansas City Expected to Climb Following U.S. Prediction of 8% Drop in Harvest," both on May 12, 1989. The *New York Times* missed badly in its front-page story by Keith Schneider, "Serious Drought Seen as Unlikely in U.S. This Year," February 20, 1989, but it turned

around by November: William Robbins, "Wheat Crop Faces Threat of Drought," November 29, 1989.

35 Telephone interview with Jeff Schmidt, district conservationist, Soil Conservation Service, Liberal, Kansas, June 21, 1989.

36 William Robbins, "Winter Wheat Farmers Fear Second Year's Crop Failure," *New York Times*, January 2, 1990.

37 Irvin Molotsky, "Drought Has Eased, U.S. Reports," *New York Times*, September 13, 1988.

38 *Scientific Assessment of Climate Change* (Geneva: Intergovernmental Panel on Climate Change, WMO, UNEP, 1990); Paul E. Waggoner, "U.S. Water Resources Versus an Announced But Uncertain Climate Change," *Science* 251 (1 March 1991): 1002.

39 "Using Forests to Counter the 'Greenhouse Effect,'" *Science* (26 February 1988): 973.

40 "Is the Greenhouse Here?" *Science* (5 February 1988): 559–61; Philip Shabecoff, "Global Warmth in '88 Is Found To Set a Record," *New York Times*, February 4, 1989; "Do We Know Enough to Act?" National Research Council, *Current Issues in Atmospheric Change* (Washington: National Academy Press, 1987), 23–27; see also the useful summary review of the evidence, its effects, and response strategies in Christopher Flavin, *Slowing Global Warming: A Worldwide Strategy*, Worldwatch Paper 91 (Washington: Worldwatch Institute, October 1989). See also Ray Bradley, ed., *Global Changes of the Past* (Boulder, Colo.: University Corporation for Atmospheric Research, 1991); Thomas J. Crowley and Gerald R. North, *Paleoclimatology* (New York: Oxford University Press, 1991); and P. E. Waggoner, ed., *Climate Change and U.S. Water Resources* (New York: John Wiley and Sons, 1990).

41 See the report by William K. Stevens, "Global Warming: Search for the Signs," *New York Times*, January 29, 1991.

42 Philip Shabecoff, "The Heat Is On," *New York Times*, June 26, 1988; Philip Shabecoff, "Global Warming: Experts Ponder Bewildering Feedback Effects," *New York Times*, January 17, 1989.

43 Jesse H. Ausubel, "Does Climate Still Matter?" *Nature* 350 (25 April 1991): 650. See also Emmanuel Le Roy Ladurie, *Times of Feast, Times of Famine: A History of Climate Since the Year 1000*, trans. by Barbara Bray (Garden City, N.Y.: Doubleday and Company, 1971).

44 Stephen H. Schneider, "The Greenhouse Effect: Science and Policy," *Science* 243 (10 February 1989): 771.

45 Author's visit to NCAR, May 1986.

46 Edward Lorenz, "The predictability of hydrodynamic flow," *Transactions of the New York Academy of Sciences* II (1963) 25:4, pp.409–32, quoted in James Gleick, *Chaos: Making of a New Science* (New York: Penguin Books, 1987), 25.

47 Reported in Richard A. Kerr, "Report Urges Greenhouse Action Now," *Science* (1 July 1988): 23–24; see also "Climatologists see sharp temperature swings over the next decade," *Newark* (N.J.) *Star-Ledger,* July 29, 1988.

48 Michael Oppenheimer, "How to Cool Our Warming Planet," *New York Times* Op-Ed page, July 23, 1988.

49 "Is a Climate Jump in Store for Earth?" *Science* (15 January 1988): 259.

50 John Noble Wilford, "His Bold Statement Transforms the Debate On Greenhouse Effect" *New York Times,* August 23, 1988; but see also Philip Shabecoff, "U.S. Data Since 1895 Fail To Show Warming Trend," *New York Times,* January 26, 1989; "Could the Sun Be Warming the Climate?" *Science* 254 (1 November 1991): 652–53; and William K. Stevens, "Earth's Temperature Has Dropped a Little After a Warm Spell," *New York Times,* December 24, 1991.

51 Stephen H. Schneider, "Climate Modeling," *Scientific American* 256, no.3 (May 1987): 77, 80; see also Michael H. Glantz and Jesse H. Ausubel, "The Ogallala Aquifer and Carbon Dioxide: Comparison and Convergence," *Environmental Conservation* 11, no.2 (Summer 1984): 123–31; Thomas R. Karl, Richard R. Heim, Jr., and Robert G. Quayle, "The Greenhouse Effect in Central North America: If Not Now, When?" *Science* 251 (1 March 1991): 1058–61; and William K. Stevens, "In a Warming World, Who Comes Out Ahead?" *New York Times,* February 5, 1991.

52 Schneider, *The Greenhouse Effect,* 772; see also J. I. Hanchey et al., *Preparing for Climate Change: Proceedings Washington DC, 27 to 29 October 1988* (Rockville, Md.: Government Institutes, 1988), 394–405.

53 Robert Lewis, "Global warming: the cold facts," *Newark* (N.J.) *Star-Ledger,* February 5, 1989; William K. Stevens, "With Cloudy Crystal Balls, Scientists Race to Assess Global Warming," *New York Times,* February 7, 1989.

54 See the critique by Raymond J. Supalla, Robert R. Lansford, and Noel R. Gollehon, "Is the Ogallala going dry?" *Journal of Soil and Water Conservation* (November–December 1982): 310–14, and Michael H. Glantz, Barbara G. Brown, and Maria E. Krenz, *Societal Responses to Regional Climate Change:*

Forecasting by Analogy (Boulder, Colo.: ESIG/EPA Study, Environmental and Societal Impacts Group, NCAR, 1988), 13.

55 Ric Jensen, "Are Things Warming Up? How Climate Changes Could Affect Texas," *Texas Water Resources* 15, no. 1 (Spring 1989); see also Judith Clarkson and Robert King, *Global Warming and the Future of Texas Agriculture: Impacts and Policy* (Austin: Texas Department of Agriculture, 1989); Daniel Dudek, "Economic Implications of Climate Change Impacts on Southern Agriculture," *Proceedings of the Symposium on Climate Change in the Southern U.S.: Future Impacts and Present Policy Issues* (Washington: EPA, 1987); Norman J. Rosenberg, "Drought and Climate Change: For Better or Worse?" in *Planning for Drought: Toward a Reduction in Societal Vulnerability* (Boulder, Colo.: Westview Press, 1987).

56 R. F. Diffendal, Jr., "Plate Tectonics, Space, Geologic Time, and the Great Plains," *Great Plains Quarterly* 11 (Spring 1991): 93–94.

57 Michael H. Glantz and Nicolai Orlovsky, "Desertification: A review of the concept," *Desertification Control Bulletin* 9 (December 1983): 15–21; see also Donald A. Wilhite and Michael H. Glantz, "Understanding the Drought Phenomenon: The Role of Definitions," *Water International* 10 (1985): 111–20; Michael H. Glantz, "Politics, Forecasts and Forecasting: Forecasts are the Answer, but What was the Question?" in Richard Krasnow, ed., *Policy Aspects of Climate Forecasting* (Washington: Resources for the Future, 1987[?]), 81–95; Michael H. Glantz, "Drought Follows the Plow," *The World & I* (April 1988): 208–13; and Jonathan G. Taylor, Thomas R. Stewart, and Mary Downton, "Perceptions of Drought in the Ogallala Aquifer Region," *Environment and Behavior* 20, no. 2 (March 1988): 150–75.

58 Glantz and Orlovsky, "Desertification," 15.

59 Ric Jensen, "Are Things Warming Up?"; see also Judith Clarkson, "Global Climate Change and Its Implications for Agricultural Productivity in Texas," *Grassroots* (Fall 1988): 3, 21–24.

60 Quoted in "The Heat is On," *Time,* October 19, 1987, 59.

61 Quoted in "The Greenhouse Effect," *Newark* (N.J.) *Star-Ledger,* June 7, 1988.

62 Quoted in "The Heat is On," *Time,* 63.

63 V. Ramanathan, "The Greenhouse Theory of Climate Change: A Test by an Inadvertent Global Experiment," *Science* 15 (April 1988): 293–99.

64 See Paul E. Waggoner, ed., *Climate Change and U.S. Water Resources* (New York: Wiley-Interscience, 1990).

65 Stephen H. Schneider, "The Greenhouse Effect: Science and Policy," *Science* 243 (10 February 1989): 781.

66 "Just Enough to Fight Over," *Time*, July 4, 1988, 14.

67 Howard Witt, "Canadians fear U.S. water grab," *Chicago Tribune*, July 11, 1988.

Chapter 9

1 Fredeick H. Newell, "Irrigation on the Great Plains," *Yearbook of the United States Department of Agriculture 1896* (Washington: USDA, 1896), 193.

2 Newell, "Irrigation on the Great Plains," 167.

3 Donald Worster, "Doing Environmental History," in *The Ends of the Earth* (New York: Cambridge University Press, 1988), 290.

4 Eugene P. Odum, "The Emergence of Ecology as a New Integrative Discipline," *Science* 195 (25 March 1977): 1292; see also E. P. Odum and J. L. Cooley, *Biological Evaluation of Environmental Impact* (Washington: Council for Environmental Quality, n.d.).

5 A. Maass and R. L. Anderson, *And the Desert Shall Rejoice: Conflict, Growth and Justice in Arid Environments* (Cambridge, Mass.: MIT Press, 1978), 5; see also F. Lee Brown et al., "Water Reallocation, Market Proficiency, and Conflicting Social Values," *Western Water Institutions in a Changing Environment* (Napa, Calif.: John Muir Institute, 1980), and Kenneth Boulding, *Western Water Resources: Coming Problems and the Policy Alternatives* (Boulder, Colo.: Westview Press, 1980).

6 See the discussion in Mark Sagoff, *The Economy of the Earth: Philosophy, Law, and the Environment* (New York: Cambridge University Press, 1988), 114ff.

7 See also Willard W. Cochrane, *The Development of American Agriculture: A Historical Analysis* (Minneapolis: University of Minnesota Press, 1979), 137, 183–86, 320.

8 See, for example, Douglas R. McManis, *Colonial New England: A Historical Geography* (New York: Oxford University Press, 1975), chaps. 1–3; Michael Williams, "Clearing the United States forests: Pivotal years 1810–1860," *Journal of Historical Geography* 8, 1 (1982): 12–28; and the many articles in W. L. Thomas, Jr., ed., *Man's Role in Changing the Face of the Earth*, 2 vols. (Chicago: University of Chicago Press, 1956).

9 See the essays in Brian W. Blouet and Merlin P. Lawson, eds., *Images of the Plains: The Role of Human Nature in Settlement* (Lincoln: University of Ne-

braska Press, 1975), and W. Eugene Hollon, *The Great American Desert, Then and Now* (New York: Oxford University Press, 1966).

10 See the collected essays of pioneer environmental historian James C. Malin in Robert P. Swierenga, ed., *History and Ecology: Studies of the Grassland* (Lincoln: University of Nebraska Press, 1984); see also Gilbert C. Fite, *The Farmers' Frontier, 1865–1900* (New York: Holt, Reinhart and Winston, 1966), esp. chaps. 3, 4, 7, and 11.

11 T. G. Jordan, "Between the Forest and the Prairie," *Agricultural History* 35 (1964): 206–16; D. R. McManis, "The Initial Evaluation and Utilization of the Illinois Prairies, 1815–1840," *Department of Geography Research Paper 94* (Chicago: University of Chicago, 1964); Carl O. Sauer, "Conditions of Pioneer Life in the Upper Illinois Valley," a 1916 essay in John Leighly, ed., *Land and Life: A Selection from the Writings of Carl Ortwin Sauer* (Berkeley: University of California Press, 1967), 11–22.

12 See Richard A. Warrick and Martyn J. Bowden, "The Changing Impacts of Droughts in the Great Plains," in Merlin P. Lawson and Maurice E. Baker, eds., *The Great Plains: Perspectives and Prospects* (Lincoln: University of Nebraska Press, 1981), 111–37.

13 See the yet unsurpassed study by Walter Prescott Webb, *The Great Plains* (Boston: Ginn and Company, 1931), chaps. 7–8, and John T. Schlebecker, *Whereby We Thrive: A History of American Farming, 1607–1972* (Ames: Iowa State University Press, 1975).

14 This is a major thesis in John Opie, *The Law of the Land: 200 Years of American Farmland Policy* (Lincoln: University of Nebraska Press, 1987); see also "How Americans Got Their Farmland Before the Constitution," *Yearbook of Agriculture 1987* (Washington: USDA, 1987), 15–20.

15 See Douglas Helms and Susan L. Flader, *The History of Soil and Water Conservation* (Washington: Agricultural History Society, 1985); Douglas Helms, *Great Plains Conservation Program: 25 Years of Accomplishment* (Washington: Soil Conservation Service Bulletin No. 300-2-7, 1982).

16 See John Opie, "America's Seventy-Year Mistake, or How We Got Fooled by Good Weather in Difficult County," *Proceedings of a Seminar on Natural Resource Use and Environmental Policy* (Ames: North Central Regional Center for Rural Development, Iowa State University, 1980), 27–56, and Pamela Riney-Kehrberg, "In God we trusted, in Kansas we busted . . . again," paper presented to the Conference on Agriculture, Climate, and History, Orono,

Maine, June 3, 1988. Another oft-maligned region, Appalachia, has been called "a frontier region frozen in time." See particularly Rodger Cunningham, *Apples on the Flood: The Southern Mountain Experience* (Knoxville: University of Tennessee Press, 1987).

17 T. Lindsay Baker, "Turbine-Type Windmills of the Great Plains and Midwest," in C. Clyde Jones and Homer E. Socolofsky, eds., *Science and Technology in Agriculture* (Washington: Agricultural History Society, 1985), 38–51.

18 See the excellent discussion in Lawrence B. Lee's introduction to *Reclaiming the American West: An Historiography and Guide* (Santa Barbara, Calif.: A B C Clio, 1980).

19 Although Donald E. Green's book, *Land of the Underground Rain* (Austin: University of Texas Press, 1973) is about irrigation on the Texas High Plains alone, it is still the best source on the technological innovations which made large-scale agricultural irrigation possible.

20 Green, *Land of the Underground Rain*, 161–62, corroborated by an early-evening visit to the irrigated fields of thirty-two-year-old Keith Allen north of Sublette, Kansas, in May 1987.

21 See the discussion in Cochrane, *The Development of American Agriculture,* esp. 8–9, 76–77, 85–88, 183–89.

22 Despite its brevity (116 pages), the Ogallala study *You Never Miss The Water Till . . . . (The Ogallala Story)* by Morton W. Bittinger and Elizabeth B. Green, is exceptionally detailed, accurate, and useful (Littleton, Colo.: Water Resources Publications, 1980).

23 Cochrane, *The Development of American Agriculture,* 137, 183–86, 320.

24 See the analysis in ibid., 321–24.

25 But see Earl O. Heady, "National and International Commodity Price Impacts," in Ernest A. Engelbert and Ann Foley Scheuring, eds., *Water Scarcity: Impacts on Western Agriculture* (Berkeley: University of California Press, 1984), esp. 280–91.

26 See William Lockeretz, ed., *Environmentally Sound Agriculture* (New York: Praeger Publishers, 1983); Gordon J. Douglass, *Agricultural Sustainability in a Changing World Order* (Boulder, Colo.: Westview Press, 1984); Joel Sokloff, *The Politics of Food* (San Francisco: Sierra Club Books, 1985); Clyde Kiker, "Comments," *Agriculture and Human Values* 3, no. 3 (Summer 1986): 71–74; and John Opie, "The Precarious Balance: Matching Market Dollars and Hu-

man Values in American Agriculture," *The Environmental Professional* 10 (Spring 1988): 36–45.

27 See the pathbreaking study by Gilbert C. Fite, *American Farmers: The New Minority* (Bloomington: Indiana University Press, 1981).

28 This tension is analyzed in Elizabeth Ann R. Bird, *Research for Sustainability? The National Research Initiative's Social Plan for Agriculture* (Walthill, Nebr.: Center for Rural Affairs, August 1991).

29 U.S. Senator Rudy Boschwitz et al., "Building a conservation-centered farm policy," *Journal of Soil and Water Conservation* 44, no.5 (September–October 1989): 451.

30 Jeffrey A. Zinn and John E. Blodgett, "Agriculture versus the environment: Communicating perspectives," *Journal of Soil and Water Conservation* 44, no.3 (May–June 1989): 184–87.

31 See the discussions in David R. Cressman, "The promise of low-input agriculture," *Journal of Soil and Water Conservation* 44, no.2 (March–April 1989): 98; and Kenneth A. Cook, "The environmental era of U.S. agricultural policy," *Journal of Soil and Water Conservation* 44, no.5 (September–October 1989): 363; one of the best analyses of contemporary American agriculture and its historic development is still Willard W. Cochrane, *The Development of American Agriculture*.

32 Zinn and Blodgett, "Agriculture versus the environment," 184–87.

33 The literature is large and growing. For example, water issues are debated in Marc Reisner, *Cadillac Desert: The American West and Its Disappearing Water* (New York: Viking Penguin, 1986), and Donald Worster, *Rivers of Empire: Water, Aridity, and the Growth of the American West* (New York: Pantheon Books, 1985). See also Paul B. Sears's 1935 classic, *Deserts on the March* (Norman: University of Oklahoma Press, 1980), now in its fourth edition, and Lawrence B. Lee's *Reclaiming the American West: A Historiography and Guide* (Santa Barbara, Calif.: ABC Clio, 1980).

34 Zinn and Blodgett, "Agriculture versus the environment," 187.

35 Tim T. Phipps and Katherine Reichelderfer, "Farm support and environmental quality at odds?" *Resources* 95 (Spring 1989): 14–16.

36 See the summary in Lester R. Brown, "Sustaining World Agriculture," *State of the World 1987* (New York: W.W. Norton and Company, 1987), 132–36.

37 Paul B. Thompson, "The Social Goals of Agriculture," *Agriculture and Human Values* 3 (Fall 1986): 41.

38 See the discussion by Thompson in ibid., 35–40.

39 Ibid., 32–43.

40 Mary Fund and Elise Watkins Clement, *Distribution of Land and Water Ownership in Southwest Kansas* (Whiting: Kansas Rural Center, 1982), 17–18.

41 World Commission on Environment and Development, *Our Common Future* (New York: Oxford University Press, 1987), 8; see also R. Boardman, *International Organization and the Conservation of Nature* (Bloomington: Indiana University Press, 1981), Lynton K. Caldwell, *International Environmental Policy: Emergence and Dimensions* (Durham, N.C.: Duke University Press, 1984), L. W. Milbrath, *Envisioning a Sustainable Society: Learning Our Way Out* (Albany, N.Y.: SUNY Press, 1989), Edward Pestel, *Beyond the Limits to Growth: A Report to the Club of Rome* (New York: Universe Books, 1989), M. Redclift, *Sustainable Development: Exploring the Contradictions* (London: Methuen Publishers, 1987), and L. Stark, *Signs of Hope: Working Towards Our Common Future* (Oxford: Oxford University Press, 1990).

42 See Timothy O'Riordan, "The politics of sustainability," in R. Kelly Turner, ed., *Sustainable Environmental Management* (Boulder, Colo.: Westview Press, 1988), 29–49.

43 D. Scott Slocombe and Caroline Van Bers, "Seeking Substance in Sustainable Development," a paper presented at the annual conference of the North American Association for Environmental Education, San Antonio, Texas, November 4, 1990.

44 See Thomas S. Kuhn, *The Structure of Scientific Revolutions,* 2d ed. (Chicago: University of Chicago Press, 1962, 1970).

45 This review of global sustainable development is based largely on *Our Common Future,* esp. 43–66, and the special issue, "Managing Planet Earth," of *Scientific American* 261, no.3 (September 1989).

46 Jim MacNeill, "Strategies for Sustainable Economic Development," *Scientific American* 261, no.3 (September 1989): 158–59, 163–64.

47 Based on the analysis offered by Bird, *Research for Sustainability?,* 2–3; see also Wendell Berry, *The Unsettling of America: Culture and Agriculture* (New York: Avon Books, 1977), Marty Strange, *Family Farming: A New Economic Vision* (Lincoln: University of Nebraska Press, 1988), Chuck Hassebrook, "Developing a socially sustainable agriculture," *American Journal of Alternative Agriculture* 5, no.2: 50, 96; National Research Council, *Alternative Agri-*

culture (Washington: National Academy Press, 1989); Gary Comstock, ed., *Is There a Moral Obligation to Save the Family Farm?* (Ames: Iowa State University Press, 1987).

48 Charles A. Francis, "Practical applications of low-input agriculture in the Midwest," *Journal of Soil and Water Conservation* 45 (January–February 1990): 66–67.

49 Bird, *Research for Sustainability?*, 27.

50 D. T. Walters, D. A. Mortensen, C. A. Francis, R. W. Elmore, and J. W. King, "Specificity: The context of research for sustainability," *Journal of Soil and Water Conservation* 45, no.1 (January–February 1990): 55–57.

51 Fred Kirschenmann, "Fundamental fallacies of building agricultural sustainability," *Journal of Soil and Water Conservation* 46, no.3 (May–June 1991): 168; see also Charles Benbrook, "Protecting Iowa's common wealth: Challenges for the Leopold Center for Sustainable Agriculture," *Journal of Soil and Water Conservation* 46, no.2 (March–April 1991): 89–95.

52 See, for example, the combined USDI, USDA and EPA analysis, *Better Federal Coordination Needed to Promote More Efficient Farm Irrigation* (Washington: General Accounting Office, June 22, 1976).

53 Collin Fallat, "What role land use planning in the restructuring of American agriculture?" *Journal of Soil and Water Conservation* 43, no.6 (November–December 1988): 470.

54 This is a primary interest in the report by the National Research Council's Committee on the Role of Alternative Farming Methods in Modern Production Agriculture, *Alternative Agriculture* (Washington: National Academy Press, 1989); see also Stuart B. Hill, "Redesigning the food system for sustainability," *Alternatives* 12, no.3 (Fall 1985): 32–36.

55 Cook, "The environmental era of U.S. agricultural policy," 366.

56 Boschwitz et al., "Building a conservation-centered farm policy," 451.

57 Ibid., 451.

58 MEY and MSY are reviewed in another context by Arthur F. McEvoy, "Toward an Interactive Theory of Nature and Culture: Ecology, Production, and Cognition in the California Fishing Industry," in Donald Worster, ed., *The Ends of the Earth: Perspectives on Modern Environmental History* (New York: Cambridge University Press, 1988), 219–29.

59 Thompson, "The Social Goals of Agriculture," 34.

60 Eugene P. Odum, "The Strategy of Ecosystem Development," *Science* 64 (April 1969): 262–70, and see Jake Vail, "Society as a Maturing Ecosystem," *The Land Report* 32 (Spring 1988): 32–33.

61 D. Scott Slocombe and Alex Grzybowski, unpublished paper "Self Organization Theories and Sociobiophysical Systems: The Case of South Moresby," presented at the annual conference of the North American Association for Environmental Education, Eugene, Oregon, September 16, 1986, 25.

62 Vail, "Society as a Maturing Ecosystem," 32–33.

63 Ibid.

Appendix

1 See Turner's essays collected in *The Frontier in American History* (New York: Henry Holt and Company, 1920); see also Ray Allen Billington, *Frederick Jackson Turner: Historian, Scholar, Teacher* (New York: Oxford University Press, 1973), and Billington's *America's Frontier Heritage* (New York: Holt, Rinehart & Winston, 1966); John Wesley Powell, *Report on the Lands of the Arid Region of the United States* (Washington: H. Ex. Doc. 73, 45th Cong., 2d sess., 1878; 2d ed. of 1879 reprinted by Harvard Common Press of Boston in 1983); Wallace Stegner's biography of Powell, *Beyond the Hundredth Meridian: The Exploration of the Grand Canyon and the Second Opening of the West* (Boston: Houghton Mifflin Company, 1953); and William H. Goetzmann, *Exploration and Empire: The Explorer and the Scientist in the Winning of the American West* (New York: Alfred A. Knopf, 1966).

2 Walter Prescott Webb, *The Great Frontier* (Austin: University of Texas Press, 1951–52, 1964), 415.

3 Ibid., 418.

4 Ibid., 15n.

5 Robert DeCourcy Ward, *The Climates of the United States* (Boston: Ginn and Company, 1925), 125f., quoted in ibid., 22.

6 Walter Prescott Webb, *The Great Plains* (Boston: Ginn and Company, 1931), 23–24.

7 Ibid., 22.

8 Ibid., 10–26.

9 Ibid., 19n.

10 Ibid., 17.

11 Paul B. Sears, *Deserts on the March* (Norman: University of Oklahoma Press, 1935, 1947, 1959, 1980).

12 Ibid., 174–84.

13 Ibid., 10–13.

14 Ibid., 85; see also 83–91, 107–16.

15 Donald Worster, *Nature's Economy* (Garden City, N.Y.: Anchor Books, 1979; reprint of original 1977 Sierra Club ed.), 209–20.

16 Ibid., 209.

17 Quoted in ibid., 211.

18 Quoted in ibid., 216.

19 Ibid., 219.

20 Malin's primary interpretations have been gathered together and introduced by Robert P. Swierenga in *History and Ecology: Studies of the Grassland* (Lincoln: University of Nebraska Press, 1984); see also the perceptive and critical comments by Donald Worster, "The Dirty Thirties: A Study in Agricultural Capitalism," *Great Plains Quarterly* 6 (Spring 1986): 107–14.

21 James C. Malin, "Dust Storms: Part One, 1850–1860," *Kansas Historical Quarterly* 14 (May 1946): 129–44, and "Dust Storms: Part Three, 1881–1890," *Kansas Historical Quarterly* 14 (November 1946): 391–413.

22 See Swierenga, *History and Ecology,* xvff.

23 Quoted in ibid., xxii.

24 See the introductory note by John Leighly in *Land and Life: A Selection From the Writings of Carl Ortwin Sauer* (Berkeley: University of California Press, 1963).

25 *Land and Life,* 386–88.

26 *Land and Life,* 389–404. Sauer gave his historical reasoning in a 1938 paper, "Theme of Plant and Animal Destruction in Economic History," 145–54.

27 See William L. Thomas, Jr., ed., *Man's Role in Changing the Face of the Earth* (Chicago: University of Chicago Press, 1956), 49–69, 350–66, 721–62, 1131–35. See also *Land and Life,* "The Morphology of Landscape," 325f.

28 See the 1916 "Conditions of Pioneer Life in the Upper Illionis Valley," the 1927 "The Barrens of Kentucky," and the 1962 "Homestead and Community on the Middle Border," 11–41.

29 Richard A. Warrick and Martyn J. Bowden, "The Changing Impacts of Droughts in the Great Plains," in Merlin P. Lawson and Maurice Baker, eds. *The Great Plains: Perspective and Prospects* (Lincoln: University of Nebraska Press, 1981), 111–37.

30 Martyn J. Bowden, "The Great American Desert and the American Frontier, 1800–1882: Popular Images of the Plains," in T. K. Mareven, ed., *Anonymous Americans: Explorations in Nineteenth Century Social History* (Englewood Cliffs, N.J.: Prentice-Hall, 1971), 48–79.

31 Donald Worster, *Dust Bowl: The Southern Plains in the 1930s* (New York: Oxford University Press, 1979).

32 See also Worster's discussion of environmental history in "Nature as Natural History: An Essay on Theory and Method," *Pacific Historical Review* 53 (February 1984): 1–19, and his opening and closing essays in Donald Worster, ed., *The Ends of the Earth* (New York: Cambridge University Press, 1988), 3–22, 289–308.

33 This is even more clearly expressed in Worster, "The Dirty Thirties: A Study in Agricultural Capitalism," 110–15; see the critique of Worster by Harry C. McDean, "Dust Bowl Historiography," *Great Plains Quarterly* 6 (Spring 1986): 121–23.

34 Worster, *Dust Bowl*, 4.

35 See, for example, the 1974 fourth edition of Ray Allen Billington's still-definitive textbook of classic frontier expansion, *Westward Expansion: A History of the American Frontier* (New York: Macmillan Company, 1974), esp. 559–629.

36 Ray Bradbury, "A Sound of Thunder," in John Stadler, ed., *Eco-Fiction* (New York: Washington Square Press, 1971), 5.

37 Bradbury, "A Sound of Thunder," 13.

38 James Gleick, *Chaos: Making a New Science* (New York: Penguin Books, 1987), 8, 20–23.

39 Frederick Kirschenmann, "Fundamental fallacies of building agricultural sustainability," *Journal of Soil and Water Conservation* 46, no.3 (May–June 1991): 165–68.

40 William E. Reed, "The ecology of sustainable development," *The Ecologist* (January–February 1990): 41, quoted in Kirschenmann, "Fundamental fallacies," 167.

41 Jesse H. Ausubel, "Does Climate Still Matter?" *Nature* 350 (25 April 1991): 650.

42 Eugene P. Odum, "The Emergence of Ecology as a New Integrative Discipline," *Science* 195 (25 March 1977): 1289.

43 See, for example, A. E. Kahn, *Kyklos* 19 (1966): 23, and W. E. Odum, *BioScience* 32 (1982): 728.

44 This is an undeveloped approach suggested by the Office of Technology Assessment, *Water-Related Technologies for Sustainable Agriculture in U.S. Arid/Semiarid Lands* (Washington: U.S. Congress, OTA-F-212, October 1983), 5, 19–21, 333 ff.

45 See the discussion in Benjamin R. Stinner and Garfield J. House, "The search for sustainable agroecosystems," *Journal of Soil and Water Conservation* 44, no.2 (March–April 1989): 114–15; see also "Academy of Sciences Endorses Low-Input Farming," *Rural Papers* 78 (October 1989): 1–2.

46 Recent discussions include Erich Jantsch, *The Self-Organizing Universe* (New York: Pergamon Press, 1980); G. Nicolis and I. Prigogine, *Self-Organization in Non-Equilibrium Systems* (New York: John Wiley, 1977); D. N. Parkes and N. J. Thrift, *Times, Spaces, and Places: A Chronogeographic Perspective* (New York: John Wiley, 1980); and H. Ulrich and G. J. B. Probst, eds., *Self-Organization and Management of Social Systems* (Berlin: Springer, Verlag, 1984); see also the broader perspectives offered in Berman and Gleick below.

47 Gleick, *Chaos,* 292–93.

48 Morris Berman, *The Reenchantment of the World* (Ithaca, N.Y.: Cornell University Press, 1981), 243.

49 Ibid., 256.

50 Unpublished paper by D. Scott Slocombe and Alex Grzybowski, "Self-Organization Theories and Sociobiophysical Systems: The Case of South Moresby," presented at the annual conference of the North American Association for Environmental Education, Eugene, Oregon, September 16, 1986; see also D. Scott Slocombe, "History and Environmental Messes: A Nonequilibrium Systems View," *Environmental Review* nos.3–4, 13 (Fall–Winter 1989): 1–14.

51 Slocombe, "History and Environmental Messes," 1–14.

52 Eugene P. Odum, "Input Management of Production Systems," *Science* 243 (13 January 1898): 177–81.

53 Quoted in Berman, *The Reenchantment of the World,* 200.

54 Cornelia Butler Flora, "Values and the Agricultural Crisis: Differential Problems, Solutions, and Value Considerations," *Agriculture and Human Values* 3, no.4 (Fall 1986): 17.

55 Gleick, *Chaos,* 298; see Hans Jonas, *The Phenomenon of Life: Toward a Philosophical Biology* (New York: Harper and Row, 1966), 183–87; see also William

399

K. Stevens, "New Eye on Nature: The Real Constant Is Eternal Turmoil," *New York Times*, July 31, 1990.

56 Berman, *The Reenchantment of the World*, 257.

57 Ibid., 200.

58 Eugene P. Odum, "Trends Expected in Stressed Ecosystems," *Bioscience* 35, no.7 (1985): 419–22; for an integrative approach, see Kenneth A. Dahlberg, ed., *New Directions for Agriculture and Agricultural Research: Neglected Dimensions and Emerging Alternatives* (Totowa, N.J.: Rowman and Allanheld, 1986), and J. Bonnen, "Historical Sources of U.S. Agricultural Productivity: Implications for R&D Policy and Social Science Research," *American Journal of Agricultural Economics* 65, no.5 (1983): 958–66.

59 Odum, "Input Management of Production Systems," 177.

60 Slocombe and Grzybowski, "Self-Organization Theories and Sociobiophysical Systems," 21.

61 Stephane Castonguay, "The Technological Function of the Environment in a Sustainable Agriculture," paper presented at the conference "The Environment and the Mechanized World," American Society for Environmental History, Houston, Texas, February 28–March 3, 1991, 5.

62 Thompson, "The Social Goals of Agriculture," 40.

63 Odum, "The Emergence of Ecology," 1292.

Index